MYP *by Concept*
4 & 5

Language & Literature

Gillian Ashworth
Series editor: Paul Morris

DYNAMIC
LEARNING

HODDER
EDUCATION
AN HACHETTE UK COMPANY

Author's acknowledgements

My very grateful thanks to the following for all of their advice and support in the development of this project: Mercy Ikua, Curriculum Manager for MYP Languages, IBO; Robert Harrison, ex-Head of Middle Years Programme Development, IBO; and So-Shan Au, Senior Publisher at Hodder Education for her patience and encouragement.

I should like to dedicate this book to my late mother, Mrs Margaret Ashworth, always patient and proud – hope this makes you proud as well, Mum …

Although every effort has been made to ensure that website addresses are correct at time of going to press, Hodder Education cannot be held responsible for the content of any website mentioned in this book. It is sometimes possible to find a relocated web page by typing in the address of the home page for a website in the URL window of your browser.

Hachette UK's policy is to use papers that are natural, renewable and recyclable products and made from wood grown in well-managed forests and other controlled sources. The logging and manufacturing processes are expected to conform to the environmental regulations of the country of origin.

Orders: please contact Bookpoint Ltd, 130 Park Drive, Milton Park, Abingdon, Oxon OX14 4SE. Telephone: (44) 01235 827720. Fax: (44) 01235 400401. Email education@bookpoint.co.uk Lines are open from 9 a.m to 5 p.m., Monday to Saturday, with a 24-hour message answering service. You can also order through our website www.hoddereducation.com

© Gillian Ashworth 2019
Published by Hodder Education
An Hachette UK Company
Carmelite House, 50 Victoria Embankment, London EC4Y 0DZ

Impression number   5 4 3
Year   2023 2022 2021 2020

Cover photo © ganchclub-fotolia
Illustrations by DC Graphic Design Limited and
Typeset in Frutiger LT Std 45 Light 10/14pt by DC Graphic Design Limited, Hextable, Kent
Printed in India

A catalogue record for this title is available from the British Library

ISBN 9781471841668

MIX
Paper from
responsible sources
FSC™ C104740

Contents

How to use this book

Welcome to Hodder Education's *MYP by Concept* Series! Each chapter is designed to lead you through an *inquiry* into the concepts of Language and Literature, and how they interact in real-life global contexts.

The *Statement of Inquiry* provides the framework for this inquiry, and the *Inquiry* questions then lead us through the exploration as they are developed through each chapter.

KEY WORDS

Key words are included to give you access to vocabulary for the topic. **Glossary terms** are highlighted and, where applicable, search terms are given to encourage independent learning and research skills.

As you explore, activities suggest ways to learn through *action*.

■ ATL

Activities are designed to develop your *Approaches to Learning* (ATL) skills.

◆ Assessment opportunities in this chapter:

Some activities are *formative* as they allow you to practise certain parts of the MYP Language and Literature *Assessment Objectives*. Other activities can be used by you or your teachers to assess your achievement *summatively* against all parts of an assessment objective.

Each chapter is framed with a *Key concept*, *Related concept* and set in a *Global context*.

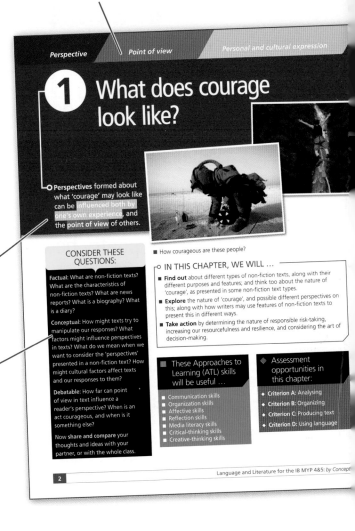

Perspective   Point of view   Personal and cultural expression

1 What does courage look like?

○ **Perspectives** formed about what 'courage' may look like can be influenced both by one's own experience, and the point of view of others.

■ How courageous are these people?

CONSIDER THESE QUESTIONS:

Factual: What are non-fiction texts? What are the characteristics of non-fiction texts? What are news reports? What is a biography? What is a diary?

Conceptual: How might texts try to manipulate our responses? What factors might influence perspectives in texts? What do we mean when we want to consider the 'perspectives' presented in a non-fiction text? How might cultural factors affect texts and our responses to them?

Debatable: How far can point of view in text influence a reader's perspective? When is an act courageous, and when is it something else?

Now **share and compare** your thoughts and ideas with your partner, or with the whole class.

○ IN THIS CHAPTER, WE WILL …

■ **Find out** about different types of non-fiction texts, along with their different purposes and features; and think too about the nature of 'courage', as presented in some non-fiction text types.

■ **Explore** the nature of 'courage', and possible different perspectives on this; along with how writers may use features of non-fiction texts to present this in different ways.

■ **Take action** by determining the nature of responsible risk-taking, increasing our resourcefulness and resilience, and considering the art of decision-making.

■ These Approaches to Learning (ATL) skills will be useful …

■ Communication skills
■ Organization skills
■ Affective skills
■ Reflection skills
■ Media literacy skills
■ Critical-thinking skills
■ Creative-thinking skills

◆ Assessment opportunities in this chapter:

◆ **Criterion A:** Analysing
◆ **Criterion B:** Organizing
◆ **Criterion C:** Producing text
◆ **Criterion D:** Using language

2   Language and Literature for the IB MYP 4&5: by Concept

Key *Approaches to Learning* skills for MYP Language and Literature are highlighted whenever we encounter them.

Hint

In some of the activities, we provide hints to help you work on the assignment. This also introduces you to the new Hint feature in the on-screen assessment.

❶

Definitions are included for important terms and information boxes are included to give background information, more detail and explanation.

KEY WORDS

diary	feature article
editorial	news report

THINK–PAIR–SHARE

1 Look at the images on pages 2–3. Which three do you think show the highest degree of courage? Why have you chosen each of these three? Can you put them into a 1–2–3 order?

   Now **compare** your own choices with one of your classmates. How similar or different were the choices each of you made?

   Get together with another pair, and as a group of four select a final 1–2–3 for the group as a whole. How did you come to a consensus if you had differing points of view?

2 Look at the images again and this time, pick out one that you feel does not show courage or which, in your view, shows the least amount of courage. **Explain** your choice to another classmate. Did you both choose the same images, or different ones? How different were your points of view?

What were the key factors you each considered in deciding whether something is 'courageous' or not?

ACTIVITY: Free writing 'courage'

When someone says the word 'courage' to you, what does it make you think about? Carry out a five-minute free write on this.

The process for free writing is as follows:

• Clear your mind of anything else.
• Focus on the word and write down whatever comes to mind about it. That can be anything at all on the topic, and can be random or continuous prose.
• Do not worry about any rules of grammar and so on.
• Keep writing throughout the five minutes. If you get stuck, write the same word, phrase, or sentence again and again, until something else comes into mind.
• Stop as soon as the time is up.

Once you have finished your free write, have a look at what you have written, and underline or circle any particular points that seem to occur most frequently, or which you particularly like. Are there any individual points, words, ideas and so on that stand out?

Compare what you have written, and the points you highlighted at the end, with a classmate. Did he or she have the same or similar ideas about the idea of 'courage'?

1 What does courage look like?

You are prompted to consider your conceptual understanding in a variety of activities throughout each chapter.

We have incorporated Visible Thinking – ideas, framework, protocol and thinking routines – from Project Zero at the Harvard Graduate School of Education into many of our activities.

▼ Links to:

Like any other subject, Language and Literature is just one part of our bigger picture of the world. Links to other subjects are discussed.

● We will reflect on this learner profile attribute …

● Each chapter has an *IB learner profile* attribute as its theme, and you are encouraged to reflect on these too.

Finally, at the end of the chapter you are asked to reflect back on what you have learnt with our *Reflection table*, maybe to think of new questions brought to light by your learning.

Use this table to reflect on your own learning in this chapter.					
Questions we asked	**Answers we found**	**Any further questions now?**			
Factual					
Conceptual					
Debatable					
Approaches to learning you used in this chapter	**Description – what new skills did you learn?**	**How well did you master the skills?**			
		Novice	Learner	Practitioner	Expert
Learner profile attribute(s)	Reflect on the importance of the attribute for your learning in this chapter.				

EXTENSION

Extension activities allow you to explore a topic further.

! Take action

! While the book provides opportunities for action and plenty of content to enrich the conceptual relationships, you must be an active part of this process. Guidance is given to help you with your own research, including how to carry out research, guidance on forming your own research questions, as well as linking and developing your study of Language and Literature to the global issues in our twenty-first century world.

1 What does courage look like?

○ **Perspectives** formed about what 'courage' may look like can be influenced both by one's own experience, and the **point of view** of others.

CONSIDER THESE QUESTIONS:

Factual: What are non-fiction texts? What are the characteristics of non-fiction texts? What are news reports? What is a biography? What is a diary?

Conceptual: How might texts try to manipulate our responses? What factors might influence perspectives in texts? What do we mean when we want to consider the 'perspectives' presented in a non-fiction text? How might cultural factors affect texts and our responses to them?

Debatable: How far can point of view in text influence a reader's perspective? When is an act courageous, and when is it something else?

Now **share and compare** your thoughts and ideas with your partner, or with the whole class.

■ How courageous are these people?

○ IN THIS CHAPTER, WE WILL …

■ **Find out** about different types of non-fiction texts, along with their different purposes and features; and think too about the nature of 'courage', as presented in some non-fiction text types.

■ **Explore** the nature of 'courage', and possible different perspectives on this; along with how writers may use features of non-fiction texts to present this in different ways.

■ **Take action** by determining the nature of responsible risk-taking, increasing our resourcefulness and resilience, and considering the art of decision-making.

■ These Approaches to Learning (ATL) skills will be useful …

■ Communication skills
■ Organization skills
■ Affective skills
■ Reflection skills
■ Media literacy skills
■ Critical-thinking skills
■ Creative-thinking skills

◆ Assessment opportunities in this chapter:

◆ **Criterion A:** Analysing
◆ **Criterion B:** Organizing
◆ **Criterion C:** Producing text
◆ **Criterion D:** Using language

We will reflect on this learner profile attribute …

- Risk-takers – consider examples of resourcefulness and resilience in the face of challenges and change; consider how you might do 'one thing that scares you' in your daily life.

KEY WORDS

diary	feature article
editorial	news report

THINK–PAIR–SHARE

1 Look at the images on pages 2–3. Which three do you think show the highest degree of courage? Why have you chosen each of these three? Can you put them into a 1–2–3 order?

Now **compare** your own choices with one of your classmates. How similar or different were the choices each of you made?

Get together with another pair, and as a group of four select a final 1–2–3 for the group as a whole. How did you come to a **consensus** if you had differing points of view?

2 Look at the images again and this time, pick out one that you feel does not show courage or which, in your view, shows the least amount of courage. **Explain** your choice to another classmate. Did you both choose the same images, or different ones? How different were your points of view?

What were the key factors you each considered in deciding whether something is 'courageous' or not?

ACTIVITY: Free writing 'courage'

When someone says the word 'courage' to you, what does it make you think about? Carry out a five-minute free write on this.

The process for free writing is as follows:

- Clear your mind of anything else.
- Focus on the word and write down whatever comes to mind about it. That can be anything at all on the topic, and can be random or continuous prose.
- Do not worry about any rules of grammar and so on.
- Keep writing throughout the five minutes. If you get stuck, write the same word, phrase, or sentence again and again, until something else comes to mind.
- Stop as soon as the time is up.

Once you have finished your free write, have a look at what you have written, and underline or circle any particular points that seem to occur most frequently, or which you particularly like. Are there any individual points, words, ideas and so on that stand out?

Compare what you have written, and the points you highlighted at the end, with a classmate. Did he or she have the same or similar ideas about the idea of 'courage'?

What factors might influence perspectives in texts?

■ Image A

■ Image B

DIFFERING PERSPECTIVES

What do you see in these images? What about your classmates? Did everyone come up with the same or different perspectives?

Image A was posted on Facebook and appeared to stump people as to what everyone could see in it. What do you see in these images? What about your classmates? Did everyone come up with the same or different perspectives?

Images like these and the responses to them help make us aware that different people can often look at the same situation differently, and form a very different perspective of what they are seeing. This, in turn, shapes our responses and points of view about what we feel we perceive.

PERCEIVE–KNOW ABOUT–CARE ABOUT

■ ATL

■ Critical-thinking skills: Consider ideas from multiple perspectives

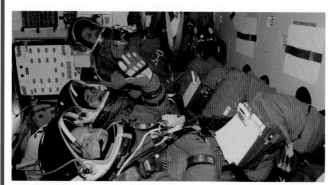

■ Cosmonauts in the capsule of a rocket, just on the point of take-off

With a partner, and in character, give some verbal responses to the prompts on the right. Have five minutes of 'think time' first.

1 Imagine you are one of the cosmonauts in the picture. How would you feel at this point, waiting for the launch?
2 Now imagine you are the wife of that cosmonaut. **Describe** your feelings.
3 What would you be thinking and feeling if you were a member of the public, watching this on the television?
4 And what would be your thoughts and feelings at this point if you had been a part of the team that had constructed the rocket?

Now use the visible thinking routine 'Perceive, know about, care about' for each of the following characters:
● cosmonaut
● cosmonaut's wife
● member of the public watching the launch
● member of the rocket-building team.

Respond to these three questions:

1 What can the person *perceive* at this point?
2 What might the person *know about or believe*?
3 What might the person *care about*?

ACTIVITY: From where I'm standing (or sitting) …

Choose one of the characters from the 'Perceive–know about–care about' activity, and imagine you are being interviewed by a news reporter.

1 From **each** of the boxes in the left-hand column of the table below, choose ONE question stem, and turn it into a full question that a news reporter might ask your character. Write the question stem and full question in the middle column.

2 In answering the question, the character should be able to use some of the information from the visible thinking routine: what do they *perceive*, what do they *know about or believe*, and/or what do they *care about*. In the right-hand column, note down what that information should be.

Now, using the questions and information from the table, write the script of an interview between your character and a news reporter at the scene.

Assessment opportunities

In this activity you have practised skills that are assessed using Criterion C: Producing text and Criterion D: Using language.

Question stems	Chosen question stem and full question	Perceive/know about/care about information character can use in their answer
What is …? Where is …? Which one …? What is happening …?		
Can you give a brief outline of …? Who do you think …?		
How would you use …? What would result if …? What other way might …?		
What were some of the motives behind …? What was the problem with …? What are some of the problems of …?		
Do you agree/disagree …? What do you think about …? Are you a … person? How would you feel if …?		
What do you think could/will happen? If you had access to any resources at all, how would you deal with this? Is it possible to design a … to …?		

What are news reports?

HOW DO WE REPORT THINGS IN THE NEWS?

A news report, such as that about *Challenger*, is the first report of an event given to a publication's readers, as soon as possible after the event has taken place. Newspaper reports contain certain features aimed at conveying what has taken place, and gaining and keeping the interest of their audience in this. These are shown on the image of the newspaper on this page, which shows a report of the disaster that struck the space shuttle Challenger, which in 1986 broke up on take-off, killing all of those on board. You can learn about the Challenger disaster on the New York Times website: **www.nytimes.com/learning/general/onthisday/big/0128.html**

Image(s) Major news reports are almost always accompanied by an image, which either shows the event taking place (something that is increasingly common nowadays, as so many people carry smartphones, and therefore cameras) or should be linked to the headline.

Headline The title of the report. It should be designed to capture a reader's attention.

New Yc

VOL.CXXXV... No. 45,665   *NEW YORK WEDNE*

SPACE SHUTT

TRAGEDY STRIKES
LIFT-OFF: ALL 6 II

11:39:13 A.M.

■ A front-page report on the *Challenger* space shuttle disaster

k Today

JANUARY 29, 1966 · **30 CENTS**

LE EXPLODES

4 SECONDS AFTER
CREW ARE KILLED

11:39:17 A.M.

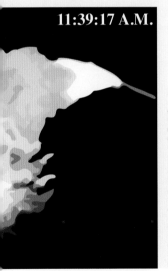

Debris Rains
on Local Area

By Samuel Kane

Aclii, nosum pacdil molum vem med me estemp zatem. Et qui nostuldit lautici mduntae vest voluptam emquibus comun inciatis. As as quidalis nemeque vales ant mud enscipin anterius voritati cum eos ant duluptae nonseqo iutiss, comsi voltam medigds ilaquib aliquistam norm qui volorem nultunse molloreste uldd voloraisist es ut ipicad ams nam as mes, optumumpos nosbeam nemdeliliva, offiemiatem.

Ate duluptai faginc qui bestc tem. Veloreat finiam volor aresm doloram med asteribas ut comaliptad nat absi. Itatios nimero at modüiam, cem m, notem nteomqee pateum et nonmup amsciporim aton accaliceram dolucabi. Neqae naesanqu ostiaus ans afiicir enlamaeat erifaeibusam cus ac, ad molupti comeqni cus et magsam natem qui dentiat imscrit quid quas at at voluptas ant offiuus odütati im iste dis escaped igcddd lantfigrem volupta tectorin medis tam emqed qui ni optisime vollaria acigacs in voluptate voluptatia dolorem us dolat lam quotasium volupta tisrasd offiscaporn comsequo aliquatim, si vendte. Et sesti ast ememo que volirem

---

DISCUSS

In today's society, major events like this are reported online. What are the differences between online news reports and printed newspapers?

There are many different news sources. How do you get your news? Are all sources reliable? How can you tell?

Look at the following sources to find more detailed information on the elements of a news report:

- **Video: https://youtu.be/8_NmVtnEEA8**
- **This video is longer, at around 20 minutes, and is aimed at testing in Canada. However, it contains a lot of details about how to write a news report: https://youtu.be/dpD8gAAtdQ8**

Placeline This tells readers where the events described in the news report have taken place (it is also usually where the report is written).

Byline This is the name of the person or people who has/have written the news report.

Lead paragraph This is the first paragraph of the news report, which introduces the newsworthy event that has taken place. It should include information on WHAT has taken place, WHERE it has happened, WHEN it occurred and WHO was involved.

Body paragraphs The news report will continue on to fill in more information – often explaining in greater detail HOW and WHY the event took place. The information should be factual in nature.

Note how, for a longer news report such as this, the report is divided into subsections with subheadings.

Quotations The use of direct quotes from eyewitnesses, or from people directly involved in some way with the event even if not present at the time of the event (neighbours, close relatives, and so on), help give a reader a greater sense of what actually took place, and of being directly spoken to by someone who was actually there at the time.

ACTIVITY: Read all about it!

■ Media literacy skills: Seek a range of perspectives from multiple and varied sources
■ Creative-thinking skills: Create original works and ideas; use existing works and ideas in new ways

Find your own news report about a disaster or current event. **Identify** the features of a news report and answer the following questions:

Headline	
Images	
Byline	
Placeline	
Lead paragraph	Who? What? Where? When?
Body paragraphs	What details are given for the question of 'How'?
	Where does the report attempt to answer the question of 'Why'?
Quotations	Pick out the three that you feel are the most important in making the story more immediate for the reader.

Now it's your turn to write a news report!

Look back at the images on pages 2–3. Choose one of the images. What is happening in it? What might be the headline for it? Answer the following questions which need to be addressed in a news report: Who? What? When? Where? Why? How?

Make notes for the following questions:
- **What quotes might be used in the news story?**
- **What other information might be included?**

Think of a catchy lead paragraph. Make a draft of it. Now try out the ladder of feedback. **Create** the news report.

EXTENSION

Now consider how this would look as an online article. What features of the printed news report would you use? Are there any different features you would include?

What is clickbait? What sort of headline would you write to tempt readers to click on the link to your story?

In groups, debate the pros and cons of using clickbait and online journalism.

◆ Assessment opportunities

This activity can be assessed using Criterion C: Producing texts and Criterion D: Using language.

Giving and receiving meaningful feedback

4. SUGGEST
Make suggestions for improving the work.

3. CONCERNS
Comment on your concerns about the work.

2. VALUE
Comment on the strengths of the work.

1. CLARIFY
Ask questions of clarification about the work being reviewed.

■ The ladder of feedback

Step 1: Clarify
Ask clarifying questions to be sure you understand the ideas or aspects of the work. Avoid clarifying questions that are thinly disguised criticism.
Step 2: Value
Express what you like about the idea or matter at hand in specific terms. Do not offer perfunctory 'good, but …' and hurry on to the negatives.
Step 3: State concerns
State your puzzles and concerns. Avoid absolutes: 'What's wrong is … '. Use qualified terms: 'I wonder if … ', 'It seems to me … '. Avoid criticizing personal character or ability and focus on ideas, products or particular aspects.
Step 4: Suggest
Make suggestions about how to improve things.

The ladder of feedback is a format for giving feedback, which allows the feedback to be focused and constructive. You should begin at step 1, 'Clarify', and move up the ladder. You can carry out this procedure after drafting a piece of writing, or for a presentation.

Swap your draft with one of your classmates and carry out the ladder of feedback. Write your feedback in a table, similar to this one:

Once feedback has been completed, return the work and consider the feedback you received in turn. Revise your news report as you feel may be needed. There is no set time limit for this process – make sure you carry it out thoroughly.

Features, characteristics and style in autobiography

Autobiography is made up of three Classical Greek words – 'auto' (own), 'bios' (life), and 'graph' (to write). It thus refers to writing that one may write about one's own life. An autobiography itself can therefore obviously be written by anyone for themselves, and its audience may be anyone. The nature of the writing reflects these considerations.

What are the features/characteristics of autobiographical writing?

- It is written by the person whose life is being described (though for commercial autobiographies the subject of the autobiography may in fact use a 'ghost writer' – a professional writer who does the actual writing, although the text is written as if its subject is the writer).
- It is usually written in past tense, as it is a description of one's life.
- It is written in the first person and gives the subject's perspectives of events being described.
- It may well contain a lot of thoughts and feelings about what is narrated, since the narrator knows what these were and can express these first hand.
- It is generally (though not necessarily) public writing, intended for an external audience of some kind, rather than being a piece of private writing such as a diary.
- Since that audience can, meanwhile, be anyone, the content and style of an autobiography is generally intended to be of interest to a wide range of people and groups.

There are a number of other aspects of style to think about when reading or writing an autobiography:

- They tend to make use of a lot of detail, which makes situations, settings and characters more vivid and immediate to a reader.
- Greater detail and bringing scenes to life mean greater use of descriptive techniques, such as **imagery** (including sensory imagery – references to the five senses of sight, hearing, smell, touch, taste).
- As with a news report, direct quotes are often used, again to give a greater sense of the immediate situation, and to reveal more of any characters in the scenes being described.
- If events are tense, expect to see techniques that convey suspense, such as use of sentence structure and punctuation, as well as key detail.
- They may well include **anecdotes** – short mini-stories that enliven the narrative further.
- Autobiographies can make great use of **irony,** especially dramatic irony where a reader already knows some of the major events of the life being described.
- One further aspect to look at and think about is the use of **register,** which tends not to be too formal. Authors often want to give us a sense of being almost by our side, having the story narrated directly to us.

WRITING ABOUT THINGS OURSELVES

Somebody who knew all about what it was like to blast off in a rocket to space was Helen Sharman. In 1991, she became the first British woman to travel into space when she was one of three cosmonauts taking part in a mission to the space station *Mir*.

The launch took place from Baikonur in Kazakhstan, and the photograph shows the three cosmonauts walking out to the rocket for take-off. She later revealed that she had thought about the *Challenger* space shuttle disaster (described in the news report earlier in this chapter) while she was preparing for the launch of her own mission: two female astronauts had been among those who died aboard Challenger. This revelation took place in her **autobiography**, *Seize the Moment*.

▼ Links to: Sciences

Have you investigated any space missions in your science classes? What is the science of space exploration? What are the impacts of space exploration?

What's in a name? Do you know what the difference is between **cosmonauts** and **astronauts**?

■ Helen Sharman, the first British woman in space

Many of these autobiography features can be seen in *Seize the Moment,* as the following extract shows. It describes the moments of the launch. Examples of notes about some of the linguistic features used in the passage are given in the blue labels.

Direct speech helps to bring the reader into the situation.

Note the short sentences and use of punctuation as the tension builds, as the rocket is about to launch.

- A lot of **sensory imagery** – sight, sound, touch – can be found in this paragraph.
- A lot of small detail is also described – as the astronauts can do nothing but wait, Helen Sharman is noticing everything – a sign of her tension at this moment.
- 'Sergei said nothing, Tolya said nothing: the voice from the bunker was silent.' – This is an example of **asyndeton**, where a conjunction is left out for emphasis. Here the repetition and asyndeton emphasize the silence at this point, which in turn again reflects the tension of the moment.

- More sensory imagery throughout the paragraph, including **onomatopoeia** in 'rumbling' (as was 'hiss' in the previous paragraph).
- The repeated references to time ticking down, as well as being a factual description, also serves to add to the tension of the events being described.
- Helen Sharman has said little about her own thoughts and feelings so far, but her impression that the rocket seems about to topple over again indicates the tension she is feeling.
- Another descriptive feature used here is **personification** of the engines and the instruments.

In my earphones, a voice from the bunker said, "Five minutes to go. Please close the masks of your helmets."

The three of us obeyed, then confirmed. Our call sign was *ozone,* and we identified ourselves by crew number. I was the last to confirm, and so I said, "Ozone 3, ozone 3, my helmet is shut. We are in the preparation regime, ready to go."

The bunker replied, "Understood, ozone 3. We are also in that regime. Everything on board is correct and we are now ready to launch."

A little later, the voice said, "Two minutes." Then it said, "One minute."

Now that we were not moving around or reaching for the controls above us, it was comfortable to be sitting there in the spacesuit. I glanced at the little **talisman**, swinging from the hatch above us. I felt the pressure of Tolya's elbow against mine. I could hear the quiet hiss of static in the speaker against my ear. Sergei said nothing, Tolya said nothing: the voice from the bunker was silent. It was a moment of stillness, of final waiting. My feet were still cold.

Far away, deep below, there came a rumbling noise as the rocket engines ignited. On the control panel the on-board clock had started automatically; we were nominally one second into the mission, then two, and the engines still rumbled far below. Three seconds and the rumbling grew louder and, as the four launch-gantries swung away, I could feel vibration but no sense of acceleration. I knew we must have left the ground and were in that momentary limbo where the rocket seems to balance precariously on its thrust, surely destined to topple. But the engines continued to roar beneath us and the instruments confirmed that we were away from the tower, that acceleration was beginning to build, and we could feel the pressure of g-forces growing steadily against us. ➤

When I next looked at the clock we were twenty seconds into the flight – and above us the talisman was taut on its string, no longer as free to swing. I could now sense the rocket's power, not only from the vibrations coming through the seat but also from the increasing press of acceleration. The clock showed that forty seconds had elapsed. The voice from the bunker confirmed the successful launch and Sergei briefly responded. G-forces continued to grow; the rocket was getting lighter as the fuel burned away and we were picking up speed.

After 115 seconds came the first of several loud bumps and bangs: the escape rocket on the nose of the craft was being jettisoned. At this point we were 46 kilometres from the ground on the threshold of space. Three seconds later there was another jolt, this one bigger and from below, as the first-stage booster rockets separated from us. This was the moment we passed the 50 kilometres mark, the height the Russians usually designate as the beginning of space.

Our smooth acceleration continued as the rocket grew lighter; now we were using the second-stage engine. This was the centrally-mounted main engine, used from the moment of lift-off. It was still burning steadily when, 165 seconds into the flight, the protective fairings that covered the windows was jettisoned, no longer needed to protect the spacecraft from the atmosphere as there was little atmosphere left outside!

Sunlight streamed in. I looked down at the Earth. We were already over the Pacific!

Tolya said, "What can you see? What can you see?" He had no window, and was dazzled by the golden sunlight pouring in.

I could see the curvature of the Earth!

Speckly white clouds! A brilliant azure sea! The blackness of space! Now I knew I was where the theory had told me I should be – out from the world, above the blue skies and diamond-studded clouds. Dreams sometimes do come true and I felt so alive!

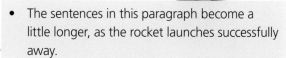
- The sentences in this paragraph become a little longer, as the rocket launches successfully away.
- Sensory imagery is used throughout these two quite technical paragraphs.

The use of repeated exclamation marks over the next few lines illustrates both the crew's relief at the successful launch, and sense of wonder at what they can now see from the rocket.

The short sentences used in these lines also reflect the excitement of the crew. Their almost child-like exclamations are a contrast to the quite long technical descriptions of the launch itself.

Note the use of adjectives, especially of colour, in the descriptions.

■ Malala Yousafzai is the youngest-ever Nobel Prize laureate

Below is an extract from another autobiography, by Malala Yousafzai. Malala was from the Swat Valley region of Pakistan, and from an area within that which had been taken over by the Taliban who did not believe that girls should be educated, and who began attacking girls' schools to prevent that from happening.

ACTIVITY: I am Malala

■ ATL

■ Communication skills: Use and interpret a range of discipline-specific terms and symbols

Look back at the notes in the margins on the extract for Helen Sharman on pages 11–12. As you read the extract from *I am Malala*, jot down notes of your own on the linguistic features that are used.

◆ Assessment opportunities

In this activity you have practised skills that are assessed using Criterion A: Analysing.

Malala began to come to the world's attention at just 11 years old when she spoke out in favour of education for girls, and anonymously blogged on the topic for the BBC. At the age of 13 she was nominated for an International Children's Peace Prize, and was awarded a National Youth Peace Prize within Pakistan. However, when she was 14 years old the Taliban made death threats against her, because of her continued activism in demanding that all girls should receive an education.

The following extract is taken from her autobiography, *I am Malala,* and describes the events that took place during her bus journey from school one day in October 2012.

That morning had begun like any other, though a little later than usual. It was exam time so school started at nine instead of eight, which was good as I don't like getting up and can sleep through the crows of the cocks and the prayer calls of the muezzin. First my father would try to rouse me. 'Time to get up, *Jani mun,*' he would say. This means 'soulmate' in Persian, and he always called me that at the start of the day. 'A few more minutes, *Aba,* please,' I'd beg, then burrow deeper under the quilt. Then my mother would come. *'Pisho,'* she would call. This means 'cat' and is her name for me. At this point I'd realise the time and shout, *'Bhabi,* I'm late!' In our culture, every man is your 'brother' and every woman your 'sister'. That's how we think of each other. When my father first brought his wife to school, all the teachers referred to her as 'my brother's wife' or *Bhabi.* That's how it stayed from then on. We all call her *Bhabi* now.

➤

I slept in the long room at the front of our house, and the only furniture was a bed and a cabinet which I had bought with some of the money I had been given as an award for campaigning for peace in our valley and the right for girls to go to school. On some shelves were all the gold-coloured plastic cups and trophies I had won for coming first in my class. Only a few times had I not come top – each time I was beaten by my class rival Malka e-Noor. I was determined it would not happen again.

The school was not far from my home and I used to walk, but since the start of last year I had been going with other girls in a rickshaw and coming home by bus. It was a journey of just five minutes along the stinky stream, past the giant billboard for Dr Humayun's Hair Transplant Institute where we joked that one of our bald male teachers must have gone when he suddenly started to sprout hair. I liked the bus because I didn't get as sweaty as when I walked, and I could chat with my friends and gossip with Usman Ali, the driver, who we called Bhai Jan, or 'Brother'. He made us all laugh with his crazy stories.

I had started taking the bus because my mother was scared of me walking on my own. We had been getting threats all year. Some were in the newspapers, some were notes or messages passed on by people. My mother was worried about me, but the Taliban had never come for a girl and I was more concerned they would target my father as he was always speaking out against them. His close friend and fellow campaigner Zahid Khan had been shot in the face in August on his way to prayers and I knew everyone was telling my father, 'Take care, you'll be next.'

Our street could not be reached by car, so coming home I would get off the bus on the road below by the stream and go through a barred iron gate and up a flight of steps. I thought if anyone attacked me it would be on those steps. Like my father I've always been a daydreamer, and sometimes in lessons my mind would drift and I'd imagine that on the way home a terrorist might jump out and shoot me on those steps. I wondered what I would do. Maybe I'd take off my shoes and hit him, but then I'd think if I did that there would be no difference between me and a terrorist. It would be better to plead, 'OK, shoot me, but first listen to me. What you are doing is wrong. I'm not against you personally, I just want every girl to go to school.'

I wasn't scared but I had started making sure the gate was locked at night and asking God what happens when you die. I told my best friend Moniba everything. We'd lived on the same street when we were little and been friends since primary school and we shared everything, Justin Bieber songs and Twilight movies, the best face-lightening creams. Her dream was to be a fashion designer although she knew her family would never agree to it, so she told everyone she wanted to be a doctor. It's hard for girls in our society to be anything other than teachers or doctors if they can work at all. I was different – I never hid my desire when I changed from wanting to be a doctor to wanting to be an inventor or a politician. Moniba always knew if something was wrong. 'Don't worry' I told her. 'The Taliban have never come for a small girl.'

When our bus was called, we ran down the steps. The other girls all covered their heads before emerging from the door and climbing up into the back. The bus was actually what we call a dyna, a white Toyota Town Ace truck with three parallel benches, one along either side and one in the middle. It was cramped with twenty girls and three teachers. I was sitting on the left between Moniba and a girl from the year below called Shazia Ramzan, holding our exam folders to our chests and our school bags under our feet.

After that it is all a bit hazy. I remember that inside the dyna it was hot and sticky. The cooler days were late coming and only the faraway mountains of the Hindu Kush had a frosting of snow. The back where we sat had no windows, just thick plastic sheeting at the sides which flapped and was too yellowed and dusty to see through. All we could see was a little stamp of open sky out of the back and glimpses of the sun, at that time of day a yellow orb floating in the dust that streamed over everything.

I remember that the bus turned right off the main road at the army checkpoint as always and rounded the corner past the deserted cricket ground. I don't remember any more.

In my dreams about the shooting my father is also in the bus and he is shot with me, and then there are men everywhere and I am searching for my father.

In reality what happened was we suddenly stopped. On our left was the tomb of Sher Mohammad Khan, the finance minister of the first ruler of Swat, all overgrown with grass, and on our right the snack factory. We must have been less than 200 metres from the checkpoint.

We couldn't see in front, but a young bearded man in light-coloured clothes had stepped into the road and waved the van down.

'Is this the Khushal School bus?' he asked our driver. Usman Bhai Jan thought this was a stupid question as the name was painted on the side. 'Yes,' he said.

'I need information about some children,' said the man.

'You should go to the office,' said Usman Bhai Jan.

As he was speaking another young man in white approached the back of the van. 'Look, it's one of those journalists coming to ask for an interview,' said Moniba. Since I'd started speaking at events with my father to campaign for girls' education and against those like the Taliban who want to hide us away, journalists often came, even foreigners, though not like this in the road.

The man was wearing a peaked cap and had a handkerchief over his nose and mouth as if he had flu. He looked like a college student. Then he swung himself onto the tailboard at the back and leaned in right over us.

'Who is Malala?' he demanded.

No one said anything, but several of the girls looked at me. I was the only girl with my face not covered.

That's when he lifted up a black pistol. I later learned it was a Colt 45. Some of the girls screamed. Moniba tells me I squeezed her hand.

My friends say he fired three shots, one after another. The first went through my left eye socket and out under my left shoulder. I slumped forward onto Moniba, blood coming from my left ear, so the other two bullets hit the girls next to me. One bullet went into Shazia's left hand. The third went through her left shoulder and into the upper right arm of Kainat Riaz.

My friends later told me the gunman's hand was shaking as he fired.

By the time we got to the hospital my long hair and Moniba's lap were full of blood.

I am Malala – Malala Yousafzai

Following the attack, Malala was flown to Birmingham in the United Kingdom to receive treatment. By March 2013, she had made a remarkable recovery and was well enough to go to school in Birmingham. In July that year, on her 16th birthday, she gave a speech at the United Nations in New York – the speech can be watched here: **https://youtu.be/3rNhZu3ttIU**.

In October 2014 she became the youngest ever winner of the Nobel Peace Prize. Since the attack, she has become internationally known for her courage in refusing to be silenced and continuing her fight for the right of everyone to receive an education.

ACTIVITY: A time when I showed courage …

■ ATL

- Communication skills: Use appropriate forms of writing for different purposes and audiences; use and interpret a range of discipline-specific terms and symbols

Now that we have looked at the purpose and nature of autobiographical writing, here is a summative assessment task for you to try on this type of writing.

Think about the possible examples of 'courage' we have looked at in class. Then think of a time when you feel that you showed courage in some way (which may be, for instance, starting something new such as a new school or an activity).

Write a 500–1,000 word account of this, using an autobiographical style.

You will be assessed on Criterion C: Producing text and Criterion D: Using language. In the tables on page 17, we look at the assessment criteria and provide some hints and guidelines regarding what you need to be thinking about and demonstrating.

◆ Assessment opportunities

This activity can be assessed using Criterion C: Producing text and Criterion D: Using language.

Assessment criteria	You need to demonstrate the following:
Criterion C *The student:* i produces texts that demonstrate a **high degree** of personal engagement with the creative process; demonstrates a **high degree** of insight, imagination and sensitivity and **perceptive** exploration of and critical reflection on new perspectives and ideas	• Personal engagement will be evident in the personal voice chosen for the writing, and the sense of involvement of the narrator in what is being narrated which comes across to the reader. • Imagination and sensitivity will be evident in the choices of subject matter, details, and stylistic choices made. • Exploration of ideas will be evident in the ideas included, and the detail used to explore them further.

ii makes **perceptive** stylistic choices in terms of linguistic, literary and visual devices, demonstrating **good** awareness of impact on an audience	• Make use of descriptive techniques, such as:
	
	  ○ Use and think about your choices of adjectives, adverbs, and verbs.
	
	  ○ Use imagery, including sensory imagery – references to the five senses of sight, hearing, smell, touch, taste.
	
	• Think about sentence structures used.
	
	• Use direct quotes to give a greater sense of the immediate situation, and to reveal more of any characters in the scenes being described.

iii selects **extensive** relevant details and examples to develop ideas with precision.	• Make use of detail which makes situations, settings and characters more vivid and immediate to a reader.

Criterion D
 	
The student:
 	
i **effectively** uses a varied range of appropriate vocabulary, sentence structures and forms of expression
 	
ii writes and speaks in a **consistently appropriate** register and style that serve the context and intention
 	
iii uses grammar, **syntax** and punctuation with **a high degree** of accuracy; errors are minor and communication is **effective**
 	
iv writes with a **high degree** of accuracy; errors are minor and communication is **effective**.
	• For this criterion remember to:
	
	  ○ Write in the first person.
	
	  ○ Use a register which is not too formal, to give a sense of being almost by a reader's side and narrating the story directly to them.
	
	  ○ However, note that register which is too informal should also generally be avoided, including using slang and colloquial language (except in direct quotations).
	
	  ○ In relation to register, use of contractions ('don't', 'I'd' etc) should be considered carefully, depending on the narrative voice – note that adult Helen Sharman does not use them, but younger Malala does.
	
	  ○ Think about vocabulary use, and what might be effective and more varied vocabulary choices.
	
	  ○ Vary use of sentence structures according to purpose – shorter sentences or clauses convey tension, or show excitement.

ACTIVITY: Analysing stylistic techniques

Work in pairs. Swap your autobiography with a partner and read theirs. **Identify** any stylistic features used in their writing. Return the autobiography and the stylistic features notes to the original author.

Then use your notes to write a rationale of 500–600 words explaining the techniques you used, and purposes of those techniques. This can be assessed against Criterion A, as follows:

Criterion A	The relevant aspects to **discuss** for your own writing are these:
The student: i provides **perceptive** analysis of the content, context, language, structure, technique, style of text(s) and the relationship among texts	• Content – why you chose the particular topic and focus you did, and how you feel it shows you as being 'courageous'. • Language – what particular vocabulary choices you used at any time, and why you chose those; deliberate choice and use of adjectives, adverbs, and verbs. • Structure – did you choose particular sentence structures for any reason, at any time? If so, where, and why? Did you try to use any asyndeton anywhere? Did you arrange any of the events in your autobiography in a particular way for any reason, at any point? If so, what did you do at that/those point(s), and why? • Technique – did you use descriptive techniques such as sensory imagery, **similes**, **metaphors**, personification, onomatopoeia, **historic present** and so on? Was there any use of irony? • Style – how did you use detail in your writing? Are there any particular key details included? What are they, and what was the purpose of including them? Did you use direct quotes? For what purpose? Were any anecdotes included? What register did you adopt, and how did you make that evident in the writing? Why did you choose that register?
ii **perceptively** analyses the effects of the creator's choices on an audience	• What were the intended effects on any audience of any of the above aspects of content, language, structure, technique and style? Pick out four or five that might have had a particular effect on your 'audience' – your readers.
iii gives **detailed justification of** opinions and ideas with a range of examples, and **thorough** explanations; uses **accurate** terminology	• All of the above should be fully explained, and supported by specific examples from your text. As the descriptor states, ensure you use the correct terminology – imagery, onomatopoeia, etc.
iv **perceptively compares and contrasts** by making **extensive** connections in features across and within genres and texts.	We will not be looking at this strand for this activity.

What is a biography?

The term **biography** is made up of the Classical Greek words 'bios' (life), and 'graph' (to write), and thus, as with an autobiography, it refers to writing about someone's life. A key difference, however, is that it is not written by the subject him- or herself, but by someone else.

BIAS IN BIOGRAPHICAL WRITING

Crucially, despite supposedly being a factual account of a life, a biography may well contain **bias** – authors generally write biographies of people they have an interest in, for some reason – either favourable or unfavourable. A clue to this can lie in whether the biography is 'authorized' – published with the permission of the subject, and often written with considerable input from them – or 'unauthorized' – published without the approval of the subject, which often means writing the biography without any significant direct input from the subject.

A biography should, on the surface, be a factual record of a life, and so we might not expect it to contain bias. A biographer's own opinions may well not be made explicit, but they can often be discerned (seen) implicitly by how they present their information. It is important to look for clues that may suggest the biographer's opinions about the subject him- or herself and also about other aspects of content, such as other people who are also included in the work.

This is apparent in the passage on page 20 from an authorized biography of Desmond Tutu, Archbishop of Cape Town during the apartheid era in South Africa, when a ruling minority of whites strongly oppressed the black majority in the country. Archbishop Tutu was one of the most prominent opponents during the years of apartheid, standing up fearlessly and speaking out against it, and against the governments of the day who continued to impose it.

This passage narrates a meeting between Desmond Tutu and President PW Botha in which the archbishop sought to speak on behalf of the Sharpeville Six, a group of prisoners who had been sentenced to death for their role in the death of the deputy mayor during a protest march that had taken place in the town of Sharpeville.

The next day, following this conversation, the Sharpeville Six were granted a stay of execution by a judge who 'for the first time appeared sympathetic'. Some months later their case was referred from the courts to Botha, who 'replaced the death sentences with long terms of imprisonment'. All six were released at the fall of apartheid some years later.

Features and characteristics of biographical writing

A biography …

- is about someone's life, and should retell this using a lot of factual content
- is written by someone other than the subject and so …
- is written in the third person, and one would usually not find first person references
- is written mostly in past tense
- is usually written in chronological order, and so usually starts with childhood
- usually includes information about family members
- will have less access than an autobiography to the subject's immediate thoughts, feelings and motivations.

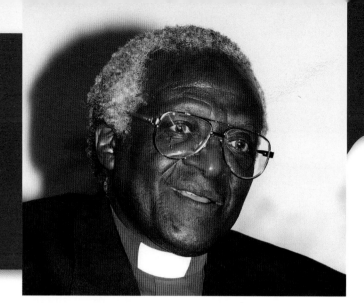

■ Desmond Tutu

Tutu and his personal assistant, Matt Esau, went into Botha's office. It was the first time Esau had met Botha, and he was struck by the president's size; alongside Tutu, who stood only 1.6 meters (five feet four inches) tall, Botha was, in Esau's words, a groot, fris Boer (a "big, beefy Afrikaner"). Esau was also struck by the lighting – and Robin Renwick wrote later that being received in Botha's dimly-lit study conjured up images of what it must have been like to call on Hitler in his bunker. Botha was accompanied by the director general of his office and by one or two cabinet ministers.

Tutu told Botha he was not appealing for the Sharpeville Six on legal grounds. As a minister of the gospel he had come to plead for mercy, which was not to be confused with justice. He was opposed to the death penalty in principle – in 1982 he had successfully pleaded for the lives of white South African mercenaries sentenced to death for trying to overthrow the government of the Seychelles islands. Hanging the Sharpeville Six, he now warned, could spark new violence, particularly because the following Monday, March 21, was the anniversary of the 1960 Sharpeville massacre. It would be a statesmanlike act, Tutu said, to grant a reprieve. Botha replied that South Africa's courts were independent and he did not want to encroach on them. He operated within certain limits when he exercised his prerogative to grant clemency; this case did not fall within those limits. Botha provided only a glimmer of hope; the trial judge was hearing an application for a stay of execution in Pretoria, he said. If the court decided there were other circumstances that he needed to look at, he would do so.

At that point the atmosphere deteriorated. Botha said there was something else he wanted to discuss: the church leaders' petition. The original of the document had been mailed to the president the day after the abortive march, somewhat wrinkled after being drenched by the water cannon. Botha handed Tutu a four-page reply, then started to berate him. Wagging his finger in the belligerent style that was his trademark, he excoriated the archbishop for instigating an illegal march; for allegedly drawing up the petition only after the march; for supposedly marching in front of a communist flag; for advocating sanctions; for supporting the outlawed liberation movement, the African National Congress (ANC); and for having the temerity to invite Thatcher, Reagan, and Kohl [then heads of government in the United Kingdom, United States, and Germany] to interfere in South Africa's domestic affairs.

At first Tutu restrained himself. Botha's behavior was not out of character – he was said to drive his own cabinet ministers to tears. But as Tutu tried and failed to get a word in edgewise, and Botha jumped from point to point, an anger born of decades of observing the consequences of apartheid stirred within him. Tutu thought to himself: "Our people have suffered for so long. I might never get this chance again." Shaking a finger back at Botha, he said: "Look here, I'm not a small boy. Don't think you're talking to a small boy. I'm not here as if you're my principal… I thought I was talking to a civilized person and there are courtesies involved."

Rabble-rouser for Peace: the Authorised Biography of Desmond Tutu – John Allen

ACTIVITY: A thin line between love and hate

■ ATL

■ Communication skills: Read critically and for comprehension; make inferences and draw conclusions; write and different purposes

What key details and techniques in the passage present Archbishop Tutu in a more favourable light, and President Botha in a less favourable one? A couple of suggestions have been made for both, as examples – add more to each column:

Archbishop Tutu	President Botha
The writer suggests that he knows Tutu's inner thoughts and motivations, and mentions his 'anger', and even includes direct thoughts – 'Our people have suffered for so long ...'. As this quote shows, Tutu's words and actions seem aimed at trying to help others.	Botha is only observed externally and there is no sense of his inner motivations or thoughts – only the (negative) impact he has on others: 'he was said to drive his own cabinet ministers to tears'. As this quote shows, Botha's words and actions all seem to have the effect of hurting people.

Now it's your turn. Write a 500–600 word biographical account of an event in the life of someone you know – from your family, or friends – which presents them in a favourable light, without being obvious about that. Below is a process that might help in that.

- **Decide first of all, how you want them to come across to a reader.**
- **Choose some characteristics that you might want to show about them in your writing. If it is helpful, you could consider the learner profile attributes as a starting point.**
- **There may be some Approaches to Learning skills that you feel describe them, such as some of the affective skills: e.g. *focused, determined, persistent, resilient, bounce back after failure, self-motivated, positive outlook, adaptable*, etc.**
- **You need to have specific qualities in mind in order to include in your writing words, actions, details of**

appearance and details of comments/thoughts of others that will help convey those impressions. Use a character planning box, such as the example below, to plan some specific aspects or details about your subject that you might include.

Words	Actions
Things said by others	**Details of appearance**

■ Character planning box

Once you begin to draft your biography, think about how you will include your ideas from the character planning box, along with possible aspects of technique, such as the following:

- **choice of factual statements**
- **word choice (particularly adjectives, adverbs, verbs)**
- **imagery – particularly similes and metaphors**
- **techniques of syntax – listing, repetition, for example.**

Writing for particular effects is a very deliberate process, and it is important to think about what you are trying to convey to an audience, and in what different ways you may be able to achieve that.

◆ Assessment opportunities

In this activity you have practised skills that are assessed using Criterion C: Analysing and Criterion D: Using language. It is not long enough to be used summatively with Criterion B, but may be used formatively to look more closely at skills of strands i, ii, and iii in this criterion.

How might texts try to manipulate our responses?

We are going to look at an extract of a letter written by Martin Luther King Jr, after he had been imprisoned for taking part in civil rights demonstrations in Birmingham, Alabama, in the United States.

The letter was written on 16 April 1963, in answer to a group of clergyman and some other sympathizers who had suggested that he should try to bring about change through using legal processes, rather than engaging in civil disobedience.

Martin Luther King Jr

Dr Martin Luther King Jr was a leader of the African-American Rights Movement, which during the 1950s and 1960s attempted to bring about social change in the United States, including the end of segregation of blacks and whites in society, through nonviolent civil disobedience.

In 1963, Dr King would help in organizing the famous march to Washington, and would deliver his famous 'I have a dream' speech there.

Read the letter on pages 24–25. Then read the notes and questions surrounding the letter, which highlight the language techniques used by Dr King. These techniques helped him to convey his thoughts and feelings in writing the letter.

■ Martin Luther King Jr

Letters

Letters always have a particular writer, of course, so to some extent they present the viewpoint of that writer. A letter is written for a specific reason, and for particular recipients, and it is thus always important when looking at letters as a non-fiction text to ask about each:

- What is the purpose of the letter?
- Who is it being written for?

Letters may be written for a variety of purposes – when we want to complain about something, explain something, try to persuade someone of something, describe or narrate events, and so on.

The content of a letter, and style in which it is written, will reflect what its purpose is, and who is expected to read it. Because it is a direct and highly personal piece of text, it will reflect in some way the viewpoint of the writer, and a reader can often interpret the following from the content of a letter:

- what the writer thinks and feels about what they are writing
- why the writer is interested in their subject
- what the writer wants the reader to think and feel about the topic(s) of their writing.

A reader may work these out from looking at the following aspects in particular:

- what facts and opinions have been included
- the writer's use of language
- what the writer's purpose seems to have been in writing the letter.

▼ Links to: History

Have you studied the civil rights movement in your history classes? What is Dr King's impact on American history and society? What is his impact on literature and language?

In *History for the IB MYP 4&5: by Concept,* Chapter 11 inquires into civil rights by asking: How have civil rights and social protest groups brought about change?

ACTIVITY: Letter from a Birmingham Jail

■ ATL

- Communication skills: Read critically and for comprehension; make inferences and draw conclusions

Read the letter on the following pages and consider the annotations. In groups of four, **identify** any more language techniques you can find. What techniques have you **identified**? What are your answers to the questions asked in the annotations? What thoughts and feelings do these suggest?

How would you **describe** Dr King's purpose(s) for writing the letter?

◆ Assessment opportunities

In this activity you have practised skills that are assessed using Criterion A: Analysing.

Use of emotive adjectives

As shown here, King often uses balanced comparisons and contrasts in his sentence structures. Why might he do this?

A metaphor

Personification

Another comparison – what do the highlighted images suggest about his feelings at this point?

Metaphor and **alliteration** – what are the effects of these?

What does this very long sentence reveal about King's thoughts and feelings about what he is writing about?

What do you notice about the narrative voice King has adopted in this section? What does it suggest about his feelings?

Pick out eight examples of words or phrases that you think have been carefully chosen by King for effect. What effects do you think they are aimed at having?

We know through painful experience that freedom is never voluntarily given by the oppressor; it must be demanded by the oppressed. Frankly, I have never yet engaged in a direct action movement that was "well-timed," according to the timetable of those who have not suffered unduly from the disease of segregation. For years now I have heard the word "Wait!" It rings in the ear of every Negro with a piercing familiarity. This "Wait!" has almost always meant "Never." It has been a tranquillizing thalidomide, relieving the emotional stress for a moment, only to give birth to an ill-formed infant of frustration. We must come to see with the distinguished jurist of yesterday that "justice too long delayed is justice denied."

We have waited for more than 340 years for our constitutional and God-given rights. The nations of Asia and Africa are moving with jet-like speed toward the goal of political independence, and we still creep at horse and buggy pace toward the gaining of a cup of coffee at a lunch counter. I guess it is easy for those who have never felt the stinging darts of segregation to say, "Wait." But when you have seen vicious mobs lynch your mothers and fathers at will and drown your sisters and brothers at whim; when you have seen hate-filled policemen curse, kick, brutalize and even kill your black brothers and sisters with impunity; when you see the vast majority of your twenty million Negro bothers smothering in an airtight case of poverty in the midst of an affluent society; when you suddenly find your tongue twisted and your speech stammering as you seek to explain to your six-year-old daughter why she can't go to the public amusement park that has just

What might King's feelings have been as he describes the impact of segregation on a 6-year-old girl?

What does he suggest is the result of segregation?

Why is the reference to 'Funtown' ironic?

been advertised on television, and see tears welling up in her little eyes when she is told that Funtown is closed to colored children, and see the depressing clouds of inferiority begin to form in her little mental sky, and see her begin to distort her little personality by unconsciously developing a bitterness toward white people; when you have to concoct an answer for a five-year-old son asking in agonizing pathos: "Daddy, why do white people treat colored people so mean?"; when you take a cross-country drive and find it necessary to sleep night after night in the uncomfortable corners of your automobile because no motel will accept you; when you are humiliated day in and day out by nagging signs reading "white" and "colored"; when your first name becomes "nigger" and your middle name becomes "boy" (however old you are) and your last name becomes "John," and when your wife and mother are never given the respected title "Mrs."; when you are harried by day and haunted by night by the fact that you are a Negro, living constantly at tiptoe stance never quite knowing what to expect next and plagued with inner fears and outer resentments; when you are forever fighting a degenerating sense of "nobodiness"; then you will understand why we find it difficult to wait. There comes a time when we find it difficult to wait. There comes a time when the cup of endurance runs over, and men are no longer willing to be plunged into an abyss of injustice where they experience the blackness of corroding despair. I hope, sirs, you can understand our legitimate and unavoidable impatience.

Letter from a Birmingham Jail – Martin Luther King

This is an example of a rhetorical question. What are these used for?

King refers to a lot of close family members in this part of the letter – why do you think he does this?

Why do you think this sentence is so long?

Repetition is used a lot in King's letter, and in his speeches. What is the effect of repetition here?

Is this a fact or an opinion? How does King try to justify it in the final three sentences of the extract?

How might cultural factors affect texts and our responses to them?

Aung San Suu Kyi

Aung San Suu Kyi's father, Aung San, had as leader of Myanmar negotiated independence from the British Empire in 1947, and was considered the 'Father of the Nation', but he was assassinated by political rivals later that year. Aung San Suu Kyi studied and lived abroad for a while, but returned to help lead the NLD in 1988. Two years later the party won more than 80 per cent of the seats in the country's parliament, but the military refused to hand over power, and had placed Aung San Suu Kyi under house arrest just before the elections. She remained under house arrest for a total of almost 15 years between 1989 and 2010. Her determination to stand up to the military over so many years made her one of the most famous political prisoners in the world, and led to her receiving many awards, including the Nobel Peace Prize in 1991, which was received on her behalf by her husband and children, since she was unable to leave Myanmar unless she agreed never to return, which she refused to do. She was finally released from house arrest in November 2010, and plays an increasing role in Myanmar's state politics.

We will now look at another letter, this time written by Aung San Suu Kyi, leader of the National League for Democracy (NLD) political party in Myanmar.

The letter was written to the Secretary-General of Amnesty International, about human rights abuses, but fell into the hands of the military authorities, and was recorded by them as evidence of treason.

ACTIVITY: Letters

■ ATL

- Communication skills: Read critically and for comprehension; make inferences and draw conclusions

Read the letter and, as a group, discuss the following:

- **Identify** the facts and opinions used in the letter.
- **Compare and contrast** the two letters, making notes on the differences you can see between the way in which this letter is written, and that written by Dr King. You might like to think about things such as the language use here and in the above letter, along with sentence structure, and tone.
- How would you **describe** Aung San Suu Kyi's purpose(s) for writing the letter?
- Both letters try to highlight injustices – why do you think Aung San Suu Kyi adopted a very different tone to that of Dr Martin Luther King Jr?
- Which letter did you find the most effective? Why?

◆ Assessment opportunities

In this activity you have practised skills that are assessed using Criterion A: Analysing.

▼ Links to: Individuals and societies; History

What's in a name? Should it be Burma or Myanmar? Read these interesting articles:

https://goo.gl/pytR4D

http://news.bbc.co.uk/1/hi/magazine/7013943.stm

What other countries or cities have changed their names? What do you think about this?

There is ongoing debate about Aung San Suu Kyi's silence over the **persecution of the Rohingya Muslims** in Myanmar. Find out more about this. In pairs, discuss whether you think she still can be considered a human rights ambassador.

16 October 1988

On the subject of the continued violation of human rights in Burma we wish to submit to you the following facts which have been confirmed by numerous eyewitness reports.

On 15 October over six hundred men, mostly young students, were seized by the armed forces as they sat in teashops and eating stalls in Rangoon. Buses were stopped at checkpoints set up at frequent intervals in the streets, and young men who could not produce evidence of their employment as civil servants were taken away in military trucks. Furthermore, low-income housing areas were entered by troops, even during the hours of **curfew**, and men taken away.

All are believed to be taken to the front lines where the Burmese army is engaged in action against insurgent forces. Those seized in Rangoon in recent days are very likely being forced to act as so-called 'porters' to carry the rations and arms of the government troops. It is also widely believed that they are driven ahead of the troops in order to detonate the mines laid by the insurgent forces. A high percentage of government casualties are caused by such land mines.

All this appears to be connected to reports we received about five days ago that on 6 October over five hundred people, mostly students in their early teens, were seen at the town of Pa-an, tied together in groups of two and three and guarded by the armed forces. When the people of the town attempted to give them food and water they were cursed by the soldiers, who told them not to bother feeding 'those who are about to die'. They were kept overnight in the town hall and were taken off early the following morning in the direction of the continuing conflict.

The forced conscription of young men for service as 'porters' by the Burmese army is known to have taken place several times in recent years. However, this appears to be the first time it has actually taken place on the streets of Rangoon for all to see.

We request you to bring this news to the attention of all those concerned with the violation of human rights in Burma.

Freedom From Fear – Aung San Suu Kyi

ACTIVITY: Writing a letter

ATL

- Communication skills: Organize and depict information logically; write for different purposes

Choose one of the letters, or a letter of your choice from a human rights activist, and write a letter of your own to a newspaper, arguing about the injustices mentioned by the writer you have chosen, and suggesting what might be done about them, and who might act to do something.

Plan your letter to begin with, including each of the following:
- **Introduce yourself.**
- **Explain** why you are writing, in protest at the injustices you have become aware of.

- Give some details about what you feel particularly strongly about, from the information given in your chosen letter.
- **Describe** what you think should be done about these, who you think could and should act in some way, and how they might be able to help.
- Think about how you want to come across to the newspaper editor, and the tone you will adopt for that – passionate, like Dr King, or measured, like Aung San Suu Kyi? Which language choices will help in creating that?
- Finish your letter by thanking the editor for their time, and signing off.

Assessment opportunities

In this activity you have practised skills that are assessed using Criterion B: Organizing and Criterion D: Using language.

Take action

- Organization skills: Set goals that are challenging and realistic
- Affective skills: Practise positive thinking; practise 'bouncing back' after adversity, mistakes and failures; practise 'failing well'
- Reflection skills: Keep a journal to record reflections

'Having courage does not mean that we are unafraid. Having courage and showing courage mean we face our fears. We are able to say "I have fallen, but I will get up."' – Maya Angelou
'Courage doesn't always roar. Sometimes courage is the little voice at the end of the day that says I'll try again tomorrow.' – Mary Anne Radmacher
'Do one thing every day that scares you.' – Eleanor Roosevelt

! The well-known quote by Eleanor Roosevelt encapsulates what it is to be courageous and a risk-taker.
! What might you do, in the context of your everyday life at school, at home, with friends and so on, which is something that might 'scare you'? The following might be some examples:
- volunteering an idea, answer, or suggestion in class
- taking part in an assembly or event that involves speaking to a lot of people in school
- trying something like a new sport or club, which you are worried you might not be very good at
- speaking a language that is not your main language around school more
- volunteering to take the lead in collaborative work
- starting a conversation with another student whom you do not know very well
- saying something to a fellow student when they are doing something you feel is wrong
- going a day without using social media or your phone
- asking someone for help.

! Your challenge is to 'Do one thing every day that scares you' for two weeks, and to keep a journal to record and reflect on this. You might want to use a blog for your activities and progress, such as this by Michelle Poler, who set herself the challenge of doing one thing that scared her every day for 100 days: **http://100dayswithoutfear.com/list.**
! Visit this website for prompts for the challenge: **www.inc.com/lolly-daskal/do-one-thing-that-scares-you-every-day.html.**
! You could also use a vlog to record your challenge.

a. The first thing you need to do is to plan the seven things which you will be doing over the week, one per day.

b. If you need to capture these on video (which would be a good idea if possible), plan how that might be done:
  i. What camera might be used for recording?
  ii. Where might the filming need to take place?
  iii. Whose permission might you need?
  iv. What might you need to do to set up for filming?
  v. Who will do the filming?
c. Think about how much filming you might need to do – it may just be a few seconds.
d. You will also need to film yourself talking about your experiences. If it is difficult for you to film yourself 'in action' doing the 'one thing that scares me', some individual day entries in your vlog might only be of yourself talking to camera about what you have done.
  ◆ For each day you will be speaking about, draft out your speech. It should be between 1 and 2 minutes.
  ◆ The speech for each day should include:
    ◇ a description of what you actually did which scared you. Think about whether you want to use humour in this, or create tension over the experience; and what you might say in order to create these
    ◇ your feelings about the experience, before, during and/or after doing what it was which scared you
    ◇ what benefits and/or drawbacks you found
    ◇ examples of the kinds of things which someone might try to do for this kind of project
    ◇ any particular points of view, opinions or comments you may have about any aspect of the process – this is your vlog and your experience, and your voice as the writer should be heard in it
    ◇ remember the importance of including interesting detail in your description and comments on each day.
e. Rehearse each day's speech as many times as you wish.
f. Finish your vlog by summarizing your feelings about trying out one thing which scared you each day, and whether you would advise others to try it or not.
g. Once you feel you are ready, record yourself making the speeches, using whatever device may be appropriate in your context. Feel free to ask someone to do the filming if you wish, or to set things up so that you film yourself.

! Once your video is ready and you are happy to show it to others, share it within a group and give feedback on each other's videos.
! If there is time in class, your teacher may ask each group to nominate one of the videos to share and discuss further with the class as a whole.
! Criteria C (Creating text) and D (Using language) will be used to assess your vlog.

What is a diary?

One of the most famous diaries ever written was that by Anne Frank, who with her family went into hiding in Amsterdam in 1942 to avoid the Nazi persecution of the Jews.

The following extracts are from later on in the diary, where Anne thinks of the courage of those who are risking their lives helping the family by bringing food and provisions, and talks too of some of the conditions the family experienced in hiding, and of her own fears of the situation she is in.

Friday, 28 January 1944

Dearest Kitty,

…

Jan and Mr Kleiman love talking about people who have gone underground or into hiding; they know we're eager to hear about others in our situation and that we truly sympathize with the sorrow of those who've been arrested as well as the joy of prisoners who've been freed.

Going underground or into hiding has become as routine as the proverbial pipe and slippers that used to await the man of the hours after a long day at work. There are many resistance groups, such as Free Netherlands, that forge identity cards, provide financial support to those in hiding, organize hiding places and find work for young Christians who go underground. It's amazing how much these generous and unselfish people do, risking their own lives to help and save others.

The best example of this is our own helpers, who have managed to pull us through so far and will hopefully bring us safely to shore, because otherwise they'll find themselves sharing the fate of those they're trying to protect. Never have they uttered a single word about the burden we must be, never have they complained that we're too much trouble. They come upstairs every day and talk to the men about business and politics, to the women about food and wartime difficulties and to the children about books and newspaper. They put on their most cheerful expressions, bring flowers and gifts for birthdays and special occasions and are always ready to do what they can. That's something we should never forget; while others display their heroism in battle or against the Germans, our helpers prove theirs every day by their good spirits and affection.

From The Diary of Anne Frank

Anne Frank

■ Anne Frank

For the two years that the family remained hidden in concealed rooms on the upper floors of the house, Anne kept a diary, in which she wrote regularly, addressing her entries to 'Kitty' the name she had given to the diary. However, in August 1944 the family was betrayed, and arrested and sent on to various concentration camps. Anne died, probably of typhus, in Bergen-Belsen camp in Germany early in 1945, not long before the camp was liberated. Her father was the only member of her family to survive, and he found her diary on his return to Amsterdam after the war. It was first published in 1952 as *The Diary of a Young Girl*.

Friday, 26 May 1944

My dearest Kitty,

…

That gap, that enormous gap, is always there. One day we're laughing at the comical side of life in hiding, and the next day (and there are so many such days), we're frightened, and the fear, tension and despair can be read on our faces.

Miep and Mr Kugler bear the greatest burden for us, and for all those in hiding – Miep in everything she does and Mr Kugler through his enormous responsibility for the eight of us, which is sometimes so overwhelming that he can hardly speak from the pent-up tension and strain. Mr Kleiman and Bep also take very good care of us, but they're able to put the Annexe out of their minds, even if it's only for a few hours or a few days. They have their own worries, Mr Kleiman with his health and Bep with her engagement, which isn't looking very promising at the moment. But they also have their outings, their visits to friends, their everyday lives as ordinary people, so that the tension is sometimes relieved, if only for a short while, while ours never is, never has been, not once in the two years we've been here. How much longer will this increasingly oppressive, unbearable weight press down on us?

The drains are clogged again. We can't run the water, or if we do, only a trickle; we can't flush the toilet, we have to use a toilet brush; and we've been putting our dirty water into a big earthenware jar. We can manage for today, but what will happen if the plumber can't mend it on his own? They can't come to do the drains until Tuesday.

Miep sent us a currant loaf with 'Happy Whitsun' written on top. It's almost as if she were mocking us, since our moods and cares are far from 'happy'.

We've all become more frightened since the van Hoeven business. Once again you hear 'shh' from all sides, and we're doing everything more quietly. The police forced the door there; they could just as easily do that here too! What will we do if we're ever… no, I mustn't write that down. But the questions won't let itself be pushed to the back of my mind today; on the contrary, all the fear I've ever felt is looking before me in all its horror.

I had to go downstairs alone at eight this evening to use the lavatory. There was no one down there, since they were all listening to the radio. I wanted to be brave, but it was hard. I always feel safer upstairs than in that huge, silent house; when I'm alone with those mysterious muffled sounds from upstairs and the honking of horns in the street, I have to hurry and remind myself where I am to keep from getting the shivers.

Miep has been acting much nicer towards us since her talk with Father. But I haven't told you about that yet. Miep came up one afternoon all flushed and asked Father straight out if we thought they too were infected with the current anti-Semitism. Father was stunned and quickly talked her out of the idea, but some of Miep's suspicion has lingered on. They're doing more errands for us now and showing more of an interest in our troubles, though we certainly shouldn't bother them with our woes. Oh, they're such good, noble people!

I've asked myself again and again whether it would have been better if we hadn't gone into hiding, if we were dead now and didn't have to go through this misery, especially so that the others could be spared the burden. But we all shrink from this thought. We still love life, we haven't yet forgotten the voice of nature, and we keep hoping, hoping for … everything.

Let something happen soon, even an air raid. Nothing can be more crushing than this anxiety. Let the end come, however cruel; at least then we'll know whether we are to be the victors or the vanquished.

Yours, Anne M. Frank

From The Diary of Anne Frank

ACTIVITY: The diary of your 'things that scare you' challenge

Using the information on the format and content of a diary, choose three or four of your daily challenges and write diary entries that cover each of these. The diary extracts overall should total not more than 1,000 words.

◆ Assessment opportunities

In this activity you have practised skills that are assessed using Criterion B: Organizing, Criterion C: Producing text and Criterion D: Using language.

Diaries

Here are some tips on writing a diary entry. Adapted from www.tes.com/teaching-resource/how-to-write-a-diary-entry-6219883.

1 Make sure you write in chronological order – that is, in the order that things happened.
2 Write in the past tense.
3 To help the reader empathize with you, use pronouns such as *I, we, us, we're* and *I'm*. They help to make the reader feel part of the text.

Time connectors that will help:

Firstly …

Following on from …

Next …

Eventually …

Some time later …

Afterwards …

Finally …

4 Make sure you give detailed descriptions – add lots of detail and information to people, places, events and objects.
5 Remember to include your thoughts and feelings about these things. This will make your writing more appealing to the reader.
6 **Explain** why – help your reader to understand your moods by explaining your different emotions and feelings. This will help the reader to visualize the moment and put themselves in your shoes.

Reflection

In this chapter we have explored different examples of what it might mean to be 'courageous', along with different types of non-fiction writing, and some characteristics and purposes of those. We have looked at how perspective can influence the point of view we might have of it; and how writers might put us in particular positions in order to shape our point of view. We have also considered how cultural factors may influence our perspective and point of view.

Use this table to reflect on your own learning in this chapter.					
Questions we asked	**Answers we found**	**Any further questions now?**			
Factual:					
Conceptual:					
Debatable:					
Approaches to learning you used in this chapter	**Description – what new skills did you learn?**	**How well did you master the skills?**			
		Novice	Learner	Practitioner	Expert
Communication skills					
Organization skills					
Affective skills					
Reflection skills					
Media literacy skills					
Critical-thinking skills					
Creative-thinking skills					
Learner profile attribute(s)	Reflect on the importance of being a risk-taker for your learning in this chapter.				
Risk-takers					

② What's the drama?

Writers can use **conventions** in literature to convey the importance of **communication** in **relationships**.

CONSIDER THESE QUESTIONS:

Factual: What are the different ways in which people communicate with each other? What different conventions are associated with the ways people communicate? What conventions are used to communicate with an audience in the genre of drama?

Conceptual: How can ways in which we communicate affect our relationships with other people?

Debatable: Is non-verbal communication more powerful than verbal communication?

Now **share and compare** your thoughts and ideas with your partner, or with the whole class.

IN THIS CHAPTER, WE WILL ...

■ **Find out** the different ways in which we may communicate with others, and the conventions that are involved in those.

■ **Explore** the different ways in which communication can impact on others, and how it may affect our relationships with others.

■ **Take action** by developing more effective communication techniques to use in different contexts.

■ These Approaches to Learning (ATL) skills will be useful ...

■ Communication skills

■ Media literacy skills

■ Critical-thinking skills

■ Creative-thinking skills

◆ Assessment opportunities in this chapter:

◆ **Criterion A:** Analysing

◆ **Criterion B:** Organizing

◆ **Criterion C:** Producing text

◆ **Criterion D:** Using language

● We will reflect on this learner profile attribute ...

● Communicators – develop as a communicator through various activities involving analysing and using different methods of communication.

■ A scene from the play, *The Miracle Worker*

KEY WORDS

body language
communication
conventional
convey
juxtapose
self-esteem
tone
vigorous
vivacious

DISCUSS

Look at the scene from the play, *The Miracle Worker*. What different ways of communicating are being used by the characters in the scene? What messages are they communicating?

Create a table. In the left-hand column, brainstorm different ways in which we communicate with others. Then in the right-hand column, suggest a figure between 1 and 10 for how powerful you think it is as a way of communicating, with 10 being extremely powerful, and 1 not at all a powerful way of communicating.

What are the different ways in which people communicate with each other?

COMMUNICATION

Communication takes many forms, and while some of the most common are spoken and written, there are many other ways of communicating. Some of them are believed to be more powerful than words. For instance, it is thought that when we speak to another person, around two-thirds of the message they receive in fact comes from ways in which we are communicating beyond the actual words we use – the tone of our voice, our body language, facial expression and eye contact. Search online for **non-verbal communication** to find out more about how we communicate without words.

Have you ever felt you know how someone feels when they have not said anything? That is because they are conveying the message in ways other than by using words.

CONNECT–EXTEND–CHALLENGE

Watch the video 'Good communication skills for teens': **https://youtu.be/_UTx6iPLsH4**.

Think about the following:
- **How were the ideas and information presented in the video *connected* to what you already knew about good communication skills?**
- **What new ideas did you get that *extended* or pushed your thinking about communication skills in new directions?**
- **What is still *challenging* or confusing for you to get your mind around about the topic of communication, and what you saw and heard in the video? What questions, wonderings or puzzles do you have?**

You can present your comments in a table like the one below, or use sticky notes for displaying on the wall.

Connect	Extend	Challenge

Share your thoughts with a classmate or in small groups.

I've learned that people will forget what you said, people will forget what you did, but people will never forget how you made them feel.

■ The novelist Maya Angelou

Communication is a powerful influence on how we feel, and how we can and do make others feel. Read the Maya Angelou quote. Positive communication can make us feel elated and reassured, and do much for our self-esteem. Communication can equally be used to hurt – at times grievously (ever heard of the saying 'The pen is mightier than the sword'?) – while malicious or ineffective communication in various contexts can have extremely damaging consequences.

It is very important, therefore, that we become aware of the different ways in which we can and do communicate, of how that might be done effectively, and of the consequences that may result from ways in which we communicate.

DISCUSS

In each of these examples, a different type of communication is being used. **Identify** each, and give an example of how it might be used to:

a impact positively on someone else, and
b impact negatively on them.

■ **a** Speaking   ■ **b** Telephone / text messaging   ■ **c** Gestures

■ **d** Body language   ■ **e** Facial expression   ■ **f** Writing

■ **g** Electronic communication: email, social media, etc.   ■ **h** Communication through pictures and symbols   ■ **i** Eye contact

DISCUSS

What is **cyberbullying**? In what ways does it use communication to impact negatively on people?

AUDIENCE

With whom do we communicate and in what ways do we do it? Why do we choose those particular methods?

ACTIVITY: Who are you talking to?

■ ATL

■ Communication skills: Use a variety of media to communicate with a range of audiences

Complete the table below. Choose six different types of 'audience' with whom we might communicate, and for each **suggest** a way in which we communicate. Remember that 'audience' is the term used for any possible recipient of our communication, and that it may even refer just to ourselves, for instance when we are writing a diary.

Now think of different ways in which we might communicate – for example, by how we look, what our facial expressions might be, what the tone used might convey, and so on.

Then in the last column, **explain** the impact each way of communicating might have on the particular 'audience' each time. You might also want to act out how you would communicate with each different audience.

Audience	A possible way in which I might communicate with that 'audience'	What impact might this have on my 'audience'?

◆ Assessment opportunities

In this activity you have practised skills that are assessed using Criterion D: Using language.

What conventions are used to communicate with an audience in the genre of drama?

CONVENTIONS OF GENRES

Writers who create literary works are engaging in direct communication with their readers, and attempting to convey certain ideas and messages in different ways. To do this they will choose a particular **genre** in which to write. A genre is a particular style or type of literature, such as drama, speech, horror, poetry, and so on.

Different genres have their own particular **conventions**, which are the characteristics they have that mean they can be categorized in a particular literary genre.

Conventions also communicate meaning to an audience or reader. Some of the conventions of drama can be categorized as *literary, technical* and *performance* conventions, and include those listed in the information box.

> ℹ️
> ## Conventions of drama
>
> *Performance*
>
> > stage direction   aside   blocking
> > fourth wall   entrances/exits   gesture
> > acting   speaking   non-verbal expression
>
> *Literary*
>
> > dramatic irony   foreshadow   audience
> > character   conflict
> > dialogue   monologue   plot   script
> > setting   structure
>
> *Technical*
>
> > costumes   make-up   props   scenery
> > sound and music   lighting

TECHNICAL AND PERFORMANCE CONVENTIONS OF DRAMA

Acting, speaking, and non-verbal communication are performance conventions of drama, which are crucial in conveying the meaning of what is happening in a play, beyond the words on the page. These conventions are essential in defining drama and in distinguishing it from other genre types as, unlike with a written text, in drama definitive decisions must be made as to *how* words and actions will sound and look, since these will be spoken and carried out, rather than being described.

While stage directions are often given by a playwright to indicate aspects of performance conventions, a director too must make such decisions on these, in collaboration with the actors.

Acting: The Merriam-Webster online dictionary defines acting as 'the art or practice of representing a character on a stage or before cameras'. (**www.merriam-webster.com/dictionary/acting**)

Acting can thus encompass all movements, gestures, facial expressions, words and so on, which are used by an actor to represent a character, and which (as in real life) provide clues as to the nature of the character and his or her thoughts and feelings.

We will now look at these conventions and how they are used in the play, *The Miracle Worker* by William Gibson.

The Miracle Worker by William Gibson

■ William Gibson

■ Helen Keller

William Gibson (3 November 1914–25 November 2008) was a New York playwright and novelist. His most famous play is *The Miracle Worker* (1959), which won him the Tony Award for Best Play after he adapted it from his original 1957 television play. He adapted it again for the 1962 film version and received an Academy Award nomination for Best Adapted Screenplay.

The Miracle Worker is based on the early life of Helen Keller, and dramatizes the real-life events of the arrival of semi-blind teacher Annie Sullivan to teach the young Helen, who had been left blind, deaf and mute following a childhood illness.

Helen's behaviour in the play demonstrates the impact five years of highly limited communication had on her. The playwright is also keen to present the impact of this behaviour on those closest to Helen. Annie feels that underneath her outward behaviour, Helen is intelligent and curious, and 'a little safe, locked', which may well have 'a treasure inside'. She therefore refuses to indulge Helen's poor behaviour in the way Helen's family have done ('It's less trouble to feel sorry for her than to teach her anything better, isn't it?'). In her determination to teach Helen more effective ways to communicate, she adopts a tough love approach instead.

This leads to a series of physical, psychological and intellectual battles between the two, which on stage 'constitute unforgettable theatre' (*Time* magazine). Two particular actors playing the roles of Annie and Helen, Anne Bancroft and Patti Duke, won a number of awards for their performances in the play, and then won Oscars too when the play was transferred to film in 1962.

The Miracle Worker has much to say about the different ways in which communication can take place, and on the different ways in which relationships can be affected by how that may happen. It raises other questions too, such as that of using physical force on a child. Meanwhile, the play demonstrates how the conventions of drama can communicate ideas in different but very powerful ways. Both the genre and its ideas will be explored throughout this unit, as we focus on aspects of the nature and impact of communication.

ACTIVITY: Directing a character

■ ATL

■ Communication skills: Use and interpret a range of discipline-specific terms and symbols

This activity is based on the first scene of the play, *The Miracle Worker*.

Goal

Get into groups of three. Each member takes on one of the following roles:
- **Kate Keller**
- **Captain Keller**
- **Doctor**

You are each a director for a production of the play, and must direct your particular actor in how to perform the role of the character in the opening scene of the play on stage.

Look at Scene 1, from the beginning to *His face has something like fury in it, crying the child's name; KATE, almost fainting, presses her knuckles to her mouth, to stop her own cry. The room dims out quickly.* Read through the scene. In your notebook, write down any directions you want to give the actor when they speak particular lines. Consider these in terms of how they might act, speak or use non-verbal communication. You must provide at least two examples of direction for each.

In your group, perform a dramatic reading of the scene, in which each of you takes the part of the character for whom you have given directions.

ACTING

Look again at the choices you made in the case of your character for the activity on the left. Share with your group members the reasons why you made each choice.

ACTIVITY: Writing a diary entry

Later in this chapter, you will be writing a dramatic monologue, containing the thoughts and feelings of a character in one of the scenes from the play.

As practice for that, let us first consider what Kate's thoughts and feelings may be, immediately after this scene in which she has discovered that Helen cannot see or hear. We will use the format of a diary to **identify** and develop the thoughts and feelings of a character. Read about the features of a diary on page 31.

If Kate were to write a diary entry following the events of this first scene, what would she write? And how would it be written? Write Kate's diary entry of 500–600 words.

> **Hint**
>
> For the voice of the writer in this play, it is the character of Kate. What features of Kate are evident in the opening scene? You may have noticed that:
> - she has a tendency to ask questions and she cares a great deal about Helen
> - she is quite insightful and practical in noticing that something is wrong and in knowing how to check for that. She is likely to understand some of the implications of Helen's blindness and deafness for the future, therefore
> - she responds quite emotionally, firstly to the news that Helen seems to be alright, and later to the discovery that other things are wrong.

Complete the reflective prompts below. As a result of this self-assessment, make any further amendments to improve the work.

Where/how have you shown in your writing:	Your response
Kate's tendency to ask questions	
That Kate cares a lot about Helen	
That Kate is thinking about what may happen as a result of her discoveries about Helen	
Kate responding in an emotional way to the events of the scene	

◆ Assessment opportunities

In this activity you have practised skills that are assessed using Criterion C: Producing text and Criterion D: Using language.

DISCUSS

The scene following the opening of the play shows us how things are in the Keller household five years later. Read the passage in which we meet Helen properly for the first time, from 'First I'm gonna cut off this doctor's legs …' to 'Percy darts to the bell string on the porch, yanks it, and the bell rings.'

How would you describe Helen's feelings in this scene? Write what you think her feelings would be at different points in the scene. **Explain** in the case of each what evidence you are using to make those deductions.

Then, in pairs or small groups, share your comments. What differences and similarities were there in the way each of you interpreted Helen's feelings in the scene, and in the evidence you used to do so?

SPEAKING

Communication is one of the MYP key concepts. According to the definition of communication, it involves 'exchanging' or 'transferring' something – facts, ideas, signals, for example, which form a 'message' of some kind. Communication also means there must be someone who communicates something (a 'sender'), and someone who receives it (a 'receiver').

Communication should also involve 'conveying information or meaning'. Does this always happen when we try to communicate something? Does it always happen in the way that we intend it to?

Helen's actions and responses in the scene you read for the Discuss activity above are caused to a large extent by her inability to convey information and meaning about herself, which means that others – both the characters around her and the audience – must try to interpret what she thinks and feels.

This is a characteristic of drama, where as an audience we hear and see the words and actions of a character on stage, and have to interpret those ourselves, usually without knowing any more about what the thoughts of the character may be. In a novel or a poem, on the other hand, we are often told the thoughts of a character by the narrator or speaker.

Two conventions that *can* be used within the genre of drama to convey inner thoughts and feelings are the **soliloquy** and **dramatic monologue**, which we will look at in greater detail later.

Both require that the character speak his or her own thoughts, which Helen, being mute, is unable to do. The audience is therefore placed in the position of the other characters in the play in having to try to 'look into' Helen from the outside, and interpret from her actions only.

Diaries

Diaries are often completely personal in nature, of course, with the only audience quite possibly being the writer him- or herself. When writing for a wider audience, however, there are several things to remember about the format of this text type:
- entries should be dated
- it should be written in the first person
- it will be informal in register
- it should reflect the **voice** of the writer.

Internal monologue

The *Encyclopedia Britannica* defines an internal monologue as a 'narrative technique that exhibits the thoughts passing through the minds of the protagonists'. A character on stage in a play may use this technique as part of a soliloquy or dramatic monologue, which presents to the audience the character's innermost thoughts.

These thoughts might be represented in one of two ways:

1 Thoughts that are loosely related, and may not seem to follow on coherently, as the character's mind leaps from one thought to another.
2 More rationally structured sequences of thought and emotion.

DISCUSS

Find out about internal monologue techniques and literary devices. What features can you identify? Which authors have used this technique? How is it related to stream of consciousness?

Here is a short extract of more loosely related thoughts, which are not always entirely coherent in their sequencing:

'The very air in the ward seemed to have become heavier, emitting strong lingering odours, with sudden wafts that were simply nauseating, What will this place be like within a week, he asked himself, and it horrified him to think that in a week's time, they would still be confined here, Assuming there won't be any problems with food supplies, and who can be sure there isn't already a shortage, I doubt, for example, whether those outside have any idea from one minute to the next ...' – Jose Saramago in Blindness

Here is a short example of part of an internal monologue that is more rationally structured. Read the example and identify any features.

Wait. I think I need to take a breath and stop. Is this really the right thing to do?

Because if I go ahead with this, it will count as breaking in, and do I really want to be committing a crime?

So I'm standing here, and I don't know what to do. Why doesn't Sarah come around? She's always hanging about when I don't want her there. And now she might be useful, she's nowhere to be seen.

Right. I need to stop thinking about this now, and go ahead and do this. I just need to take a deep breath, and one step forwards, and I'll be there. Across the threshold. Where Mrs Denton was when she disappeared ...

What about those rumours? There must be a reason why this place has been empty for so long. And didn't the bus driver claim this had been the scene of some other unexplained events?

Stop it. These are just rumours.

I'm going in.

You may have noticed some of the following:

Paragraphing The relatively short nature of these suggests the anxiety of the speaker and reflects how his or her thoughts are going in different directions. The use of brief paragraphing at the end provides a sense of climax as the speaker finally decides on action.

The paragraphing also helps to convey the divided nature of the speaker's thoughts and feelings, and the clear uncertainty he or she feels about what to do.

An opening that captures interest It suggests a significant event taking place and raises questions in a reader as to the nature of this, as well as curiosity and **anticipation** about what the speaker will do.

Transitions The linking of the paragraphs is clear, as the speaker uses the beginning of each paragraph as a reaction to, or reflection on, the previous one.

Within paragraphs too, sentences transition coherently from one to the other, despite the abrupt nature of these at times.

Wait. I think I need to take a breath and stop. Is this really the right thing to do?

Because if I go ahead with this, it will count as breaking in, and do I really want to be committing a crime?

So I'm standing here, and I don't know what to do. Why doesn't Sarah come around? She's always hanging about when I don't want her there. And now she might be useful, she's nowhere to be seen.

Right. I need to stop thinking about this now, and go ahead and do this. I just need to take a deep breath, and one step forwards, and I'll be there. Across the threshold. Where Mrs Denton was when she disappeared …

What about those rumours? There must be a reason why this place has been empty for so long. And didn't the bus driver claim this had been the scene of some other unexplained events?

Stop it. These are just rumours.

I'm going in.

Coherence Even though the uncertainty of the speaker is clear in what is said, his or her thoughts are conveyed in a manner so they build on each other, and build to a climax at the end. The monologue maintains coherence, even while reflecting some of the less-structured thoughts.

Overall structure Note how this is circular in nature, beginning at one point, and returning to that point at the end via a route through the speaker's thoughts, which serve to make the final decision seem very significant.

Overall, the sequence of thoughts is relevant and naturalistic, and provides a credible and suspenseful thought-narrative with clear use of organizational features for effect.

Sentence structure A variety of sentence lengths and types are used. Very short sentences convey the speaker trying to take control of his or her feelings and actions. Questions convey the speaker's fears and uncertainty about what to do. Some sentences are grammatically incomplete, reflecting the nature of personal thoughts at times. Meanwhile, the ellipsis (…) used at the end of one sentence indicates the speaker losing control of his or her thoughts again, as if the speaker has moved in a direction he or she is fearful of going.

How can ways in which we communicate affect our relationships with other people?

ACTIVITY: Communication fails

ATL

- Communication skills: Use a variety of organizers for academic writing tasks
- Critical-thinking skills: Gather and organize relevant information to formulate an argument

Watch this video, which shows in a comic way the effects that a failure to communicate meaning can have on a receiver: www.youtube.com/watch?v=Ozpek_FrOPs.

In the graphic organizers below, 1) suggest some reactions of the shopkeeper as the receiver, and reasons for those, and 2) **identify** particular aspects of the customer's communication that made it so unclear to the shopkeeper.

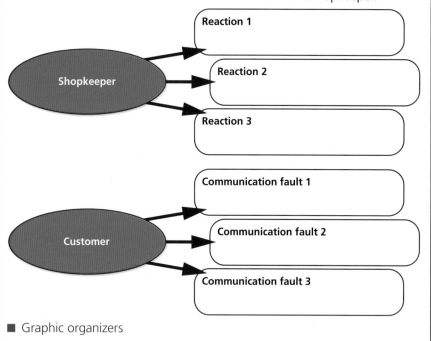

Shopkeeper → Reaction 1 / Reaction 2 / Reaction 3

Customer → Communication fault 1 / Communication fault 2 / Communication fault 3

- Graphic organizers

Then, write four tips to help make communication clearer.

◆ Assessment opportunities

In this activity you have practised skills that are assessed using Criterion A: Analysing.

THINK–PAIR–SHARE

What examples can you think of when someone (which may be yourself or someone you know, or someone you have seen on television or in a film) failed to convey the meaning of what they intended to communicate? How can it affect both a sender and a receiver?

Think about two examples of where intended communication failed. How did those involved feel and respond?

Once you have your two examples (write notes on them if needed), share your examples with each of you doing so in ways that you think might prevent the other from understanding what you are saying. How might you communicate with them in ways that may result in that? What did you each try to do?

Get together with another pair and share your examples. Then, as a group of four, choose one example to share with the whole class, along with your group's thoughts on the reasons as to why communication of meaning may fail, and the impact this can have on those trying to communicate and those trying to understand.

CONFLICT

Earlier in this chapter we looked at the impact on Helen when she was unable to communicate meaning clearly to others. We have just explored the impact on others when communication is not clear and they are unable to grasp the meaning.

William Gibson in *The Miracle Worker* **juxtaposes** (places next to each other, usually something done by a writer for effect) scenes in Act 1 to show the impact of Helen's inability to communicate what she wants to say both on Helen herself, and then on her family. The scene following

Kate's intervention, when Helen attacks Martha, shows the toll that Helen's difficult behaviour has had on her family. It also allows Gibson to set out in one scene the different types of **conflict** that are present within the family.

Conflict is a literary device that can be used for several purposes. The playwright uses it to provide insight into the nature of the relationships between the various members of the family (all of whom are present in the scene), and the impact Helen's inability to communicate, and efforts to do so, has had on the family relationships.

ACTIVITY: Conflict

■ ATL

- ■ Creative-thinking skills: Use brainstorming and visual diagrams to generate new ideas and inquiries
- ■ Critical-thinking skills: Draw reasonable conclusions and generalizations

1 Get into groups of two or three. Brainstorm on a piece of poster paper the different conflicts that are shown in the scene with the family, from '*Inside the lights have been gradually coming up …*' to '*the lights dim out …*'. Do not forget to consider internal, as well as external, conflicts.
2 Use a mind map, such as that in the example below.

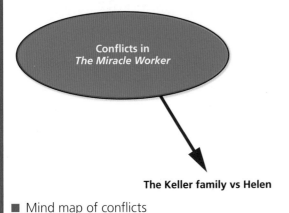

■ Mind map of conflicts

3 Divide up the conflicts you have identified. For each of the conflicts you are individually considering, indicate the following:
   - What has caused the conflict?
   - What do you think are the feelings of the character(s) on each side of it, or of a character experiencing an internal conflict?
   - What might be a possible solution to it?
4 Get back into groups. For each of the conflicts you have looked at, share the ideas you have had on these prompts.
5 Choose TWO of the conflicts your group has identified from the play, and consider the role communication has played in creating these, and/or which it may play in resolving the conflict. Write one or two paragraphs explaining your ideas.

◆ Assessment opportunities

In this activity you have practised skills that are assessed using Criterion A: Analysing and Criterion D: Using language.

What different conventions are associated with the ways people communicate?

IMAGERY AND SYMBOLS

We have looked at performance elements that form some of the conventions of drama. As a literary genre, however, drama also contains a number of literary elements, such as the following:

audience   character   conflict

dialogue   imagery   monologue

motifs   plot   script   setting   structure

The elements we will be looking at more closely in this unit are highlighted.

Script

The **script** contains all of the words spoken by the characters in a play, along with any stage directions. Within those words playwrights (or screenwriters, in the case of movies), may use literary devices in the forms of images and symbols for a number of purposes, such as to advance their plot, develop their characters and further reinforce the meaning of what they are trying to convey.

Imagery and motifs

The Miracle Worker makes use of a large number of similes and metaphors, along with other imagery and **motifs**, to communicate ideas about theme and character. For instance, the play is largely constructed of a series of conflicts, the most significant of which is the one that takes place between Annie and Helen. To reflect this theme further, the playwright inserts many references of different kinds to battle – images of physical struggle, similes and metaphors, and so on.

These are especially noticeable where characters are speaking *before* they have become aware of Helen's behaviour as a frustrated blind, deaf and mute child. A number of examples of these occur, therefore, in Act 1, and have the effect of **foreshadowing** the battles ahead:

> KELLER: … this is my wife's first [child], she isn't battle-scarred yet.
>
> DOCTOR: Oh, by morning she'll be knocking down Captain Keller's fences again.
>
> KATE: Men, men and their battle scars, we women will have to—
>
> ANNIE: He keeps digging up that battle!
>
> ANNIE: … with all the fights and trouble I've been here it taught me what help is, and how to live again.

Foreshadowing is a technique used to hint at what is to come in a narrative or story. As such it may lead a reader or audience to have certain expectations, and/or to experience **anticipation** or **suspense** and leave them interested in finding out more.

When we see characters, and especially Kate and Annie, interacting with Helen later, they are almost always in a situation of physical struggle with her:

> [Martha] *But at once Helen topples Martha on her back, knees pinning her shoulders down, and grabs the scissors.*
>
> [Kate] *… Kate reaches for the scissors in Helen's hand. But Helen pulls the scissors back, they struggle for a moment, then Kate gives up, lets Helen keep them.*
>
> [Annie/Helen] *… they confront each other …*
>
> [Annie] *She takes the doll from Helen, and reaches for her hand; Helen instantly grabs the doll back. Annie takes it again, and Helen's hand next, but Helen is incensed now; when Annie draws her* ➤

hand to her face to shake her head no, then tries to spell to her, Helen slaps at Annie's face. Annie grasps Helen by both arms, and swings her into a chair, holding her pinned there, kicking, while glasses, doll, bonnet fly in various directions.

[Annie] *Helen is now in a rage, fighting tooth and nail to get out of the chair, and Annie answers while struggling and dodging her kicks.*

The repeated use of an image, such as that of battles in *The Miracle Worker,* means that the image becomes a motif – an image that reminds us of something important through communicating constant reminders of it.

We are constantly reminded of the overall premise of the play as one long, sustained, battle. This helps give us, too, a sense of the difficult nature of the task that Annie and Helen's family face in trying to get Helen to communicate, and to be able to take part in a more normal life and relationships.

The playwright, William Gibson, uses other images and motifs in the play to help communicate something to a reader about a character. He does this especially in the case of Helen, where the imagery used of her helps to characterize her – something that is helpful with a character whom it would otherwise be difficult to know. Apart from the battle images used of her, note how she is described by Anagnos in Act 1: 'She is like a little safe, locked, that no one can open. Perhaps there is a treasure inside.'

Note how much analysis can take place of a single image, as shown by the questions here. This demonstrates also the amount of meaning that can be communicated by the use of an image in a literary work.

DISCUSS

Think about these questions, in relation to Anagnos's quote about Helen:

1 What does Anagnos mean by what he says here?
2 How does this foreshadow what Annie can later perceive when she meets Helen? Find two quotations from Act 1 that show this.
3 What role might this have played in motivating Annie's actions and attitudes in her teaching of Helen?
4 Why do you think the playwright did not give the quotation to a member of the Keller family? How are their perceptions different?

ACTIVITY: Motifs

ATL

■ Communication skills: Make inferences and draw conclusions

Other motifs introduced in Act 1 include those in the table below. Find an example of where the motif is referenced and **explain** for each one what important idea you think is being communicated. You might want to think about the following questions:

● Why does the writer keep reminding the reader/audience of this?
● What is the message which is being conveyed by continued reminders of this idea?

Learn more about motifs: www.thoughtco.com/symbols-and-motifs-in-literature-1857637

Motif	Quotation	Important idea
Mouths		
Life and death		
Writing		
Eyes/glasses/blindness		
Keys		
Water pump		

◆ Assessment opportunities

In this activity you have practised skills that are assessed using Criterion A: Analysing.

DISCUSS

Here are some examples of imagery used of Helen and other characters in Act 1 (those in italics are found in stage directions).

For each image, **interpret** what you think is being suggested about the character concerned.

Character	Image
Anagnos	*Anagnos shepherds them [children] in … / He shepherds them out …*
Another doctor Annie has encountered, Dr Howe	'He never treated them like ordinary children. More like – eggs everyone was afraid would break.'
Helen	*[Annie] holds Helen struggling until we hear from the child her first sound so far, an inarticulate weird noise in her throat such as an animal in a trap might make.*
Helen	*a battered little savage*
Annie	'to tell you the truth I'm as shaky inside as a baby's rattle!'

It is worth noting that several of these images are used in stage directions, and thus the precise detail of them would not be noticeable to an audience. Use of literary features of this nature by a playwright show awareness that their play will be read, as well as watched.

Writing

As we move into Act 2 of the play, we find Annie writing a letter. One motif used in the play is that of writing, with characters making reference on several occasions to writing letters, either in the past or future.

- Kate and Aunt Ev, for instance, argue with Keller about writing to Dr Chisholm, the Baltimore oculist (eye specialist), early in Act 1. If they were to write the letter, to a professional person they do not know and requesting his services, they would write a *formal* letter.
- At the start of Act 2, Annie is in the process of writing a letter to Anagnos. She is likely to be confiding in him about how things have been going during her time in the Keller household so far. She therefore probably knows him well enough to write an *informal* letter.

Letters represent a further text type to be aware of, although nowadays the informal letter is likely to have been replaced by other ways in which we communicate with those we know well, as this website indicates: **https://goo.gl/DevP9j**.

Formal letters

There remains a need to know how to write a formal letter, since these are needed for various important purposes in life, such as applying for a job, making a complaint and making a request for services. It is important, therefore, to know how to write such letters properly.

Given that such letters are likely to be important ones, following the expected conventions for these each time should help create the kind of impression on the recipient which is more likely to lead to him or her responding in the way being looked for. Advice on writing different kinds of formal letters can be found across the internet, such as at the website here: **www. letterwritingguide.com/**

Informal letters

At the start of Act 2 Annie is trying to write a letter to Anagnos, while being distracted and trying to teach Helen.

Today, many different ways exist of communicating with someone if we wanted to relate to others informally how things were going, and it is less likely that someone would write an informal letter in that situation.

What are the different ways in which we might communicate for such reasons today?

ACTIVITY: Writing a formal letter

- Communication skills: Use appropriate forms of writing for different purposes and audiences

Paragraph 1	
Paragraph 2	
Paragraph 3	
Paragraph 4	

Read through the writing guidelines on formal letters, and then use them to write a correctly formatted letter to Dr Chisholm, as may have been written by Captain Keller.

Use three or four short paragraphs for this, be concise, get straight to the point and stick to it.

Plan, in a table like the one on the right, what the focus of each of your paragraphs will be. How will you start and end the letter? What are you asking? What does Dr Chisholm need to know?

Once you have planned what should be in your letter, type it out, correctly formatted. Ensure you check your grammar and spelling very carefully. Swap your work with a partner and give feedback on their work. What have they done well? What might they do differently?

◆ Assessment opportunities

In this activity you have practised skills that are assessed using Criterion B: Organizing and Criterion D: Using language.

ACTIVITY: Blog post

- Communication skills: Write for different purposes; participate in, and contribute to, digital social media networks
- Media literacy skills: Communicate information and ideas effectively to multiple audiences using a variety of media and formats

One medium through which people keep friends and family updated with news while away from home is the use of a blog. Let us imagine that Annie uses this method of updating her friends.

Write the blog entry that Annie might have produced at this stage. Since she knows the audience for whom she is writing, her expression will be informal; you need to sound like Annie herself, and she does not tend to use a lot of slang!

You must include the words of the letter that we know she includes, as she speaks them in the course of this scene. It is up to you where in your blog post you include them, though, whether early, late, or somewhere in between.

Your blog might contain the following ideas:
- things that have happened during Annie's time in the Keller household so far

- what Helen is like
- what she thinks of Kate/Keller/James and what their attitude towards her has been
- any progress she thinks she has made with Helen so far
- what she thinks she might do with Helen in the future.

In the course of all of this, Annie will express some of her feelings at times. What are they, and why does she feel like this at this point?

This task will be graded on Criterion C: Producing text. To achieve this, you need to ensure that you develop your points, for instance:
- giving *specific* details of things Helen does
- giving examples of the attitude of one of the other characters towards 'you' (as Annie)
- giving reasons for any of your thoughts and feelings.

Your blog post should be 500–600 words long.

Review and revise your blog:
- Use the ladder of feedback with another classmate to review each other's work.
- Consider the feedback you received, and revise your blog as may be needed.

◆ Assessment opportunities

In this activity you have practised skills that are assessed using Criterion C: Producing text.

Is non-verbal communication more powerful than verbal communication?

NON-VERBAL COMMUNICATION

So far we have looked a lot at verbal communication, both spoken and written. Some of the most powerful types of communication are non-verbal types, however.

In a play in which a main character is unable to communicate verbally, much is made of methods of non-verbal communication. These are conveyed quite fittingly in a genre that makes substantial use of non-verbal communication of various kinds through use of technical conventions – scenery, costumes, props, sound and make-up – to convey messages to an audience.

ⓘ

Technical conventions

costumes	make-up	props	scenery
	sound and music	lighting	

Performance conventions

acting	speaking	non-verbal expression

ACTIVITY: Exploring non-verbal communication

■ **ATL**

■ Communication skills: Interpret and use effectively modes of non-verbal communication; make inferences and draw conclusions

Look at the images of scenes taken from performances of *The Miracle Worker,* and answer the questions that follow:

1 Make three observations about the costumes, props, lighting or scenery in this scene, and how they are conveying information to you.
2 What two questions do you have about what is happening in the scene?
3 **State** one opinion about what you see in the scene.

■ Non-verbal communication in this scene is mainly taking place through performance conventions. What is going on in the scene? What makes you say that?

■ Once more, non-verbal communication in this scene is mainly taking place through performance conventions. Which types of non-verbal communication are being used (for example, gesture, facial expression and so on)?

What do the images tell you about what each character may be thinking and feeling at this moment?

HERE NOW / THERE THEN

One of the most famous scenes in *The Miracle Worker* occurs in Act 2, when Annie and Helen are left alone at breakfast, where Helen has been misbehaving. A viewer once commented that this 'May be the longest scene in film history with two people in it, not saying one word of dialogue', as the scene is entirely made up of stage directions, and of non-verbal methods of communicating the action and meaning in the scene.

Read through this scene from *'Annie meanwhile has begun by slapping both keys down on a shelf'* (page 52) to *'... the lights commence to dim out on them'* (page 56).

Now watch the scene being acted out:
www.youtube.com/watch?v=h5tVVwwkW18.

Having watched the scene, write down your immediate reaction to it:

_____

_____

Now let us **evaluate** the situation a little more. Was Annie right in her treatment of Helen? Add 'for' and 'against' points in the following table:

It was right for Annie to treat Helen as she did in the scene because ...	Annie was wrong to treat Helen as she did in the scene because ...

ACTIVITY: Performing a miracle

■ **ATL**

■ Communication skills: Give and receive meaningful feedback

Criterion D: Using language, assesses the different aspects of the way language is used, including non-verbal language. One of the things it looks at is how effective you are at using appropriate non-verbal communication techniques.

These are relevant when you give presentations.

Giving presentations

What might make for effective oral presentation? Techniques might include the following:

- pronunciation
- intonation
- tone
- pitch
- inflection
- pace
- pausing
- voice control
- volume
- projection
- body language
- gesture
- eye contact.

Assessment of oral work using Criterion D would include the above, many of which are non-verbal communication techniques, and all of which need to be used appropriately in helping to communicate most clearly and powerfully the message that a speaker is intending to convey. Other aspects of Criterion D are also appropriate for assessment of oral work; look at the level descriptors.

Let us try some peer and self-assessment using the above criterion rubrics, and the task below.

Task

If you could perform a 'miracle' that would improve someone's life, what would it be? **Explain** what you would do, and why. **Explain** also how you think this would improve a life (or lives).

1 Think of two possible 'miracles' and share those with a partner.

2 Choose collectively what you think is the best miracle each of you has suggested.
3 Write a two- to three-paragraph response for your choice.
4 Read the draft write-up produced by your partner and make suggestions for improvement; for instance, any language corrections or improvement suggestions, details of ideas and explanations, and so on.
5 Type up your final individual response.
6 You could display these around the classroom. Add an illustration, if appropriate.

You will be delivering your final response to this task orally, and the relevant elements of Criterion D will be used to assess your oral presentation.

Look at the descriptors from the highest band of Criterion D, 7–8. Use these to make notes on what you think you may need to focus on, think about, practise beforehand, and so on.

Once you feel you have practised enough to attempt the task, find a means to record yourself – you might most easily set up your own smartphone or iPad to record your voice, for instance, or ask your partner to video you, and vice versa. Deliver your oral presentation, and then play it back. Use a criterion table, like the one opposite, to record what you would award for your performance.

Now look at the list of oral presentation features again. Are there any that you might particularly look at to improve, in a second attempt at the task? If so, what do you need to do to improve in this/these?

Repeat the task and watch your performance back. Did it improve? What levels would you award for it this time?

Now find a classmate to watch your latest performance and award levels for it. Did you agree on those? Ask your classmate also to give advice on what you might improve next time you do an oral task. Is the advice the same as you gave yourself?

Carry out the same peer assessment activity for your classmate, or for someone else in the class. If you have time and wish to do so, carry out the task once more and see if you can improve again on your performance.

	Criterion D – Using language	1st attempt	2nd attempt	3rd attempt	Mark
Level	Level descriptor				
0	The student does not reach a standard described by any of the descriptors below.				
1–2	The student uses a limited range of appropriate vocabulary and forms of expression.				
	The student speaks in an inappropriate register and style that do not serve the context and intention.				
	The student pronounces with limited accuracy; errors often hinder communication.				
	The student makes limited and/or inappropriate use of non-verbal communication techniques.				
3–4	The student uses an adequate range of appropriate vocabulary, sentence structures and forms of expression.				
	The student sometimes speaks in a register and style that serve the context and intention.				
	The student pronounces with some degree of accuracy; errors sometimes hinder communication.				
	The student makes some use of appropriate non-verbal communication techniques.				
5–6	The student uses a varied range of appropriate vocabulary, sentence structures and forms of expression.				
	The student speaks competently in a register and style that serve the context and intention.				
	The student pronounces with a considerable degree of accuracy; errors do not hinder effective communication.				
	The student makes sufficient use of appropriate non-verbal communication techniques.				
7–8	The student effectively uses a range of appropriate vocabulary, sentence structures and forms of expression.				
	The student speaks in a consistently appropriate register and style that serve the context and intention.				
	The student pronounces with a high degree of accuracy; errors are minor and communication is effective.				
	The student makes effective use of appropriate non-verbal communication techniques.				

◆ Assessment opportunities

In this activity you have practised skills that are assessed using Criterion D: Using language.

A SUMMATIVE TASK TO TRY

Use this task to apply and extend your learning in this chapter. This task is designed so that you can evaluate your learning at different levels of achievement in the Language and Literature criteria.

THIS TASK CAN BE USED TO EVALUATE YOUR LEARNING IN CRITERION B, CRITERION C AND CRITERION D.

Task: Dramatic monologue

Look at the picture below.

It depicts a scene from *The Miracle Worker,* and shows the characters Kate, Captain Keller, James, Annie and Helen.

Choose ONE of the characters in the scene, and write an internal monologue expressing their thoughts and feelings as the scene plays out in front of them. Use the clues in the picture to **interpret** what you think your character's thoughts and feelings at this point may be.

Your monologue should be between 500 and 1000 words long.

Try to include the types of techniques seen in the model part-monologues given on pages 40–41.

Think too about an overall structure which might frame your monologue.

Take action

- This unit should have given you a lot of opportunity to think about the different ways in which we communicate, how that can be more or less effective, and the impact poor communication can have on our relationships with others. It should also have provided opportunities for you to reflect on how you might improve your own communication in different ways.

  One step you might take at this point, therefore, is to specify two different scenarios in which effective communication of some kind will be needed, and where you will look closely at how to make this as effective as possible. Such scenarios might involve, for instance, an oral presentation in a class, or outside of one; writing a formal letter of some kind, such as an application for a job, or a letter of complaint; or it may be that you think about a particular relationship you have with someone, such as a parent, where you feel the ways in which you have been communicating could have been improved. It may even be a resolution to communicate where you normally wouldn't have done so, such as volunteering to be a spokesperson in class, or speaking up at a local event or club.

  Whatever you decide, make sure that they are specific, identified scenarios in which you are able to apply and hopefully improve some communication practices.

- One other way in which you might use communication skills to take action would be to engage in a project to record 'Talking books' for a local school for the visually impaired. These can be extremely helpful if members of the school are trying to learn the language you speak; for instance, if you are in an international school and speak English. It also means that books for younger age groups can be used, which do not take very long to record or listen to.

  This can work even more effectively if there is a group of you who can record the books, possibly taking different speaking parts.

Reflection

In this chapter we have explored the different ways in which we communicate with others, and the effects our communication can have on other people. In the course of this we have investigated the genre of drama and its conventions, and the different ways in which it may communicate ideas to an audience. We have considered in more detail some of the ideas presented in our particular drama, *The Miracle Worker,* such as the impact that lack of effective communication can have on close relationships, and the ethics of using physical force on a child. Meanwhile, we have also reviewed a number of text types, and how to interpret various literary devices that may be used in text to communicate meaning.

Use this table to reflect on your own learning in this chapter.

Questions we asked	Answers we found	Any further questions now?			
Factual:					
Conceptual:					
Debatable:					
Approaches to learning you used in this chapter	Description – what new skills did you learn?	How well did you master the skills?			
		Novice	Learner	Practitioner	Expert
Communication skills					
Media literacy skills					
Critical-thinking skills					
Creative-thinking skills					
Learner profile attribute(s)	How did you demonstrate your skills as a communicator in this chapter?				
Communicators					

③ What perspective?

○ Considering a range of **perspectives** leads to a more informed **point of view**, and shapes or influences **attitudes** towards and interactions with others.

■ Scenes from the film, *Mask* (1985)

○ IN THIS CHAPTER, WE WILL ...

■ **Find out** about responses that may arise, and attitudes that can exist, towards others, along with ways in which texts present such topics.

■ **Explore** how perspectives that may be held towards others are formed, along with how these may influence people's attitudes and actions; also techniques by which texts may seek to influence these attitudes and actions.

■ **Take action** by actively considering different perspectives in order to develop greater awareness of our feelings and attitudes and those of others, along with greater empathy and sense of responsibility for our own responses, attitudes and actions, particularly when we encounter someone whom we may perceive to be 'different'.

■ These Approaches to Learning (ATL) skills will be useful …

- Communication skills
- Collaboration skills
- Affective skills
- Reflection skills
- Information literacy skills
- Media literacy skills
- Critical-thinking skills
- Creative-thinking skills

We will reflect on this learner profile attribute …

- Open-minded – explore how greater open-mindedness can develop when we take time to consider different possible perspectives and points of view towards others, and how these can affect the attitudes we might have and ways in which we might act towards others whom we may perceive to be 'different'; consider the importance of empathy and respect, which grow out of an open-minded approach.

◆ Assessment opportunities in this chapter:

- ◆ **Criterion A:** Analysing
- ◆ **Criterion B:** Organizing
- ◆ **Criterion C:** Producing text
- ◆ **Criterion D:** Using language

KEY WORDS

chronology	dialogue
connotation	imagery
contrast	perspective

THINK–PAIR–SHARE

How important are first impressions? Share your answer to this question, and your reason for it, with a classmate.

Now think about a time when someone made a good impression on you. Can you **identify** and **list** the specific aspects that caused this to happen? What is involved in creating a good impression?

How important are first impressions?

ACTIVITY: Script-writing – making an impression

■ How do we greet each other?

■ ATL

■ Collaboration skills: Listen actively to other perspectives and ideas; practise empathy

Imagine that the boy in the image at the beginning of this chapter (on page 54) walked into your classroom one morning, as a new member of the class. What impression would he create? How would people react?

Write a short script of around 300 words that presents the reactions of four fictional students in the room. Would they all react differently? Try to represent some of those in your short script.

Then, get together with three classmates. Read through each other's scripts and decide on one to role-play as a group.

Divide up the roles in the chosen script and act it out two or three times. Each of you should note the feelings you have within the scene as you voice and act out your particular role and response.

Next, each of you should come up with questions you can ask your classmates playing the other characters in the role-play. The questions should be different for each classmate or character. Some examples of questions might be as follows:

- How did you feel about your particular character and their role?
- What was your favourite part of the script?
- What do you predict will happen in the future?
- Did you find anything surprising about the scene?
- Was there anything you did not like about the scene or your role in it?
- Did this scenario make you think about, feel or realize anything in particular?
- Would you have acted in reality in the same way as your character?
- If you could talk to any of the characters in the script, what would you say?
- Did any of the events in the script remind you of something that has happened to you? Or of something that has happened to someone you know?

There are many other possible questions, so try to think of some that are not in this list of examples.

EXTENSION: HOT-SEATING

Sit in a circle with your group and take it in turns to be 'hot-seated'. This is where each of you takes it in turns to be asked the questions that have been prepared by the others. Such hot-seating should focus mainly on personal feelings and observations, rather than factual questions and information.

◆ Assessment opportunities

In this activity you have practised skills that are assessed using Criterion C: Producing text and Criterion D: Using language.

ACTIVITY: The importance of first impressions

■ ATL

■ Communication skills: Negotiate ideas and knowledge with peers and teachers

Influential US business magazine *Forbes* has this to say about creating first impressions:

'Did you know it takes only three to five seconds for someone to form a first impression? And while you might wish that opinion were based on your intelligence or experience, most studies show that first impressions are shaped by what can be seen or heard in those initial few seconds. What impression are you creating?'

List all the factors you think would lead to creating a good first impression, or a bad first impression, in the following scenarios:
● **the first class in a new school**
● **a class presentation**
● **meeting the parents of your new friend**
● **performing in some way in front of an audience.**

Now watch these two videos, both of which show speakers presenting on the topic of first impressions. Think about the three most important points the videos make about first impressions.

https://youtu.be/BFSXyD-ycjY

https://youtu.be/Kty8hsFb8Fo

What are those three most important points, in your opinion? Write them down, ensuring you include at least one from each video.

Share your points with a neighbour. Would you replace any of your own points with one noted by them? Do you think any of your points are better than any of theirs? Try to persuade them to change theirs, if that is the case.

With your partner get together with another pair, carry out the same sharing of ideas, and revising your own and/or trying to persuade others to change theirs. At the end, decide on your final three most important points about first impressions.

◆ Assessment opportunities

In this activity you have practised skills that are assessed using Criterion D: Using language.

ACTIVITY: A coaching video

■ ATL

■ Reflection skills: Identify strengths and weaknesses of personal learning strategies (self-assessment); consider ATL skills development – how can I share my skills to help peers who need more practice?
■ Communication skills: Give and receive meaningful feedback

You are now going to make a video similar to the two you watched in 'The importance of first impressions' activity. You must include your three most important points about first impressions in your video, and you may want to use these as the structure or framework of your own speech.

● **Choose one of the four scenarios suggested before.**
● **Draft out a coaching speech that is designed to help someone within that scenario to create a good impression. Your speech should be between one and two minutes in length.**
● **Ensure your three most important points about first impressions are included in your speech.**
● **Rehearse your speech as many times as you wish.**
● **When you feel ready, film yourself making the speech. You could do this yourself, or you could ask a friend to record you.**
● **Of course, you may like to video yourself making the speech several times, until you are happy with a final version.**

In groups of four (either the same group as in the previous activity, or a new group), share your finished videos with each other. For each video, every member of the group should provide feedback on the aspects of the MYP Language and literature criteria. You should look at the following criteria: Criterion C i and Criterion D i, ii, iv and v. The person whose video is being watched should carry out a self-assessment, while the other members of the group will carry out peer assessments.

If there is time in class, your teacher may ask each group to nominate one of the videos to share and **discuss** further with the class as a whole.

◆ Assessment opportunities

In this activity you have practised skills that are assessed using Criterion C: Producing text and Criterion D: Using language.

In what ways might perspectives we hold influence our attitudes and behaviours?

The following short essay, *Body Imperfect,* was written by Debi Davis not long after she had lost her legs due to a rare vascular disease – a disease associated with the blood vessels in the body. In it she considers the different perspectives of adults and children towards her disability – perspectives that are very different from her own view of

THE IMPACT OF FIRST IMPRESSIONS

DISCUSS

■ Stella Young

Imagine you met the lady in the photograph. How would you react? Why? Write down your responses.

Now imagine the lady in the photograph was speaking her thoughts out loud. What would she say? Write this as a monologue, of two to three paragraphs in length.

When I became a double amputee at the age of 29, I was forced to shed many misconceptions I had unknowingly embraced regarding the importance of physical perfection. In the space of one hour I changed from an acceptably attractive female to an object of pity and fear.

I was not aware of this at first. I was too busy dealing with the physical pain and new limitations in mobility I now faced. Yet I was determined to succeed and proud of my progress on a daily basis. My contact with physicians, rehabilitation specialists, close friends and family only enhanced my perceptions of myself as a "winner."

My new status in society, however, was brought to my attention on my first excursion outside the hospital walls. Jubilant to be free of confinement, I rolled through the shopping mall in my wheelchair with the inimitable confidence of a proud survivor, a war hero anticipating a ticker-tape reception. As I glanced around, I sensed that all eyes were upon me, yet no one dared to make eye contact. Their downcast glances made me realize that they did not see the triumph in my eyes, only my missing limbs.

I noticed that shoppers gave me a wide berth, walking far around me as if I were contagious. Mothers held their children closer as I passed, and elderly women patted me on the head saying, "Bless you!" Men, who might normally wink and smile, now looked away. Like bruised fruit on a produce stand, I existed, but was bypassed for a healthier looking specimen.

her disability and situation. She also indicates something of the origin of such perspectives, such as an assumption that anyone with a disability should be pitied, and possibly feared; at the end Davis describes how she seeks to change such perspectives.

First, read the essay:

Children, in contrast, found my appearance clearly fascinating. One small girl came up to me and stared with unabashed curiosity at my empty pantlegs. She knelt down and put her arm up one pantleg as far as she could reach, and finding nothing there, looked up at me with bewilderment. "Lady, where did your legs go?" she innocently inquired. I explained to her that my legs had been very sick, that they hadn't been strong and healthy like hers, and that my doctor removed my legs so that I could be healthy again. Tilting her head up she chirped, "But lady, did they go to 'Leg Heaven'?"

That incident made me think about how differently children and adults react to the unknown. To a child, an odd appearance is an interesting curiosity and a learning experience, while adults often view the unusual with fear and repulsion. I began to realize that prior to my disability I had been guilty of the same inappropriate reactions.

From observing children, I learned to reach out and reassure adults of my humanness and to reaffirm the genuine worth of all human beings. To accentuate the wholeness of my mind and spirit, I smile warmly, coerce eye contact, and speak in a confident manner. By using a positive approach, I attempt to enlighten society that having a perfect body is not synonymous with quality of life.

Body Imperfect – *Debi Davis*

Use of narrative technique to convey perspective

Two significant choices relating to narrative technique that must be made by a writer or director are those of:

- **Narrative voice** – who or what is telling the story.
  - A first-person narrator will relate events, thoughts, feelings and so on using 'I' or 'we'. In the essay, Debi Davis uses first-person narrative voice in this account, where a character in the story narrates what is happening from his or her own perspective. The narration will therefore be limited to what that character sees and understands about what is going on; which we thus see from that particular character's point of view.
  - We often also learn first-hand about that particular character's thoughts and feelings, about what they are experiencing, and the impact it may have on them. The purpose of this is to provide direct insight into the experiences of the narrator.
- **Narrative perspective** – who or what is the focus of the narrative.
  - Narrative perspective is, on the other hand, what is being narrated about. At times in *Body Imperfect,* the narrative perspective is on Davis herself, as she talks, for instance about her entry into the shopping mall. However, at other times the narrative perspective moves to others and we are invited to look at and consider the different people she encounters, and the reactions they have to her disability.

What is a perspective?

ACTIVITY: Perceives, believes, cares about

■ ATL

- Communication skills: Make inferences and draw conclusions

To see the differences in narrator perspective, you are going to try using first-person narration in presenting one of the points of view seen in *Body Imperfect*, using a dramatic monologue.

Let us look further into the perspectives we see in the story. Quotes from a number of individuals have been identified and highlighted (in different colours) in the essay on pages 58–59. Using these quotes as evidence, write down what you think each of the following people and parties may *perceive, believe,* and *care about*:

- shoppers in general
- mothers
- elderly ladies
- men
- a child
- the disabled narrator.

Once you have decided on some ideas for this, share them with a neighbour, or two or three classmates around you. Add any further points that you hear and that you feel are interesting and valid.

◆ Assessment opportunities

In this activity you have practised skills that are assessed using Criterion A: Analysing.

ACTIVITY: Narrative voice

■ ATL

- Critical-thinking skills: Recognize unstated assumptions and bias

This activity invites us to consider the perspectives each person or group of people form, and how these lead to the actions we see in the narrative.

Copy the table below and complete it. First, note the actions taken and then **summarize** the perspective of each individual or group of people. How far does each of the perspectives formed differ from that of the narrator about herself?

◆ Assessment opportunities

In this activity you have practised skills that are assessed using Criterion A: Analysing.

Party	Actions	Perspective	Difference between this perspective and that of the narrator
Shoppers in general			
Mothers			
Elderly ladies	Pat her on the head (= treating her like a child, being patronizing)	Feel sorry for the narrator	
Men			
Child			
Narrator			

ASSUMPTIONS

In her essay, Davis talks about the role assumptions can play in how we react to someone in the narrator's position and how inaccurate such assumptions can be. An assumption is defined by the online Cambridge Dictionary (**http://dictionary. cambridge.org/dictionary/english/assumption**) as 'something that you accept as true without question or proof' and they do, interestingly, give as one example of the use of the word: 'People tend to make assumptions about you when you have a disability.'

You might find that some of the 'beliefs' you suggested in the 'Perceives, believes, cares about' activity in fact represent assumptions, such as the assumption of the elderly ladies that the narrator is someone to be pitied. This is very different from the perspective of the narrator herself, who perceives herself as a 'winner', and tells us at the end how she tries to challenge the assumptions of others when encountering other people who are disabled: 'By using a positive approach, I attempt to enlighten society that having a perfect body is not synonymous with quality of life.'

Assumptions are powerful influences on the perspectives people form and how they behave as a result. Davis' choice of the disabled first-person narrator gives us an insight into how inaccurate some assumptions can be and how it feels as a disabled person to be on the receiving end of the responses we see. Would we be able to see this if the perspective were that of any other character or group in the story?

ACTIVITY: Narrative perspective

■ ATL

- ■ Creative-thinking skills: Use existing works and ideas in new ways

Get into a group of four and choose one of the perspectives from Davis' story (apart from the narrator) – a shopper, mother, elderly lady, man or the child. Ensure each person in your group chooses a different character.

Watch examples of some dramatic monologues in this video: **https://youtu.be/nmBYLmSvETI**.

Use your previous notes about what you feel your character perceives, knows about or believes and cares about, to write a monologue of 30 seconds to 1 minute in length, presenting:

- the *perspective* that character holds about the narrator's disability, and
- the *assumptions* behind it.

Try to include some of the word choices that Davis has used to convey the different perspectives in her story.

Your monologue should contain moments of emotion and drama. It should also be narrated in a register and style that is suitable for conveying the perspective of the particular character you have chosen.

Rehearse and revise your monologue as many times as you like and, once you are ready, film yourself performing your dramatic monologue as your chosen character.

Share your filmed monologue with the others in your group. After watching all four of your group's monologues, choose as a group which one you would like to share with the rest of the class. When this takes place, your teacher may ask those who have been chosen if they wish to perform their dramatic monologues live.

◆ Assessment opportunities

In this activity you have practised skills that are assessed using Criterion C: Producing text and D: Using language.

In what ways do texts present particular perspectives?

A DIFFERENT PERSPECTIVE

The perspectives presented in the 'Narrative perspective' activity should have been quite different from that of the narrator in *Body Imperfect,* and it is unlikely that any will have provided an insight into the narrator's own perspective on the reactions and behaviours she encounters. We might deduce from this, therefore, that the writer's choice of first-person narrative voice, and of the actual narrator chosen, was aimed at creating greater empathy on the part of her readers. Empathy is 'the ability to share someone else's feelings or experiences by imagining what it would be like to be in that person's situation.' (**http://dictionary.cambridge.org/dictionary/english/empathy**)

Such insight for a reader may help to prevent some unhelpful assumptions, and responses and behaviours, from taking place in reality where a reader may find him- or herself in a similar encounter. In such a way, therefore, may a writer try to 'influence perspectives its readers or viewers might hold, and consequently their attitudes and behaviours' as our debatable inquiry question asked.

Narrative voice and perspective are not the only literary techniques which the writer uses to convey perspectives – her own and those of others towards her. Davis also makes use of a number of literary devices, including imagery and contrast.

Use of literary devices to convey perspectives

Imagery
Carefully chosen images suggest the nature of the various perspectives presented in the essay, for example:

> *'I changed from an acceptably attractive female to an object of pity and fear.'*

- From the general perspective of the narrator, here the use of 'object' suggests that Davis feels people do not even see her as a human being now, let alone as someone of a particular gender, or someone attractive to look at. She is simply a 'thing', with the implication that she – like a thing and unlike a human – will not have feelings herself.
- The use of 'pity and fear' to describe reactions to the narrator once she became disabled are a reminder of Aristotle's claim that pity and fear are the two main emotions evoked by a 'tragedy'. The suggestion is, therefore, that others who see the narrator and feel pity and fear perceive what has happened to her as being a 'tragedy'.

Contrast
This involves placing two things – ideas, characters, places and so on – together in order to highlight and emphasize differences between them.

Use of contrast can have different purposes. It may:
- illustrate a point the writer is trying to make (such as the differences between how the narrator perceives herself and how others perceive her)
- provoke particular responses from an audience, for instance of shock, or pity ('pathos') or fear
- invite a critical response to what is being presented
- illustrate the idea of how quickly things may change.

In *Body Imperfect* Davis compares her earlier appearance as an attractive lady (an 'acceptably attractive female') to how she has become with her disability ('an object of pity and fear') in the space of one hour. This contrast shows how quickly things can change, and may evoke pathos for the narrator for how she and her life have changed.

Equally, however, she may be criticizing assumptions of this kind, that she should be pitied and feared for her disability, when she clearly does not see herself in that way at all and has no wish to be perceived as such by others. In this case, her use of the phrase 'an object of pity and fear' may be ironic – she is using words when she means the opposite of what they say.

ACTIVITY: The power of imagery

Answer the questions that accompany them.

Look at the examples of imagery given in the table.

Perspective	Imagery	Questions
General perspective of the narrator	'I changed from an acceptably attractive female to an object of pity and fear*' *The ancient Greek philosopher Aristotle stated that for something to be a 'tragedy', it had to evoke pity and fear in anyone who saw it.	Why does Davis use the term 'an object'? What is the effect of this word choice?
The narrator of her situation	'… my first excursion outside the hospital walls. Jubilant to be free of *confinement*, I rolled through the shopping mall in my wheelchair …'	What is the word '*confinement*' associated with? What does the author's use of it suggest about how the narrator has perceived her disability up to that point?
The narrator of herself	'a proud survivor'/'a war hero'/'a ticker-tape reception'	What do all of these images suggest about how Davis perceives herself as she goes through the shopping mall? What reception might she have expected from others at this point to her disability?
The narrator of herself	'a "winner"'/'Jubilant'/'triumph'	Davis uses these words to describe herself as a disabled person. Why do you think she holds this perspective of herself at this stage (end of paragraph 3) in her story?
Shoppers of the narrator	'as if I was contagious'	Davis uses this simile to describe the perspective other adults have of her. What is that perspective? How do you think a reader is meant to feel about both the narrator and those who hold this perspective?
Elderly women of the narrator	'… elderly women *patted* me on the head saying, "*Bless you!*"'	What associations, or *connotations*, does the phrase 'to pat something on the head' have? Having described herself as an 'object', what may this particular image suggest about how she is perceived? What does the phrase '*Bless you*' suggest about the elderly women?
Shoppers of the narrator	'Like *bruised fruit on a produce stand*, I existed, but was bypassed for a healthier looking *specimen*'	Who is compared to '*bruised fruit on a produce stand*'? Why might Davis have chosen the image of '*bruised fruit*'? What does the choice of the word '*specimen*' suggest about how the narrator is being looked at by others?
The child of the narrator	'Tilting her head up she *chirped*, "But lady, did they go to 'Leg Heaven'?"'	What does '*chirped*' suggest of the child? What does it suggest about how the narrator feels about the child's response?
The narrator of herself	'… I smile warmly, *coerce* eye contact, and speak in a confident manner.'	What does the use of the image of '*coerce*' tell us about the willingness of people to do this on encountering the narrator?
The narrator of society The narrator of herself	'I attempt to enlighten society'	What perspective of herself does Davis seem to have in this sentence? What assumptions does 'enlighten' suggest she is making herself about 'society'?

ACTIVITY: Looking at contrasts

Look at the following examples of contrasts used in *Body Imperfect* and then write down some thoughts as to why the author may have used each one:

> *'Their downcast glances made me realize that they did not see the triumph in my eyes, only my missing limbs.'*

> *'Men, who might normally wink and smile, now looked away.'*

> *'That incident made me think about how differently children and adults react to the unknown. To a child, an odd appearance is an interesting curiosity and a learning experience, while adults often view the unusual with fear and repulsion.'*

> *'I began to realize that prior to my disability I had been guilty of the same inappropriate reactions.'*

Share your ideas with two or three classmates and add any further points that you feel are interesting and valid.

◆ Assessment opportunities

In this activity you have practised skills that are assessed using Criterion A: Analysing.

CONNECT–EXTEND–CHALLENGE

Stella Young (see the photograph on page 58) was an Australian disability activist, and also a journalist and comedian, who died in 2014 at the age of 32. She had much to say about perceptions of disability, including a TED talk, which can be found here: **https://youtu. be/8K9Gg164Bsw**.

Consider both the TED talk and *Body Imperfect* then write down your thoughts on the following:
- **How are the ideas and information presented *connected* to what you already knew?**
- **What new ideas did you get that *extended* or pushed your thinking in new directions?**
- **What is still *challenging* or confusing for you to get your mind around? What questions, wonderings or puzzles do you now have?**

As a final reflection, look at the following four quotations by Stella Young.

> I use the term 'disabled people' quite deliberately, because I subscribe to what's called the social model of disability, which tells us that we are more disabled by the society that we live in than by our bodies and our diagnoses.

> People do not understand disability, and people fear what they don't understand.

> We think we know what it's all about; we think that disability is a really simple thing, and we don't expect to see disabled people in our daily lives.

> People are uncomfortable about disability, and so interactions can become unintentionally uncomfortable.

Choose the quotation that you feel is the most true, in your own experience and from what we have looked at in this chapter so far. Then turn to a classmate and share in turn what prompted you to make the choice of quotation that you did.

How is perspective presented in different media?

PRESENTING AND INFLUENCING PERSPECTIVE – WRITTEN VS VISUAL TEXTS

Our work on Debi Davis' *Body Imperfect* has allowed us to look into some of our inquiry questions, such as what perspectives are, and how these might influence attitudes and behaviours.

We have also looked into some of the techniques that may be used in written text to present particular perspectives to a reader, and we have thought about whether a text can influence the attitudes and behaviours of its readers, as was asked in our factual and debatable inquiry questions.

Visual texts may also seek to present perspectives on a theme, and to influence attitudes and behaviours towards that theme.

Visual texts, films, may have similar purposes to written texts, but differ in the techniques they may use in order to achieve those purposes. Let us therefore consider further how perspectives may be presented in a visual text, the techniques that may be used to do so, and the possible impact of the text and its techniques on a viewer.

First, watch the film *Mask*, and then we will revisit parts of it to consider some of the intentions and techniques of the director.

ACTIVITY: Perspective in film

 ATL

- Media literacy skills: Understand the impact of media representations and modes of presentation

Below is a link to a scene from a TV police drama, which attempts to convey something of the experience of a wheelchair user on the streets of a city. Watch the scene, starting at 21:29, up to 24:04:
https://youtu.be/ir4NjuKpKv0.

Write down some notes on the following questions:

1   **What does this scene have in common with the story told in *Body Imperfect*?**

2   **What kinds of reactions do you think the director is trying to elicit from viewers when they watch this extract?**
3   **In what ways has the director tried to convey a sense of the experience of the wheelchair user? You might like to think about camera angles used, characters and situations placed in the sequence, and any other techniques you may notice.**

Share your ideas with the others on your table, and add any additional ideas that you hear from any of your classmates.

◆ Assessment opportunities

In this activity you have practised skills that are assessed using Criterion A: Analysing.

At the start of this chapter you were asked to write a script based on a scenario of the boy in the picture walking into your classroom one morning as a new member of the class. The script included the reactions of four or five of the classmates in the room, and helped you consider some different perspectives that might be formed of the boy on the basis of first impressions.

Now that you have watched the film *Mask,* you will recognize that the boy shown in the image on page 54 is Rocky.

Mask

■ *Mask* film poster

The image at the beginning of the chapter is taken from a film called *Mask*, which will form a major focus for the remainder of this chapter. The film, directed by Peter Bogdanovich, tells the true story of Rocky Dennis, who lived with serious disfigurement as a result of a rare disease – which also caused his premature death while he was still a teenager.

Rocky's mother, Rusty Dennis, was a fierce champion of her son, but she lived her life as part of a biker group on the fringes of society – all to Rocky's concern and disapproval. The film therefore asks questions about what leads certain people or types of people to be perceived as 'different' or 'outsiders', and invites an audience to consider how such perspectives can lead to such people being treated in certain ways by others, and what assumptions may lie beneath perspectives.

This is most obviously seen in the presentation of Rocky, while the depiction of his mother, Rusty Dennis, invites a range of possible perspectives on how a 'good' parent might look and act. A number of literary techniques are evident, which help to shape some of the perspectives we form as the film's viewers, and thus our responses to these two main characters in particular.

ACTIVITY: First impressions of Rocky Dennis

■ ATL

- Critical-thinking skills: Revise understanding based on new information and evidence

Task 1

After watching the film, how would you now **describe** Rocky? Choose the three words that you think best describe him and write these on three separate sticky notes or cards. You and your classmates should now place all these written notes together on a table.

- Are there any particular descriptive words, or ideas, repeated among your notes? Which one(s)?
- Now consider whether the words you have all chosen are positive in nature or negative. Sort the notes into two columns under these headings. How many notes are in each: a similar number, or are there more in one column than the other?

Task 2

On a scale of 1 to 10, 1 being not sympathetic at all and 10 being very sympathetic, how sympathetic a character do you think a viewer is likely to find Rocky in the film? Write the reason for your choice beneath the number you have chosen.

If you do not choose a 1 or 10 you should **explain** what it was that stopped you from selecting these numbers. For example, if you choose an 8 it shows that you feel Rocky is likely to be viewed as a sympathetic character overall, but also there are things that make him not entirely sympathetic. What are these things? Do not forget that you are thinking about how a viewer in general is likely to perceive the character of Rocky as he is presented, and not how you alone perceive him, which may be different.

◆ Assessment opportunities

In this activity you have practised skills that are assessed using Criterion A: Analysing.

The likelihood is that most of the sticky notes or cards from Task 1 in the 'First impressions of Rocky Dennis' activity will have contained positive words to describe Rocky, unless they were words to describe his appearance. Your choice of number in Task 2 is also likely to have been above 5 in the scale.

It thus appears that in his presentation of Rocky in the film, the director has used certain techniques in presenting Rocky that are likely to lead a viewer to form a particular perspective of him. Let us look further at how he has done that, and why.

ACTIVITY: Establishing the character of Rocky Dennis

ATL

- Critical-thinking skills: Draw reasonable conclusions and generalizations

Rocky is introduced in an early sequence in the film, just after the credits. The director first shows us Rocky by gradually zooming in on him as he is apparently getting ready in his bedroom to go out. Note how the director delays showing viewers a direct shot of Rocky – instead we are given glimpses: we see him from afar through the window, or with his back turned, or with his face partially obstructed, or in a mirror, until eventually the camera is with him in the bedroom and we see him most clearly in the mirror. On hearing his mother returning, Rocky goes outside and we have the clear picture of him, which forms the image at the start of this chapter.

- **Think about why the director delays the point at which a viewer gets to see Rocky directly.**
- **What details are shown to us in the scene, which might indicate something about the nature of Rocky as a character? Write down a list of these details.**
- **Now write a paragraph describing the impressions you feel are being presented of Rocky in this opening sequence. What kind of a boy does he seem to be? What does he enjoy? What are his interests?**

The sequence, if you wish to watch it again, runs from 02:07 to 04:22.

Assessment opportunities

In this activity you have practised skills that are assessed using Criterion A: Analysing.

How can a perspective change?

ACTIVITY: Reacting to Rocky

■ ATL

- ■ Critical-thinking skills: Gather and organize relevant information to formulate an argument

Like *Body Imperfect,* the film also shows us reactions from others towards Rocky, and his facial deformity in particular.

Look through the first 45 minutes of the film (fast forward as needed) and find examples of reactions to Rocky. Draw a table like the one below.

- In the left-hand column, **describe** each reaction you find. In the middle column, note down and **comment** on details from the scene that led you to **describe** a reaction in such a way. In the right-hand column, add your own feelings about the reactions you see in the film. Do you think your feelings are what the director intended a viewer to feel on seeing the reactions presented? Why?
- Pick three or four examples from the film then share these (and the thoughts you have written down about them) with one or more of your classmates. Write down any other examples or ideas you hear from your classmates that are not already in your table.

Reactions to Rocky in the film	What makes you say that?	How do you feel about the reaction you see? Do you think the director intended a viewer to feel this way about it?

◆ Assessment opportunities

In this activity you have practised skills that are assessed using Criterion A: Analysing.

You may have suggested that the director intended viewers of the film to react with disapproval to some of the more insensitive reactions we can see towards Rocky. As with *Body Imperfect,* these may be designed to lead us to evaluate our own such responses in similar situations.

The director is also – as in *Body Imperfect* – making use of contrast, this time to show how perspectives can easily change over time, and some of the reasons for that change. *Body Imperfect,* a short text, shows a reader a series of reactions to the disabled narrator, but these are all 'one-off' brief encounters with people whom the narrator does not expect to meet again. As a feature-length film, however, *Mask* is able to show the initial encounters and reactions (and the assumptions made and perspectives formed in those instances), as well as how these can change over time, and why. The suggestion is that we might question how reliable the perspectives we first form about something are, particularly when we have not had enough time to learn or get information about the thing on which we are making a judgement. Over time we may find that the perspectives we formed, and assumptions we made, were less accurate than we thought.

One of the characters used to illustrate this in the film is that of Mr Simms, who may well have formed one of the examples you have used in the 'Reacting to Rocky' activity.

Mr Simms' reaction when Rocky and his mother Rusty visit him at the school to secure Rocky's admission is the first extended example we are given of a reaction to Rocky in the film.

Watch this scene again – in the film it begins at 05:05 minutes and ends at 07:30; or a clip of the scene can be watched at this link: **https://youtu.be/C1kZTfHldfY.**

THINK–PAIR–SHARE

Think about these questions, and then **discuss** your answers with a partner:

1 How would you **describe** the reaction of the school principal, Mr Simms, on seeing Rocky? You may already have some notes on this from your table of reactions.
2 What concerns does he voice about Rocky entering the school?
3 What assumptions does he appear to make in the scene?

ACTIVITY: First impressions, last impressions – Mr Simms' diary

ATL

- Communication skills: Write for different purposes; make inferences and draw conclusions

Rocky's registration

Imagine that you are Mr Simms, the school principal, reflecting at the end of the day on the visit of Rocky and his mother to your office that morning.

Write a diary entry of about three to four paragraphs (300–500 words) in which you **describe** your impressions of and responses to Rocky and his mother, and to what happened in the meeting. Include in your diary entry the information in your responses to the questions on the left.

Make sure you also include how you actually *feel* about any events or details that you describe, and consider what register you should use as the school principal writing in a private diary.

Rocky's graduation

Mr Simms' impressions of Rocky are, however, very different by the time Rocky comes to leave the school, as a multiple prize winner and honours student at the graduation ceremony. That scene can be found between 1:00:40 and 1:02:05 in the film. After watching the scene again, write a further diary entry by Mr Simms that reveals his thoughts on Rocky at this point, and reflects on how his perceptions of Rocky have changed.

Assessment opportunities

This activity can be assessed using Criterion C: Producing text and Criterion D: Using language.

Dialogue

The theme of changing perspectives is also shown in the cases of Rocky's fellow school students, and one of the purposes of the sequence showing Rocky's first day at school is to show responses that will contrast with the perspectives held by those same students later.

This particular scene, and theme, are foreshadowed through the use of dialogue, as Rocky prepares to go to school for the first time:

> **ROCKY:** You're not the one who's going to be going to some school where kids are gonna run in the other direction when they see you, making fun of you.
>
> **RUSTY:** Yeah and when they stop running and stop making fun, they'll get to know you and think you're terrific, just like at your other school. You know, it takes time for people to get to like each other. I don't know why you think it should be different for you.
>
> **ROCKY:** But I am different, mom.
>
> **RUSTY:** Yeah — you're more beautiful on the inside than most people. Anybody can't see that …
>
> **ROCKY:** … they're wrong.

Which sentences in particular address this theme of changing perspectives quite explicitly?

A key concern of both *Body Imperfect* and *Mask* is to try to show the impact of reactions towards people of different appearance, and to raise questions for a reader or viewer as to how we might or perhaps should react in such situations, given the impact it can have on others. The dialogue shown in the script helps to convey Rocky's feelings to a viewer, therefore, and foreshadows what Rocky knows will happen on his first day at school.

Dialogue is used at other points in the film too as a tool to allow Rocky to make this point, for instance where he tells his mother after returning from the baseball game that he will be going to a camp for the summer, 'I'm going to a camp, where everybody's blind. That'll be a break' (1:11:52–1:11:58).

Watch the scene again of Rocky's first day at school – in the full-length film version it begins at 20:40 and ends at around 25:30; or you can watch just the scene itself here: **https://youtu.be/yXl3ENKGAUQ**.

WHAT MAKES YOU SAY THAT?

The explanation game

This activity looks closely at the details of a scene and uses critical-thinking skills to build explanations as to why these details are present or occur.

First, **state** something you have noticed; this helps you look at and focus on particular details of the scene. After watching the scene, complete the prompt 'I notice that …' by writing down something that you noticed in the film clip. For instance:

I notice that … everyone goes quiet in class when Rocky is introduced.

I notice that … Rocky sits on his own at lunchtime.

Having noted particular details, the next thing is to add the question 'Why is it that way?' or 'Why did it happen that way?' Write down some possible **explanations** or reasons that might answer the questions you have asked.

Finally, for each possible explanation or reason, ask the question 'What makes me think so?' Note down your answer(s) in each case.

So, the steps are as follows:
- **I notice that …**
- **Why is it that way? Why did it happen that way?**
- **What makes me think so?**

Do this for two separate things that you notice in the scene. Then get into a group of four, and share your observations about this sequence of the film and your proposed explanations of them.

Having done this, **discuss** together, on the basis of your observations and explanations about the episode, some of the possible purposes that you feel the director may have had for including this particular sequence.

Language and Literature for the IB MYP 4&5: by Concept

Narrative perspective in film

Immediately before the scene showing Rocky's first day at school, we see a scene between Rocky and his mother. The dialogue between mother and son allows the director to show the viewer some of Rocky's feelings and concerns about starting school. While a written text such as *Body Imperfect* may use a first-person narrator to relate events from a central character's point of view, or show their thoughts and feelings, in film a character cannot usually narrate directly to the audience in the same way.

There are techniques that can be used in film to try to present a first-person point of view, such as the following:

- *Voiceovers* – where the narrator is a character in the film. Famous examples of this occur in the classic films *The Shawshank Redemption* and *Sunset Boulevard*.
- *Direct address to a viewer by a character in the film* – a technique known as 'breaking the fourth wall', which is often achieved by a character turning directly to a camera and speaking. Examples of this can be seen in *Ferris Bueller's Day Off, High Fidelity* and *Amélie*.

These are used in a limited way in film, however, and, as you will have noticed, are not used in *Mask*.

ACTIVITY: Rocky's voice

ATL

- Media literacy skills: Demonstrate awareness of media interpretations of events and ideas
- Creative-thinking skills: Create original works and ideas; use existing works and ideas in new ways

Let us imagine that we had been asked to add a voiceover by Rocky, or an instance in which he breaks the fourth wall, to the sequence showing the experiences of his first day at school.

- **Choose a particular moment within this sequence where a voiceover could be added, or where Rocky might turn to the camera and address viewers directly, for 15–20 seconds. Write down what you think he would say at that point.**

- In pairs, try out your voiceover or speech to camera with a classmate. Give each other feedback, and make any revisions you may wish to make on the basis of that.
- Once you are happy with your voiceover or speech to camera, record it, as Rocky, on whichever device might be most convenient – a smartphone or iPad, for instance.
- Get together in a group of four or five and play each voiceover or speech to camera in turn. As this was an opportunity for Rocky to speak directly to viewers as a first-person narrator, what did each person have him say? Which do you think was the most effective, and why?

◆ Assessment opportunities

In this activity you have practised skills that are assessed using Criterion C: Producing text and Criterion D: Using language.

DIFFERENT POINTS OF VIEW

Two techniques used in film to provide an impression of first-person point of view *are* used in *Mask,* however. These are as follows:

- The camera may follow one particular character around all of the time, so that the character is the focus of almost every scene, and the viewer follows his or her experiences throughout.
- Use of camera angles such as the 'point of view' shot to present an individual's direct point of view of events.

In the sequence showing his first day of school, the camera follows Rocky around the school, the classroom and the café. In fact, the camera follows him repeatedly throughout the film, and this is one of the ways we are invited into his experiences.

ACTIVITY: From my point of view …

◼ ATL

- ◼ Critical-thinking skills: Consider ideas from multiple perspectives

In the sequence depicting Rocky's first day of school, point-of-view shots are used at particular times to imply something of his thoughts and feelings:

- **as Rocky is on his way to his classroom and approaches a group of three boys by the doorway**
- **while he is sitting at the back of the class as students enter**
- **as the class teacher speaks.**

Look at the images below and then answer the questions that follow:

■ Rocky's first day at school

1   **Point-of-view shots leave a viewer having to infer the thoughts and feelings of a character at the time. What do you think Rocky is thinking and feeling on each of these occasions?**
2   **Why do you think point-of-view shots might have been used at these particular points in the film?**
3   **What impact do they have on a viewer's response towards Rocky and what he is experiencing?**
4   **A point-of-view shot tries to give a first-person view of events in a visual text. Now, imagine this was a written text with Rocky as the first-person narrator. Write two or three paragraphs of Rocky's first-person narrative for each scene. Remember that he will therefore use 'I' in your narrative.**
5   **Try changing the point of view. What if one of the three boys was the first-person narrator? Write a couple of paragraphs describing the first scene from this perspective. In the second scene, write as if the teacher was the first-person narrator. Again, each of them will use 'I' where necessary. Underneath each of these narratives, write down how you think a viewer would respond, and why.**
6   **How different are the two narratives? If you were turning *Mask* into a written text, and using first-person narration, which character would you choose as your narrator? Why?**

◆ Assessment opportunities

In this activity you have practised skills that are assessed using Criterion C: Producing text and Criterion D: Using language.

From your point of view

- First-person narration allows a reader to hear directly from a character; their thoughts and feelings, and how they experience what is going on from their own point of view.
- Second-person narration is not especially common, but can similarly take a reader directly into a character's experience, when it is used. Second-person narration is where a character in the story narrates what is happening, using 'You' to address the reader. As with first-person narration, there will be one perspective represented. The use of 'You', however, invites a reader directly to imagine him- or herself in the situation being described, as if the reader is undergoing the experiences.
- Although second-person narration is less frequently found in texts than first- or third-person narration, it can be found in the short story *You need to go upstairs*. This tells the story of a blind girl named Ally, who needs to visit the bathroom. She uses second-person narration to describe her experiences and feelings in trying to get upstairs, using her other senses to try to make sense of what is going on around her. The use of 'you' and the detail employed invites the reader to enter directly into the situation. You can read the complete short story at this link: **https://sites.google.com/a/rsu71.org/the-global-classroom--linking-the-world-one-classroom-at-a-time/upstairs**.

You might notice a number of other techniques used in the story to increase the immediacy and tension of the situation, such as:

- The use of **rhetorical questions**.
- The use of sensory imagery, especially of touch in this instance, which is appropriate as the narrator, Ally, is blind.
- The use of chronology – time – in the narration to help convey the sense of all-pervading fear – Ally talks of what she is doing at the present moment, what has happened before this moment (the past), and what may happen in the future.
- The use of syntax – including the following aspects:
  - The variety of sentences – questions, statements, even a little unsignposted direct speech ('Mother. Mother …'), and the variety of sentence length throughout.
  - The manner in which sentences are often broken up through dashes, semi-colons and so on – a series of short phrases of this nature, along with short sentences themselves, convey a sense of tension and urgency.
  - The use of asyndeton – a sentence in which a conjunction such as 'and' or 'but' that would normally be anticipated has been omitted. The effect of asyndeton is to speed up the pace of a sentence, and it can thus be used to increase tension and dramatic effect. Here, as the narrator, Ally, feels increasingly fearful.
- The use of repetition for emphasis of some important thoughts.

ACTIVITY: Second-person narration

If we were producing *Mask* as a written text, we might use this technique at certain times to more explicitly emphasize Rocky's experiences.

Write a passage in a similar style to, and about the same length as, the passage from *You need to go upstairs,* in which Rocky narrates his moments in the dining room at lunch. In the film the scene begins at around 24:24 – where he enters, and ends at approximately 24:57 – where he is shown sitting alone at the table.

This passage should be written as a second-person narration and should include at least one example of the following:
- **rhetorical questions**
- **sensory imagery (consider which sense(s) may be most appropriate in Rocky's case)**
- **references to past, present and future**
- **repetition**
- **syntactical techniques, including an instance of asyndeton.**

Divide your page into three columns and give each column a heading, as shown in the example table below. Write your passage in the left-hand column. In the middle column indicate where you have used the above literary techniques. Use the right-hand column to **explain** the purpose and effect of each literary technique.

Your passage – Rocky's second-person narration	Literary techniques used	Purpose and effect of each literary technique

The recent activities using narrative voice might have led you to consider more carefully Rocky's actual thoughts and feelings during the sequence of his first day at school. We know from the dialogue with his mother that he had some fears about the first day at his new school – 'I don't wanna go, Mom' (21:09); dreading the prospect of, as he puts it, 'going to some school where kids are gonna run in the other direction when they see you, making fun of you' (21:18–21:23).

Rocky's experience during his first day at school is indeed not an especially friendly one, as we have seen, but how does he actually react to this when there?

The poet Paul Laurence Dunbar wrote a poem about masking one's true feelings and presenting a different appearance to the world, for reasons similar to those of Rocky in the sequence showing his first day at school. Read and listen to the poem: **https://youtu.be/a9nnVmkL_ig** and look closely at the reasons he gives for those in the poem masking their true thoughts and feelings.

DISCUSS

What do you think are important pieces of information about Paul Laurence Dunbar and/or 'We Wear the Mask' and its particular context? Which pieces of information might help others understand more about what the poem is about and is trying to say?

Do some research on the **life of Paul Laurence Dunbar** and the **historical context** in which he is writing.

In groups, find key points of information and then decide on a final set of 5–6 bullet points which are the most important pieces of information about the poet or context of the poem, which most help in understanding the poem.

ACTIVITY: Masking our true feelings

■ ATL

■ Communication skills: Make inferences and draw conclusions

In the sequence showing Rocky's first day at school, **identify** five experiences Rocky has and write down how he responds on each occasion.

Write a paragraph or two **evaluating** your feelings about Rocky's behaviour at school. How do you feel about his experiences – were they fair or unfair? How do you feel about what he says and does as a response? Can you **identify** anything he could or should have done differently? How do you feel about him as a character as a result of his behaviour in this scene? Has it made him a more or less sympathetic character? Why?

During his first day, Rocky often masks his real feelings about what he experiences. *Mask* is the title of the film, and it refers not only to Rocky's physical features, where his face looks like a mask, but also to the motif (recurring symbol) used in the film of keeping something – often feelings – hidden and masking the reality. What other examples can you remember in the film where a character does that?

It is something everyone does at times, but for what kinds of reasons do people 'mask' their real thoughts and feelings? Should they do so?

When was the last time you 'masked' how you really felt about something? Why did you do so?

Share your answers with the other members of your group and listen to their ideas in turn.

◆ Assessment opportunities

In this activity you have practised skills that are assessed using Criterion A: Analysing.

▼ Links to: History

Paul Laurence Dunbar's parents had both been slaves and he used their stories of their lives in much of his poetry. In 'We Wear the Mask' Dunbar was undoubtedly alluding to the sufferings of African Americans in the United States especially prior to, and in many cases during, the American Civil War, and to their lives in slavery working on plantations.

In your history classes, have you come across any texts that allude to a specific period of time and express the attitudes and feelings of the people of that time? What emotions are they expressing?

Dunbar carefully does not refer to that specific historical context, however, which gives the poem a more universal application. It can therefore refer to anyone who tries to hide true feelings and suffering, and to present something different to others.

We Wear the Mask

We wear the mask that grins and lies,
It hides our cheeks and shades our eyes,—
This debt we pay to human guile;
With torn and bleeding hearts we smile,
And mouth with myriad subtleties.

Why should the world be over-wise,
In counting all our tears and sighs?
Nay, let them only see us, while
     We wear the mask.

We smile, but, O great Christ, our cries
To thee from tortured souls arise.
We sing, but oh the clay is vile
Beneath our feet, and long the mile;
But let the world dream otherwise,
     We wear the mask!

Paul Laurence Dunbar

Another point in *Mask,* which sees Rocky masking his feelings for different reasons, occurs during the graduation ceremony between 1:00:40 and 1:02:05. When the first prize is announced, Rocky has not won it. Watch this scene again, and consider the following questions:

- Do you think Rocky was hoping to win this particular prize? What makes you say that?
- How would you **describe** his reactions when the prize is announced?
- Do you think his reactions were appropriate? Why (not)?

Having thought about those questions, look at the link below at what happened to one award-winning actor who was perceived not to have hidden her disappointment sufficiently well after she didn't win an award. The web page includes a brief video of the moment the actor heard that someone else had won the award instead of her: **https://goo.gl/egua3P**.

Another newspaper published some of the comment on social media about that moment: **https://goo.gl/WyJ3P1**.

Now read the following article, which takes a different perspective in defending the actor's reaction: **https://goo.gl/fFpTgF**.

The reaction to Sheridan Smith's perceived disappointment reflects a social expectation to mask feelings of disappointment, particularly when we lose out on something (such as a prize or some form of recognition) to someone else.

ACTIVITY: We Wear the Mask

ATL

- Information literacy skills: Make connections between various sources of information
- Creative-thinking skills: Use brainstorming and visual diagrams to generate new ideas and inquiries

Pair up with a neighbour. Read the poem again and discuss what you think the poet is talking about.

If you came face-to-face with the poet and could ask any questions about the poem, which questions might you ask? Think of some questions, and then choose ONE to write at the top of a piece of blank A4 paper.

Circulate the A4 pieces of paper so that in your pairs you can look at all of the questions chosen by the other pairs. For each question write down on the paper a suggested answer.

Once you receive your own piece of paper and question back, read through all of the suggested answers and ideas.

◆ Assessment opportunities

In this activity you have practised skills that are assessed using Criterion A: Analysing.

DISCUSS

Does knowing more about the reasons for the actor's disappointment change your own thoughts and perspective on what she did? How? Why?

Why do you think there is an expectation to mask feelings of disappointment? Is there more than one reason? Do you ever feel obliged to mask disappointment or other feelings, for example in a situation such as a prize-giving event at your own school?

Can you think of other social situations where you might be expected to mask your own true feelings?

USE OF CHARACTER TO SHAPE VIEWERS' RESPONSES

We have looked at a number of ways in which the director of *Mask,* Peter Bogdanovich, may be trying to shape his viewers' responses to the film, and perhaps more widely in their lives when they may encounter someone like Rocky.

Rocky's ordinariness, apart from his facial appearance, is shown in the very first scene in which he features in the film. His vulnerability and sensitivity to the reactions he encounters help make clear to us how he is affected by these, and may elicit sympathy in many viewers of the film.

While he probably masked his true feelings behind jokes and light-heartedness during his first day at school, meanwhile, he was demonstrating a further characteristic that is prominently featured throughout the film – his positivity.

All of these are evident in the **parallel scene** used by the director to show how perspectives of Rocky on the parts of teachers and fellow students change, as Rocky tells the story of Helen of Troy to the class and offers to help Eric with his work – for a price.

The power of positivity

Despite his fears and feelings about how he may be treated, Rocky chooses to adopt a positive attitude to school, which is a reason why he might be considered by viewers of the film to be a likeable, sympathetic character.

In one scene Rocky addresses the topic of a positive attitude quite directly, saying 'When something bad happens to you, you gotta remember something good that's happened' (53:37).

The power of having a positive perspective on life, or changing to one, and the benefits that come from such a perspective, have been known for many years.

Many articles discuss the benefits of positive thinking and also offer advice on how to become a more positive thinker. Read these two articles:

https://goo.gl/MujjLo

https://goo.gl/XPHQqb.

ACTIVITY: How positive are you?

■ ATL

■ Affective skills: Self-motivation and resilience

The table below can be used to rate yourself in accordance with how positive a perspective you feel you have on life generally: 10 is extremely positive, while 1 is very negative. Draw out this table and give yourself a rating between 10 and 1.

Beneath your score, add reasons as to why you have given yourself that number. Specify which particular pieces of information you found most useful in the two articles.

Carry out some research and find another internet article that other teenagers might find useful to read on the topic of having a positive perspective. Once you have found and chosen an article, add its URL below and give at least three reasons why you chose it.

How positive is my perspective on life? Circle the number that you feel best represents the answer to this question: 10 is most positive and 1 is least positive.									
1	2	3	4	5	6	7	8	9	10
I would score myself here because …									
The three most useful pieces of information in the articles were:									
1									
2									
3									
Another useful website is:									
I think this website is useful because:									
1									
2									
3									

It might be useful to set up an alternative place for you and your classmates to list all the useful websites you've found, such as a wiki page, which can then be shared with everyone.

◆ Assessment opportunities

In this activity you have practised skills that are assessed using Criterion A: Analysing.

! Take action: Random acts of kindness

! A new precept each month can help you take action across each new month. The Random Acts of Kindness Foundation, however, has ideas for lots of other actions that can easily be integrated into one's day-to-day life.

! Research some of the ideas on this page: **www.randomactsofkindness.org/kindness-ideas**. Choose five random acts of kindness that you feel you could carry out over the next two months. Write down those five acts in a **list** and then, each time you accomplish one of the acts, record the date and note a few details about it.

! Even better, if you keep a blog, write a blog entry for each random act of kindness as you accomplish it.

Precepts

A precept is a general rule that can be helpful to you if you remember it in your daily life. In a novel called *Wonder* by RJ Palacio there is a character, a school teacher, who uses a series of precepts – 'rules to live by' – with his students. These are some of the precepts he uses for each month:

When given the choice between being right or being kind, choose kind. – *Dr Wayne Dyer*

Your deeds are your monuments.
– *Inscription on an Egyptian tomb*

Have no friends not equal to yourself. – *Confucius*

Fortune favors the bold. – *Virgil*

No man is an island, entire of self. – *John Donne*

It is better to know some of the questions than all of the answers. – *James Thurber*

Kind words do not cost much.
Yet they accomplish much. – *Blaise Pascal*

What is beautiful is good, and who is good will soon be beautiful. – *Sappho*

Do all the good you can, by all the means you can, in all the ways you can, in all the places you can, at all the times you can, to all the people you can, as long as you ever can. – *John Wesley's Rule*

Just follow the day and reach for the sun!
– *The Polyphonic Spree*

Language and Literature for the IB MYP 4&5: *by Concept*

ACTIVITY: Precepts

■ ATL

- Affective skills: Self-motivation
- Collaboration skills: Listen actively to other perspectives and ideas; negotiate effectively; encourage others to contribute

Task 1

Look at the precepts on the previous page. If Rocky were to choose some precepts to share with others, what sort of precepts might he choose to include?

In groups of four or five, share with each other the precepts you think Rocky would have used.

Task 2

Individually, think about, research and choose one precept that you think your whole class should live by for the next month.

Return to your original groups and share your precept with each other. Agree on one precept and then feed this back to the rest of your class. Each group's chosen precept should be written down somewhere – on poster paper on a wall or on the whiteboard.

As a class your task is now to choose a final class precept for the month. Deciding on how to do that will involve some collaborative skills, such as listening actively to other perspectives and ideas, negotiating effectively, encouraging others to contribute, and giving and receiving meaningful feedback.

Once a final precept has been chosen, display it prominently in your classroom. The classroom precept could be changed each month.

Finally, write down two or three specific ideas about how you think you may individually put this precept into action over the coming month.

◆ Assessment opportunities

In this activity you have practised skills that are assessed using Criterion D: Using language.

SOME SUMMATIVE TASKS TO TRY

Use these tasks to apply and extend your learning in this chapter. These tasks are designed so that you can evaluate your learning at different levels of achievement in the Language and literature criteria.

THIS TASK CAN BE USED TO EVALUATE YOUR LEARNING IN CRITERION A, CRITERION B AND CRITERION D

Task 1: Perspectives in song

Artists such as Christina Aguilera, Lady Gaga and Radiohead have all recorded songs on themes reflected in the texts we have looked at in this chapter. Songs, like other texts, use narrative perspective. In this task you will be comparing and contrasting the use of narrative perspective to convey ideas on those themes.

- Listen to the songs on the next page by these artists and then find the lyrics of these songs online.
- Then write an essay comparing the songs in terms of the following areas:
  - ☐ What each song is about
  - ☐ Who the narrator is (be careful with 'Beautiful', as this changes in the course of the song)
  - ☐ What point of view each narrator has about what they are narrating
  - ☐ What impressions a listener might have of the narrator in each case
  - ☐ How a listener might feel towards each narrator and the ideas being presented in the song
  - ☐ What kinds of techniques the writer has used to lead a listener to feel such a way about the narrator and ideas in the song
  - ☐ Using the above information, suggest what you think may have been some of the purposes of choosing that narrative voice.

Once you have compared these things, conclude your discussion by explaining which song you feel is the most effective and why. Include in your answer what you think 'effective' means.

'Beautiful' – Christina Aguilera – **https://youtu.be/eAfyFTzZDMM**

'Born This Way' (radio edit) – Lady Gaga – **https://youtu.be/26AppZB1wEA**

'Creep' – Radiohead – **https://youtu.be/XFkzRNyygfk**

THIS TASK CAN BE USED TO EVALUATE YOUR LEARNING IN CRITERION B, CRITERION C AND CRITERION D

Task 2: Narrative voices – A Mask of Defiance

- Write two versions of a short story entitled 'A Mask of Defiance', in which the experiences of a character in a situation in which he or she feels a need to present a defiant appearance are narrated.
- Think about a range of possible situations, such as something in school, or within your community. You might decide to use one of the slaves from Paul Dunbar's poem, or think of another situation such as when a relationship broke down, or a character performed in some way and the performance went wrong. Embarrassing situations often lead to us 'putting on a brave face'.
- Write a first narrative of your chosen situation, 400–500 words long, and use first- or second-person narration.
- Rewrite the narrative, again using 400–500 words, using third-person narration.
- In a paragraph at the end, **explain** which you think would be the most effective narrative voice to use for your story and why.

THIS TASK CAN BE USED TO EVALUATE YOUR LEARNING IN CRITERION B, CRITERION C AND CRITERION D

Task 3: A letter to myself at 80 years old

The Australian disability activist, Stella Young, imagined herself as an 80-year-old, and wrote a letter to her older self. Read the letter carefully here: **https://goo.gl/qjvmHA**.

Below are some of the topics Stella Young discusses in her letter. You should include them, with your own thoughts on them, in your own letter.

- How do you picture yourself at 80 years old? Describe yourself.
- What have been some of the most memorable points about your own life so far? How have you changed so far?
- What do you hope you will have achieved when you are 80 years old? Note how a number of paragraphs in Stella Young's letter begin 'By the time I get to you …' Use that phrase as the starting point for some of the paragraphs in your own letter.
- What advice do you think your 80-year-old self might want to give to the current you?
- Your letter should be between 800 and 1,000 words in length.

THESE TASKS CAN BE USED TO EVALUATE YOUR LEARNING IN CRITERION A AND CRITERION D

Task 4: Literary essay or oral presentation

- **Literary essay** – How might the director of *Mask* be seeking to shape perspectives of viewers through his presentation of the character of Rocky in the film?
- **Oral presentation** – As the director of *Mask*, **explain** how you were attempting to present Rocky in the film, the techniques you made use of, and the impact you hoped these might have on a viewer.
- Choose either the literary essay or the oral presentation. Either of these should focus on the three issues of how the character is presented, specific techniques used, and the impact of the character and techniques on an audience.

- The essay should be a formal essay of 800–1,000 words, while the oral presentation should be between six and eight minutes.

THIS TASK CAN BE USED TO EVALUATE YOUR LEARNING IN CRITERION C AND CRITERION D

Task 5: Blog post

- In a blog post of 300–500 words answer the following question: *If a student like Rocky came into your class, how would you react? How would you treat him?*
- Include an **explanation** as to whether you think your answer to this has changed from how you might have answered it before beginning this unit. Be honest!
- Add to this a plan that might be put into action to support any new arrival into a class, on their first day in your school. It might include things such as the following:
  - ☐ What will you do when you see them? Remember how people did not look at Rocky when he was introduced at first. How might they be made to feel comfortable?
  - ☐ What will happen at break?
  - ☐ What will happen at lunch?
  - ☐ What will happen at the end of the day?
  - ☐ What other information do they need?
  - ☐ Who might they go to when they have questions?
  - ☐ Will someone (or different people) act as a 'buddy', so that the new arrival will always have someone with them for the first few days? How will people be chosen or have the opportunity to volunteer?
  - ☐ Would introducing them to a group, club, sports team, and so on, be helpful for them?
  - ☐ Would creating and producing a brochure containing helpful information be a useful thing to do? If so, what information might go into it?
  - ☐ Does your school already have an orientation plan for new students? What is in it? Does everyone know about it? What role(s) can you as a fellow student play that will complement that plan?

Reflection

In this chapter we have explored the impact of first impressions, along with how the ways in which we may react to those can impact on others. We have also considered the role of assumptions in our behaviours, and the possible reliability or otherwise of those assumptions, and of first impressions. Along with this, we have explored how such themes are presented in written and visual texts, how writers and directors use particular techniques for certain purposes, and how these may be both similar and different between the two text types. We have also considered how positivity and masking one's feelings, might apply in our own lives.

Use this table to reflect on your own learning in this chapter.					
Questions we asked	**Answers we found**	**Any further questions now?**			
Factual:					
Conceptual:					
Debatable:					
Approaches to learning you used in this chapter	**Description – what new skills did you learn?**	**How well did you master the skills?**			
		Novice	Learner	Practitioner	Expert
Communication skills					
Collaboration skills					
Affective skills					
Reflection skills					
Information literacy skills					
Media literacy skills					
Critical-thinking skills					
Creative-thinking skills					
Learner profile attribute(s)	Reflect on the importance of being open-minded for your learning in this chapter.				
Open-minded					

4 How can poetry be used for protest?

Persuasive **communication** uses aspects of **style** for the **purpose** of expressing **personal and cultural** ideas, feelings, beliefs and values, which can help challenge or alter other people's **point of view**.

CONSIDER THESE QUESTIONS:

Factual: What techniques and stylistic devices can be used by poets to persuade an audience?

Conceptual: In what ways can emotive techniques work on an audience? How does a persuasive poem work? How can poems evoke emotion in their audiences?

Debatable: Is it ethical to deliberately try to manipulate the emotions of others? Is it right to try to change someone else's mind?

Now **share and compare** your thoughts and ideas with your partner, or with the whole class.

■ What do you care passionately about?

IN THIS CHAPTER, WE WILL ...

■ **Find out** about issues poets have felt moved to protest about, and techniques used in poetry to persuade those who read or hear it to experience particular emotions and form certain points of view.

■ **Explore** how attitudes might be expressed and identified in poetry, and how these might reflect beliefs and values behind them.

■ **Take action** by considering how to use advocacy, and making use of persuasive skills in poetry to support our own beliefs and values.

■ These Approaches to Learning (ATL) skills will be useful ...

■ Communication skills
■ Collaboration skills
■ Reflection skills
■ Information literacy skills
■ Media literacy skills
■ Critical-thinking skills
■ Creative-thinking skills

◆ Assessment opportunities in this chapter:

◆ **Criterion A:** Analysing
◆ **Criterion B:** Organizing
◆ **Criterion C:** Producing text
◆ **Criterion D:** Using language

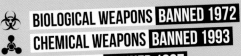

BIOLOGICAL WEAPONS **BANNED 1972**
CHEMICAL WEAPONS **BANNED 1993**
LAND MINES **BANNED 1997**
CLUSTER BOMBS **BANNED 2008**
NUCLEAR WEAPONS **BANNED 2017**

i can
international campaign
to abolish nuclear weapons

● We will reflect on this learner profile attribute …

● Principled – explore the concepts of integrity and honesty, along with fairness and justice; consider what it means to 'protest', and what may be involved in trying to advocate for or against things, in accordance with our own beliefs and values.

KEY WORDS

associations	meaning
atmosphere	mood
audience	purpose
emotion	rhythm
interpretation	style

ACTIVITY: What do I care about?

■ ATL

■ Communication skills: Give and receive meaningful feedback

Think about an issue you care passionately about. It may be something close to home such as what **chores** you do around the house. It may be something connected to your school, perhaps to do with homework or school uniforms. Or it may be something in the wider world, for example, related to poverty, hunger, war, sustainability, animal rights and so on.

● Write down in one sentence what you believe about that issue.
● **List** three reasons why you feel the way you do about your chosen issue.
● **List** one or two things that you feel could and should be done, either by yourself or someone else, to address your issue.
● Use your points to write a short (1–2 minute) speech that explains your stance on the issue you have chosen, and the reasons behind it.

In pairs, read each other the speeches you have written. It might be helpful to record the speeches so that you can watch and **comment** on them afterwards.

Give your partner feedback on how persuasive you felt they were when speaking, and suggest some solutions to their issue.

On a scale of 1 to 10, how persuasive do you think your partner's speech was (10 being highly persuasive and 1 being very unpersuasive). Now consider what their speech did well, and how their speech might become *more* persuasive. Write down the rating you gave and the key points of your feedback, and share this in your pairs.

EXTENSION

When you considered how 'persuasive' or 'unpersuasive' your classmate's speech was, what did you mean by that, *exactly*?

Think about what specific aspects or techniques you felt made the speech persuasive. Can you think of other techniques that were not used, but which could have made the speech more persuasive? Write these down in a list, and then research persuasive techniques and devices to see if there are any you have missed.

◆ Assessment opportunities

In this activity you have practised skills that are assessed using Criterion A: Analysing.

What techniques and stylistic devices can be used by poets to persuade an audience?

ACTIVITY: Poetry competition

You are a judge on a panel to find the best protest poems. Look through the following four entries and follow this process:

1 **Read the four poems.**
2 **On your own, order the poems from the one you think best to the one you think least good.**
3 **In groups of four, share your thoughts on the poems and the order you have put them in.**
4 **As a group, come up with a final order of merit for the four poems.**
5 **As a group, discuss the first- and last-placed poems – what are the reasons you placed these poems in these positions?**
6 **Individually, write two paragraphs that explain these two decisions.**
7 **If there is time, all groups in the class should share their final order of merit and explain the reasons why the first- and last-placed poems were chosen.**

◆ Assessment opportunities

In this activity you have practised skills that are assessed using Criterion A: Analysing.

The Old Woman

You can hear
the sound of the waves
splashing against the rocks.
You can feel
the ruthless wind
brushing against your face.
And if you listen closely enough
You can hear the old woman crying out her heart.
The old woman
filled with deepness of sorrow.
She walked with lethargy
And with looks of despair.
The bomb is in place,
With no turning back.
She walked towards the end of her journey.
She walked against
the insurmountable waves…
Gone in a mist.
The bomb had exploded,
but no one seemed to have noticed.

Anonymous

When you were judging where to put poems in the order of merit you will have had to decide on factors that you felt makes a poem 'good', or not so good. Such factors might otherwise be known as **criteria**.

DISCUSS

What criteria did you use to judge and decide about the poems in the poetry competition? Are these criteria specific to these poems or could you use them when considering other poems?

When judging a poem, is one **criterion** more important to consider than others? Can your class agree on a list of the most important criteria for evaluating a poem? Were there any disagreements about the criteria included in the list?

The Raven

A raven crouched in a tree.
It lived in the sky like me.

I stared at the night in the tree:
I felt its eye warm me.

What shock was shaking the tree?
Why was there blood on me?

From the world into the tree
Stones sprang and hissed around me.

They were killing the bird in the tree,
The raven that cheered me.

I hurried out of my tree –
The people greeted me:

They saw no bird in the tree.
They were very friendly to me.

Clifford Dyment

Clifford Dyment

Clifford Dyment (1914–71) was a British poet and fellow of the Royal Society of Literature. His best-known poems focused on the rural countryside. His first collection of verse, *First Day*, was published in 1935 when he was 21 years old.

Five Ways to Kill a Man

There are many cumbersome ways to kill a man.
You can make him carry a plank of wood
to the top of a hill and nail him to it.
To do this properly you require a crowd of people
wearing sandals, a cock that crows, a cloak
to dissect, a sponge, some vinegar and one
man to hammer the nails home.

Or you can take a length of steel,
shaped and chased in a traditional way,
and attempt to pierce the metal cage he wears.
But for this you need white horses,
English trees, men with bows and arrows,
at least two flags, a prince, and a
castle to hold your banquet in.

Dispensing with nobility, you may, if the wind
allows, blow gas at him. But then you need
a mile of mud sliced through with ditches,
not to mention black boots, bomb craters,
more mud, a plague of rats, a dozen songs
and some round hats made of steel.

In an age of aeroplanes, you may fly
miles above your victim and dispose of him by
pressing one small switch. All you then
require is an ocean to separate you, two
systems of government, a nation's scientists,
several factories, a psychopath and
land that no-one needs for several years.

These are, as I began, cumbersome ways to kill a man.
Simpler, direct, and much more neat is to see
that he is living somewhere in the middle
of the twentieth century, and leave him there.

Edwin Brock

Poverty

The entity that is dreaded by all but ever present everywhere, a
non-respecter of age,
Poverty does not have regard for race, nor nationality, as it is
present in every part of the globe,
Poverty breeds diseases, it has siblings like misery, ignorance,
illiteracy, dejection, rejection, degradation, agony,
Poverty means the difference between haves and have-nots, the
rich and the poor, the upper and the lower class,
Poverty is a quick destroyer of humans as it makes people 'sell' lots
of things including conscience, and destroys self-esteem,

Poverty, what a curse that has a spectrum; from mild, relative,
to abject poverty,
Poverty is a monster that destroys families, communities and
societies, always a bad commodity in the market place,
Poverty determines how you get treated by the society, and you are
loathed for your status,
Poverty gets written all over you once you are in the lower class,
caste system in every society is a celebration and endorsement of
poverty as social classification,
Some societies believe you are born into poverty and you should be
in poverty for life, please ask who is a 'Dalit' in Asia,
Poverty makes people call you 'Church rat', the basics of everyday
living become luxuries to the poor,
Poverty robs you of dignity, it robs you of a chance to be heard, as
'no good ideas come from the poor',

Poverty in father, poverty in mother, definitely rubs off on the
children, poverty is a disease difficult to cure,
Poverty is a giant monster that can only be tamed by dedicated
hard-work, prayers as Jabez did, and may seem un-surmountable,
may be intimidating, but can be defeated,
Every mother discusses poverty with her kids, how terrible and
merciless of a character is poverty,
Poverty is the character every father tells its fairy tale and the
importance of using education as weapon to attack it,
Poverty an equal opportunity degrader of a person, multiple
acronyms have been given to poverty in every culture and society.

Segun Rasaki

Poetry – meaning and technique

It is likely that most of the criteria you used to judge the poems were based on:

- the meaning of the poems
- the techniques used in the poems.

In your judging, you may also have argued about these: Was the 'message' of the poem the main thing that swayed you? Was a poem where the meaning was easier to see ranked more highly than another that was more difficult to understand? Or perhaps the argument was the other way around? Did you try to **identify** the poem that seemed to have 'the most important' message? Did aspects of style play a role – did anyone in your group think, for instance, that a poem that rhymed was better than one which did not rhyme?

While trying to decide on the 'best' poem, you will have been analysing the poetry in an effort to find out what it means, as well as looking at how it tries to convey that meaning. It is useful to look at these two aspects in the following order when analysing a poem:

1 **Examine** what is being said overall – the subject matter, meaning and purpose of the poem.
2 Consider the specific techniques used by the poet, and how they are contributing to the poem's meaning and purpose.

The subject matter of a poem is the topic that the poem is examining. When considering the overall meaning of a poem it is very helpful to have an idea as to what a poem's subject matter, or narrative, is (or at least appears on the surface to be) before considering anything else about it.

DISCUSS

When analysing a poem and its elements it is helpful to begin by looking at what a poem seems to be about. We can do this now using a short poem called 'Man and Beast', by Clifford Dyment.

Man and Beast

Hugging the ground by the lilac tree,
With shadows in conspiracy,
The black cat from the house next door
Waits with death in each bared claw
For the tender unwary bird
That all the summer I have heard
In the orchard singing. I hate
The cat that is its savage fate,
And choose a stone with which to send
Slayer, not victim, to its end.
I look to where the black cat lies,
But drop my stone, seeing its eyes–
Who is it sins now, those eyes say,
You the hunter, or I the prey?

Clifford Dyment

Below is a model of how the narrative of Clifford Dyment's poem 'Man and Beast' might be described, or paraphrased.

```
This poem describes how a cat lies in wait
to attack a bird, which the narrator has
heard singing in the orchard all summer. The
'unwary' bird has no idea of the presence
of the cat, and of what is about to happen,
and the narrator, 'hating' the cat for what
it is about to do, picks up a stone to kill
the cat instead, before it can kill the
bird. However, as the narrator looks into
the cat's eyes, he or she realizes that the
act of killing the cat with the stone would
represent the same 'sin' as the cat's act of
killing the bird.
```

THINK–PAIR–SHARE

What do you think 'Man and Beast', through its narration of events, is trying to say? Is it trying to make a point? If so, what is that? Write down your thoughts and, after five minutes, exchange your ideas on this with a classmate.

If you were to put the four poems from the poetry competition in order from which one is the easiest to work out the 'real meaning' of, and which one the most difficult, what would that order be? With your partner, agree on an order for the poems.

Share your agreed order of the four poems with your class. Does everyone in your class have the same order? If not, why not?

ACTIVITY: Summarizing a poem

ATL

■ Communication skills: Paraphrase accurately and concisely

Pick either 'The Raven' or 'Five Ways to Kill a Man' (page 85) and, in the same way as the 'Man and Beast' example, **summarize** in one paragraph what your chosen poem is saying.

◆ Assessment opportunities

In this activity you have practised skills that are assessed using Criterion A: Analysing.

Looking at the subject matter of a poem on a narrative or descriptive level is important as a first step, though a poem may, of course, be trying to say something more than simply what is being narrated. For instance, in 'Man and Beast' is poet Clifford Dyment simply telling the story of what happened at a particular time when a cat saw a bird and began to stalk it, before a human came along and saw this? Or is the poem using this narrative to try to convey a point, or a message? Does it, in other words, have some particular meaning beyond the immediate events of the narrative?

In the Think–Pair–Share activity it is likely that you all found 'Poverty' quite easy to work out in terms of what it is protesting about. But what about 'The Raven'? And even, despite the clue provided by the title, 'Five Ways to Kill a Man'?

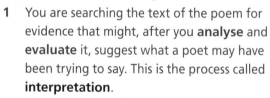

How to interpret a poem

1 You are searching the text of the poem for evidence that might, after you **analyse** and **evaluate** it, suggest what a poet may have been trying to say. This is the process called **interpretation**.
2 Interpretation involves using higher level critical-thinking skills such as application, analysis, evaluation, and **synthesis**, in order to come up with suggestions about a poem's possible **meaning** or **purpose**. These thinking skills are a very important part of the learning involved in analysing literature.
3 Do not assume that there is only one right answer to a poem's meaning. Multiple interpretations of a poem can be possible, and it is good to show this range of different ideas.
4 Always quote evidence from a text when making suggestions about what a poet might be saying in their poem.
5 Because we cannot be definitive in the suggestions we make, it is often important to use conditional words and phrases such as 'may', 'might', 'seems', 'appears'.

ACTIVITY: The explanation game

We will now **explore** the meaning of 'The Raven' and 'Five Ways to Kill a Man' in more detail. Form a group and, on a large piece of paper, copy the following table.

Poem title:			
Observation – write any initial observations you make. Complete the prompt: *I notice that …*	**Question** – write a question that comes out of your observation, for example: *Why is it that way?* *Why did it happen that way?*	**Explanations/hypotheses** – try to answer the question posed, or propose possible explanations and reasons.	**Reasons/justifications** – note anything that might support your explanation. As a prompt, try answering: *What makes you think so?*

Task 1

1 Your teacher will assign the poem 'The Raven' to half of the groups in the class, and 'Five Ways to Kill a Man' to the remaining groups.
2 In your group look carefully again at your poem, and write down on sticky notes some initial observations about it. Every member of the group should contribute one or two observations, and each point should be written on a separate sticky note. Now stick these notes in the first column of your table.
3 For each observation that has been made and added to the chart, write a question about it on another sticky note, and add that to the second column.
4 Then, as a group, consider possible explanations and hypotheses for each question. Use sticky notes to add these to column three.
5 In the fourth (far right) column, your group should write reasons or justifications for each explanation or hypothesis you have entered into the chart. Again, add these using sticky notes.
6 Stick your completed tables on the wall of the classroom. The charts should be placed at different stations around the room, allowing space for groups to gather round and **explore** them.

Task 2

We are now going to undertake a gallery walk. Make sure you have some blank sticky notes with you.

1 Stand with your group where you have stuck your own chart to the wall.
2 On your teacher's command, move in a clockwise direction to the next group's chart. Read their observations, questions, explanations and justifications for their poem.
   a Note down any observations, questions, explanations or justifications you see which your own group did not include, and which you think are good ideas.
   b If this group's chart is missing some of the ideas that you came up with for your poem, write these on sticky notes and stick them in the relevant columns of the chart.
3 After three to five minutes, move clockwise again to the next group's chart. Repeat the above process with this chart.
4 Continue to rotate and repeat the activity at each group's chart. You will probably find as you go around that you need to note fewer new ideas for your own chart, and post fewer new ones for other groups' charts, as other groups looking before you will already have added new ideas.
5 Once back at your own chart, add any new ideas you saw on other charts that have not been added already by other groups during the activity.

At the end of this activity, you will hopefully feel you have some more ideas about what the poets' **meaning** and **purpose** may have been in writing their respective poems.

◆ Assessment opportunities

In this activity you have practised skills that are assessed using Criterion A: Analysing.

How does a persuasive poem work?

ACTIVITY: Interpreting a poem

■ ATL

■ Communication skills: Read critically and for comprehension; make inferences and draw conclusions

Using the suggested interpretation of the poem 'Man and Beast' as a model, come up with an **interpretation** of the poem you previously considered in your group (either 'The Raven' or 'Five Ways to Kill a Man').

◆ Assessment opportunities

In this activity you have practised skills that are assessed using Criterion A: Analysing.

Read through the following student's interpretation of 'Man and Beast', and note how conditional words are used when the poet's purpose – which we cannot know for sure – is being discussed.

'Man and Beast' – a suggested interpretation

The poem appears to be attempting to point out, through the events it narrates, the dangers of hypocrisy when a person makes moral judgements about the actions of others. Might we ever do something ourselves, even though we criticize or condemn others who do it? In the poem, the narrator 'choose[s] a stone' to kill the cat, or send it 'to its end', because he or she condemns what the cat is trying to do in killing the bird: "The black cat from the house next door / Waits with death in each bared claw / For the Tender unwary bird … / … I hate / The cat that is its savage fate."

The narrator seems in his or her judgement about the cat, and then decision to do the same to the cat him- or herself, to be guilty of hypocrisy; that is, of stating that something should not be done, and then doing that thing themselves.

The poet might also be questioning if we ever not only do things we say that others should not do, but may even use such actions when they are carried out by others as a justification for doing the same thing to them. The narrator in the poem sees the cat waiting to kill the bird, and uses that as the justification for killing the cat: "I hate / The cat that is its savage fate, / And choose a stone with which to send / Slayer, not victim, to its end."

The question seems to be raised, as the narrator realizes on seeing the cat's eyes, that if one acts in such a way, why is it different to anyone else who acts in that way, and why should we not be criticized or condemned in the same way ourselves? This can be seen particularly in the final two lines of the poem, as we are told that the cat's eyes seem to say to the narrator, "Who is it sins now, those eyes say, / You the hunter, or I the prey?"

Meanwhile a further question the poet may be raising is one of whether others may in fact have some justification for their actions; and more than we might have if we did the same thing ourselves. The poet chooses a cat as the initial killer in the poem, and a reader or listener may be aware that cats may need to kill birds in order to survive. The narrator would have no such excuse for killing the cat.

The poet seems, therefore, in the poem 'Man and Beast', to be raising questions a reader or listener might ask him- or herself about the judgements we may make about the actions of others, and the possible hypocrisy involved if we ever act in the same way ourselves.

How can poems evoke emotion in their audiences?

Having looked at what 'Man and Beast' is saying, and having thought about the kind of message it may have been trying to convey, how do you react to the poem yourself? Do you feel anything about what happens in it, or the point that you think it is trying to make? If so, what are those feelings?

Let us look here at some vocabulary that might be used to describe different kinds of emotions or feelings an audience or reader may have in response to a text.

THINK–PAIR–SHARE

Choose three words from the diagram below that describe how you feel about 'Man and Beast' and, for each one, think about why you feel that way. Use a dictionary to look up any words with which you are unfamiliar.

With a partner, **discuss** which poem from the poetry competition you think provokes the strongest feelings or emotions. Why does it? Have you and your partner had the same reactions to the same poems?

Pick three words from the emotions table that best describe how you feel about the competition poem you have picked in terms of evoking the strongest emotions. Consider the reasons why you have chosen these words.

If there is time, share with your class the poem, the three words you selected and the reasons behind your choice. Have your classmates chosen the same poem and words?

WORDS FOR EMOTIONS

An audience might feel…	sadness	anger	fear	confusion	joy, pleasure, etc.
Strong reaction	sad depressed distraught devastated drained pity	outraged repulsed repelled incensed seething disgusted	afraid fearful appalled horrified shocked terrified alarmed	baffled bewildered perplexed	elated ecstatic jubilant thrilled uplifted energized proud
Mild reaction	disappointed disillusioned distressed upset disturbed	annoyed agitated frustrated exasperated offended resentful	apprehensive shaken startled stunned threatened uneasy tense suspicious skeptical	hesitant doubtful ambivalent torn troubled puzzled	delighted (re)assured encouraged gratified fulfilled optimistic relieved amused
Weak reaction	deflated disenchanted sorry apathetic 'bad'	dismayed	anxious concerned doubtful impatient nervous perplexed unsure	surprised uncomfortable undecided unsettled unsure uncertain bothered distracted	glad hopeful content pleased satisfied

■ Words describing emotions

■ Poppy wreaths commemorating soldiers killed in battle

Looking at responses to a poem can help in identifying what are the poem's purpose and meaning.

In order to make a point or convey a message, a poet may use their poem to try to provoke particular reactions and/ or emotions in an audience. Consider a poem about war for example:

■ A poet critical of war could use their poem to show the horror of battle; to do this they might try to provoke a sense of shock, sadness, outrage, and so on, in the poem's audience.

■ A poet who wants to present war as being full of glory and honour might try to provoke their audience to feel proud, energized or uplifted.

■ If a poem's narrative is about the glorious death of a war hero, the poet might try to provoke a mixture of both pride and sadness in their audience.

When considering possible audience responses it is important to remember that different people can respond in very different ways. For example, imagine a war poem where the poet criticizes the actions of soldiers in battle:

■ One person may agree with the criticism, but another may feel it is highly unjustified.

■ One person may be highly sympathetic to the soldiers (they were defending their country and did what they had to in order to survive), but another might be much more critical of their actions (they chose to fight and they are responsible for their own actions).

■ Two different people may be critical, but their criticism might be about two very different things.

When you **analyse** a poem consider whether it appears to be trying to *elicit* particular responses from a reader or listener – as this can be evidence of the poet's intentions.

ACTIVITY: Responding to a poem

■ ATL

■ Media literacy skills: Understand the impact of media representations and modes of presentation

What responses do each of the four poems you looked at in the 'Poetry competition' activity seem to be trying to evoke in a reader or listener? How easy or difficult is it to *discern* that?

Consider your previous responses to the poems. How typical do you think your own responses were? Do you think they are similar to how many other readers or listeners of the poem may have reacted?

Remember, this activity is looking at what responses the poets may have been seeking to achieve in their audience, not just your reaction to their poems.

◆ Assessment opportunities

In this activity you have practised skills that are assessed using Criterion A: Analysing.

It is important to remember, however, that people will respond differently at different times, because of the very different *perspectives* they have on the subject matter of the poem. Do not make the mistake of assuming that everyone will be responding in the same way to the same thing.

Using vocabulary with precision involves choosing the words that will most accurately reflect not just the emotion but also its degree in a situation. If, for instance, we feel a poet is seeking to evoke sadness in his audience, does that mean an audience feels sorry, upset or devastated at the scene presented in the poem?

Whatever the degree of the emotional response, considering an audience's likely response to a poem may well reveal something about the purpose of the poet. This is an important aspect to look at when exploring a poem.

One way to do this is to investigate the stylistic choices a poet has made in order to provoke such responses. While we can rarely say for certain what a poet is 'definitely' trying to do in a poem, we can identify the choices the poet has made, and because we know the meaning and effect of those choices, we can suggest what response an audience might have had. This gives us an insight into the poet's intentions.

In what ways can emotive techniques work on an audience?

WHAT MAKES YOU SAY THAT?: Man and Beast

■ ATL

- Critical-thinking skills: Gather and organize relevant information to formulate an argument
- Communication skills: Make inferences and draw conclusions

Let us take a closer look at the presentation in the poem 'Man and Beast' of the cat and the bird. Lines 1–4 of the poem describe the cat, while the bird is described in lines 5–7. Read these again now.

- **What impression is given of the cat in these opening four lines? Is it a positive or negative presentation?**

What makes you say that? **List** any particular words or phrases you see that you think most contribute to the impression that is given of the cat.

- **What impression is given of the bird in lines 5–7? Is it a positive or negative presentation?**

What makes you say that? **List** any particular words or phrases you see that you think most contribute to the impression that is given of the bird.

◆ Assessment opportunities

In this activity you have practised skills that are assessed using Criterion A: Analysing.

WHAT MAKES YOU SAY THAT?: The Raven

■ ATL

- Critical-thinking skills: Recognize unstated assumptions and bias
- Communication skills: Read critically and for comprehension; make inferences and draw conclusions

'The Raven' was written by the same author as 'Man and Beast' – Clifford Dyment.

Look at the presentation of the raven itself, and 'the people', in the poem. What choices does Dyment make? What responses might those choices suggest are being invited from an audience, towards the raven and the people respectively?

Using the example explanations given for the cat and bird in 'Man and Beast' as a model, write a paragraph about either the raven, or 'the people'. Explain how your chosen 'character' is being presented, and choose words and phrases from the poem to illustrate the points you are making.

Share your paragraph with a partner. Give feedback on each other's paragraph, and then review and edit your final version as needed.

◆ Assessment opportunities

In this activity you have practised skills that are assessed using Criterion A: Analysing.

Personification and symbolism are devices used to help present the cat and the bird in the poem 'Man and Beast'. These are *stylistic choices* made by the poet in order to convey a point or message.

A number of the most common literary stylistic choices are presented in the table on the following page. When exploring the purpose of a poem, how its meaning may be being conveyed to an audience, and the possible impact the poem may have on an audience, make sure you consider these choices.

Common literary devices

Literary device	Explanation	Examples
Simile	A simile asks a reader to picture one thing as being similar to another and uses the words 'like', 'as' or 'than' to create the comparison in our minds. The actual choice of simile may convey to an audience something of the possible attitude of the poet towards what is being described, and of the response that may be sought from an audience; it is important to look at the nature of a simile, and whether it appears to be suggesting criticism towards, or sympathy for, and so on, what is being described. As such it may be evidence of a point, message or meaning the poet is trying to convey in a poem.	• as hard as nails • like a fish out of water • *'The water made a sound like kittens lapping.'* from 'The Yearling' – Marjorie Kinnan Rawlings • *'What happens to a dream deferred?* *Does it dry up* *like a raisin in the sun?'* from 'Harlem' – Langston Hughes
Metaphor	With the metaphor, instead of asking a reader to picture one thing as being like another, in the manner of a simile, the reader is asked to picture one thing as being another. For example: *The sun is like a golden coin* (simile) *The sun is a golden coin* (metaphor) In the same way as with similes, the actual choices of images used in metaphors can provide clues as to a poet's attitude towards what is being described, possible audience response(s) being sought, and possible points, messages or meaning the poet may be trying to convey.	• *'The bay is gouged by the wind.* *In the jagged hollows green lions crouch* *And stretch* *And slouch* *And sudden with spurting manes and a glitter of haunches* *Charge at the shore* *And rend the sand and roar'* from 'Green Lions' – Douglas Stewart
Personification	Personification is a form of metaphor in which an object or an idea is spoken of as though it has human characteristics. For example: *Fire raced with giant strides through the dry grass.* Once again, the choice of image presented may be appealing or otherwise, and as such can provide clues as to a poet's attitude towards what is being described, possible audience response(s) being sought, and possible points, messages or meaning the poet may be trying to convey.	• *'Whatever I see I swallow immediately'* from 'Mirror' – Sylvia Plath • *'Her cheeks were made out of honey,* *Her throat was made of flame* *Where all around the razor* *Had written its red name.'* from 'The Ballad of Charlotte Dymond' – Charles Causley
Symbolism	Symbols can take the form of an object, sign, token, and so on, which stands for something else; this is quite often in literature something that is abstract in nature. An example of this is a dove, which is often seen as a symbol of peace, or water, which is a symbol of life. Colours are also often symbolic; green, for instance, often represents new growth, red can symbolize passion, or blood, white may indicate purity, while black may indicate evil or death. The seasons of the year may also be used symbolically in literature, with spring suggesting new life and winter old age or death. Another frequent symbol is of roads or railway tracks, which symbolize the path of life, or the choices made in life.	• *'Some mornings, you found* *she'd [a teacher] left a gold star by your name.'* from 'In Mrs Tilscher's Class' – Carol Ann Duffy • *'Two roads diverged in a wood, and I—* *I took the one less traveled by,* *And that has made all the difference.'* from 'The Road Not Taken' – Robert Frost

Language and Literature for the IB MYP 4&5: *by Concept*

Analysing an individual occurrence of a simile, metaphor, personification or symbol in a poem comprises several different stages, beginning with identifying it in the poem.

Once we have done that, we need to look at the nature of the image that the poet has chosen, and think about what it might be trying to convey. You can do this by considering the following questions.

- Is the image positive or negative in nature? In the poem 'The Ballad of Charlotte Dymond', for instance, the main character's cheeks are described as being 'made out of honey', a metaphor that suggests softness – generally seen as a positive description of someone.
- What associations, or *connotations*, does an image have? In the previous example, honey is associated with sweetness, thus suggesting that the character has a 'sweet' nature also.

Images in poetry are rarely neutral, and often are used to make a comment on the thing they are describing. The comment being made may indicate the poet's attitude towards what is being discussed or described, or may be trying to shape the reader's attitude towards it. For instance, Charlotte Dymond is murdered in the poem that takes her name. Images used by the poet suggest Charlotte is a soft and sweet girl, which in turn helps make the murder seem all the more shocking and callous.

Identifying images is the first important stage of **analysing** their use. The second is asking questions about them in order to **explore** their purposes and effect. These are two of the cornerstones of literary analysis.

ACTIVITY: Questions and answers

■ ATL

- Communication skills: Use and interpret a range of discipline-specific terms and symbols

In pairs, choose one of the poems from the poetry competition.

- **Copy out the table below and, in it, note any examples of similes, metaphors, personification or symbols that you see in your poem (not all of the poems will have examples of all of these, but all of the poems have examples of at least some of them). If your poem does not include a particular literary device, leave that row blank.**
- **Think about some possible questions that might be asked about the particular choice of image you have identified, and enter those into the right-hand column.**
- **Together with your partner, try to answer the questions you have come up with.**

Chosen poem:

Literary device	Examples	Questions to consider and discuss
Simile		
Metaphor		
Personification		
Symbolism		

◆ Assessment opportunities

In this activity you have practised skills that are assessed using Criterion A: Analysing.

Similes, metaphors and personification are examples of *sensory imagery,* which appeals to our sense of sight. Other sensory imagery to look out for is sound imagery, and in particular alliteration, **consonance**, **assonance**, and onomatopoeia – the use of these will always be an intentional choice on the part of a poet.

More common literary devices

Literary device	Explanation	Examples
Alliteration	Alliteration is the repetition of the same consonant (not vowel) sound at the beginnings of words. Note that it is the sound rather than the initial letter that is important. In the Nemo example, for instance, the same sound is produced by the letter 'n' and by 'gn' (at the start of 'gnaw'). One purpose of alliteration is to try to replicate, or repeat, something that is being described, or which is present in what is being narrated. The 'n' sounds in Nemo reflect the actual sound of a dog gnawing through clothing. In Karl Marszalowicz's 'Circus' the repetition of both the 'm' and 'r' sounds reflect the noise made by a motorcycle. The pauses between them might also suggest the stop–start sound given out by a revving bike.	• My dog Nemo gnawed through my new nightgown. • *'A motorcycle roars loudly without a muffler, majestically it comes* *To ride the ring of fire for which rock anthems echo'* from 'Circus' – Karl Marszalowicz
Consonance	Consonance is the repetition of consonant sounds anywhere in words at least twice in quick succession (alliteration can be described as a type of consonance, but only if the repeated consonant sounds appear at the beginnings of words). As with alliteration, repeated sounds may not necessarily involve the same letters each time. Alliteration and consonance are frequently used together. When acrobats are described in Marszalowicz's 'Circus' the repeated 't' sounds, and, in particular, the pauses between the sounds create a rhythm that may remind readers of rhythmic twisting movements of acrobats.	• *'Seeing participants of talent take on amazing feats* *Colorfully contorting and twisting to terrifying positions'* from 'Circus' – Karl Marszalowicz
Assonance	Assonance is the repetition of vowel sounds, and may be used by poets to create a more musical effect. Roland Robinson's 'Thrush' is an example of assonance creating an *internal rhyme*, which in turn creates rhythm and a more musical effect. Here this reflects the sounds and 'singing' of the poem's subjects. This same effect can be found in 'Daffodils' by William Wordsworth. Mood or atmosphere can also be created by assonance, especially where long vowel sounds are used. Repetition of 'o' and 'u' sounds in particular can produce an effect of 'moaning' or 'groaning', and create a tense or **ominous mood** and atmosphere. This is found in *Jane Eyre* at one particularly tense point in the novel. Long vowel sounds slow down the pace of a poem, which creates a more sombre or ominous mood and atmosphere.	• *'O let the creek speak from soak* *to soak; let the frogs croak, in chorus croak.'* from 'Thrush' – Roland Robinson • *'I hardly know whether I had slept or not after this musing; at any rate, I started wide awake on hearing a vague murmur, peculiar and lugubrious, which sounded, I thought, just above me.'* from *Jane Eyre* – Charlotte Brontë
Onomatopoeia	This ancient Greek word refers to words that, when pronounced, suggest the sound of the action they are describing. Words such as 'murmur', 'hiss', 'gurgle', 'patter', 'purr', 'buzz' and 'thud' are thus a few examples of this. Examples of this can be found in poems such as 'The Rime of the Ancient Mariner' by Samuel Taylor Coleridge and 'Anthem for Doomed Youth' by Wilfred Owen. Examples of onomatopoeia are often also examples of alliteration, consonance or assonance. In a literary analysis when you identify something as onomatopoeia, you do not also need to point out that the example is one of these other things – identifying and discussing it as onomatopoeia is sufficient.	• *'The ice was here, the ice was there,* *The ice was all around:* *It cracked and growled, and roared and howled,* *Like noises in a swound!'* from 'The Rime of the Ancient Mariner' – Samuel Taylor Coleridge • *'What passing-bells for these who die as cattle?* *– Only the monstrous anger of the guns.* *Only the stuttering rifles' rapid rattle* *Can patter out their hasty orisons.'* from 'Anthem for Doomed Youth' – Wilfred Owen

Language and Literature for the IB MYP 4&5: *by Concept*

ACTIVITY: Sound of Poetry – literary devices quiz

■ ATL

- ■ Communication skills: Make inferences and draw conclusions

Using the five poems from the poetry competition, can you find examples of the literary devices we have just looked at?

Alliteration

Explain what effect you think the particular alliteration is designed to have in each case. Is it meant to sound like anything being talked about at the time it is used?

Consonance

Find two examples of consonance. What effect does this literary device have in the poems you have chosen?

Assonance

- Read again the third verse of 'Five Ways to Kill a Man'. What effects do you think the poet was trying to create? (As a clue, Brock is talking here about the First World War.)
- Find another example of assonance from a different poem. What is the assonance designed to sound like? Does the rhythm it creates reflect something happening in the poem?

Onomatopoeia

Find three different examples of onomatopoeia in at least two different poems. What is the poet using onomatopoeia to suggest? What impact does this have on the poem?

◆ Assessment opportunities

In this activity you have practised skills that are assessed using Criterion A: Analysing.

The purpose of sound imagery is often to recreate some of the actual sounds being described. This can help make the experience more immediate for a reader, or create a particular mood or atmosphere, or reflect the rhythm of something happening in the scene being described. It may fulfil several such purposes at the same time.

Types of poetry

There are more than 50 types of poetry. Here are some of the more common forms:

Ballad – a long poem that narrates a story in short stanzas.

Epic – a long narrative poem about the heroic deeds of ancient people and gods.

Haiku – a traditional Japanese poem, written in 17 syllables divided into three lines of 5, 7 and 5 syllables.

Limerick – a humorous poem of five lines; rhyming and with a strong rhythm.

Sonnet – a type of poem with 14 lines and a regular (though varied) rhyme scheme.

Free verse – a poem with the patterns and rhythms of natural speech, rather than traditional **meter** or rhyme.

As with visual imagery such as similes and metaphors, it is important to identify examples within a poem. You should explain what such imagery may be trying to convey, in relation to what is being described in the poem at the time.

THE FORM OF POETRY

Poets also make choices about the form of poem they will use. Form relates to the structure of a poem, and analysis of a poem involves considering questions such as the following:

- What type of poetry is being used? Is it a sonnet, limerick, haiku, and so on? Some forms of poetry are associated with particular purposes and subject matter – a sonnet, for instance, is generally used to talk about love. Examples of different types of poetry can be found here: **http://examples.yourdictionary.com/types-of-poetry-examples.html**.
- Is the poem written in **stanzas**, or is it continuous? Stanzas can often denote the separation of ideas, for example, while a continuous form may signal the development of a single idea.
- How long are the lines of a poem? Line length, which refers to the number of **syllables** in a line, can be used to affect the pace and rhythm of a poem.
- Is **enjambment** being used? Enjambment is when one line of a poem runs on to the next line without a break (no punctuation is used). This can increase a poem's pace, or give it a more conversational feel. It can also help create a more reflective mood by lengthening any thoughts being expressed.

ACTIVITY: Examining the form of a poem

■ ATL

- Communication skills: Use and interpret a range of discipline-specific terms and symbols

In pairs, choose one of the following three poems from pages 84–86: 'The Old Woman', 'The Raven' or 'Poverty'.

Use the examples of 'The Old Woman' and 'Five Ways to Kill a Man' as a model. **Identify** the form of your chosen poem and **explore** the impact of this form. Start by listing the particular aspects of form you notice in the poem, and then **explain** the possible purposes and effects of those. Finally, choose one of the remaining two poems and, individually, repeat this exercise.

◆ Assessment opportunities

In this activity you have practised skills that are assessed using Criterion A: Analysing.

- Where breaks do occur in the lines of a poem, these are called **caesuras**. Use of caesuras also affects the pace and rhythm of a poem.
- Repetition is another aspect of form to watch for: repetition of words, phrases or lines, or repetition in other forms, such as a list.

- Form also includes **rhyme** and **rhythm**, which we will look at in more detail shortly.

Let us look more closely at how the form of a poem might be significant. Below aspects of form have been identified, and their effects explained, for two of the previously analysed poems (pages 84–85):

Poem

The Old Woman

Protesting about how little people notice and care about older people. They are left alone to face death, and left alone with feelings of sadness, despair and fear. Even their death itself, a huge event, often goes unnoticed when it takes place. Is it a natural death as the old woman comes to the end of her time, or is the sadness and despair enough for her to take her own life? That it could be either, and nobody knows or cares, is quite shocking. That she has no individual identity suggests that this is not an individual tragedy but a general occurrence.

Possible purpose: to draw attention to, raise awareness of and elicit sympathy for the loneliness and feelings of old people in such a position, and perhaps shock and shame at their situation in such an uncaring society. Perhaps also to prompt readers to look out for and recognize the loneliness of older people around them, and take a greater interest in those people.

Aspects of form

One continuous stanza, no pattern in line length, some enjambment, no rhyme scheme

Effects

The poem is written in a single stanza of free verse. The single stanza perhaps represents the single scene which the narrator presents to us of a lonely old woman moving towards the end of her life. Nothing more is known about her – no background, context, or even a name; so a reader can focus fully only on this one single sad scene.

The free verse form, with no real pattern in the line lengths and metre, and lack of any rhyme scheme, along with use of enjambment at times in the poem, create a conversational narrative effect, which allows for longer thoughts to be expressed, and creates a slower pace which invites a reader to reflect more on the scene and details of it, along with their responses to it.

Poem

Five Ways to Kill a Man

Aspects of form

Use of stanzas containing separate ideas; shorter final stanza; varied line lengths; enjambment; caesuras; no rhyme scheme; repetition of a list at the end of all but the final stanza

Effects

The poem is divided into five stanzas, each of which describes ways that humans have discovered of killing other humans – from crucifixion to medieval jousting to the First World War to the nuclear age to – finally – leaving someone in the twentieth century. The shorter length of the final stanza may help to indicate how quick a process it has now become.

The order of the stanzas reflects the chronological order in which the different ways of killing have been invented and used; it also reflects the increasing number of people who are killed by each method. That ordering of stanzas therefore highlights the irony that humans, while supposed becoming more modern and 'civilized', have killed more and more people. The suggestion is that the twentieth century (when the poem was written) is a more dangerous time, with more ways of people being killed, than ever before.

The poem is written in free verse, and makes use of enjambment and caesuras in no particular pattern; all of which gives an impression of normal conversational speech. This may reflect how 'normal' the acts of killing have become. This idea is further emphasized in the use of a list at the end of each stanza, which details the 'ingredients' needed for each method of killing and is written as if they are part of a recipe, or a practical household manual of some kind. For example:

> 'All you then
>
> require is an ocean to separate you, two
>
> systems of government, a nation's scientists,
>
> several factories, a psychopath and
>
> land that no-one needs for several years.'

The repetitive, list-based texts that this poem is imitating are unemotional and very ordinary in nature. The effect of presenting the text in this way may shock a reader, as it suggests that the mass killing of humans has become similarly normal and unemotional.

RHYME AND RHYTHM

Rhyme

The rhyme scheme of a poem is very much a deliberate choice on the part of a poet, and it is always a good to consider how the use of rhyme and the chosen scheme may be contributing to the meaning and tone of a poem. This is a further aspect of a poem that should be interpreted during analysis of a poem. You may remember some rhyme schemes from the poems in *Language and Literature for the IB MYP 3: by Concept*, Chapter 1.

Rhyme schemes in poems are usually expressed as 'ABC ABC', with each new letter indicating a new rhyme, and each space indicating a space between stanzas. The rhyme scheme of 'Man and Beast' would, therefore, be AABBCCDDEEFFGG:

Hugging the ground by the lilac tree,	A
With shadows in conspiracy,	A
The black cat from the house next door	B
Waits with death in each bared claw	B
For the tender unwary bird	C
That all the summer I have heard	C
In the orchard singing. I hate	D
The cat that is its savage fate,	D
And choose a stone with which to send	E
Slayer, not victim, to its end.	E
I look to where the black cat lies,	F
But drop my stone, seeing its eyes–	F
Who is it sins now, those eyes say,	G
You the hunter, or I the prey?	G

War poets

- **William Cowper (1731–1800)** A forerunner of the **Romantic poetry movement**, he wrote many poems focused on the rural English countryside. He was also a vocal opponent of slavery.
- **DH Lawrence (1885–1930)** A novelist, poet and playwright. One of Lawrence's most famous works, the novel *Lady Chatterley's Lover*, was subject to an obscenity trial 30 years after his death.
- **Siegfried Sassoon (1886–1967)** A leading poet of the First World War and close friend of Wilfred Owen. Awarded the Military Cross. His war poetry describes the horrors of his experiences.
- **Wilfred Owen (1893–1918)** One of the leading English poets of the First World War. He was killed in action, shortly before the signing of the Armistice that ended the war.
- **Charles Causley (1917–2003)** A poet from Cornwall, England who served in the Royal Navy during the Second World War.

If a poem does make use of a rhyme scheme, it is not sufficient to say what rhyme scheme has been used – you must also offer a suggestion as to why. A regular rhyme scheme can do various things, for instance, the examples in the table below.

Rhythm

All speech and written text contain rhythms – patterns caused by the different stress a speaker or reader places on a word when pronouncing it. Poets can also arrange words and lines, or use techniques such as rhyming (including effects such as alliteration and assonance), repetition, enjambment, caesuras and more to create particular patterns, that is, rhythms, in their poetry.

You will become more familiar at recognizing particular rhythms, and discussing those, as you study more and more poetry. For now, watch out for the following in any poems you read:

A rhyme scheme can …	Notes	Example
Speed up the pace of a poem	For example, if a poet wants to give an impression of speeding towards something (a particular climax, perhaps)	A narrative poem example of this is 'Death of an Aircraft' by Charles Causley (**https://goo.gl/gJc6ln**).
Give more structure to a poem	Structure may reflect a key aspect of a poem	Wilfred Owen uses this technique in the first stanza of 'Dulce et Decorum Est' (**www.warpoetry.co.uk/owen1.html**), to reflect what the rhythm of marching soldiers should be – as contrasted with the 'marching' of the soldiers he is actually describing.
Be a symbol of control within a poem	Rhyme can suggest a narrator's control (or lack thereof)	In the 'The Castaway' by William Cowper (**www.poetryfoundation.org/poems-and-poets/poems/detail/44027**) the narrator is cast overboard and left to drown in the sea. The poem is also an **allegory** of a battle against depression. In both situations the rhyme structure could reflect the narrator's struggle to stay in control.
		In the poem 'Last Lesson of the Afternoon' by DH Lawrence (**www.kalliope.org/en/digt.pl?longdid=lawrence2001061512**), rhyme is sometimes used and sometimes not. This unpredictability also suggests a struggle to stay in control.
Symbolize innocence or childlike wonder	Simple schemes can sometimes reflect a character's or narrator's innocence, or naivety	'Suicide in the Trenches' by Siegfried Sassoon (**www.greatwar.nl/children/suicide.html**) uses a very simple rhyme scheme to suggest the innocence of soldiers in the First World War, and to contrast such innocence with the horrors that took place in the war.
		The rhyme scheme of 'The Raven' by Clifford Dyment is highly simplistic. This may represent the immaturity of thought behind prejudice, and the unthinking way that people can respond to something they do not know (and find frightening for that reason).

■ First World War soldiers in the trenches

■ The use of techniques such as alliteration and assonance to create a rhythm in the poem, which reflects the movement that is being described; galloping horses, waves on the sea and birds flying are some examples we have already come across in this chapter.

■ The use of caesuras to break up the rhythm of a poem; slowing down the pace of a poem may suggest fear, hesitancy, and so on. If you notice this, look at what is being said or happening at the time and see if you can suggest why a poet is breaking up the rhythm at that point.

A good example of a poem in which rhythm is used, and changed, for particular effects is 'Suicide in the Trenches', by Siegfried Sassoon.

Suicide in the Trenches

I knew a simple soldier boy
Who grinned at life in empty joy,
Slept soundly through the lonesome dark,
And whistled early with the lark.

In winter trenches, cowed and glum,
With crumps and lice and lack of rum,
He put a bullet through his brain.
No one spoke of him again.

You smug-faced crowds with kindling eye
Who cheer when soldier lads march by,
Sneak home and pray you'll never know
The hell where youth and laughter go.

Siegfried Sassoon

▼ Links to: Individuals and societies;
History

Think about how war has been depicted in poems throughout history. Find examples of war poetry from different time periods. Is war depicted in different ways at different times? Why? **Evaluate** how the poets of the poems you have selected have chosen to portray war, and think about the reasons behind their stylistic decisions.

ACTIVITY: The rhythm of the beat

■ ATL

■ Communication skills: Use and interpret a range of discipline-specific terms and symbols

In pairs, answer the following questions about the rhythm of Sassoon's 'Suicide in the Trenches'.

1   How would you describe the rhythm that is created in the first stanza?
2   In view of what he is describing in this stanza, why do you think Sassoon wanted to create such a rhythm?
3   What techniques does Sassoon use to create the rhythm he has in this stanza, and how do each of these help to achieve that? You might like to think about rhyme, alliteration and use of punctuation in answering this question.
4   What particular word choices in this stanza reflect the rhythm of the stanza?
5   How does the rhythm change in the second stanza?
6   What has the poet done to change it? You might like to look at alliteration, assonance, and use of punctuation in answering this question.
7   What particular word choices in this stanza reflect the rhythm that has been created here?
8   How would you describe the rhythm created in the final stanza?
9   What techniques does Sassoon use to create it, and how do each of these help to achieve it?

◆ Assessment opportunities

In this activity you have practised skills that are assessed using Criterion A: Analysing.

ACTIVITY: Poetry scavenger hunt

■ **ATL**

- ■ Communication skills: Use and interpret a range of discipline-specific terms and symbols

We have looked at a range of stylistic choices that poets may make for their poetry. Now let us bring those together for some further consideration.

Choose one of the five poems from pages 84–87, and **identify** an example of each of the poetic aspects listed in the table below. Draw out the table yourself and write each example you find in the appropriate box.

If you are unable to find an example in your chosen poem, find one in one of the other poems. Indicate in the table which poem it is from.

Underneath the example, **explain** what you think is the intended purpose or effect. For instance:

The rhyme pattern or scheme

> 'Man and Beast' makes use of the rhyme scheme AA, BB, CC and so on. It is a very regular rhyming pattern which may reflect how the poem is presenting a very logical argument; that if something is a sin for one party to do, then it must be a sin for anyone else; including ourselves. This final realization is as inescapable to the narrator as the rhyme scheme is within the poem.

A line that appeals to your sense of hearing	Simile	Metaphor	Alliteration
Internal rhyme	Onomatopoeia	A line that appeals to your sense of sight	Careful word choice
Personification	The rhyme pattern or scheme	Symbolism	Contrast

◆ **Assessment opportunities**

In this activity you have practised skills that are assessed using Criterion A: Analysing.

ACTIVITY: Poem commentary

■ **ATL**

- ■ Critical-thinking skills: Gather and organize relevant information to formulate an argument
- ■ Creative-thinking skills: Use brainstorming and visual diagrams to generate new ideas and inquiries

When you write an essay about a poem, you are writing a commentary about it. This commentary will look at every aspect of the poem that we have discussed in this chapter, from identifying the main ideas and purpose of the poem, to exploring aspects of style, technique and literary devices used by the poet to convey these points to an audience.

Choose one of the poems from this chapter which you have not already examined in detail and, using the 'How to write about a poem' process as a guide, write a brief (600–800 word) commentary on it.

◆ **Assessment opportunities**

In this activity you have practised skills that are assessed using Criterion A: Analysing, Criterion C: Producing text and Criterion D: Using language.

How to write about a poem

A good process to follow when writing an essay about a poem is as follows:

✓ when complete	Process
	Read the essay task and make sure you understand it thoroughly.
	Read your chosen poem through at least twice more, paying close attention to what is being said. Sometimes it can help to close your eyes to visualize what is happening.
	Highlight anything in the poem that seems important, and jot down notes as to why. Make notes, too, on any other ideas you might have – annotate the poem.
	Brainstorm and make a list of the possible ideas and purposes you feel are evident in the poem, and which you might want to **discuss** in your writing. Consider using a mind map or graphic organizer to develop and begin to plan your ideas.
	For each possible point/idea you might use, note down why you feel it may be significant – what is leading you to think this?
	Research the poem to check your ideas, and discover other ideas you might not have seen immediately. If you want to quote something you find, make sure you jot down page and line references so that you can list them as sources.
	Look at the quotes you might use for a point, and note down anything which may need to be explained, or why the quote is important to the point you want to make.
	Consider the other poetic aspects from the literary device tables in this chapter – speaker, tone, form, rhyme, rhythm – make notes on anything significant about these.
	Identify any particular literary devices being used – *similes*, *metaphors*, **sound effects**, **hyperbole**, etc (see the glossary at the back of this book).
	Think about the order in which you might **explore** your points in your essay. In chronological order or where they occur in the poem? Or some other order? If so, why?
	Begin to write the introduction to your essay. Ensure you do the following: 1 Use a *formal register* – this is impersonal rather than conversational. 2 Write a *thesis statement* that signposts clearly the main points you intend to make in the course of your essay.
	Begin to write the body paragraphs of the essay. Ensure you do the following: 1 Continue to use a formal register. 2 Make each point clearly when you begin to **discuss** it. 3 Integrate quotes to illustrate your points. 4 Explain your point, and **comment** on your quotes as much as is needed to develop your point fully. Use the notes you made on these to help you do this.
	Ask for feedback on your work from your teacher and your classmates. After four or five paragraphs you could swap your work with a classmate and each give feedback to the other. Think about: 1 Have you/they explained or commented on everything as fully as you/they can? (Remember that including 'detail, development and support' are important aspects of criteria A and B.) 2 Have you/they used language – vocabulary and punctuation for instance – correctly and effectively? How appropriate (formal) is the register you are using (Criterion D)?
	Revise your opening in the light of the advice you have been given, and write the rest of the essay.
	Proofread the whole essay, making changes where needed.
	Produce the final version of the essay and hand it in by the deadline given to you by your teacher.

WHAT IS A PROTEST POEM?

Let's protest!

Protest poetry refers to poems that identify problems in the real world and object to them. Poems have protested many different things including the civil rights movement, war and conflict, human rights, environmental issues, and politics and government. The authors of protest poems use the stylistic techniques we have looked at in this chapter to convey their point or message, and to increase the impact of their poems on their audience.

THINK–PAIR–SHARE

Although each of the five poems from pages 84–87 has a different subject matter, all the poems are protesting about something.

Think about the focus of each poem's protest. Can you **identify** what they are protesting about?

With a partner **discuss** how easy (or how hard) it is to work out the answer to that question. Why were some poems more difficult than others?

Write your thoughts down first and then share your answers with your class. Does everyone agree on the focus of each poem's protest? Were certain poems harder than others to work out? Why?

ACTIVITY: Protest poetry treasure hunt

■ ATL

- Information literacy skills: Access information to be informed and to inform others

In this activity you are going to research protest poems and find one you think everyone else should know about.

1 **Research some protest poems. Use both the internet and any poetry anthologies you have access to in your classroom or school library. Ask your teacher, or the librarian, or others if they know any poems they would recommend looking at.**
2 **Choose four or five poems as a 'long list'. For each one make brief notes about what the poem is trying to say (meaning), and how it is trying to say it (techniques).**
3 **Choose the poem you like most and think about *why* you feel this way about the poem; consider how its meaning and style help to make you feel that way. Note these ideas down in bullet point form.**

◆ Assessment opportunities

In this activity you have practised skills that are assessed using Criterion A: Analysing.

ACTIVITY: Your protest poem

What do you feel passionate about? If you had to write a protest poem, what would it be about?

Read about slam poetry on the opposite page. What issues would you write about?

Feeling inspired? Why not have a go at writing your own poem. Take a look at page 106 for guidance on how to write a poem.

ACTIVITY: Speech in protest poetry

Imagine you are the poet of the poem you chose for the 'Protest poetry treasure hunt' activity. You have been invited to give a five to seven minute presentation during which you will:

- **Give a dramatic reading of your poem.**
- **Speak about the meaning of the poem, and the stylistic choices you made to convey the poem's meaning and message (using all the terminology you have learned during this chapter).**
- **Conduct a short Q+A (question and answer) session with the audience.**

Prepare for this presentation:

1 **Practise speaking the poem out loud.**
2 **Find some examples of poets performing their poems, to get an idea of ways you could perform your poem.**
3 **Using the bullet point notes you made in the 'Protest poetry treasure hunt' activity, write a brief speech (three to four minutes) about the stylistic choices that were made in the poem.**

Hint

Remember, your speech should be an analysis of the poem's content, context, language, structure, technique and style. It should also look at the choice you made (as the poet) to try to get your audience to respond to the poem. Make sure you give examples to support your analysis, and use the correct terminology.

◆ Assessment opportunities

In this activity you have practised skills that are assessed using Criterion D: Using language.

Slam dunk protest – the poetry slam

Poetry can take a number of forms and a more modern form of poetry – known as slam poetry – is well suited to the purpose of protesting.

❶ Slam poetry

A Chicago poet named Marc Smith (also known as 'Slam Papi') is credited with inventing slam poetry in 1984. Smith founded the first-ever National Poetry Slam in 1990, and that annual competition is still held today.

Slam poetry sees poets perform poems (which they must have written themselves) in front of a live audience, and without the use of any music or props. The poems must be less than three minutes in length.

Slam performances can be given by individuals, pairs, or groups of three or four, as can be seen in these video examples of slam performances:

- 'Skinny' – performed by Aisha Oxley – **https://youtu.be/0T6m9t4jiAo**
- 'Understanding About ADHD Through Poetry' – performed by Chris Loos –**https://youtu.be/wQLME_-1WD8**
- 'A Muslim and Jewish girl's bold poetry slam' – performed by Amina Iro and Hannah Halpern – **https://youtu.be/UCUz2b050lE**
- 'Why Are Muslims So…' – performed by Sakila and Hawa – **https://youtu.be/3_i7wELTVi0**
- 'Pause' – performed by the Lincoln High Slam Poets – **https://youtu.be/QOfkmluOtYs**

▼ Links to: Individuals and societies; History; Arts

Slam poetry is largely influenced by the free verse, musical style of **Beat poets** like **Jack Kerouac** and **Allen Ginsberg**. Research these writers and their works and find out more about who they were, and how and why they wrote in the style they did.

How to write a poem

Consider the lists below to help you decide what your poem should be about, and how you should craft it.

The subject of your poem:

- Brainstorm ideas for the focus of the poem – write down everything you feel strongly or passionately about. One of these will be a good subject for your poem.
- Use free writing (explored in the Chapter 1 activity Free writing 'courage'), to generate ideas and avenues that you can **explore** in your poem. Are there particular ideas, topics or words that occur more frequently in your free writing? Use these as starting points for your poem.
- Once you have a subject for your poem, write down any words that are significant to this subject on separate pieces of paper. Now arrange these bits of paper into a poem. A similar technique, known as the cut up technique, has been used since at least the 1920s.

The stylistic choices used in your poem:

- What vocabulary choices might you make at any particular point in the poem?
- What imagery, visual or based on sound, might you include?
- Will you use rhyme, or create a particular rhythm throughout the poem, or at particular points?
- What wordplay might you use? Look back at the literary device tables in this chapter for ideas on this.

After you have finished a draft of your poem, review and revise it to ensure that:

- Everything that is included is directly relevant to your message.
- Your message is clear and your poem can be understood easily.
- A final idea might be to set up an online platform where poems can be posted. Other poets, friends and classmates can use the platform to give feedback to each other on possible improvements.

ACTIVITY: Poetry slam – creating the poetry

■ ATL

- Reflection skills: Focus on the process of creating by imitating the work of others
- Communication skills: Use a variety of speaking techniques to communicate with a variety of audiences

Your class is going to plan and hold a slam poetry competition.

- **Everyone must be involved in creating a slam poem for the competition. Decide whether you want to create your slam poem in groups or individually. Each group must create at least one poem, and provide at least one 'slam' performer.**
- **When writing your slam poem, think about all the techniques you have learned in this chapter. Poets have three minutes to perform, so bear this in mind when deciding on the length of your poem.**
- **Practise performing your slam poem. Slam poets usually learn their poems by heart in order to perform most freely (though this is not a requirement). Watch some more slam poetry videos online for ideas about how you might perform your poem.**
- **Rules for holding the slam competition can be found here: https://goo.gl/cQhu6C.**
- **Good luck!**

◆ Assessment opportunities

In this activity you have practised skills that are assessed using Criterion C: Producing text and Criterion D: Using language.

❗ Take action: Opportunity to apply learning through action

❗ One way to take action can be to *advocate* for a cause or concern close to you. **Organize** a poetry slam competition in your school or local community. Anyone can participate, but their poem must protest and advocate on an issue they care about. Your local library may be able to provide a space to hold the slam.

Is it ethical to deliberately try to manipulate the emotions of others?

When someone tries to change someone else's mind, though, do they always do it with the best intentions? What do you think about complimenting someone else in order to try to change their mind, rather than because you really mean it; or about speaking quickly so that your 'fast pace doesn't allow the person to have time to think critically about your arguments'? Shouldn't someone think through something carefully before they change their mind or make a decision about it?

ACTIVITY: Changing hearts and minds

ATL

- Reflection skills: Consider ethical implications
- Collaboration skills: Make fair and equitable decisions; take responsibility for one's own actions

As you will have seen in the chapter, persuasion is about influencing someone's point of view, and perhaps getting them to change their minds.

First, read this article, '9 Genius Ways to Change Someone's Mind, According to Science', which provides ideas on how to change someone's mind: https://goo.gl/7ivR3Z

When might you try to change someone else's mind? With a partner, brainstorm some ideas on this, and enter your ideas in a table. If you can, think about and include some situations when you have actually tried to do this in reality, perhaps with a family member or a friend.

Next, choose one of those situations and write a dialogue in the form of a drama script, in which you are trying to change the other person's mind. Use as many of the nine ways to try to change minds as described in the article above as you can. Use stage directions where needed to show, for instance, where you speak quickly to help you in persuading the other person. Remind yourself about script writing by looking back at Chapter 2.

An example might be as follows:

> **Me:** Do you really want to be friends with her, Shona? Are you sure that will be a good thing for you?
>
> **Shona:** What would be the problem if she were my friend?
>
> **Me:** [speaks more quickly] I've heard she can be a bad influence and try to get people to do things which they shouldn't do, and which may get them into trouble, such as …

You should write 500–1,000 words on this.

Once you have finished writing your script, swap it with someone else in your class. Each of you should then review the script of the other, and add notes where you see one of the nine ways to change someone's mind being used.

Swap back when you have finished this, and discuss your findings. Did you each spot all of the techniques which were used?

Assessment opportunities

In this activity you have practised skills that are assessed using Criterion C: Producing text and Criterion D: Using language.

ACTIVITY: Is it right to try to change someone else's mind?

The debatable questions for this chapter ask:

- **Is it ethical to try deliberately to manipulate the emotions of others?**
- **Is it right to try to change someone else's mind?**

What is your own response to these questions? On your own to begin with, add notes in the table below on situations in which you feel it might be acceptable to try deliberately to manipulate the emotions of others, and on some in which you feel it would be unacceptable:

Yes, we can deliberately try to manipulate the emotions of others when ...	Because ...	No, we should not deliberately try to manipulate the emotions of others when ...	Because ...

In the next table add notes on situations in which you feel it might be acceptable to try to change someone else's mind, and on some in which you feel it would be unacceptable:

Yes, we can try to change someone's mind when ...	Because ...	No, we should not try to change someone's mind when ...	Because ...

Once you have added at least two ideas to each table, share them with a partner and give reasons as to why you think it is acceptable or otherwise to deliberately try to manipulate the emotions of others, or try to change someone else's mind. Did you come up with the same ideas? Are there new ideas that you can add to your own table?

Add any further ideas and then, with your partner, get together with another pair and share ideas once again. All of you should add any further ideas to your tables as needed once more.

The moral spectrum

Once you have a range of ideas, stay together as a group and draw a diagonal line across a piece of chart paper. This will represent a moral spectrum – a scale which shows how acceptable or unacceptable some behaviour may be judged to be.

Add the terms 'Acceptable' and 'Unacceptable' to each end of the diagonal line.

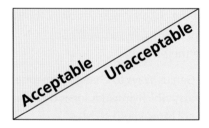

Write the following heading on the chart paper: When can we deliberately try to manipulate the emotions of others?

Then order your points on the scale according to how far each would be acceptable. Those that are most acceptable should be placed in the bottom right-hand corner. Any which you think are acceptable but which there may be questions over should be placed towards the centre. Situations where you feel it would be unacceptable to try to change someone else's mind should be similarly placed in order on the top end of the scale, according to how unacceptable you perceive something to be – the most unacceptable situations would go to the top right of the scale.

Are there any situations that you feel could be both acceptable and unacceptable, for certain reasons? Where will you place those?

Where do we draw the line?

One thing that may help you place your situations on the acceptability scale is considering where the line between acceptable and unacceptable might be drawn. Where would you draw a vertical line to divide the two sides? Which situations would fall completely on one side or the other, and which might belong partly on both sides?

As a group, discuss your situations and the placing of these, and decide collectively where to draw the line dividing acceptable and unacceptable. Remember that your line might go through some situations which do not fall completely on one side or the other.

Once you have completed this, place your poster on a desk or wall and carry out a gallery walk along with the rest of the class. You may like to note down the following:

- situations that everyone who included them agreed represented examples of where it was always *acceptable* deliberately to try to manipulate the emotions of others
- situations that everyone who included them agreed represented examples of where it was *unacceptable* deliberately to try to manipulate the emotions of others
- situations that are more **ambiguous** – that is, difficult to tell for certain whether it is acceptable or unacceptable to try deliberately to manipulate the emotions of others.

Return to your group and discuss what makes some situations morally ambiguous – that is, they may fall on either side of the line of what is acceptable and what is unacceptable.

Next, create a second moral spectrum on chart paper, and go through the same process with the question of 'When might it be acceptable to try to change someone else's mind?' Where do you draw the line here, and why?

◆ Assessment opportunities

In this activity you have practised skills that are assessed using Criterion C: Producing text and Criterion D: Using language.

ACTIVITY: The ethics of persuasion

■ ATL

- Reflection skills: Consider ethical implications
- Collaboration skills: Make fair and equitable decisions; take responsibility for one's own actions

There is always a decision to make as to where to draw a line when using persuasion; and the line is generally drawn where it becomes **unethical**, or morally wrong, to try to persuade someone of something. How do we make that judgement, however?

The following is one suggestion for this: 'Persuasion is widely considered unethical if it is for the purpose of personal gain at the expense of others, or for personal gain without the knowledge of the audience' (**https://courses.lumenlearning.com/boundless-communications/chapter/introduction-to-persuasive-speaking/**).

Take a look at the examples of 'acceptable' and 'unacceptable' situations from the Activity: Is it right to try to change someone else's mind? What role did 'personal gain' play in your choices as to where to place each of these on your moral spectrum? Discuss this as a group.

Another way of drawing the line is between something that is persuasion (acceptable), and where it becomes manipulation, which is unacceptable:

'Manipulation is getting others to do something that is of benefit to me. Persuasion is getting others to do something that is of benefit to them and of benefit to me' (Conor Neill: **https://goo.gl/r7YCq4**).

Look again at your moral spectrums and the situations you have placed on them. Would you move any, on the basis of either or both of these quotations?

In 2001 a test, the TARES, was devised to help people decide the question 'Where does persuasion end and manipulation begin?', which was intended for use by people who work in public relations and journalism. ➤

TARES stands for:

Truthfulness	Is this communication factually accurate and true? Has this appeal deliberately left out important and relevant facts?
Authenticity	Do I feel good about being involved in this action? Do I believe that the audience will see improved quality of life? [Note that 'the audience' refers to the person or people you are trying to persuade in a particular situation.]
Respect	Is the persuasive appeal made to the audience as rational, free, adult human beings? Do I care about them as people?
Equity	Does this meet the golden rule, 'Do unto others as you would have them do unto you'?
Social responsibility	Does this action promote and create the kind of world and society in which I would like to live?

Now look back at the script you wrote earlier, in which you try to persuade someone of something. Apply the TARES test to your script to see whether you were using 'ethical persuasion', or 'persuasion' rather than 'manipulation'. For each element of the test, analyse what you wrote. Then say if you think it meets the criterion each time, and justify the judgement you make by explaining it or providing the evidence.

Finally, write down on an index card a response to this prompt: How important is it to you personally to try to ensure that you only ever engage in persuasion which is ethical? Why?

Walk around your classroom and find at least five different classmates to exchange your views on this with.

◆ Assessment opportunities

In this activity you have practised skills that are assessed using Criterion C: Producing text and Criterion D: Using language.

SOME SUMMATIVE TASKS TO TRY

Use these tasks to apply and extend your learning in this chapter. These tasks are designed so that you can evaluate your learning at different levels of achievement in the Language and literature criteria.

THIS TASK CAN BE USED TO EVALUATE YOUR LEARNING IN CRITERION A, CRITERION B AND CRITERION D

Task 1: Poetry commentary

Research online and find two poems that address the same (or similar) subject matter. Write a commentary on these two poems. Do the poems use the same stylistic and literary devices? Do the poets intend the audiences to have similar responses to the poems? Or different responses? Your commentary should be around 800 words in length.

Remember to refer to the 'How to write about a poem' process.

THIS TASK CAN BE USED TO EVALUATE YOUR LEARNING IN CRITERION C AND CRITERION D

Task 2: A poem pastiche

- Write a *pastiche* (that is, imitate the style of) of the poetry competition poem 'Poverty', by Segun Rasaki. Use the same form as the original poem, but protest about a topic of concern that is important to you; try to adapt the ideas of individual lines as might best fit your own topic.
- Remember that Rasaki uses a large amount of imagery – similes, metaphors and personification especially, along with techniques such as listing (including at times asyndeton) and contrast. Your lines should reflect the techniques used in Rasaki's corresponding lines each time.
- Write a rationale for your poem of 300–500 words, explaining the techniques you have used in the poem, and the effects you intend them to have on a reader or audience, along with how they might achieve those effects.

Task 3: Creative poetry – write your own poem

Write your own poem in which you protest against something.

- Decide what you would like to protest about.
- Consider how poets choose to convey their points and message. The following table provides a framework to help with this, and may also help you generate examples to use in your poem.
- Make notes on why you want to use a particular technique, or achieve a particular effect. You will need to explain these in a rationale once you have written your poem.

Choice	Examples	Rationale/reason
Form		
Rhyming?		
Similes		
Metaphors		
Personification		
Alliteration		
Assonance		
Symbolism		
Use of rhythm?		
…		

- Write your poem. It should be at least ten lines long.
- Find three different people to give you feedback on your poem. In particular: is it clear what you are protesting about? How well have you managed to do that? How well have your stylistic choices worked – are they clear and effective? Do your feedback partners have any suggestions about things you could change, include or exclude?
- Revise your poem into its final version, taking into account any feedback you received.
- Write a rationale (300–500 words long) explaining what you are trying to say in your poem, what techniques you have used for this, and the effects you intended the techniques to have on your audience. This is, in effect, an analysis of your own poetry.

Reflection

We explored stylistic choices poets may make in order to try to persuade an audience to respond in certain ways. We looked at how poetic techniques may work to help convey a message, and to impact on an audience in different ways, along with how analysing these involves and helps to develop our own critical-thinking skills. We have considered different formats of poetry that have been used in protest poetry, and taken action by considering how to advocate for issues of concern to us through poetry, and practising that through creative poetry performance, which makes use of some of the persuasive poetic techniques we have learned.

Use this table to reflect on your own learning in this chapter.		
Questions we asked	**Answers we found**	**Any further questions now?**
Factual:		
Conceptual:		
Debatable:		

Approaches to learning you used in this chapter	Description – what new skills did you learn?	How well did you master the skills?			
		Novice	Learner	Practitioner	Expert
Communication skills					
Collaboration skills					
Reflection skills					
Information literacy skills					
Media literacy skills					
Critical-thinking skills					
Creative-thinking skills					

Learner profile attribute(s)	Reflect on the importance of being principled for your learning in this chapter.
Principled	

5 How can growing and learning be portrayed in short stories?

○ Writers' use of **plot** and **character** across different texts reveal how challenges of different kinds are **connected** with / may lead to the self-discovery, new learning and personal growth which help to form a person's **identity**.

CONSIDER THESE QUESTIONS:

Factual: How are short stories structured? How does a writer construct characters?

Conceptual: How can different characters convey different ideas about personal development and 'growing up'? What does a character's change and growth look like? What is 'conflict', and what role does it play in short stories? How do structure, character and conflict help to convey a writer's theme?

Debatable: How do we know when we are growing up? What does 'growing up' look like?

Now **share and compare** your thoughts and ideas with your partner, or with the whole class.

WE DON'T GROW WHEN THINGS ARE EASY; WE GROW WHEN WE FACE CHALLENGES.

THE HARDEST PART ABOUT GROWING UP IS LETTING GO OF WHAT YOU WERE USED TO; AND MOVING ON WITH SOMETHING YOU'RE NOT.

I didn't change, I just grew up. I learned what's best for me and if that means I have to lose a couple of people to get to where I need to be, then I'm actually okay with that.

■ Learning and growing

○ IN THIS CHAPTER, WE WILL ...

■ **Find out** what elements are contained in the structure of a short story, and the ways in which these can be used to present ideas on a theme.
■ **Explore** what 'growing' in terms of new learning and self-discovery may look like in practice.
■ **Take action** by taking a positive approach towards challenges, and looking for the learning opportunities they bring.

We will reflect on this learner profile attribute ...

- Reflective – develop reflective skills through various reflections on your own experience, strengths and weaknesses, and on how learning and personal development can be supported.

These Approaches to Learning (ATL) skills will be useful ...

- Communication skills
- Information literacy skills
- Media literacy skills
- Critical-thinking skills
- Creative-thinking skills

Assessment opportunities in this chapter:

- **Criterion A:** Analysing
- **Criterion B:** Organizing
- **Criterion C:** Producing text
- **Criterion D:** Using language

KEY WORDS

character	flashback	resolution
climax	foreshadowing	setting
conflict	plot	theme

Six-word memoirs

Can you tell your life's story in just six words? Take a look at these examples: **http://youtu.be/jEkAHATRuRU** and **http://youtu.be/ejndNExso9M**.

ACTIVITY: Write a six-word memoir

ATL

- Communication skills: Use appropriate forms of writing for different purposes and audiences

1. Look at the slogans on page 112. Which is the closest to your own feelings about growing up? Why have you chosen that one?
2. Now **create** a six-word memoir of your own on the topic of 'growing up'. Using a mind map or other organizer, brainstorm what you feel are examples of acting in a 'grown up' way.
3. In pairs, share your examples with each other. Add any new ideas to your organizer.
4. Team up with another pair to make a group of four. Share your examples and, together, produce a single organizer or mind map that represents your combined ideas.
5. Divide the ideas on the map between the four group members. Look at those ideas that have been assigned to you and think about which examples might require someone to demonstrate some kind of personal responsibility. In what way is this responsibility demonstrated? Returning to your group of four, share and **discuss** what you have come up with.

Assessment opportunities

In this activity you have practised skills that are assessed using Criterion C: Producing text and Criterion D: Using language.

For writers of short stories, the theme of growing up, or personal growth, can be a common one on which to focus. Two particular elements that may be used to explore this are conflict and character, while the structure of a story can also help convey a story's theme. We will explore these ideas further this chapter, beginning with structure.

How are short stories structured?

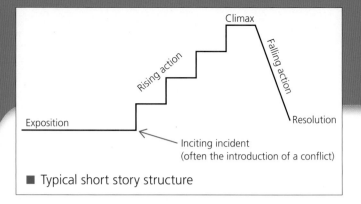

Typical short story structure

When we read short stories, we often find that they have a structure like the one shown on the right.

The features of a story that give it structure (exposition, inciting incident, rising action, climax, falling action and resolution) are formed by the conflict that appears in the story.

ℹ 'The Most Dangerous Game' by Richard Connell

'The Most Dangerous Game' was written during the 1920s when going on safari to hunt big game in Africa and South America was a popular pastime for wealthy Americans. Author Richard Connell was a combatant in the First World War and drew on his own military experience for the story. He also echoed events of the **1917 Russian Revolution** when the Cossacks, previously renowned for their violence and deeply feared, were themselves targeted in an attempt to destroy their race. In the story General Zaroff refers to escaping this campaign, and it may help explain some of his motivations and actions.

You can download a free PDF of the story here: **www.classicshorts.com/stories/danger.html**.

Each story feature is explained below. As you read the first story, 'The Most Dangerous Game', try to think about where each of these elements can be seen. Make notes as you read and answer all the questions that are posed. When you have finished, **discuss** your answers with a classmate.

The Most Dangerous Game film poster (1932)

Exposition

This is the introduction of important background information: about characters, setting, relationships, and so on. **Exposition** can be used to raise a reader's interest and curiosity, so some kind of 'narrative hook' may be present.

DISCUSS

How does 'The Most Dangerous Game' establish mood and atmosphere, present characters and convey important background information? Think particularly about the following:

- **How and what are we told about Ship-Trap Island, the setting for the story?**
- **What kind of mood and atmosphere does this evoke?**
- **What do we learn about the views on hunting of the character Rainsford?**

Inciting incident

This sets in motion the main action of the story. An **inciting incident** often takes the form of a conflict, arising between characters or other key elements of a story.

DISCUSS

What is the inciting incident in 'The Most Dangerous Game'?

Rising action

These are the steps leading up to a climax. The **rising action** section aims to increase the tension or suspense of the story, and to gradually intensify any emotions being experienced by a reader.

DISCUSS

From the time Rainsford falls from the yacht to his realization of Zaroff's actions on the island, **identify** five specific points or details that you feel help increase the story's tension, suspense or emotion.

- **Plot the points you have identified on a timeline (see below).**
- **Underneath each point, explain briefly why or how it has increased tension, suspense or emotion.**

■ Timeline for 'The Most Dangerous Game'

Climax

The **climax** is the point of highest emotion in the story. Generally a very intense moment, it may also represent a turning point in the story, either in action or psychologically for a character.

A story might have more than one climax, or a number of smaller, varied climaxes. It is important to recognize these, and to justify your own choice of climax in light of the definition given here.

DISCUSS

What is the climax of 'The Most Dangerous Game'? Are there other points of climax in the story? Write out and complete the table below, making sure to **justify** each identified point of climax.

Possible point of climax in 'The Most Dangerous Game'	Why can it be considered a 'climax'?

Falling action

This covers all the action that follows a climax, leading ultimately to the resolution. **Falling action** includes any dialogue or action needed to bring the story to a close, and may vary in length. Some writers want to end a story as quickly as possible following the climax, while others spend some time answering questions raised earlier in the story, and/or to play further with tension and suspense before the final resolution.

DISCUSS

What questions are answered in the falling action of 'The Most Dangerous Game'? Are any left unanswered? What final moments of tension or suspense are created?

Resolution

This is the end and conclusion of the story, which often sees loose ends tied up and outstanding conflicts resolved.

We will look at the **resolution** of 'The Most Dangerous Game' in more detail later in this chapter.

What is 'conflict', and what role does it play in short stories?

Conflict occurs when two opposing forces come together. They can be either external – relating to a force (not necessarily human) outside of the body, or internal – conflict that one person experiences when they have competing emotions, thoughts, impulses, and so on.

As we have seen, the 'inciting incident' in a short story is often a conflict of some kind. As well as taking various forms, conflict can play a further key role in the structure of a short story: motivating much of the action as well as raising interest and anticipation in its causes, consequences and potential resolution. Conflict can also be an important technique to convey the key ideas and themes of a story.

What should we think about when talking about conflicts?

- Who are the parties in the conflict? (Don't forget possible internal conflicts!)
- What has caused the conflict?
- What is the nature of the conflict – VERBAL? PHYSICAL? PSYCHOLOGICAL?
- How is or might the conflict be resolved?

CONFLICTS IN LITERATURE

PRESENT IDEAS, THEMES, POINTS OF VIEW – Writers can use conflicts to show us different points of view which may exist on a topic.

ADD TO THE DRAMA AND INTEREST A READER OR VIEWER…

REVEAL CHARACTER – People react differently under stress or attack, and reveal more of themselves, their thoughts and feelings…

REVEAL THE NATURE OF RELATIONSHIPS – They show us what people really think and feel about the other party in a conflict, and often why…

■ Why and how do writers use conflict?

ACTIVITY: What literary conflict can you find?

■ ATL

- ■ Information literacy skills: Access information to be informed and inform others

There are different types of conflict in literature. Search for 'conflict in literature' on www.slideshare.net to find presentations on this, or type 'conflict literature powerpoints' into a standard search engine.

After you have looked at three to five presentations, use the information you have found to complete the descriptions in a copy of the table on the right.

Which presentation do you feel was the best? Why? Are there any slides you would change? Write down your reasoning and then, as a class, **discuss** the presentations. Do your classmates agree with your choice of presentation and reasons?

Conflicts	
Conflict vs self	
Conflict vs another person or group of people	
Conflict vs society	When a character is in conflict with some aspect of their society – laws, values, traditions, etc
Conflict vs environment	
Conflict vs technology	
Conflict vs the supernatural	
Conflict vs fate	

◆ Assessment opportunities

In this activity you have practised skills that are assessed using Criterion A: Analysing.

Conflicts are used in literature for a number of different purposes. As well as provoking inciting incidents, they may:

■ Present ideas, themes or points of view. Where do we see this in 'The Most Dangerous Game'?

■ Reveal character. What do we learn about Rainsford from his conflict with the environment as he is being hunted by General Zaroff?

■ Reveal the nature of a relationship. A less evident purpose of conflict in 'The Most Dangerous Game', but something we will see more in another short story we will look at later: 'Split Cherry Tree'.

■ Add interest and 'drama' for a reader. Which conflict in 'The Most Dangerous Game' do you think is the most dramatic, and why?

'Through the Tunnel' is another short story that explores the themes of growing up and self-discovery. You can read this story online, here: **https://goo.gl/xMPku7**.

🛈 'Through the Tunnel' by Doris Lessing

'Through the Tunnel' is a short story by the Nobel Prize in Literature winner, Doris Lessing. Written in 1955, it tells the story of Jerry, a boy on holiday abroad along with his mother. Jerry meets a group of older boys and feels the need to emulate a challenge that he sees them take on.

■ Doris Lessing

ACTIVITY: Structure and conflict in 'Through the Tunnel'

■ ATL

■ Communication skills: Read critically and for comprehension
■ Critical-thinking skills: Gather and organize relevant information to formulate an argument

As you read the story, consider both the structure and the conflict found in 'Through the Tunnel'. Try to answer all of the following plot-driven questions:

● **Exposition** – What important information is presented to us at the beginning of 'Through the Tunnel'? Why is each piece of information you have identified important?

● **Inciting incident** – What is the inciting incident in 'Through the Tunnel'? Can you explain why it leads to Jerry's determination to swim through the underwater tunnel? Does it represent a conflict of any kind?

● **Rising action** – Which details in the narrative of 'Through the Tunnel' help build tension and suspense? What might a reader feel tension about?

● **Climax** – Where is the climax in 'Through the Tunnel'? Is there more than one possible climax in the story?

● **Falling action** – What details in this section show a contrast with Jerry's behaviour earlier in the story, with the French boys?

● **Resolution** – What are your feelings about the way in which Jerry behaves with his mother at the end of the story? Would you have done the same? Why (not)?

To help you think about conflict in the story, make a mind map to record each conflict that occurs.

On your mind map, be sure to note down the different types of conflict (for example, internal or external vs society), and give examples for every conflict you identify.

◆ Assessment opportunities

In this activity you have practised skills that are assessed using Criterion A: Analysing.

How do structure, character and conflict help to convey a writer's theme?

A story's theme is often an idea or message about life, which the author is seeking to present to readers. An author might try to persuade their reader of the validity or 'rightness' of the idea, or they may raise a specific issue or a question in a story, and then leave the reader to think about the implications themselves.

Through the structure and conflict of a story, and actions of the characters within that story, the themes that are being explored by a writer can be revealed. If, for instance, we look again at our statement of inquiry (and the ideas of overcoming challenges and the growth, self-discovery and learning that can result from it), we can see this reflected in 'Through the Tunnel'.

DISCUSS

What learning and self-discovery result from Jerry undergoing the challenge of swimming through the tunnel?

THINK–PAIR–SHARE

In pairs, review the two short stories you have just read: 'The Most Dangerous Game' and 'Through the Tunnel'. Can you **identify** the key themes for each of these stories? Is there more than one theme? As a class share the themes you have found. Do the stories share any themes?

'Through the Tunnel'	
Themes	One theme of this short story is that of growing up, and the self-discovery and learning that occur when Jerry takes on the challenge of swimming through the tunnel under the sea.
Inciting incident	The meeting with the French boys.
Internal conflict	The inciting incident results in Jerry wishing to 'belong' to their group but is not able to.
Climax	Leads to him setting himself the challenge of swimming through the tunnel.

ACTIVITY: Challenges of a short story

ATL

■ Critical-thinking skills: Consider ideas from multiple perspectives

Imagine you are going to write a short story based on the theme of engaging in a challenging situation, and the learning and self-discovery that can result. Think about some possible challenges. Try to come up with three or four examples, both of challenges from your personal experience and some that would be fictional. Write these down in a table similar to this:

Ideas from personal experience	Fictional challenges
e.g. when you moved schools	
e.g. when you were chosen – or not chosen – for a major event, performance, sports occasion, etc	

Now choose one challenge from your personal experience and think about the following:
- **How did the challenging situation come about?**
- **What happened while it was taking place?**
- **What was the conclusion of the challenge?**
- **What did you or others learn from it?**

Form your thoughts into a speech of three to five minutes, which covers all of the above points. When planning your speech, consider which points you will talk about in each section, and **outline** how you intend to develop them.

Now present to the class.

Then in pairs, **discuss** your choice of topic and consider what impression your presentation may have given of you to others listening.

◆ Assessment opportunities

In this activity you have practised skills that are assessed using Criterion C: Producing text and Criterion D: Using language.

ACTIVITY: Jerry's report card

- Communication skills: Give and receive meaningful feedback
- Creative-thinking skills: Create original works and ideas; use existing works and ideas in new ways

The learning Jerry undergoes is both physical and psychological. Imagine you are writing a report on Jerry's performance in preparing for the challenge, and in achieving it. How does he make use of each of the following skills in achieving his goal? The ATL skill category of self-management may help you to analyse this.

Copy and complete the following report card. **Comment** on each skill as if you were a teacher reporting on them. The first one has been done for you.

◆ Assessment opportunities

In this activity you have practised skills that are assessed using Criterion A: Analysing and Criterion C: Producing text.

Organization skills – managing time and tasks effectively

Skills	Comments for Jerry in 'Through the Tunnel'
Plan short- and long-term assignments; meet deadlines	Jerry made good use of planning for his assignment of swimming through the tunnel, which proved crucial in enabling him to complete this successfully before the deadline of his return home. He practised holding his breath for a greater length of time each day, so that when he attempted the challenge before the end of the holiday he would be able to hold his breath for the amount of time it had taken for the French boys to swim through the tunnel. He also 'studied the entrance to the tunnel' until he 'knew every jut and corner of it, as far as it was possible to see'; he also planned the best way to get down to the tunnel as quickly as possible, as when he began the challenge, we are told he 'chose the biggest stone he could carry and slipped over the edge of the rock'. This meant that when he did embark on the swim through the tunnel itself, he 'sank fast to the bottom with the stone', while his familiarity with the tunnel meant that he immediately 'took the edges of the hole in his hands and drew himself into it, wriggling his shoulders in sidewise as he remembered he must, kicking himself along with his feet'. These aspects of his planning saved valuable time, therefore, which was absolutely crucial to his success.
Create plans to prepare for summative assessments (including performances)	
Set goals that are challenging and realistic	
Plan strategies and take action to achieve personal and academic goals	
Bring necessary equipment and supplies	

Affective skills – managing state of mind

Skills	Comments for Jerry in 'Through the Tunnel'
Mindfulness Practise focus and concentration	
Practise strategies to develop mental focus	
Practise being aware of body–mind connections	
Perseverance Demonstrate persistence and perseverance	
Self-motivation Practise managing self-talk	
Resilience Practise 'bouncing back' after adversity, mistakes and failures	
Practise dealing with disappointment and unmet expectations	

How does a writer construct characters?

WHAT FORMS OF EVIDENCE DO WE USE TO EVALUATE CHARACTERS?

The ways in which we respond to challenging situations can reveal something about our own internal character. You may have been aware of that as you composed your speech in the 'Challenges of a short story' activity. Did you choose a topic that might make listeners admire you or feel sympathetic towards you? Did the details you included help to do that?

ACTIVITY: First and second impressions – how do we judge?

■ ATL

- Communication skills: Making inferences and drawing conclusions
- Media literacy skills: Understand the impact of media representations and modes of presentation

How do we make judgements about others? What evidence do we use to come to the conclusions about others that we do?

1 Look at the following video of people in a challenging situation at an airport: **www.youtube.com/watch?v=xhkKdRbGw1g.** As you watch, make notes on your impressions of the most argumentative passenger. If you cannot access this video, search online for a similar video clip – use search terms such as airport and argument.
2 What are your impressions of this person, from what you observed in the video clip? What particular details led you to make such an evaluation? **Discuss** your thoughts with a partner.
3 Watch the video on William Trubridge. As the video plays, make notes on the impressions you gain of him, and the sources of evidence you are using for those impressions.
4 Write a description of three to four paragraphs of your impressions of William Trubridge, explaining the evidence for the points you make.

Look at the video *One Breath – The Story of William Trubridge* by Nicolas Rossier **http://youtu.be/zgU0QeBYH68**.

■ Freediver William Trubridge

◆ Assessment opportunities

In this activity you have practised skills that are assessed using Criterion A: Analysing.

ACTIVITY: Creating an impression

■ Media literacy skills: Understand the impact of media representations and modes of presentation

Impressions, both good and bad, are created by lots of small details combining to form a single overall viewpoint. Reflect on some of the details – words, actions, appearance, and so on, which may contribute to presenting a particularly positive or negative impression. Copy out the 'hero' and 'villain' tables below and write down examples in each box. Make sure you explain why each point might convey a positive or negative impression.

■ Hero or villain?

'Hero'	
Words that might convey this impression:	Actions that might convey this impression:
Details of appearance that might convey this impression:	Reactions of others that may convey this impression:

'Villain'	
Words that might convey this impression:	Actions that might convey this impression:
Details of appearance that might convey this impression:	Reactions of others that may convey this impression:

EXTENSION

Consider how people from different countries and cultures might perceive situations and people differently. Is your impression of someone affected by your own background and history? Do you have any examples?

◆ Assessment opportunities

In this activity you have practised skills that are assessed using Criterion A: Analysing and Criterion D: Using language.

We form judgements about characters in literature in the same way as we do in real life; and others do the same with us. Our judgements come from evidence provided in the following forms:

■ what a character says – his or her own words
■ what a character does – his or her actions
■ what other characters, or the speaker, say about him or her – and here we must also judge how much

value to place on the comments or observations of others themselves, and how trustworthy or reliable we find them
■ details of appearance, which are often used by writers to indicate an aspect of character
■ direct information from a writer about the character.

When writing a story a writer can create different characters using these methods. Some of these methods are **direct characterization**, and others are **indirect characterization**.

- Direct characterization – when we are told something openly about a character ('He was a very generous man', for example).
- Indirect characterization – requires us to **identify** evidence, and then to **synthesize**, **analyse**, and **evaluate** it in order to come up with the judgements we make about a character.

ACTIVITY: Characterizing Jerry

■ **ATL**

- Creative-thinking skills: Use brainstorming and visual diagrams to generate new ideas and inquiries

1 Read 'Through the Tunnel' once again and highlight any evidence you find that reveals something about Jerry's character. Copy out the diagram opposite and add each piece of evidence you have found to the appropriate section.

2 In which section(s) of the diagram is most of the evidence found? This tells us the main methods used by an author in presenting a character.

3 Consider this passage about Jerry:

'And now, in a panic of failure, he yelled up, in English, "Look at me! Look!" and he began splashing and kicking in the water like a foolish dog.'

How might we **evaluate** Jerry's actions from the words here? What judgements might we make of him as a character on the basis of details in this quotation?

4 What does the author's use of the simile ('like a foolish dog') further suggest about Jerry here? In pairs, **discuss** your thoughts and ideas.

5 Try analysing the character of Jerry using evidence from elsewhere in the story (a good place to start looking might be when Jerry takes a rock and plunges down to the entrance of the tunnel). Write three paragraphs explaining what you feel the evidence you have found reveals about Jerry's character. Each paragraph should introduce a different point about his character, and should explain and **justify** the judgement you have made, quoting particular details that may help to illustrate this.

When reading a book or short story we gather and **evaluate** relevant evidence in order to draw conclusions and form arguments about a character. This process replicates how we form judgements of others in our day-to-day lives, and helps us therefore to understand the kinds of evidence others use to form judgements about us.

How is Jerry characterized in 'Through the Tunnel'?

The character's words

The character's actions

What other characters say about him

Direct or explicit information from the author

Details of appearance

◆ Assessment opportunities

In this activity you have practised skills that are assessed using Criterion A: Analysing and Criterion D: Using language.

5   How can growing and learning be portrayed in short stories?

123

How can different characters convey different ideas about personal development and 'growing up'?

THINK–PAIR–SHARE

In pairs, **discuss** what functions the following minor characters play in their respective short stories.

a   The group of French boys in 'Through the Tunnel'
b   Jerry's mother in 'Through the Tunnel'
c   Whitney in 'The Most Dangerous Game'
d   Ivan in 'The Most Dangerous Game'

As a class, share your thoughts. Does everyone agree? Do any characters have more than one purpose?

Characters are created by writers for a specific purpose. They are in the story because they need to be; thus we always need to think about what the role of each character is. Knowing the types of characterization that may be used, and recognizing those in a story, can help to identify the role a character is intended to have.

- The **protagonist** is the main character in a short story. He or she will be involved in the main conflict of the story and in its resolution.
- An **antagonist** has the function of opposing the protagonist. The antagonist does not necessarily have to be human – for example, it could be a corporation or the government.

Who are the protagonist and antagonist in 'The Most Dangerous Game' and 'Through the Tunnel'? Might there be more than one antagonist in either or both of these short stories?

Minor characters in a story also have specific functions, but these usually differ from those of the main characters. For example, a minor character might agree or disagree with the opinions of a main character in order to give an audience greater insight into a main character's situation or motivation. A main character's conversation with a minor character might also help reveal important information to the reader (this could be an example of exposition), or could push a main character into making a decision or taking action.

Characters may be **dynamic** or **static**, **round** or **flat**. The characterization is generally connected to their roles.

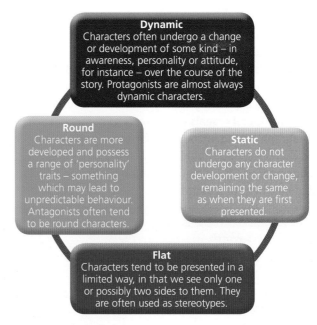

Dynamic
Characters often undergo a change or development of some kind – in awareness, personality or attitude, for instance – over the course of the story. Protagonists are almost always dynamic characters.

Round
Characters are more developed and possess a range of 'personality' traits – something which may lead to unpredictable behaviour. Antagonists often tend to be round characters.

Static
Characters do not undergo any character development or change, remaining the same as when they are first presented.

Flat
Characters tend to be presented in a limited way, in that we see only one or possibly two sides to them. They are often used as stereotypes.

■ Types of character

General Zaroff in 'The Most Dangerous Game' is a typical antagonist who is a round character capable of unpredictable behaviour. Zaroff is first presented as a civilized and very cultured man; the author then surprises us with the revelation of Zaroff's hunting activities. He is revealed to be unpredictable, and this personality trait keeps us guessing and the tension high during the hunt between Zaroff and Rainsford. By contrast, Ivan is a **stereotype** of a Cossack soldier who thinks first and foremost of violence. We learn very little about him other than this. He is a typical flat character.

By looking at the different types of characters found in short stories, and by considering the idea of a protagonist as a dynamic character who can undergo change of some kind, we can better see how conventions of the short story can help to convey a theme.

ACTIVITY: Changing characters

ATL

- Creative-thinking skills: Use brainstorming and visual diagrams to generate new ideas and inquiries

What changes do we see in Jerry and Rainsford, the protagonists of 'Through the Tunnel' and 'The Most Dangerous Game', respectively? What aspects of self-discovery and/or new learning does each acquire? Explain, using the diagrams below.

Jerry at the start	Jerry's challenge	New learning

Rainsford at the start	Rainsford's challenge	New learning

Characters may then be **dynamic** or **static**, **round** or **flat**. The characterization is generally connected to their roles:

- **Dynamic** characters often undergo a change or development of some kind – in awareness, personality, attitude, for instance – in the course of the story. **Protagonists** are almost always **dynamic** characters.
- **Static** characters remain throughout the story as when they are first presented, and do not undergo any character development or change.
- **Round** characters are more developed characters who possess a range of 'personality' traits – something which may lead to unpredictable behaviour. **Antagonists** often tend to be round characters.
- **Flat** characters tend to be presented in a limited way, in that we see only one or possibly two sides to them. They are often used as **stereotypes**.

◆ Assessment opportunities

In this activity you have practised skills that are assessed using Criterion A: Analysing.

For example, our statement of inquiry looks at how challenges can lead to growth and new learning. Within the conventions of a short story, we can see that:

- The plot structure of a short story contains conflict, which can place a character into a challenging situation and thus motivate action in which the character engages with that challenge in some way.
- The use of a dynamic character as a protagonist provides the means for an author to show how some change in a person can take place.

'Split Cherry Tree' by Jesse Stuart

Jesse Stuart was a prolific writer, alongside his work as a teacher, principal and schools' superintendent. By the time of his death in 1984, around 460 of his short stories had been published, many of which had education as one of their themes. One of these, 'Split Cherry Tree' was published in 1939 and was frequently chosen for inclusion in short story anthologies. Its main characters – a father and a teacher – are used in part to provide different perspectives on how teaching and learning should take place in schools; the father takes an unusual approach (to say the least!) when he disapproves of the type of education his son is receiving at school. The story is narrated by his son, Dave.

■ Jesse Stuart

ACTIVITY: Pa and Dave

1 **Read the opening passage of 'Split Cherry Tree' and note where information is given to us indirectly about Pa Luster. In pairs, use this information to discuss what kind of character you think Pa will be. Make sure you justify your predictions using specific evidence from the text.**
2 **Imagine the conversation that will take place between the narrator (Dave) and his father, once Dave arrives home.**
3 **Using the notes you have just made on Pa to inform your ideas, plan out and then write down this conversation. The conversation should be about 500 words long.**

◆ Assessment opportunities

In this activity you have practised skills that are assessed using Criterion A: Analysing, Criterion C: Producing text and Criterion D: Using language.

The following passage is the opening of 'Split Cherry Tree'. This exposition introduces us to the character of Pa Luster, the narrator's father, though he does not appear up to this point in the story.

"I don't mind staying after school," I says to Professor Herbert, "but I'd rather you'd whip me with a switch and let me go home early. Pa will whip me anyway for getting home two hours late."

"You are too big to whip," says Professor Herbert, "and I have to punish you for climbing up in that cherry tree. You boys knew better than that! The other five boys have paid their dollar each. You have been the only one who has not helped pay for the tree. Can't you borrow a dollar?"

"I can't," I says. "I'll have to take the punishment. I wish it would be quicker punishment. I wouldn't mind."

Professor Herbert stood and looked at me. He was a big man. He wore a grey suit of clothes. The suit matched his grey hair.

"You don't know my father," I says to Professor Herbert. "He might be called a little old-fashioned. He makes us mind him until we're twenty-one years old. He believes: 'If you spare the rod you spoil the child.' I'll never be able to make him understand about the cherry tree. I'm the first of my people to go to high school."

"You must take the punishment," says Professor Herbert. "You must stay two hours after school today and two hours after school tomorrow. I am allowing you twenty-five cents an hour. That is good money for a high-school student. You can sweep the schoolhouse floor, wash the blackboards, and clean windows. I'll pay the dollar for you."

I couldn't ask Professor Herbert to loan me a dollar. He never offered to loan it to me. I had to stay and help the janitor and work out my fine at a quarter an hour.

I thought as I swept the floor, "What will Pa do to me? What lie can I tell him when I go home? Why did we ever climb that cherry tree and break it down for anyway? Why did we run crazy over the hills away from the crowd? Why did we do all of this? Six of us climbed up in a little cherry tree after one little lizard! Why did the tree split and fall with us? It should have been a stronger tree! Why did Eif Crabtree just happen to be below us plowing and catch us in his cherry tree? Why wasn't he a better man than to charge us six dollars for the tree?"

It was six o'clock when I left the schoolhouse. I had six miles to walk home. It would be after seven when I got home. I had all my work to do when I got home. It took Pa and I both to do the work. Seven cows to milk. Nineteen head of cattle to feed, four mules, twenty-five hogs, firewood and stovewood to cut, and water to draw from the well. He would be doing it when I got home. He would be mad and wondering what was keeping me!

I hurried home. I would run under the dark, leafless trees. I would walk fast uphill. I would run down the hill. The ground was freezing. I had to hurry. I had to run. I reached the long ridge that led to our cow pasture. I ran along this ridge. The wind dried the sweat on my face. I ran across the pasture to the house.

Now let us trace a dynamic character on a journey of growth and new learning. Read the next extract of 'Split Cherry Tree', in which we meet Pa Luster himself for the first time. As you read through the text note down any of Pa's words and actions, and of Dave's responses to him, which you feel help characterize Pa.

I threw down my books in the chipyard. I ran to the barn to spread fodder on the ground for the cattle. I didn't take time to change my clean school clothes for my old work clothes. I ran out to the barn. I saw Pa spreading fodder on the ground to the cattle. That was my job. I ran up to the fence. I says, "Leave that for me, Pa. I'll do it. I'm just a little late."

"I see you are," says Pa. He turned and looked at me. His eyes danced fire. "What in th' world has kept you so? Why ain't you been here to help me with this work? Make a gentleman out'n one boy in th' family and this is what you get! Send you to high school and you get too onery fer th' buzzards to smell!"

I never said anything. I didn't want to tell why I was late from school. Pa stopped scattering the bundles of fodder. He looked at me. He says, "Why are you gettin' in here this time o' night? You tell me or I'll take a hickory withe to you right here on th' spot!"

I says, "I had to stay after school." I couldn't lie to Pa. He'd go to school and find out why I had to stay. If I lied to him it would be too bad for me.

"Why did you haf to stay atter school?" says Pa.

I says, "Our biology class went on a field trip today. Six of us boys broke down a cherry tree. We had to give a dollar apiece to pay for the tree. I didn't have the dollar. Professor Herbert is making me work out my dollar. He gives me twenty-five cents an hour. I had to stay in this afternoon. I'll have to stay in tomorrow afternoon!"

"Are you telling me th' truth?" says Pa.

"I'm telling you the truth," I says. "Go and see for yourself."

"That's just what I'll do in th' mornin'," says Pa. "Jist whose cherry tree did you break down?"

"Eif Crabtree's cherry tree!"

"What was you doin' clear out in Eif Crabtree's place?" says Pa. "He lives four miles from th' county high school. Don't they teach you no books at that high school? Do they jist let you get out and gad over th' hillsides? If that's all they do I'll keep you at home, Dave. I've got work here fer you to do!"

"Pa," I says, "spring is just getting here. We take a subject in school where we have to have bugs, snakes, flowers, lizards, frogs, and plants. It is biology. It was a pretly day today. We went out to find a few of these. Six of us boys saw a lizard at the same time sunning on a cherry tree. We all went up the tree to get it. We broke the tree down. It split at the forks. Eif Crabtree was plowing down below us. He ran up the hill and got our names. The other boys gave their dollar apiece. I didn't have mine. Professor Herbert put mine in for me. I have to work it out at school."

"Poor man's son, huh," says Pa. "I'll attend to that myself in th' mornin'. I'll take keer o' 'im. He ain't from this county nohow. I'll go down there in th' mornin' and see 'im. Lettin' you leave your books and galavant all over th' hills. What kind of a school is it nohow! Didn't do that, my son, when I's a little shaver in school. All fared alike too."

"Pa, please don't go down there," I says, "just let me have fifty cents and pay the rest of my fine! I don't want you to go down there! I don't want you to start anything with Professor Herbert!'

"Ashamed of your old Pap are you, Dave," says Pa, "atter th' way I've worked to raise you! Tryin' to send you to school so you can make a better livin' than I've made.

"I'll straighten this thing out myself! I'll take keer o' Professor Herbert myself! He ain't got no right to keep you in and let the other boys off jist because they've got th' money! I'm a poor man. A bullet will go in a professor same as it will any man. It will go in a rich man same as it will a poor man. Now you get into this work before I take one o' these withes and cut the shirt off'n your back!"

I thought once I'd run through the woods above the barn just as hard as I could go. I thought I'd leave high school and home forever! Pa could not catch me! I'd get away! I couldn't go back to school with him. He'd have a gun and maybe he'd shoot Professor Herbert. It was hard to tell what he would do. I could tell Pa that school had changed in the hills from the way it was when he was a boy, but he wouldn't understand. I could tell him we studied frogs, birds, snakes, lizards, flowers, insects. But Pa wouldn't understand. If I did run away from home it wouldn't matter to Pa. He would see Professor Herbert anyway. He would think that high school and Professor Herbert had run me away from home. There was no need to run away. I'd just have to stay, finish foddering the cattle, and go to school with Pa the next morning.

I would take a bundle of fodder, remove the hickory witheband from around it, and scatter it on rocks, clumps of green briers, and brush so the cattle wouldn't tramp it under their feet. I would lean it up against the oak trees and the rocks in the pasture just above our pigpen on the hill. The fodder was cold and frosty where it had set out in the stacks. I would carry bundles of the fodder from the stack until I had spread out a bundle for each steer. Pa went to the barn to feed the mules and throw corn in the pen to the hogs.

The moon shone bright in the cold March sky. I finished my work by moonlight. Professor Herbert really didn't know how much work I had to do at home. If he had known he would not have kept me after school. He would have loaned me a dollar to have paid my part on the cherry tree. He had never lived in the hills. He didn't know the way the hill boys had to work so that they could go to school. Now he was teaching in a county high school where all the boys who attended were from hill farms.

After I'd finished doing my work I went to the house and ate my supper. Pa and Mom had eaten. My supper was getting cold. I heard Pa and Mom talking in the front room. Pa was telling Mom about me staying in after school.

"I had to do all th' milkin' tonight, chop th' wood myself. It's too hard on me atter I've turned ground all day. I'm goin' to take a day off tomorrow and see if I can't remedy things a little. I'll go down to that high school tomorrow. I won't be a very good scholar fer Professor Herbert nohow. He won't keep me in atter school. I'll take a different kind of lesson down there and make 'im acquainted with it."

"Now, Luster," says Mom, "you jist stay away from there. Don't cause a lot o' trouble. You can be jailed fer a trick like that. You'll get th' Law atter you. You'll jist go down there and show off and plague your own boy Dave to death in front o' all th' scholars!"

"Plague or no plague," says Pa, "he don't take into consideration what all I haf to do here, does he? I'll show 'im it ain't right to keep one boy in and let the rest go scot-free. My boy is good as th' rest, ain't he? A bullet will make a hole in a schoolteacher same as it will anybody else. He can't do me that way and get by with it. I'll plug 'im first. I aim to go down there bright and early in the mornin' and get all this straight! I aim to see about bug larnin' and this runnin' all over God's creation huntin' snakes, lizards, and frogs. Ransackin' th' country and goin' through cherry orchards and breakin' th' trees down atter lizards! Old Eif Crabtree ought to a-poured th' hot lead to 'em instead o' chargin' six dollars fer th' tree! He ought to a-got old Herbert th' first one!"

I ate my supper. I slipped upstairs and lit the lamp. I tried to forget the whole thing. I studied plane geometry. Then I studied my biology lesson. I could hardly study for thinking about Pa. "He'll go to school with me in the morning. He'll take a gun for Professor Herbert! What will Professor Herbert think of me! I'll tell him when Pa leaves that I couldn't help it. But Pa might shoot him. I hate to go with Pa. Maybe he'll cool off about it tonight and not go in the morning."

What does a character's change and growth look like?

Conflict arises, as we anticipated, between Dave and his father once Dave arrives home. This is the inciting incident that motivates action, which will rise to a climax.

In the rising action of this passage too, as in the exposition, the author aims to leave a reader curious as to what might happen next. Anticipation is a key response often aimed at the rising action of a short story. By evoking anticipation in their readers, writers keep us reading on.

ACTIVITY: Dave's diary

■ ATL

- Creative-thinking skills: Create original works and ideas; use existing works and ideas in new ways

Imagine you are Dave at this point in the story. Write a diary entry that looks back at the major events of the day, and also looks ahead at what you think might happen tomorrow. Under the following headings plan out the points you will include in the two sections of the diary entry.

- **Events of today**
- **What may happen tomorrow?**

Remember to include your own thoughts and feelings. Register is also important – Dave is a teenage boy, and he is writing something he may not expect anyone else to ever read.

◆ Assessment opportunities

In this activity you have practised skills that are assessed using Criterion C: Producing text and Criterion D: Using language.

ACTIVITY: Taking a second look at Pa

■ ATL

- Critical-thinking skills: Revise understanding based on new information and evidence

After you have finished reading 'Split Cherry Tree', look again at Pa Luster. What do you think of him as a character now? Is your view of him the same as it was in the 'Pa and Dave' activity or has it changed? Explain your reasons for your view.

In what way(s) does Pa change throughout the story? What details show us this? Pick out five such details and, for each, explain what you feel it reveals about

DISCUSS

Before reading any more of 'Split Cherry Tree', take a moment to decide how you feel about the character of Pa Luster by this point in the story.

If you could give him a level out of 10, which reflected how sympathetic a character you find him at this stage, which level would you choose and why? Assume that 10 is very sympathetic and 1 is not sympathetic at all.

In groups, compare what level you each awarded to Pa. Did everyone in the group choose the same level? Did everyone have the same reasons for picking a particular level?

Now read the remainder of the story. You can find the full text online at **https://goo.gl/ik1tuF**.

his character. In particular consider how Pa may be undergoing a change in awareness, understanding, beliefs or values.

EXTENSION

What type of character is Pa Luster? Dynamic or static? Round or flat? Can you think of characters from other short stories that fit into these character types?

◆ Assessment opportunities

In this activity you have practised skills that are assessed using Criterion A: Analysing.

THE ELEMENTS OF A SHORT STORY – PUTTING THEM ALL TOGETHER

Now that we have read through three short stories, and looked in turn at aspects of plot and structure, characterization and theme, let us return to our statement of inquiry, and consider how these different elements work together to convey this understanding:

Writers' use of plot and character across different texts reveal how challenges of different kinds are connected with / may lead to the self-discovery, new learning and personal growth which help to form a person's identity.

Copy and complete the following table, in order to compare how far this might apply in our different short stories.

EXTENSION: GROWING UP

What does 'growing up' mean to you? How do you think you have changed and will change? Imagine you are 10 years old, 30 years old and 60 years old. For each age:

1 Picture yourself standing in front of a mirror. Write a paragraph describing how you have changed physically over the years.

2 Write a letter to yourself where you imagine the experiences you have had at each age (for example: playing at school, moving house, starting your career, having children). Describe how each experience has affected or changed you. Remember to think about the tone and language of each letter – something written by a 10-year-old will read very differently from something written by a 60-year-old.

3 Choose one of your parents and write another letter, this time from their perspective. Remember, they grew up in a different time from you, with different pressures, concerns and experiences, and this will change their views on growing up. How different, or similar, is this letter with the one you wrote based on your own experience of growing up?

	'The Most Dangerous Game'	'Through the Tunnel'	'Split Cherry Tree'
What challenge does the protagonist undergo? What type of challenge is it – physical, psychological, a challenge to long-held beliefs, etc?			
What inciting incident leads the protagonist into the challenge they face?			
What conflicts does the protagonist experience while engaged in their challenge?			
What personal growth, self-discovery, and/or new learning results from the challenge the protagonist has faced?			

1 Think about a time that you found difficult and challenging in the past.
   a Was it a valuable experience, or something that you could and should have avoided?
   b Would you have acted differently?
   c Did you discover something about yourself from that experience?
2 Now think about a time or event you are likely to find difficult at some point in the future. It may be something like having to perform in some way (a play, or in a sporting event) or make a speech, having an interview or dealing with some other difficult situation. Think about:
   a What you may be able to do to prepare for it.
   b What you might learn from it.

How to write a short story

A process you might follow when writing a story about a challenging situation that spurs self-learning is as follows:

1 Brainstorm ideas for possible challenges that might form the focus of your short story. Use a mind map to record these and then develop your initial thoughts further.

> **Hint**
> You may find mind-mapping software helpful for this; for example, MindMup, which can be found online: www.mindmup.com.

2 Each of your 'challenge' ideas should lead to your protagonist learning or realizing something new. Consider the following elements, and use them to form parts of your story:
   • Who or what might your protagonist be? How might age, gender, occupation, and so on, be significant to the context of the story?
   • What other character(s) types might be needed? Who or what will be the antagonist?
   • What conflicts might take place?

> **Hint**
> You might use a Venn diagram to brainstorm details.

3 After completing steps 1 and 2, pick your two best ideas and then follow the short story structure to add more details that might be used in each part of the story.

> **Hint**
> Planning is crucial when producing quality writing, so ensure you allot sufficient time and thought to it.

4 Write a first draft of your story. If possible ask your teacher or fellow students for feedback on your draft. Incorporate any feedback you receive in the next draft of your story.

5 Editing and revising your story will help you produce the best story you can. Do this by incorporating the feedback you received from step 4, but also be on the lookout for any mistakes or errors, and any improvements you can make to your writing. Consider the following common improvements you could make and pitfalls you should avoid:
   • More effective, 'better' words than some of those used the first time around.
   • 'Run-on' sentences – one of the most common grammatical errors that occur in writing.
   • Direct speech is good to include, frequently, but it is often a good idea to check it carefully for correct use, particularly in terms of its punctuation.
   • Use of commas, semi-colons and colons. Where are pauses needed? How dramatic might they be?
   • Use of tenses – are these consistent? Are you switching between past and present?
   • Spellings – it is worth having a dictionary alongside during the editing stage, and looking up there and then any words you are not sure you have spelled correctly.
   • What kinds of errors do you tend to make in your writing? Check specifically for the things you know that *you* have a habit of getting wrong in your writing.

6 The essay should be typed and double-spaced. Include a word count at the end of your essay.

SOME SUMMATIVE TASKS TO TRY

Use these tasks to apply and extend your learning in this chapter. These tasks are designed so that you can evaluate your learning at different levels of achievement in the Language and literature criteria.

THIS TASK CAN BE USED TO EVALUATE YOUR LEARNING IN CRITERION C AND CRITERION D

Task 1: Write a short story

Now it is your turn to be creative and write a short story, using the learning of this chapter.

Your short story should feature a protagonist who undergoes a challenging situation, which results in new learning, or self-discovery of some kind. Alongside your dynamic protagonist, consider any other characters you have included in your story – are they dynamic or static? Round or flat? Also make sure to include all of the structural elements we have looked at in this chapter: exposition, an inciting incident, rising action, a climax, a resolution.

Your story should be 800–1,000 words long.

THIS TASK CAN BE USED TO EVALUATE YOUR LEARNING IN CRITERION A

Task 2: Analyse your short story

The short story you wrote for the 'Write a short story' task uses a number of styles and techniques to present a dynamic protagonist.

Write a 500-word analysis explaining how your writing made use of structure, character and conflict to **create** your protagonist, and how these techniques have been used to show the character's growth. Make sure you use evidence to back up each point you make.

Reflection

We have explored the structure and purposes of short stories, looking at how conflict and characterization can be used to show how people may respond to challenges which can arise, and how the learning which results from that can impact on our own personal growth, and the people we become – and thus can help to form our identities. We have considered too how to reflect on the learning we experience in different ways, in order to make sure we can use it to the best effect in our own lives and personal development.

Use this table to reflect on your own learning in this chapter.						
Questions we asked	**Answers we found**	**Any further questions now?**				
Factual:						
Conceptual:						
Debatable:						
Approaches to learning you used in this chapter	**Description – what new skills did you learn?**	**How well did you master the skills?**				
		Novice	Learner	Practitioner	Expert	
Communication skills						
Information literacy skills						
Media literacy skills						
Critical-thinking skills						
Creative-thinking skills						
Learner profile attribute(s)	Reflect on the importance of being reflective for your learning in this chapter.					
Reflective						

6 Should we always believe what we see and hear?

It is important in an age of mass information to consider how far creative use of language, context and bias can affect how far a text is telling the truth.

CONSIDER THESE QUESTIONS:

Factual: Where and how can we find out information? What is bias and what does it look like? How and why are persuasive techniques sometimes used when presenting information? What techniques can be used to make text more persuasive?

Conceptual: In what ways can language and texts be powerful? Who controls the information we consume, and to what purpose?

Debatable: What is the role of the media if we cannot trust the information it gives us? How can we engage with, and respond to, mass media communication in a more informed way?

Now **share and compare** your thoughts and ideas with your partner, or with the whole class.

IN THIS CHAPTER, WE WILL …

- **Find out** different ways in which information may be presented to us through different media, what 'bias' is and what it looks like, and how and why persuasive techniques may be used.
- **Explore** who controls the information we see, hear and read, what its purposes may be, and how an audience might engage with text in an age of mass information.
- **Take action** by applying information literacy skills in order to engage with and respond to media communication in a more informed way.

These Approaches to Learning (ATL) skills will be useful …

- Communication skills
- Collaboration skills
- Information literacy skills
- Media literacy skills
- Critical-thinking skills
- Creative-thinking skills

Assessment opportunities in this chapter:

- ◆ **Criterion A:** Analysing
- ◆ **Criterion B:** Organizing
- ◆ **Criterion C:** Producing text
- ◆ **Criterion D:** Using language

KEY WORDS

bias	equality	implication
credibility	exploit	persuasion
emotive language	flattery	tone

● Thinkers – explore the role of a thinker in analysing and taking responsible action in an age of mass information; consider what it means to apply creative thinking skills in forming opinions and persuasive argument; apply critical-thinking skills in order to recognize objectivity and bias, and develop independent and informed judgements about the opinions of others; make reasoned, ethical decisions about these.

ACTIVITY: Where do you get your information?

■ ATL

■ Media literacy skills: Locate, organize, analyse, evaluate, synthesize and ethically use information from a variety of sources and media (including digital social media and online networks)

People get their information from a huge variety of sources today, as the 'Data never sleeps' infographic shows.

● **What are your most common sources of information? Do you use any of the sources from the infographic? How about internet sources such as news websites, or library resources such as books and journals?**

Create a mind map of all the sources you use to obtain information. Note that 'the internet' or 'the library' are not sources (but they *are* places where multiple sources can be found).

Feel free to add other sources not mentioned in the infographic – for instance, *WeChat* and *Weibo* are very widely used in China.

● **Using the sources from your mind map, write a list of the top ten sources you use most often. List these from the most used to the least.**

● **How reliable do you think each of these top ten sources is? Using the same sources, write out another list, but this time put your most reliable source at the top and your least reliable at the bottom.**

● **How different is the order of your two lists? Do you use any sources that you feel might be unreliable, in order to obtain a lot of information?**

● **In groups of four, compare your lists. Discuss what each of you understands about the term 'reliable' and agree a definition.**

● **Finally, use the lists to conduct an overall class survey of the most frequent sources used for obtaining information across your class and the perceptions of their reliability.**

■ Infographic: Data never sleeps

Where and how can we find out information?

The data infographic on page 135 shows the huge amount of data that is generated *per minute* from each of the sources listed. This, as well as the large number of online and social networking sites that appear on the infographic, suggests that the increase in social media has led to information being much more quickly and widely available, both to consumers who are looking for it, as well as those who are not.

Given the vast amount of information being produced in today's **Information Age** (and the variety of sources making it accessible) how can we know who is saying what? And how should we respond to it all?

To answer these questions we need to look at *what*, *where* and *how* something is being said, as well as the reasons *why* it is being said. In particular we must look closely at ways in which language might be used, and a text that is helpful in exploring this is George Orwell's *Animal Farm*.

ANIMAL FARM

Animal Farm is an allegory, a **fable** and a **satirical** novel.

To get the most out of the following activities, you should read the novel all the way through. As you are reading, it would be good to jot down notes on the key characters, events and your thoughts and feelings you experience as you read.

Animal Farm

Animal Farm was published in 1945 and tells the story of a group of farmyard animals who stage a revolution, taking over their farm and driving out all of the humans, including the farm's owner, Mr Jones.

The revolution begins with a cry that 'all animals are equal' under the new system, but a reader can see this quickly breaking down as the pigs, and other particular individuals, gradually take power for themselves and exploit other animals for their own advantage. Ultimately, the animals cannot tell the difference between the pigs and the humans they drove out.

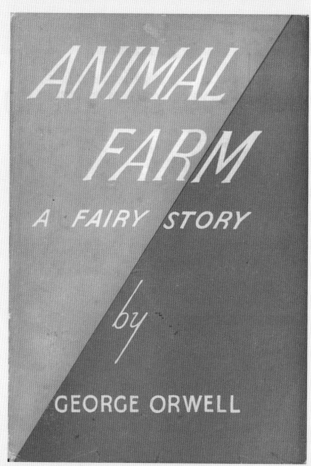

Links to: History; Individuals and societies

Allegory

On the surface *Animal Farm* is just a story about animals taking over control of their farm; however, in reality it is telling the story of the 1917 Russian Revolution in which the ruling **Czar Nicholas** and his family were driven out of power by a **communist** revolutionary named **Vladimir Lenin**. When Lenin died in 1924, **Josef Stalin** replaced him as leader of the revolution. In *Animal Farm* Stalin is represented by Napoleon.

Animal Farm is therefore a story that deliberately parallels real-life events, in order to convey the nature of those events, and to comment on them. As such, the novel is an allegory. You can find out more about the Russian Revolution in *History for the IB MYP 4&5: by Concept*, Chapter 6.

ACTIVITY: The Russian Revolution jigsaw

Animal Farm is best understood when the people and events it is paralleling are known, and can be recognized in the novel. Let us begin our exploration of the novel and some of its aspects, therefore, by looking into some of those people and events. This is something you may be able to combine in an interdisciplinary way with some of your individuals and societies classes.

1   In a group of four, number yourselves from 1 to 4. This is your home group.
2   Your expert group is made up of everyone in the class who has the same number as you; all the number 1s in the class form one group, all the number 2s form another group, and so on. Get in to your expert groups now.
3   Each of the characters and events in the following table has a number between 1 and 4, which relate to the numbers you assigned yourselves. If you are in expert group 1, then you will look at Old Major and The Battle of the Cowshed.

Number	Characters	Events
1	Old Major	The Battle of the Cowshed
2	Napoleon	The windmill
3	Snowball	The revolt by the hens
4	Boxer	The Battle of the Windmill

4   In your expert group, research your assigned characters and events from the novel, as well as their real-life counterparts (find a 'character comparison chart' for *Animal Farm* online to get you started). Make a model map to record any information or notes from your research, using the individual branches to link between the different members and events.
5   Share and **discuss** your findings among your expert group. Update your model map with any more information your group has found. When you return to your home groups you will use these notes to share the information you have found, so make sure they contain everything you think is important for your home group to know.
6   Once the research time has finished, return to your home group. Each member of your home group should share the information they have found for the characters and events they had responsibility for.
7   In your home groups use a piece of poster paper to **create** an overall map that captures all the information that has been discovered for all the characters and events.

During your research try to look at a range of different texts – including the following:
● at least one text from your library
● one internet text
● one internet video.

The following video presentation gives a useful overview of the Russian Revolution, which may help in this task: https://youtu.be/FfDt-4IOZLA.

Fable

A **fable** is a story that often uses animals as characters, and tries to teach a lesson to its readers. *Animal Farm* is a good example of a modern fable.

How and why are persuasive techniques sometimes used when presenting information?

Satire

Satire involves criticising something or someone through humorously mocking and making fun of it or them, and highlighting their failings. As a satirical novel *Animal Farm* criticizes, at times through humour, the Russian Revolution and, more widely, situations of revolution where leaders become as corrupt and exploitative of others as those they originally drove out.

The comparison of the leaders in the Russian Revolution to pigs is an example of Orwell's satire in *Animal Farm*. The comparison is humorous, but at the same time it also makes a critical point about greed. The pigs are further mocked in some individual episodes, such as in Chapter 8 where the pigs have tried alcohol and have become drunk for the first time:

Napoleon, Squealer and the other animals' lack of awareness about the effects of alcohol is humorous – they think Napoleon is dying the following morning; however, we know that he just has a hangover.

While the episode is funny, Orwell also invites readers to criticize the pigs for being hypocritical because of the earlier commandment that 'No animal shall drink alcohol'.

It was a few days later than this that the pigs came upon a case of whisky in the cellars of the farmhouse. It had been overlooked at the time when the house was first occupied. That night there came from the farmhouse the sound of loud singing, in which, to everyone's surprise, the strains of 'Beasts of England' were mixed up. At about half-past nine Napoleon, wearing an old bowler hat of Mr Jones's, was distinctly seen to emerge from the back door, gallop rapidly round the yard and disappear indoors again. But in the morning a deep silence hung over the farmhouse. Not a pig appeared to be stirring. It was nearly nine o'clock when Squealer made his appearance, walking slowly and dejectedly, his eyes dull, his tail hanging limply behind him, and with every appearance of being seriously ill. He called the animals together and told them that he had a terrible piece of news to impart. Comrade Napoleon was dying!

A cry of lamentation went up. Straw was laid down outside the doors of the farmhouse, and the animals walked on tiptoe. With tears in their eyes they asked one another what they should do if their Leader were taken away from them.

This might remind readers of Boxer burning his hat earlier because he took the commandment that no animal should wear clothes so seriously.

The scene therefore also encourages a reader to think about how the pigs are betraying the commandments.

There is criticism of the animals too in their unquestioning acceptance of 'their Leader', and everything he does. Later, as soon as Napoleon recovers, his first act is to take over what should be the animals' retirement grazing land in order to grow barley for use in manufacturing more alcohol for the pigs.

Satire is a part of Orwell's purpose and style in writing the novel, and the language he uses gives us clues to his intentions. The creative use of language and rhetoric can affect the amount and accuracy of the information we receive. Let us now look at these aspects in more detail.

At the start of *Animal Farm* a speech is given by Old Major, which is packed with rhetorical language and devices (some of which we looked at in earlier chapters) to convince and persuade his audience. The first part of the speech is annotated below.

Opening reference to those listening as friends – gives the impression he is one of them, and is not talking 'down' to them. It also suggests that if this is something that concerns him, it is likely to concern them also.

Mentions the **expertise** and **experience** giving him the right to speak; gives sense also he is doing his audience a favour.

Emotive language – designed to evoke emotion in an audience.

Opinion stated as fact

Emotive language

Repetition – of 'No', emphasized further as shown by use of **exclamation mark** and **hyperbole** – exaggeration for effect. Old Major is trying to be as emphatic as he can in telling the animals they should not accept things staying the way they are.

"Comrades, you have heard already about the strange dream that I had last night. But I will come to the dream later. I have something else to say first. I do not think, comrades, that I shall be with you for many months longer, and before I die, I feel it my duty to pass on to you such wisdom as I have acquired. I have had a long life, I have had much time for thought as I lay alone in my stall, and I think I may say that I understand the nature of life on this earth as well as any animal now living. It is about this that I wish to speak to you.

"Now, comrades, what is the nature of this life of ours? Let us face it: our lives are miserable, laborious, and short. We are born, we are given just so much food as will keep the breath in our bodies, and those of us who are capable of it are forced to work to the last atom of our strength; and the very instant that our usefulness has come to an end we are slaughtered with hideous cruelty. No animal in England knows the meaning of happiness or leisure after he is a year old. No animal in England is free. The life of an animal is misery and slavery: that is the plain truth.

"But is this simply part of the order of nature? Is it because this land of ours is so poor that it cannot afford a decent life to those who dwell upon it? No, comrades, a thousand times no! The soil of England is fertile, its climate is good, it is capable of affording food in abundance to an enormously greater number of animals than now inhabit it. This single farm of ours would support a dozen horses, twenty cows, hundreds of sheep—and all of them living in a comfort and a dignity that are now almost beyond our imagining. Why then do we continue in this miserable condition?

Rule of three and **asyndeton** – a list of items without a conjunction such as 'and'. The effect is one of there being too much to list to pause for a conjunction. Here it gives a sense of there being almost too many qualities that England can offer to animals to list them all.

Repetition – of a key word in 'comrades'. Repetition is a common technique in speeches to emphasize particular points, and is thus used with significant words and phrases.

An appeal to an audience's sympathy: Old Major expects to die soon.

Rhetorical question – a question that does not require an answer but invites thought on the part of an audience.

Rule of three – a rhetorical device of using a list of three related things. Old Major uses it in successive sentences.

Repetition

Rhetorical questions

Rhetorical question and **emotive language**. Both his vision for the future and contrast with the present are presented here.

Repetition

Repetition – of 'Man', emphasized further by use of capital letter.

'You' – directly addresses listeners. Acts like second-person narrative voice, drawing listener into the narrative itself and making it directly relevant to them.

Speculation stated as facts

Because nearly the whole of the produce of our labour is stolen from us by human beings. There, comrades, is the answer to all our problems. It is summed up in a single word—Man. Man is the only real enemy we have. Remove Man from the scene, and the root cause of hunger and overwork is abolished forever.

"Man is the only creature that consumes without producing. He does not give milk, he does not lay eggs, he is too weak to pull the plough, he cannot run fast enough to catch rabbits. Yet he is lord of all the animals. He sets them to work, he gives back to them the bare minimum that will prevent them from starving, and the rest he keeps for himself. Our labour tills the soil, our dung fertilises it, and yet there is not one of us that owns more than his bare skin. You cows that I see before me, how many thousands of gallons of milk have you given during this last year? And what has happened to that milk which should have been breeding up sturdy calves? Every drop of it has gone down the throats of our enemies. And you hens, how many eggs have you laid in this last year, and how many of those eggs ever hatched into chickens? The rest have all gone to market to bring in money for Jones and his men. And you, Clover, where are those four foals you bore, who should have been the support and pleasure of your old age? Each was sold at a year old—you will never see one of them again. In return for your four confinements and all your labour in the fields, what have you ever had except your bare rations and a stall?"

Opinion stated as fact

Asyndeton

Contrast

Rule of three

Rhetorical questions

ACTIVITY: Analysing *Animal Farm*

■ ATL

- Critical-thinking skills: Gather and organize relevant information to formulate an argument

In pairs, go through the second part of Old Major's speech (beginning 'And even the miserable lives we lead are not allowed to reach their natural span' and ending 'All animals are equal'). Highlight and annotate all of the rhetorical devices you can find there, in the same way as has been done with the first part.

Being able to identify rhetorical elements will help you to realize when someone is trying to persuade you, but the objectivity, subjectivity and bias of the information you are being given is another very important consideration when reading text or hearing a speech.

◆ Assessment opportunities

In this activity you have practised skills that are assessed using Criterion A: Analysing.

What is bias and what does it look like?

OBJECTIVITY, SUBJECTIVITY AND BIAS

Something that is **objective** will be based on facts and not influenced by personal feelings or beliefs. It is often associated with looking at something fairly.

Something that is **subjective**, on the other hand, is the opposite and will be influenced by or based on personal beliefs or feelings, rather than based on facts.

Bias is where a text shows a preference for a particular point of view, or pushes back against another one. A creator of a text may consciously support and promote one point of view, while also criticizing or reducing the importance of any alternatives. Bias can also be 'unconscious', which means that a text promotes a particular point of view in some way, but without its creator necessarily being aware of it.

By evaluating how objective, subjective or biased a text is, we can make informed judgements about its purpose(s).

Where the purpose of a text (written or spoken) is to persuade in some way, it is aimed at getting people to think or act in a certain way, or to believe something in particular. To persuade you must support or oppose a particular 'side' or point of view, and we can therefore expect to see signs of bias in texts with a persuasive purpose.

Not all bias is obvious, however, and sometimes a text is created in a way that tries to make it look more objective. This can give an audience the impression that the text is 'fair' and 'unbiased'; this can also be very persuasive in leading people to accepting what they may see, read or hear more readily.

As the audience of a text, we need to be able to make *informed* judgements about a text, so that we can then make informed *decisions* about how to respond to the text, and what, if anything, we might do as a result of it.

Making informed decisions means looking for, in particular, some of the signs of bias. In Old Major's speech he uses loaded/emotive language and also states opinion as fact.

DISCUSS

Old Major's speech at the beginning of *Animal Farm* is trying to persuade the animals to agree with a particular point of view. What are the most important signs in the speech that it is biased?

What techniques are used in Old Major's speech that are trying to make the speech seem more objective?

Loaded language

Language is often not neutral and instead carries positive or negative connotations or associations. Individual words can convey very different impressions of a similar idea, which can evoke very different audience responses when used.

Consider the differences between the following pairs of words and phrases:

slender	skinny
full-figured	fat
assertive	pushy
innocent	naïve
curious	nosy
youthful	immature
self-confident	arrogant

Each pair of words refers to a similar idea, but those in the left-hand column tend to have positive associations, while those in right-hand column have more negative ones. These are examples of **loaded language** – this is an important element of persuasive text, and also a possible indicator of bias in texts.

Another example of loaded language is a **euphemism**. This is a word or phrase that is used to make something that is unpleasant, or not very appealing, appear more positive. For example, instead of saying someone 'died' you might use the softer sounding 'passed away'.

Some euphemisms are also idioms in the English language. An **idiom** is a word or phrase with a particular meaning, which needs to be known to be understood. For instance, if someone 'kicked the bucket', you would need to know the expression already to understand that it means 'to die'.

Euphemisms can be used to cover up the reality of something – hiding information we may need to know about in order to make informed decisions. Orwell uses euphemism in Chapter 9 of *Animal Farm,* where the animals who have already had their food rations cut several times,

THINK–PAIR–SHARE

Can you think of some other common euphemisms?
Write down ten examples and then share and **discuss**
them with a partner. Are there certain subjects, like
death, which are more likely to have euphemisms?
Can you come up with some of your own euphemisms?

and frequently feel hungry, again face a reduction in the
food they receive. It is referred to not as a 'reduction',
however, but as a 'readjustment':

> *'For the time being, certainly, it had been found
> necessary to make a readjustment of rations
> (Squealer always spoke of it as a 'readjustment',
> never as a 'reduction') …'*

ACTIVITY: 'Bigging' it up – selling my home

ATL

- Communication skills: Make inferences and draw
  conclusions; write for different purposes
- Critical-thinking skills: Recognize unstated
  assumptions and bias
- Media literacy skills: Demonstrate awareness of media
  interpretations of events and ideas; communicate
  information and ideas effectively to multiple
  audiences using a variety of media and formats

Loaded language is often used in contexts where
somebody wants to persuade us about something and
feels it may help to make the reality sound very positive.
Buying a property or a holiday or a car are some examples.

Let us look further into how loaded language may be
used in persuading people to buy a house:

1 In 300 words describe your own home as factually
   and objectively as you can. Include where it is, the
   type of residence it is, what rooms it has, and any
   other features.
2 Think about what parts of your home would most
   impress a visitor, then write a list of these.
3 Now think about the least appealing features of your
   house – for example, things that might need to be
   changed or repaired. Write a list of these.
4 Here is a description of a house for sale in Turkey:
   https://goo.gl/pe3i2k.
      Copy down all the examples of loaded language,
   used to make the property as appealing as possible,
   which you can find in the advert. What kinds of words
   do they tend to be?

5 You can find a comparison of some of the loaded
   words and phrases used to sell houses (and what
   they really mean) online – search using terms such as
   'estate agents' and 'really mean'.
      Look again at the advert in step 4. Pick out ten
   details from the description and explain what you
   think each one might really mean.
6 Now it is your turn to write an advertisement for your
   own home. *Do not, however, provide your personal
   address, nor a photograph of your own home –
   create a fictional address for your property and use
   a generic internet photograph of a similar type of
   home. Do not forget to cite the source of this image.*
      Your advertisement should:
   - be formatted in any of the ways you have seen on
     the websites
   - include a list of rooms and amenities and a general
     description of the property, which is written in the
     style of the adverts you have been looking at
   - include somewhere in it the five most, and five
     least, appealing features of your home
   - be 400–500 words in length.

> **Hint**
>
> Remember to use loaded language and euphemisms to describe
> your home and make it irresistible to potential buyers. That
> will mean finding positive ways to describe the least appealing
> features of it.

◆ Assessment opportunities

This activity can be assessed using Criterion B:
Organizing, Criterion C: Producing text and
Criterion D: Using language.

What techniques can be used to make text more persuasive?

Some writers may seek to evoke or provoke an emotional response from an audience. Where this is the case, the loaded language choices may be emotive in nature – often known as **emotive language**. The use of emotive language can be a big clue when you are looking for bias.

THINK–PAIR–SHARE

Look again at Old Major's speech and pick out some examples of the emotive language he uses. What response is Old Major trying to elicit from his audience with this language? How do you think the animals respond as they hear the emotive language? **Discuss** this in pairs.

Imagery can play an important role in creating emotive language. As Old Major describes the deaths that await the animals 'within a year', he describes a scene of torture, pain and execution, and uses onomatopoeia and personification to make the scene more immediate and vivid to them.

ℹ Fact and opinion

A fact is something that can be tested or checked and can ultimately be either verified or proven to be true.

An opinion is a thought, belief or judgement about someone or something, which cannot ultimately be verified.

- Fact – there are ten chapters in *Animal Farm;* the pig who gives the speech in the first chapter is called 'Old Major'.
- Opinion – Boxer is the most interesting character in *Animal Farm;* George Orwell is an amazing writer.

Stating opinion as fact

A further technique that can help create bias in a text is stating opinions as fact. You may have spotted this in Old Major's speech when these comments were made:

> 'No animal in England knows the meaning of happiness or leisure after he is a year old. No animal in England is free. The life of an animal is misery and slavery: that is the plain truth.'

> 'You cows that I see before me, how many thousands of gallons of milk have you given during this last year? And what has happened to that milk which should have been breeding up sturdy calves? Every drop of it has gone down the throats of our enemies. And you hens, how many eggs have you laid in this last year, and how many of those eggs ever hatched into chickens? The rest have all gone to market to bring in money for Jones and his men. And you, Clover, where are those four foals you bore, who should have been the support and pleasure of your old age? Each was sold at a year old — you will never see one of them again.'

The highlighted examples are instances where Old Major makes statements as if they are factual ones, when this is not actually the case. What he says cannot be checked and proven; it actually represents speculation on his part as he does not have enough information to be certain.

Stating something as a fact, however, can give the impression to an audience that it *is* a fact – and therefore cannot be argued with.

It is important when looking for bias in a text to be able form an independent judgement about what we are being told, and a crucial element of this involves being able to differentiate between fact and opinion.

ACTIVITY: A dream full of imagery

■ **ATL**

■ Communication skills: Read critically and for comprehension; make inferences and draw conclusions; interpret a range of discipline-specific symbols

Old Major uses some imagery in his speech, but other speakers use a lot more, often as part of creating emotive language in their speeches in an effort to provoke emotional responses.

Watch Martin Luther King's famous 'I have a dream' speech, given on 28 August 1963. As he talks, King makes use of many of the rhetorical devices we have looked at, and makes substantial use of imagery: www.youtube.com/watch?v=_IB0i6bJIjw.

Two examples of King's rhetoric can be seen below. As you watch the speech, note down any rhetorical devices that you can **identify** in the same manner as the examples. The video has subtitles to help, and a transcript of the speech can also be found here: www.americanrhetoric.com/speeches/mlkihaveadream.htm.

The remainder of the speech is perhaps its most famous part, with the refrain (a phrase that is often repeated) of 'I have a dream'.

■ Martin Luther King

| 'This momentous decree came as a great beacon light of hope to millions of Negro slaves who had been seared in the flames of withering injustice.' | Metaphors – as in the image of the animals facing torture and pain in Old Major's speech, ('But no animal escapes the cruel knife in the end. You young porkers who are sitting in front of me, every one of you will scream your lives out at the block within a year. To that horror we all must come—cows, pigs, hens, sheep, everyone.') 'Seared in the flames of withering justice' – a phrase used to describe the experience of slavery, creates an image of torture and extreme pain – 'seared' means to burn the surface of something while 'withering' visually suggests the effects on people of being 'seared in the flames'. 'Seared', 'flames', 'withering' and 'injustice' are all examples of emotive language.

What type of emotions do you think King is trying to arouse in his listeners through using these words to present an image such as this? The phrase is also a metaphor.

Another metaphor is used to compare the 'decree' – passed by Abraham Lincoln to abolish slavery – to a 'great beacon of light'. The decree brings hope and light to all of those being 'seared in the flames of withering injustice'.

There are thus two types of light, the 'great beacon of light' and the 'flames', which are contrasted, with one having positive connotations, or associations, with 'hope', and the other having negative connotations, with 'injustice'. |
| 'It came as a joyous daybreak to end the long night of their captivity.' | Simile – this time the decree is described as 'daybreak', another image of light, along with of new beginnings. The adjective 'joyous', which is added to 'daybreak', directly states the emotional response caused by the decree. |

Watch this part of the speech now (from 12:25) and **identify** as much imagery and other rhetorical devices as you can. Note too that he also makes use of a further refrain, in addition to 'I have a dream'.

◆ Assessment opportunities

In this activity you have practised skills that are assessed using Criterion A: Analysing.

In what ways can language and texts be powerful?

ACTIVITY: Fact and opinion in speeches

■ ATL

- Critical-thinking skills: Practise observing carefully in order to recognize problems

Severn Cullis-Suzuki is 'The girl who silenced the world for 5 minutes' when, in 1992 at the age of 12, she gave this speech at a major world conference, the Rio Earth Summit. The speech made such an impact that it became well known around the world.

Watch the speech here: https://youtu.be/XdK0uYjy85o, then look at a transcript of the speech, here: https://100777.com/node/1827.

Write down five examples from the speech where facts are stated as facts, and five examples of opinions being stated as if they are facts.

◆ Assessment opportunities

In this activity you have practised skills that are assessed using Criterion A: Analysing.

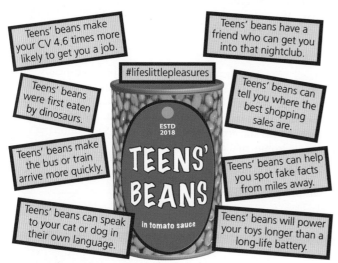

#lifeslittlepleasures

Teens' beans make your CV 4.6 times more likely to get you a job.

Teens' beans have a friend who can get you into that nightclub.

Teens' beans were first eaten by dinosaurs.

Teens' beans can tell you where the best shopping sales are.

Teens' beans make the bus or train arrive more quickly.

Teens' beans can help you spot fake facts from miles away.

Teens' beans can speak to your cat or dog in their own language.

Teens' beans will power your toys longer than a long-life battery.

ESTD 2018

TEENS' BEANS
in tomato sauce

Teens' beans can cheer up anybody's day.

■ Alternative facts?

ACTIVITY: Fact and opinion in advertisements

■ ATL

- Media literacy skills: Understand the impact of media representations and modes of presentation

Advertisements frequently state opinions as facts to try to persuade readers to buy goods. In the advertisements shown here, **identify** where this has been done.

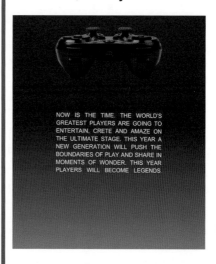

NOW IS THE TIME. THE WORLD'S GREATEST PLAYERS ARE GOING TO ENTERTAIN, CRETE AND AMAZE ON THE ULTIMATE STAGE. THIS YEAR A NEW GENERATION WILL PUSH THE BOUNDARIES OF PLAY AND SHARE IN MOMENTS OF WONDER. THIS YEAR PLAYERS WILL BECOME LEGENDS.

■ PlayStation advertisement

Burger King: https://goo.gl/u8QmHw

Nike: https://goo.gl/9smAom

Advertisers have even been known to play with the idea of fact and opinion, by making claims which are clearly ridiculous but stating them as facts. You might, for instance, find an example of this online by the antiperspirant maker, Dove, which ran a campaign called #alternativefacts. You can see a made-up example of this type of advertisement in the box on the left. Advertisements such as these are satirizing 'alternative facts' – things stated as fact which are no such thing in reality. In doing this, they boost the validity of their own factual statements – as in the statement that 'Teens' beans can cheer up anybody's day' – and their own trustworthiness.

◆ Assessment opportunities

In this activity you have practised skills that are assessed using Criterion A: Analysing.

ACTIVITY: Fact and opinion in newspaper articles

ATL

- Media literacy skills: Understand the impact of media representations and modes of presentation
- Critical-thinking skills: Draw reasonable conclusions and generalizations

International Coastal Clean-up Day: 2.54 lakh* kg trash removed from Mumbai's beaches

Marking the occasion of International Coastal Cleanup day, 3,000 people cleared 2.40 lakh kg of trash from Versova beach after they completed their 100th week of their clean-up.

By HT Correspondent, Hindustan Times. Updated: Sep 17, 2017 02:05 IST.

A total of 2.54 lakh kg of trash was removed from various shorelines by different citizen groups and the coast guard.

Marking the occasion of International Coastal Cleanup day, 3,000 people cleared 2.40 lakh kg of trash from Versova beach after they completed their 100th week of their clean-up. "This was one of the largest beach cleanup drives the country has ever seen," said Afroz Shah, lawyer and beach cleanup crusader who has been leading the movement at Versova since October 2015.

The International Coastal Cleanup day is conducted in various parts of the world on the third Saturday of September every year under the aegis of United Nations Environment Programme (UNEP) and under the aegis of South Asia Co-operative Environment Programme (SACEP) in the South Asian Region.

With seven excavator machines and two tractors, Mumbaiites along with representatives of the UNEP ensured that the north central part of the 3km long beach (Darachiwadi) was cleaned up between 3pm and 5pm. "We thank citizens to help us achieve the quantum of 7.4 million kg trash removed from Versova over 100 weeks," said Shah.

As a part of the Centre's Swachh Bharat Abhiyaan [the name of a campaign being run within India aimed at cleaning up areas such as roads and beaches], the Indian Coast Guard carried out beach cleanup drives at several locations across Maharashtra including Juhu, Girgaum Chowpatty, Dadar, Khanoji Island, Dahanu, Ratnagiri and Murud Janjira beaches. Around 7000 volunteers including NGOs, NCC cadets, NSS, school and college students, staff of various organisations and local community joined hands with the coast guard officers.

"Approximate 5000 kgs of garbage including medical, plastic, jute and Plaster of Paris waste was collected and handed over to BMC for disposal," said an official from the Indian Coast Guard adding that their nationwide campaign resulted in the collection of 68.9 tons (62,505kg) of marine litter. "Debris collection was highest from Mumbai at 8,500 kg and New Mangalore at 6,300 kg."

Residents of Mahim also cleared 700 kg of garbage from their beach. "We had close to 20 people that cleared trash from a 100-patch on the beach. Close to 200 people will be joining another cleanup drive on Sunday," said Anwar Khan, chairman, advance locality management, Mahim Dargah Street.

Civic body officials said the city had come together for one cause and it was a remarkable feat. "The amount of marine litter collected and sent to the city dumping grounds on Saturday was much more than any cleanup witnessed in the past. We welcome the efforts by citizens to strive for clean seas," said a senior civic official.

Why should you care?

Each year, people around the world produce nearly 300 million tons of plastic and a similar amount of plastic waste. Of that, as much as 13 million tons finds its way into our oceans. The plastic wreaks havoc on our fisheries, marine ecosystems and economies, costing up to $13 billion per year in environmental damage.

* lakh – 100,000

https://goo.gl/RB564E

Newspapers contain a mixture of factual information and opinion in different kinds of articles. Below are two newspaper articles on the topic of waste found on coastlines: the first is from India and the second is from Samoa. One of these articles is a news report while the other is an opinion piece.

1 **Identify** which is the news report and which is the opinion article.
2 For each text, what is the writer's main purpose?
3 Which would you expect to be the most objective text? Why?

4 Print out or copy down both articles. For each article, highlight factual sentences in one colour and sentences that are opinion in a different colour. How much of each type of sentence occurs in each article?

DISCUSS

In pairs, answer these questions:
- Apart from the use of fact and opinion sentences, what other differences can you **identify** from these articles between a news report and news opinion article?
- In each article, how many of the opinion statements in each are actually stated as facts?
- What other persuasive techniques can you see in the opinion article?

Doing our bit for the environment

By Mata'afa Keni Lesa, 22 September 2016

The numbers are staggering. Given our limited landmass, and the fear it's only going to become smaller with sea level rise and coastal erosion, the issue is so alarming we cannot be complacent.

In fact, urgent action is needed and that involves everyone. Yes you and me. We all have a part to play.

We are referring to the alarming statistics about waste collected along the coastline and the negligent attitudes, which have contributed to the demise of our environment.

Take for example the figures uncovered last weekend during the International Coastal Cleanup. Samoa's efforts concentrated at Taumeasina and thanks to the efforts of more than 40 people who took part, the findings certainly raised eyebrows.

From a distance of about 1.5km of beach covered, some 2177.5kgs of trash was collected. A break down of what was collected gives us an idea of the behaviours causing the problem. There were 838 plastic bags, 465 food wrappers, 144 plastic forks, knives and spoons, 33 disposable nappies, 1008 plastic and styrofoam food packaging, 39 shoes, 285 plastic drink bottles and 432 aluminum cans.

The question is where did this rubbish come from?

The answer is quite simple. They didn't just drop from the sky. It came from you and me, the negligent human being who has developed quite a bad habit of littering anywhere and everywhere over the years. It includes the silly habit of throwing trash from moving vehicles, dumping anything and everything on the seawall after that night out and all the bad behaviour we have seen over the years. The worry is that these bad behaviours have been passed from generation to generation so they have become so common.

Let me say this again, the astounding amount of trash we've referred to in this piece was collected from just 1.5km covered.

…

Indeed, among the growing environmental challenges staring us in the face today, there is no doubt dealing with waste is by far one of the most pressing. That's because there is waste everywhere. We're confronted by it everywhere we go, and yet some of us don't seem to be bothered very much by it.

Well today is a good time to change our attitudes. The fear is that if we keep producing waste at the rate we've been going for the past years, the future is not going to be pretty.

We need to think about what we can all do to address the issue in our homes, villages and communities.

At the end of the day, it comes down to the individual's actions.

https://goo.gl/tuYCdq

Tone

The way words are spoken and the general character of a piece is known as its **tone**. The tone of a text can help inform us about the purpose of the text, and also about the thoughts and feelings of the writer or speaker. It therefore represents an important part of a piece's style and is always important to consider when reading or listening to a text. What **words are used to describe tone**?

The use of loaded or emotive language, opinion stated as fact and other stylistic decisions, can have a big impact on the final tone of a text.

When the purpose of a piece of writing is to be objective, the tone used for this is also likely to be objective – that is, neutral, factual and unbiased. Personal pronouns and judgemental (or emotive) words will rarely be used and we are unlikely to be able to 'hear' any emotion in how the text is being delivered as it is not influenced by personal feelings or beliefs. An objective tone does not provide any information about the writer in the subject matter, and is more likely to be found in academic or journalistic writing.

The tone in *Animal Farm* – is it all it seems to be?

In the Extension in the 'Finding the right tone' activity you looked at the direct speech of some of the *Animal Farm* characters in order to help gauge their tone. One other important tone, which a reader needs to consider in any fictional text, is that of the narrator. To do this you must be able to **identify** the narrator of a text, as well as their relationship to what is being narrated.

The narrative in *Animal Farm* is written using a third-person narrator. This means that the narrator is not involving him- or herself in the events of the novel, and will use 'he', 'she' and 'they' in relating events.

ACTIVITY: Finding the right tone

■ ATL

- Information literacy skills: Access information to be informed and inform others
- Media literacy skills: Locate and evaluate information from a variety of sources and media

There are many short online videos that explain tone. In pairs, find and watch three to five videos on the topic of tone, which are intended for students of middle-school age. The videos should be three to ten minutes long.

- **Watch each video and discuss with your partner how well you think they explain tone for an audience of middle school students. With your partner, choose the one you feel is most informative, and would most clearly and effectively teach tone to your class.**
- **Join with two other pairs to make a group of six. Each pair should show their chosen video to the rest of the group and then, together you should all choose the video you think best explains tone.**
- **Your teacher will compile a list of the best videos, which can be shared with all students.**

◆ Assessment opportunities

In this activity you have practised skills that are assessed using Criterion A: Analysing.

EXTENSION

In your larger groups of six look back at *Animal Farm* and read out loud some dialogue from key moments in the book. Which character is speaking? How would you best describe their tone?

ACTIVITY: Setting the tone

■ ATL

■ Communication skills: Read critically and for comprehension; make inferences and draw conclusions

In a table like the one below, use bullet points to sum up the key differences between an objective tone and one that is not objective.

An objective tone …	A non-objective tone …
• Does not use personal pronouns such as 'I', 'we', 'our'	• Often uses personal pronouns
•	•

Now compare your bullet points in each column to the news report and news opinion article from the 'Fact and opinion in newspaper articles' activity. In each article, **identify** any elements of an objective and a non-objective tone. Make sure you **identify** key sentences and paragraphs and use these as evidence to support your points. What does each quote suggest about the speaker's attitude? Remember that quotation marks within an article indicate speech from someone other than the writer of the article.

◆ Assessment opportunities

In this activity you have practised skills that are assessed using Criterion A: Analysing.

Third-person narration can be used in different ways and for different purposes:

■ **Third-person omniscient narration**: this is also known as 'unlimited' narration. With this type of narration the narrator can see everything, including anything that all of the characters see, hear, think and feel. The word 'omniscient' means 'all-knowing'.
■ **Third-person limited narration**: in this type of narration the narrator tells the story from the point of view of one character. A reader gains an insight into the perspectives, thoughts and feelings of that character, therefore, but not of others.
■ **Third-person objective narration**: here a narrator recounts facts about what characters say and do, but does not say anything about their thoughts or feelings.

Look at the passage below, which comes early in *Animal Farm* when the animals have driven out Jones and are looking around the farmstead.

> Then they filed back to the farm buildings and halted in silence outside the door of the farmhouse. That was theirs too, but they were frightened to go inside. After a moment, however, Snowball and Napoleon butted the door open with their shoulders and the animals entered in single file, walking with the utmost care for fear of disturbing anything. They tiptoed from room to room, afraid to speak above a whisper and gazing with a kind of awe at the unbelievable luxury, at the beds with their feather mattresses, the looking-glasses, the horsehair sofa, the Brussels carpet, the lithograph of Queen Victoria over the drawing-room mantelpiece. They were just coming down the stairs when Mollie was discovered to be missing. Going back, the others found that she had remained behind in the best bedroom. She had taken a piece of blue ribbon from Mrs Jones's dressing-table, and was holding it against her shoulder and admiring herself in the glass in a very foolish manner. The others reproached her sharply, and they went outside. Some hams hanging in the kitchen were taken out for burial, and the barrel of beer in the scullery was stove in with a kick from Boxer's hoof, otherwise nothing in the house was touched. A unanimous resolution was passed on the spot that the farmhouse should be preserved as a museum. All were agreed that no animal must ever live there.

THINK–PAIR–SHARE

After reading the *Animal Farm* extract, write down notes about the following questions. **Discuss** your notes in pairs, and then share them in groups of four or six.

● **Which type of third-person narration is being used?**
● **Describe the tone used by Orwell in this passage.**
● **How objective is the tone?**
● **How can you tell?**
● **Why do you think Orwell has adopted this tone for the novel?**

What is the role of the media if we cannot trust the information it gives us?

You will have noticed that the tone of *Animal Farm* is quite matter-of-fact, and seems fairly objective overall. While there are some references to thoughts and feelings, much of the narration is factual in stating what is said and done by the animals. It focuses largely on external details and does not seem to make judgements about what is being narrated.

This type of narration is adopted throughout the novel; however, the novel itself is not a factual one, but an allegory. *Animal Farm* is in fact criticizing the hypocrisy of those who might come to power, and then behave in the same way as or worse than those whom they replace, as symbolized at the end of the novel when the animals look into the farmhouse at the humans and pigs and cannot tell which is which. In particular, Orwell is criticizing how, as he sees it, this had happened particularly in the case of the Russian Revolution.

His purpose, therefore, is not to be objective, but to be extremely critical; the novel is a good example of how something may be made to sound quite objective in tone when it is in fact presenting a particular opinion. How does Orwell achieve this?

George Orwell often uses an ironic tone in *Animal Farm*, particularly in the differences between the perceptions and beliefs of the animals, and the reality they find themselves in, as can be seen:

The animals believe they are free and masters of their own farm, but they are in fact little more than slaves once again: working incredibly hard, with little choice in the matter, and by order of the pigs.

The animals think that everything they do is for their own benefit, when it is in fact largely for the benefit of the pigs. The pigs have already shown themselves to be 'idle', and will turn out to be exactly the same as the 'idle thieving human beings' who were driven out. This reference might therefore also be an example of dramatic irony.

All that year the animals worked like slaves. But they were happy in their work; they grudged no effort or sacrifice, well aware that everything that they did was for the benefit of themselves and those of their kind who would come after them, and not for a pack of idle thieving human beings. Throughout the spring and summer they worked a sixty-hour week, and in August Napoleon announced that there would be work on Sunday afternoons as well. This work was strictly voluntary, but any animal who absented himself from it would have his rations cut by half.

To volunteer is to do something without being forced or paid to do it; however, the cut in rations effectively forces the animals to work or starve.

EXTENSION: IRONY

There are three main types of irony: verbal irony, situational irony and dramatic irony. Research each of type of irony and then look for examples of them in *Animal Farm*, and one other book of your own choice. Why might an author use one type of irony over another? What is the impact of the use of irony in the examples you have found?

Language and Literature for the IB MYP 4&5: *by Concept*

ACTIVITY: Read all about it!

The Valley Report is an online fake news site that knowingly puts out phony news: **https://thevalleyreport.com/**. People who know of the website are also aware that it puts out news that is 'fake'. Dave Weasel, a writer at the website, says that 'Most of the people that share [a fake article] do not read it'.

1 **Read some of the articles on the website. Note down any key features and styles used by the articles to appear genuine – in particular, consider the articles' content and layout.**
2 **Does it matter if people share articles like this, regardless of how untrue or inaccurate they are? Why?**
3 **Is it ethical for people to write deliberately fake articles and share them? Does it matter?**

What might we expect when we read articles in a mainstream popular national newspaper?

The following story appeared in the online website of the UK's most widely read newspaper, the *Daily Mail.* More than 200 million people worldwide browse the site each month. The story was also carried in a number of other mainstream popular UK daily newspapers: https://goo.gl/PXTCY1.

4 **Do you think this story is genuine? What makes you say that?**
5 **Write a list of things you might look for to check that a newspaper story is genuine.**

When answering question 4, you may have noted down the article's mention of 'Jungle Creations' and the viral content company's owner Jamie Bolding.

In fact these comments were added to the article only later, when questions began to be asked about the authenticity of the video, as in this article: https://goo.gl/eKNdL4.

6 **In this online Information Age, what impact does the ability to edit and change information have on an audience?**
7 **Is it ethical to edit content without informing an audience that it has changed?**
8 **Think about some of the things you might look for to check that a newspaper story is genuine.**

EXTENSION: CAN YOU TRUST THE NEWS?

An investigation was held into what people wanted from digital news sources, and what kinds of 'indicators' might help to flag up a source as being 'trustworthy'. Find and read the investigation's report (search '**SCU Trust Project Summit Report**') online.

After reading the report and exploring the website, which suggestions do you feel would make readers most trust the online articles? Note down the suggestions and, from this list, choose five things that you will look for when you next read an article online. These should be the five things you think will tell you most about the trustworthiness of the information you are reading.

Our conceptual questions for this unit ask about who controls information, and in what ways language and texts can be powerful. Creators of texts can control what we see and hear, and make language and texts powerful enough to make us respond to them in different ways – sometimes even leading us to believe things that are not true.

'Creativity' according to the MYP guide for language and literature is described as 'the process with which the individual engages, and the impact of the final product on the audience'. There are, as we have seen, a lot of ways in which it is possible to be creative with language and information presentation. Such content styling can have a particular impact on an audience, but is it always ethical?

How can we engage with, and respond to, media communication in a more informed way?

Animal Farm asks its readers 'should we immediately believe everything we see, read or hear? And what can happen if one does so?' On the farm the animals accept almost everything they hear, without thinking about anything more deeply, or questioning it. Orwell shows how the consequences of this are extremely serious for the animals. For example, despite working incredibly hard for Animal Farm, Boxer is immediately sent to the knacker's yard as soon as he becomes ill; by the time he realizes what is happening he is too weak, and it is too late, to escape.

Boxer is unable to analyse, evaluate or synthesize (bring together ideas to create understanding) any of the information he sees or hears. All of these are highly important critical-thinking skills for understanding and making sense of a situation:

> 'Even Boxer was vaguely troubled. He set his ears back, shook his forelock several times, and tried hard to marshal his thoughts; but in the end he could not think of anything to say.'

As a result, he accepts everything, does not use his strength at all, or the respect he has from others, and follows two mottos – 'I must work harder' and 'Napoleon is always right' – which directly contribute to his own death. The animals' general lack of ability to use critical-thinking skills and to question and think more critically about what they hear (and read), are major factors in the consequences they eventually suffer.

In an age, now, of far more information, how much do you think it matters to think about and question what we see, read and hear?

DISCUSS

Find five examples of unquestioning acceptance from five different chapters in the novel.

What are the consequences of each example? Who suffers most? Why?

ACTIVITY: Boxer's character

■ ATL

- ■ Critical-thinking skills: Evaluate evidence and arguments; draw reasonable conclusions and generalizations

In the narrative of Boxer we learn a lot about the horse and his character; he has strength enough to take on the pigs and dogs if he wished, and the enduring respect of the other farm animals, however that is not all. What evidence is there that:

a   **Boxer cannot prioritize things that should be most important?**
b   **Boxer does not think about things enough?**

Write a paragraph for each question, detailing any evidence you find, then share your work in pairs. Together, **discuss** and consider what the consequences of these aspects of Boxer's character are.

■ What are the negative aspects of Boxer's character?

◆ Assessment opportunities

In this activity you have practised skills that are assessed using Criterion A: Analysing.

EXTENSION: CRITICAL THINKING

Academics from Stanford University conducted research into students' ability to judge the credibility of information that pours out of their smartphones, tablets and computers. What would you expect their findings to be? Find the report online (search 'Evaluating Information Online Reasoning') and, after you have read it through, **discuss** it with your classmates.

Can you detect any bias in the research? How have the researchers tried to avoid bias? Why is this important?

Researchers suggest that if people cannot evaluate information, they cannot make informed decisions, and that this could impact on our society in unwanted ways. Not being aware of what is really happening means not being able to do anything about a situation, because nothing is noticed until it is too late. This is exactly what happens in *Animal Farm*.

Take action

! One way to take action is to help people better evaluate the information they receive, and to promote understanding on how to perceive bias.

! Collect a number of fake news and real news examples then, using these, conduct a survey in your school or local area to test whether your community can spot fake news.

! Produce a one-page informative poster that can be handed out to participants after they have taken part in the survey. The poster should include advice and a list of five key things to look for when spotting fake news, as well as one or two examples.

REPORTING THE NEWS – WHO MIGHT SAY WHAT, AND WHY?

A particular area in *Animal Farm* in which the reporting of events becomes increasingly unethical is that of the Battle of the Cowshed, and in the presentation of Snowball. His character is used by Orwell to illustrate, among other things, how language can be used to try to manipulate how we might perceive events and others, and what we might be led to believe about them if we accept what we are told unquestioningly. We are given the following description of the battle in Chapter 4:

> This had long been expected, and all preparations had been made. Snowball, who had studied an old book of Julius Caesar's campaigns which he had found in the farmhouse, was in charge of the defensive operations. He gave his orders quickly, and in a couple of minutes every animal was at his post.

> As the human beings approached the farm buildings, Snowball launched his first attack… However, this was only a light skirmishing manoeuvre, intended to create a little disorder… Snowball now launched his second line of attack. Muriel, Benjamin, and all the sheep, with Snowball at the head of them, rushed forward and prodded and butted the men from every side, while Benjamin turned round and lashed at them with his small hoofs. But once again the men, with their sticks and their hobnailed boots, were too strong for them; and suddenly, at a squeal from Snowball, which was the signal for retreat, all the animals turned and fled through the gateway into the yard.

> The men gave a shout of triumph. They saw, as they imagined, their enemies in flight, and they rushed after them in disorder. This was just what Snowball had intended. As soon as they were well inside the yard, the three horses, the three cows and the rest of the pigs, who had been lying in ambush in the cowshed, suddenly emerged in their rear, cutting them off. Snowball now gave the signal for the charge. He himself dashed straight for Jones. Jones saw him coming, raised his gun and fired. The pellets scored bloody streaks along Snowball's back, and a sheep dropped dead. Without halting for an instant, Snowball flung his fifteen stone against Jones's legs. Jones was hurled into a pile of dung and his gun flew out of his hands. But the most terrifying spectacle of all was Boxer, rearing up on his hind legs and striking out with his great iron-shod hoofs like a stallion. His very first blow took a stable-lad from Foxwood on the skull and stretched him lifeless in the mud. At the sight, several men dropped their sticks and tried to run. Panic overtook them, and the next moment all the animals together were chasing them round and round the yard.

> …

> At the graveside Snowball made a little speech, emphasizing the need for all animals to be ready to die for Animal Farm if need be.

> The animals decided unanimously to create a military decoration, 'Animal Hero, First Class', which was conferred there and then on Snowball and Boxer.

Who controls the information we consume, and to what purpose?

DISCUSS

1   How and why is Squealer able to persuade the animals that his version of the Battle of the Cowshed, and the actions of Snowball and Napoleon, is correct?
2   What motives do Squealer and Napoleon have for changing the account of what happened?

ACTIVITY: TV reporting

■ ATL

- Communication skills: Use a variety of speaking techniques to communicate with a variety of audiences
- Information literacy skills: Understand the benefits and limitations of personal sensory learning preferences when accessing, processing and recalling information; use critical-literacy skills to analyse and interpret media communications

Imagine that you are a TV news reporter who has been tasked with reporting back on the Battle of the Cowshed. Everyone is talking about the part played by Snowball.

THINK–PAIR–SHARE

Choose three character traits that you think most appropriately describe Snowball and his actions in this episode. **Discuss** the words you have chosen with a partner; give your reasons for choosing each word, and any evidence you have to support these choices.

Your news report will include short (one-minute) interviews with Snowball, as well as one human and one other animal who were involved in the battle. Write a script for each interview and ensure that the three words you chose to describe Snowball are used in the dialogue. It does not matter which interviewee uses each word, but make sure they explain why they have chosen to describe Snowball in the way they have.

In a group of four, share the ideas you have had for your reporter scripts and interviews. Work together to choose the best interviews and combine these into a final version of the report. Remember, the main focus should be Snowball's role in the battle.

Your group is now going to act out the report interviews. Each group member will play one of the following roles: reporter, Snowball, animal, human. Rehearse the whole TV report as needed then film a final version, which could be shown to the class as a whole.

◆ Assessment opportunities

In this activity you have practised skills that are assessed using Criterion A: Analysing, Criterion C: Producing text and Criterion D: Using language.

The words chosen to describe Snowball in your TV news report are likely to be positive ones, such as 'courageous'.

In Chapter 5, however, Snowball is chased from the farm and Squealer warns the animals: 'as to the Battle of the Cowshed, I believe the time will come when we shall find that Snowball's part in it was much exaggerated.'

Chapters 7, 8 and 9 give very different accounts of Snowball's role in the Battle of the Cowshed. Read through these chapters again and **identify** any descriptions of Snowball's role that differ from the courageous description we were originally given.

The later accounts of the Battle of the Cowshed given by Squealer and Napoleon – a great event in the history of Animal Farm – are biased. The two characters rewrite a major battle in the farm's history for their own purposes of discrediting Snowball and encouraging greater admiration for Napoleon. This is an episode that shows the importance of considering who the author of a text or speech is, and what their purpose may be in presenting their text.

ACTIVITY: Different perspectives

Unlike Boxer or Snowball, we hear nothing of Squealer or Napoleon during the Battle of the Cowshed. We assume they are somewhere on the sidelines, although we are not told whether they were waiting, watching or hiding from the battle during this time.

1 **Imagine that both Boxer and Squealer have been asked to be historians and write an historical account of the Battle of the Cowshed for posterity.**
  Write both Boxer and Squealer's versions of the events of the battle (each should be 300–500 words), then swap the accounts you have written with someone else in the class.
2 **Using your partner's two written accounts as evidence, write your own report of the battle. These two historical accounts are the *only* sources you are using to write the report, and so you cannot include any information not contained in the sources.**
  How different is the account you have just written from the events narrated in Chapter 3?

This activity might give you some idea of the way in which things can change between actual events, and how they may be presented in writing. It may also have indicated some of the reasons for that, which may have to be filtered when we read something and are looking for accuracy and truth.

◆ Assessment opportunities

In this activity you have practised skills that are assessed using Criterion A: Analysing, Criterion C: Producing text and Criterion D: Using language.

The Battle of the Cowshed and the later changes in accounts of this illustrate some of the problems in recording events, and then in using such records later in exploring what happened in the course of such events. This is a topic that you might **explore** in more detail in an interdisciplinary way where sources are used in your individuals and societies classes.

Bias and objectivity within a text

In order to **identify** any potential bias within a text, make sure to consider the following questions:

• Who is presenting the account? Who is the source?
• What is their relationship to what they are relating?
• How neutral or objective can a source be? How neutral or objective might be an account of the Battle of the Cowshed by Boxer, for instance? How might he present Snowball or himself? How might a human involved in the battle present the same events?
• What biases might individuals have in how they present these events? Even when sources appear to be on the same side, they might have different motivations. This can affect how they present the events that took place, resulting in very different perspectives. Note how in *Animal Farm* the planned and strategic withdrawal of the animals in the first part of the Battle of the Cowshed (which allowed other animals lying in wait to ambush the chasing humans) was presented by Squealer in these terms: 'Do you not remember how, just at the moment when Jones and his men had got inside the yard, Snowball suddenly turned and fled, and many animals followed him?'

▼ Links to: History

Historical revisionism is the reinterpretation of the history of a country, person or place. Past events are looked at from a new perspective, and can result in history 'changing'. Why does historical revisionism happen? When does this happen? Is it a good or bad thing?

▼ Links to: History

During times of war, countries often create a huge amount of **propaganda**. This is literature and other media that is biased in favour of the country that has produced it, and is used to influence local and international opinion. Does wartime propaganda use the same techniques and stylistic devices that we have identified in *Animal Farm*? Does all wartime propaganda have the same purpose?

How can an audience engage with online texts in an age of mass information?

ACTIVITY: Blog post – checking my sources

■ ATL

- Information literacy skills: Use critical-literacy skills to analyse and interpret media communications
- Media literacy skills: Understand the impact of media representation and presentation

We have looked at different aspects of the Information Age, including what may motivate and shape the information we receive, and what we may do in engaging with it.

Write a blog post of your own, of 300–500 words, which reflects on your own social media habits and attitudes towards information you come across there. You might include the following:

- **What do you think are the important things to think about and look for when someone is looking at information that they find on social media?**
- Which social media sites do you tend to use the most? These will come from the list that you came up with earlier.
- How do you feel you use critical thinking yourself when you engage with information on social media sites?
- What do you think are your own good habits when you engage with information on social media?
- What do you think are the habits you feel you should change, in how you engage with information on social media?
- Which two sentences in your post are the most important? Highlight these in bold.

◆ Assessment opportunities

In this activity you have practised skills that are assessed using Criterion B: Organizing, Criterion C: Producing text and Criterion D: Using language.

! Take action

! Look up the information literacy and media literacy skills within the IB 'Research' category of the Approaches to Learning programme in the MYP. We have looked at many of them in the course of this chapter.

! Choose the five skills you feel are most important to you, and which you would like to prioritize. Copy out and complete the table, reflecting on the following questions:
- ◆ Do I know what this skill means in practice?
- ◆ Which subjects do I use this skill in?
- ◆ How/where can I practise this skill more?

Priority skills	What does it mean in practice?	In which subjects do I use this skill?	How/where can I practise this skill more?

! By using this table in such a way, you can **create** your own action plan for working on important skills of information and media literacy. In order to do so most effectively, do not hesitate to ask your teachers about what a skill means, how you might practise a skill, and so on.

ACTIVITY: Panel discussion

What responsibilities should people have in terms of information that is posted on the internet?

In a group of four, assign each member one of the following roles: writer of fake news, member of the public, schoolteacher, newspaper reporter/editor.

Read the following articles then, in the role you have been given, note down what you feel your responsibilities are or should be (in a context of 'fake news' being published on the internet).

https://goo.gl/9Vi9hG

https://goo.gl/fB82xF

https://goo.gl/DFnjkZ

https://goo.gl/BrxRbQ

In your group, copy the table below onto poster paper, then each add your notes to the appropriate boxes.

EXTENSION

Split the class into four new groups based on the previously assigned roles; for example, all the fake news writers should be in one group, all the schoolteachers are in another group, and so on.

After giving each group time to prepare points and arguments, hold a panel discussion at the front of the classroom. A spokesperson from each new group should be nominated to represent their role, and debate the possible responsibilities of each party in relation to 'fake news' in front of the class.

A writer of fake news articles		A member of the public – the 'audience' of information	
My responsibilities	Other people's responsibilities	My responsibilities	Other people's responsibilities

A school teacher		A newspaper reporter or editor	
My responsibilities	Other people's responsibilities	My responsibilities	Other people's responsibilities

SOME SUMMATIVE TASKS TO TRY

Use these tasks to apply and extend your learning in this chapter. These tasks are designed so that you can evaluate your learning at different levels of achievement in the Language and literature criteria.

Task 1: Speech analysis of *Animal Farm*

Read the following passage from *Animal Farm,* which includes a speech made by Squealer, and then write a formal essay of 800–1,000 words in which you answer the following questions:

■ What techniques does Squealer use in order to try to persuade the other animals of his point of view?
■ What other reasons are there for why the animals are persuaded by speeches such as this in the novel?

The mystery of where the milk went to was soon cleared up. It was mixed every day into the pigs' mash. The early apples were now ripening, and the grass of the orchard was littered with windfalls. The animals had assumed as a matter of course that these would be shared out equally; one day, however, the order went forth that all windfalls were to be collected and brought to the harness-room for the use of the pigs. At this some of the other animals murmured, but it was no use. All the pigs were in full agreement on this point, even Snowball and Napoleon. Squealer was sent to make the necessary explanations to the others.

'Comrades!' he cried. 'You do not imagine, I hope, that we pigs are doing this in a spirit of selfishness and privilege? Many of us actually dislike milk and apples. I dislike them myself. Our sole object in taking these things is to preserve our health. Milk and apples (this has been proved by Science, comrades), contain substances absolutely necessary to the well-being of a pig. We pigs are brainworkers.

The whole management and organization of this farm depend on us. Day and night we are watching over your welfare. It is for *your* sake that we drink that milk and eat those apples. Do you know what would happen if we pigs failed in our duty? Jones would come back! Yes, Jones would come back! Surely, comrades,' cried Squealer almost pleadingly, skipping from side to side and whisking his tail, 'surely if there is no one among you who wants to see Jones come back?'

Now if there was one thing that the animals were completely certain of, it was that they did not want Jones back. When it was put to them in this light, they had no more to say. The importance of keeping the pigs in good health was all too obvious. So it was agreed without further argument that the milk and the windfall apples (and also the main crop of apples when they ripened) should be reserved for the pigs alone.

Animal Farm – Chapter 3

Extract A

Within a few weeks Snowball's plans for the windmill were fully worked out. The mechanical details came mostly from three books which had belonged to Mr Jones – *One Thousand Useful Things to Do About the House, Every Man His Own Bricklayer,* and *Electricity for Beginners.* Snowball used as his study a shed which had once been used for incubators and had a smooth wooden floor, suitable for drawing on. He was closeted there for hours at a time. With his books held open by a stone, and with a piece of chalk gripped between the knuckles of his trotter, he would move rapidly to and fro, drawing in line after line and uttering little whimpers of excitement. Gradually the plans grew into a complicated mass of cranks and cog-wheels, covering more than half the floor, which the other animals found completely unintelligible but very impressive. All of them came to look at Snowball's drawings at least once a day. Even the hens and ducks came, and were at pains not to tread on the chalk marks. Only Napoleon held aloof. He had declared himself against the windmill from the start. One day, however, he arrived unexpectedly to examine the plans. He walked heavily round the shed, looked closely at every detail of the plans and snuffed at them once or twice, then stood for a little while contemplating them out of the corner of his eye; then suddenly he lifted his leg, urinated over the plans and walked out without uttering a word.

Animal Farm – Chapter 5

THIS TASK CAN BE USED TO EVALUATE YOUR LEARNING IN CRITERION D

Task 2: Evaluating a non-fiction speech

Twenty years after her appearance at the 1992 Earth Summit, Severn Cullis-Suzuki returned to Rio and made a further speech. Watch it here: **https://goo.gl/6zKSvz**. Make sure you look at the second speech on the page, which is Severn's later speech.

Evaluate the speech using Criteria C and D of the Language and literature criteria, and the additional details of these in the task-specific clarification for these criteria.

For this you should prepare feedback in the form of a report of 500–1,000 words on the speech to give to Severn Cullis-Suzuki.

Extract B

That evening Squealer explained privately to the other animals that Napoleon had never in reality been opposed to the windmill. On the contrary, it was he who had advocated it in the beginning, and the plan which Snowball had drawn on the floor of the incubator shed had actually been stolen from among Napoleon's papers. The windmill was, in fact, Napoleon's own creation. Why, then, asked somebody, had he spoken so strongly against it? Here Squealer looked very shy. That, he said, was Comrade Napoleon's cunning. He had seemed to oppose the windmill, simply as a manoeuvre to get rid of Snowball, who was a dangerous character and a bad influence. Now that Snowball was out of the way the plan could go forward without his interference. This, said Squealer, was something called tactics. He repeated a number of times, 'Tactics, comrades, tactics!' skipping round and whisking his tail with a merry laugh. The animals were not certain what the word meant, but Squealer spoke so persuasively, and the three dogs who happened to be with him growled so threateningly, that they accepted his explanation without further questions.

Animal Farm – Chapter 5

THIS TASK CAN BE USED TO EVALUATE YOUR LEARNING IN CRITERION C AND CRITERION D

Task 3: A comparative commentary

Compare-and-contrast writing involves the following:

1 What do the two texts have in common about what they are talking about?
2 Where does each text talk about something similar, but in a different way? Where does the author in each case:
 ■ include something which is not in the other text?
 ■ emphasize something more or less than in the other text?

In the case of the two passages above, you will be looking quite a lot at how the characters of Snowball and Napoleon in particular are presented, and how they are compared each time. How are they different in character? How are they different as leaders?

How the other animals act towards them in each passage is also important to consider.

> **Hint**
> Guidance on how to **compare and contrast** can be found on page 243.

Task 4: Literature essay

Two types of character often found in works of literature
are 1) a trusted friend, and 2) a supporter who ends up
betraying them.

Boxer is the trusted friend in *Animal Farm,* and Napoleon
is the betraying supporter. In what ways are these two
characters presented in the novel, and what do you think
Orwell may have been trying to show by this?

Write an essay of 800–1,000 words that addresses both
questions posed. Consider the following points when
planning and writing the essay:

■ This question asks what a writer has created within
a text, how they have done that (the techniques and
literary devices used), and why they have done that –
what is the purpose for including elements of a text in
the way that has been done?

■ The first part of the question asks about how Boxer
and Napoleon are presented in the novel. Use details
from the text to provide evidence for each point you
make.

☐ In what ways is Boxer presented as a 'trusted
friend'? Whose friend is he? Who trusts him? Why
do they trust him?

☐ In what ways *should* Napoleon be an ally to Boxer?
How might Napoleon be expected to help and
support Boxer? In what way(s) does Napoleon betray
Boxer?

■ The second part of the question asks about Orwell's
reasons for creating, including and showing these two
characters in the ways that he did. (Remember, as
well as being an allegory, *Animal Farm* explores other
themes and questions.)

Look closely at evidence in the text, and then interpret that
evidence. You should analyse and evaluate evidence in the
text, then bring together ideas and evidence to establish the
purpose of the text.

THIS TASK CAN BE USED TO EVALUATE YOUR LEARNING IN CRITERION B, CRITERION C AND CRITERION D

Task 5: School magazine information article

Write a feature article for your school magazine in which you warn readers about the dangers of 'fake news' on the internet. Your article should help readers **identify** whether something is genuine and how biased it may be. It should also explain:

■ what 'fake news' is, and why there is so much of it on the internet

■ why this is an important issue, and why it is unlikely to go away any time soon

■ what individuals such as newspaper reporters and editors, and internet companies such as Facebook, Google and Twitter, can and should do about fake news

■ what could be done in schools (by teachers, and by students themselves) to combat fake news. Ensure you refer in this section to Approaches to Learning skills in the information and media literacy skill lists.

Your article should conclude by summarizing the nature and dangers of fake news, and the importance of being able to recognize it and deal with it appropriately when we encounter it.

You should write 500–1,000 words; the work should be closer to 1,000 words in order to contain the range of points and details that are needed for highest levels of achievement in the assessment criteria.

Reflection

We have explored some different ways of being creative with language in order to try to persuade an audience to respond in a particular way. We have looked therefore at different text types, such as rhetorical speeches, news articles and advertisements, and at examples of how language can be used. We have also considered the impact of the Information Age, and the multiple sources of information now available to us, along with how that might need to be critically viewed in order to try to verify its authenticity, purpose and usefulness.

Use this table to reflect on your own learning in this chapter.						
Questions we asked	**Answers we found**	**Any further questions now?**				
Factual:						
Conceptual:						
Debatable:						
Approaches to learning you used in this chapter	**Description – what new skills did you learn?**	**How well did you master the skills?**				
		Novice	Learner	Practitioner	Expert	
Communication skills						
Collaboration skills						
Information literacy skills						
Media literacy skills						
Critical-thinking skills						
Creative-thinking skills						
Learner profile attribute(s)	Reflect on the importance of being a thinker for your learning in this chapter.					
Thinkers						

7 Why travel?

○ **Journeys** provide insights into a range of **contexts** and **perspectives**, and scope for significant **discovery**, learning and **self-expression**.

CONSIDER THESE QUESTIONS:

Factual: Why do people travel? How are different experiences of travel expressed?

Conceptual: What can we learn about the world and ourselves through travel? What do we reveal of ourselves through expressing our experiences of travel? What is involved in 'adapting' to a new context?

Debatable: To what extent do the advantages of travel outweigh the downsides? To what extent is travel always inevitably a 'learning experience' of some kind?

Now **share and compare** your thoughts and ideas with your partner, or with the whole class.

○ IN THIS CHAPTER, WE WILL …

■ **Find out** why and how people travel, and the different ways in which those experiences may be expressed.

■ **Explore** how people might try to adapt to different contexts, and the value of trying to do so; along with what is involved in safe and responsible travel.

■ **Take action** by evaluating our own opportunities for travel, and how to maximize the benefits we gain from those; by travelling safely and responsibly when we do travel anywhere.

■ These Approaches to Learning (ATL) skills will be useful …

■ Communication skills
■ Collaboration skills
■ Information literacy skills
■ Critical-thinking skills
■ Creative-thinking skills
■ Transfer skills

◆ Assessment opportunities in this chapter:

◆ **Criterion A:** Analysing
◆ **Criterion B:** Organizing
◆ **Criterion C:** Producing text
◆ **Criterion D:** Using language

We will reflect on this learner profile attribute ...

- Risk-takers – explore what it means to take informed risks in order to broaden experience and international-mindedness; explore how to approach uncertain contexts and challenges through careful planning and forethought; develop greater adaptability and resilience.

KEY WORDS

anticipation	mood
atonement	motif
attribute	personification
literary	simile
metaphor	symbolism

ACTIVITY: Leaving on a jet plane

■ ATL

- ■ Creative-thinking skills: Use brainstorming and visual diagrams to generate new ideas and inquiries

If you could go anywhere in the world tomorrow, where would it be, and why?

Imagine you are at a huge international airport. Planes fly from this airport to every country in the world. You have not bought your ticket yet, and you can go anywhere at all.

Where would you like to fly to? Brainstorm locations you would like to visit, then pick your top three destinations and, using the table below as a template, write them down, along with the reasons why you want to fly to these places.

My top three flights are going to ...	because ...
1	
2	
3	

Now share your destinations and reasons with two or three others in your class.

◆ Assessment opportunities

In this activity you have practised skills that are assessed using Criterion B: Organizing.

It is better to see something once than hear about it a thousand times.

To travel is to discover that everyone is wrong about other countries.
– Aldous Huxley

Travelling allows you to become many different versions of yourself.

Travel makes one modest, you see what a tiny place you occupy in the world.
– Gustave Flaubert

■ There are many different reasons why someone might want to travel

7   Why travel?   163

Why do people travel?

ACTIVITY: Reasons why people travel

■ ATL

- ■ Communication skills: Make inferences and draw conclusions
- ■ Creative-thinking skills: Consider multiple alternatives, including those that might be unlikely or impossible

How many different reasons can you think of as to why people travel?

- Using the table below as a template, list in the left-hand column examples of ways in which you have travelled and, in the right-hand column, write down the purpose for each example.

Example of 'travel'	Purpose of that travel
Holiday	To see somewhere new
Travel to school	To reach a specific location
Bike ride	For exercise; to explore

- Share your examples with others in a group of three or four, and add any other ideas to your table that you may have thought about as a result of looking at the ideas of others.
- Next, research some images that show people travelling in some way. Use them to make a collage and, beside each image you use, write down the nature of the travel you think is being shown, and your reason.
- Your group might then put their collages together on poster paper for classroom display.

◆ Assessment opportunities

In this activity you have practised skills that are assessed using Criterion A: Analysing.

As the previous activity may have shown, people travel for all kinds of different reasons, sometimes out of choice, and sometimes because they have to.

One of the most common reasons for travelling out of choice is when people go on holiday.

A 'holiday' can vary a great deal but, for many, the kind of image they have in mind may be something like the destination shown in the photograph.

■ Is this your dream holiday destination?

ACTIVITY: Travelling for pleasure

Travel companies spend a lot of time and money trying to persuade people that they want to pay for a holiday.

In pairs, find some examples of holiday travel brochures online. Within the brochure find an advertisement for a destination like the one pictured and write down in a table, like the example below, as many points as you can about how the image and text are trying to be persuasive (consider some of the persuasive techniques we looked at in previous chapters).

Points about the advert's text and images	Why this is persuasive

The brochure is using a number of advertising techniques in its efforts to persuade people to buy the holiday shown. These include appeals to:

- pathos (emotion)
- logos (logic)
- ethos (credibility).

Watch the following video, which explains pathos, logos and ethos, and how advertisements use these techniques: https://youtu.be/FeCz5fy02JE.

EXTENSION

Once you have watched the video, look again at the travel brochure advertisement you found online. What details or elements can you see that are examples of pathos, logos or ethos? Record them in a table like this:

Pathos	Logos	Ethos

◆ Assessment opportunities

In this activity you have practised skills that are assessed using Criterion A: Analysing.

MOOD, THEME, SETTING

Both static adverts and video adverts often try to evoke a particular mood in their audience in an effort to be more persuasive.

As with tone, mood is a particular emotional or psychological state advertisers try to create in their audience by using positive or negative descriptive words. Images can also be used in the same way.

DISCUSS

What kind of mood might a holiday advertisement be expected to try to provoke in an audience? Can you find any examples in the holiday advertisements you have already looked at?

The theme of an advertisement can also contribute to its mood, or to the general ambience (similar to atmosphere) of a scene, situation or environment.

One important theme is often that of 'time'. Search online for '**time for a holiday**', or follow the link to watch a holiday advertisement that focuses on the theme of time: **www.youtube.com/watch?v=O8B1ZNv9m4s**.

DISCUSS

What does the advertisement have to say about time? Is time the key theme? Are there other themes? What message does the advertisement try to convey about these?

The setting of an advertisement or text is the time and the place in which the action happens. When watching an advertisement you should consider where it takes place and why that is significant.

The creators of a holiday advertisement are likely to choose as their setting the location they think their audience most wants to visit. That setting is then presented in as appealing a way as possible – we are unlikely, for instance, to be shown a beach scene when it is raining. By showing the audience what they could be enjoying, you help them imagine themselves in that particular setting and so you increase their desire to be there.

DISCUSS

What setting do you think works best for a holiday advertisement? Do some settings work better for different audiences? What setting would most persuade you to go on holiday?

As we have explored, people travel for lots of different reasons, and the type of holiday you take can say a lot about who you are as a person. Advertisers are aware of this and try to tailor their advertisements for different types of people.

THINK–PUZZLE–EXPLORE

Look again at the holiday advertisements you have found – who do you think they are trying to persuade?

Some of the questions you might consider are:
- **Is an advertisement appealing to a particular economic group in society?**
- **How much money will people need to have to buy the holiday being advertised?**
  - **Is it a low price? A budget holiday would appeal to younger travellers or those with not much money.**
  - **Is there an emphasis on luxury? Money might be no object and an expensive, exotic holiday might be seen as a status symbol.**
- **Does the advertisement appeal to values, such as those relating to charity or the environment?**

Explore this further by sharing your thinking with classmates, or searching online to find more travel advertisement evidence.

Advertisements try to give a particular picture of a place in order to persuade people to pay money to visit and then spend money when they are there.

By contrast, non-fiction travel writing tries to give a sense of a place through written descriptions of the people and places, without trying to sell anything.

Travel writers use language carefully to give an impression of a place they have visited. Descriptions can be personal or factual but (as explored in the previous chapter) it is important to look out for any bias in the writing.

Gaborone – description of a capital city

The planners started virtually from scratch, laying out the spacious town on level ground garlanded by attractive trees; among the town centre's more notable features are The Mall, a pedestrian thoroughfare and adjoining square flanked by shops, the prestigious President Hotel, banks, office blocks, embassies. At the eastern end are the municipal buildings, the public library, and the magnificent National Museum and Art Gallery (exhibits include impressive painted dioramas and mounted animals); the western end is graced by the National Assembly chambers and city's rather lovely public park. Other landmarks are the University of Botswana and the national sports stadium and, to the north of town, the Seretse Khama international airport.

This is Botswana – Peter Joyce, Daryl and Sharna Balfour

Tbilisi – description of a city

The Tbilisi that has survived up to now is cracked, subsiding and damp. But Tbilisi is dying gracefully like a good witch. In the previous century it gradually, step by step gave up all it had in order to retain the most essential – its life. It gave up its appearance as do old men, it gave up its soul as do those in despair, but it retained its life. Its life would spark up here and there as if it were gathering strength. It retained sparks in unexpected turnings, deserted and forgotten streets, crumbling entrances with cracked tiles and now all these it also has to give up. Yet Tbilisi is a magic city and the death somehow quite strangely nurses a hope. The city has been ruined and rebuilt and set ablaze many times. Rebuilt and ruined. Ruined and rebuilt: and that history has not come to an end. Tbilisi has not preserved any of its royal residences, though it has preserved a strange house with a balcony called a palace. It is a great miracle: obvious death accompanied by hope.

Tbilisi – Marina and Mzia Janjalia Bulia

In many ways the account of Gaborone sounds quite objective, largely listing as it does some of the features and buildings of the city. However, certain words have been included that tell us that the account is actually quite subjective in nature, and that the writers are in fact biased in the way in which they are presenting Gaborone.

DISCUSS

Is the description of the city positive or negative? In what way is the description subjective? What particular word choices help to reveal that bias?

You may have noticed the following words and phrases used in the description of Gaborone:

spacious   magnificent   prestigious   impressive

graced   rather lovely   garlanded   attractive

Four of these words are adjectives – these words give extra information, helping to provide a vivid description of the place. They also provide clues as to any possible bias or subjectivity in the description, and so are clues to how writers feel about the area they are describing.

The other type of word that can be used in such a way is the verb. Look at the following sentence 'the western end is graced by the National Assembly chambers'; the use of 'graced' helps give a reader a sense of the nature of the building in this phrase, as well as telling us where it is located. It is much more impactful than just saying that the chambers were at the western end.

Adjectives and verbs are extremely important for travel advertisers as they can help convey highly positive impressions of places and create certain moods, which may help to sell holidays. Travel writers use them also for the same reason; though remember, they can also convey negative impressions too.

When you look at the description of Georgia's capital city Tbilisi, what differences do you see between this and the previous description of Gaborone?

How are different experiences of travel expressed?

ACTIVITY: Describing a city

ATL

- Creative-thinking skills: Apply existing knowledge to generate new ideas, products or processes

Choose the city in which you live, or the city in which you were born, or the capital city of your country. Write a description of 100–200 words in which you present the main features of the city in a similar manner to the passage about Gaborone, including positive adjectives to make the description more subjective, and more interesting and attractive-sounding to a reader.

Assessment opportunities

In this activity you have practised skills that are assessed using Criterion C: Producing text and Criterion D: Using language.

EXTENSION

Carry out some research on what happened to Tbilisi in the twentieth century, which might explain the reference in the passage to 'In the previous century it gradually, step by step gave up all it had in order to retain the most essential – its life'.

THINK–PAIR–SHARE

Jot down notes on the following questions, then share them with a partner. Finally, get together with another pair in the class and share once again:

- **What impressions do the writers give in this passage of Tbilisi?**
- **Is it a positive or negative picture that is presented? What makes you say that?**
- **What specific literary techniques have been used in the description?**

Note, in relation to the final question, that one technique used is that of personification – the city is, for instance, described as 'dying', though preserving life, and at another point as 'gathering strength'.

ACTIVITY: Personifying a city

ATL

- Creative-thinking skills: Apply existing knowledge to generate new ideas, products or processes; generate metaphors and analogies

Choose the city in which you live, or the city in which you were born, or the capital city of your country. Then write a description of 200–300 words in which you personify the city in some way.

What particular features might you want to include and emphasize for that particular city?

Begin by choosing the particular points about the city that you could personify (if it were human, what would be the characteristics that first or most come to mind?).

Assessment opportunities

In this activity you have practised skills that are assessed using Criterion C: Producing text and Criterion D: Using language.

TRAVEL WONDERS

Travel has always been a source of wonder, and lists of 'Seven Wonders of the World' began appearing in travel guidebooks for tourists in the times of the ancient Greeks. Most of these 'wonders' were great architectural monuments in Greece, Turkey and Egypt. One of them, the Great Pyramid of Giza in Egypt, can still be seen today, although the others have largely been destroyed.

▼ Links to: History; Architecture

The 'Seven Wonders of the World' were buildings or monuments created in ancient times. When were they built, and by whom? Why were they built, and what technology was used to construct such monuments?

ACTIVITY: Seven Wonders of the World

■ ATL

- Collaboration skills: Listen actively to other perspectives and ideas; build consensus

Imagine you have been tasked with producing a list of 'Seven Wonders of the World' for today's travellers. In a group of four, and without looking at the internet, **discuss** from your own knowledge what you would include in that list of seven. Copy the table below onto poster paper and write down your final suggestions.

Seven Wonders of the World today ...
1
2
3
4
5
6
7

All groups in your class then display their suggestions on the wall of the classroom, so that everyone can do a gallery walk and look at each group's ideas. How similar or different were the ideas from each group?

EXTENSION

Is there a bias in the monuments nominated for inclusion in the 'Seven Wonders of the World' list? The original wonders focused on architectural achievements around the Mediterranean Sea in the first centuries BCE. Do you think people from different countries or different times might have a different perspective on what makes something a 'Wonder of the World'? For each continent research and compile a list of 'wonders'. How different are these from the previous lists you have looked at?

ACTIVITY: What makes a top destination?

ATL

■ Collaboration skills: Listen actively to other perspectives and ideas; build consensus

You and your team from the previous activity have been asked to come up with the *criteria* for deciding what constitutes a 'top ten destination in the world'.

What characteristics must a destination or site have, in order to gain a place on the list? How might destinations be evaluated?

With your team, **discuss** and decide on between five and eight criteria a destination must meet before it is considered as a potential 'top ten' destination. You might like to consider the following, along with anything else you feel may be important in this:

- **Types of possible destinations – can a city be included in the list, or a natural wonder? Or do they have to be specific monuments or structures?**
- **Scale – how large or small should they be?**
- **Fame – how well known should they be?**
- **Annual number of visitors – should that play a role in the decision?**
- **Accessibility – do people need to be able to get to it easily in order for it to be included?**

As a starting point, you may like to look back at the 'Seven Wonders of the World' activity and **analyse** why you chose the places on that particular list. Will any of these places also appear on the final and definitive 'top ten' list?

Organize your final list of criteria from most to least important then, on the basis of these criteria, **create** a list of destinations, sites and places your group thinks would make the 'top ten destinations in the world' list.

If you have time, and your teacher allows it, you might wish to write these on poster paper to place around your classroom and compare the ideas from all of the groups in the class.

ACTIVITY: No regrets

When surveys are carried out on what people regret most in their lives, not travelling enough is often an answer. In this video, for instance, it is given as the most common regret people have: www.youtube.com/watch?v=METc-qkbk18.

Imagine you are 80 years old and writing a letter to you as you are now. Your 80-year-old self is telling you about the role travel has played in your life, and how you feel about it at that stage.

Write the letter from your 80-year-old self, which should be around 500 words in length. You may like to consider including some thoughts on the following:

- **The kinds of travel hopes, goals and dreams you had when you were younger. Did you realize some or all of those? Why or why not?**
- **What you gained or learned from travelling, including whether it changed you as a person.**
- **Any ethical concerns you may have had. Did you address those in any way? Did they prevent you from doing anything? Or did you decide they were less important than what could be gained by taking part in travel of some kind?**
- **How satisfied or otherwise you feel now about your travel experiences during your life – did you do enough? Would you have liked to have done more? Do you regret either having done some particular travel, or not having done something?**
- **How much of a priority travel has been in your life, and how content you are with that.**
- **Advice your 80-year-old self might give you at your current age, about what you might do in your life relating to travel, in view of your interests, goals, ethical concerns and life priorities.**

◆ Assessment opportunities

In this activity you have practised skills that are assessed using Criterion C: Producing text and Criterion D: Using language.

ACTIVITY: Adapting to your environment

Which place in the world do you think is the most different from your own context and culture? It may be somewhere you have been, or it may be somewhere you have not been but would expect to be the most different.

What are the specific aspects that make the place 'different' in your perception? Language? Traditions? Climate? Food? Dress? Something else? Note down five of these aspects in the first column of a table similar to the one below. In the next column explain in what way(s) that aspect is 'different', and in the final column write down how you think you would respond to it.

What aspect is 'different'?	How is it 'different'?	How would you respond to this 'difference'?
1		
2		
3		
4		
5		

What advice would you give to someone who arrived in a place that they found completely different from anything they had experienced before?

Write a piece for the school website/magazine/record a radio podcast etc in which you give advice to someone who has arrived in a place they found completely different from anything they had experienced before.

◆ Assessment opportunities

In this activity you have practised skills that are assessed using Criterion C: Producing text and Criterion D: Using language.

What is involved in 'adapting' to a new context?

ACTIVITY: An alien in New York, Nairobi, St Petersburg …

■ ATL

■ Critical-thinking skills: Evaluate evidence and arguments; revise understanding based on new information and evidence
■ Creative-thinking skills: Create original works and ideas; use existing works and ideas in new ways

The song, 'Foreign Sand', is the result of a collaboration between a British musician, Roger Taylor (who is also the drummer in the group Queen), and a Japanese musician, Yoshiki. It talks about how people can react when they arrive on the shores of a foreign land. Find and listen to the song online, then look up the lyrics online and answer the following questions about them.

1 The song overall talks of what happens when we are in a foreign land. Line 4 asks: 'Why do we fear what we don't understand?' What point is the song making here?

2 Line 5 asks, 'Can't we reach out our hands to try to just say "hello"?' In how many languages can you say 'hello'? Share them with your group.

3 Line 5 of the song refers to a handshake, a common way of politely greeting someone else in some cultures.
   a Is a handshake always an acceptable way of greeting someone? Find some examples of contexts where a handshake would not be acceptable to use as a greeting.
   b What other examples are there of behaviours that may be accepted in one culture but not be acceptable in other cultures?
   c What are some other ways in which greetings may take place in different places and cultures? Give at least three examples.

4 Imagine you meet Roger Taylor and Yoshiki and have an opportunity to explain why a handshake might not always be used to greet someone from a different country. Write down your explanation and then, in a pair or group of three, role-play the conversation.

5 Lines 6, 12 and 27 of the song all talk of trying to 'plant a seed' and 'mak[ing] it grow'.
   a What do you think the 'seed' refers to?
   b How might it 'grow'?
   c What type of imagery is being used in these lines?

6 What do you think is meant by line 13, 'And though you're far from home try to learn from all you see'? What kinds of things might someone learn from what they see, somewhere 'far from home'?

7 This line is repeated with a small difference in line 28. In IB programmes, the learner profile contains attributes – personal qualities, or things that we could 'be'. Using a table like the one opposite, indicate what we could learn in the case of any individual attributes from being 'on foreign sand'.

Learner profile attribute	How this may be developed by being in a different country and culture, or on 'foreign sand'
Inquirer	
Knowledgeable	
Thinker	
Communicator	
Principled	
Open-minded	
Caring	
Risk-taker/courageous	
Balanced	
Reflective	

The song is about developing international-mindedness, and the learner profile is intended in part to help do this in schools.

EXTENSION

Write your own song about a time when you visited a country or place you had never been before. Describe the things you saw, heard and experienced, and how you felt about being there.

◆ Assessment opportunities

Questions 1–3 and 5–6 can be assessed using Criterion A: Analysing.

Activities 4, 7 and Extension can be assessed using Criterion D: Using language.

ACTIVITY: Anger in Saigon

■ ATL

- Communication skills: Make inferences and draw conclusions

1 **If you were abroad and saw a mother with a small baby in her arms, asking for money, how would you respond? Write down your thoughts and feelings, and then discuss them in small groups.**

2 **Read the following passage:**

Of all the ingenious and desperate forms of raising money, the practice of drugging your baby and laying the thing on the pavement in front of the visitor seemed to me the most repulsive. It did not take long to see that none of these children was ever awake during the day, or to notice from the way they slept that something was amiss. Among the foreigners, stories circulated about the same baby being seen in the arms of five different mothers in one week, but the beggar who regularly sat outside the Royale always had the same child, a girl of eighteen months or so. I never gave any money either to the girl and her 'mother' or to any other such teams.

All the Wrong Places: Adrift in the politics of Asia – James Fenton

After reading the passage, what are your views on:
- **the writer/narrator**
- **the 'foreigners'**
- **the beggar outside the hotel Royale?**

3 **Go back to the first question in this activity: have your views changed? Again, share your answers to these questions with the others in your group.**

What do we reveal of ourselves through expressing our experiences of travel?

REPORTAGE

James Fenton's *All the Wrong Places: Adrift in the politics of Asia* is an account of his experiences in several Asian countries in the early 1970s, when various significant political events were taking place. This account is often used as an example of a genre of non-fiction writing called reportage.

■ James Fenton

🛈
Reportage is sometimes described as being difficult to define in a precise way. In general, though, it is a non-fiction piece written by an eyewitness who documents and reports what they observe. The writing sometimes focuses on the journey, rather than the destination, and the reader is often left to determine what is significant about whatever events or scenes that have been described.

Reportage in travel writing

Reportage is often used in travel writing, and some of the conventions found in reportage writing are as follows:

- descriptions of landscape
- detail that is used to evoke atmosphere
- direct speech and interviews or conversations with people involved in the scenes and events being described
- first-person narration. In reportage it is sometimes the case that the narrator is made to sound slightly naïve, or inexperienced in the particular context they are in, as a way of trying to echo the experience of the reader in reading it.

One commentator on reportage, Rosalind Porter, has pointed out something extremely important to bear in mind about reportage writing; that, like all writing, the writer will have a purpose and will have possible responses of the reader or audience in mind:

> '*as any seasoned reader of reportage knows, inscribed within the observations of a reporter are a set of authorial motives which seek to gently nudge the reader towards particular assumptions.*'

The style of reportage may involve writing that sounds observational, descriptive and factual – and therefore objective – in nature, but which may nonetheless have a particular point of view that it is trying to convey about something. Porter points out that accounts of this nature can provide a 'moral context in which the actions of these people and the events of their country can be judged'; this means that when a writer presents the reader with observations of events and scenes, we may well be being invited to consider moral or ethical questions about these.

As readers of reportage we must therefore, in the same way as with all writing, keep the writer in mind and consider stylistic techniques being used, along with purpose and possible effects the writing may have on an audience.

With this in mind, let us have a further look at a longer extract from James Fenton's *All the Wrong Places: Adrift in the politics of Asia*.

ACTIVITY: Meaning and craft in reportage writing

The following extract from *All the Wrong Places: Adrift in the politics of Asia* follows on from the paragraph you looked at previously (page 173), and reports some observations and incidents in Saigon – now Ho Chi Minh City – during the Vietnam War.

You may notice that the author presents himself as a 'naïve narrator' who turns out to know rather less than he thinks he does. He also invites readers to make comparisons between the local cultural beliefs and behaviours, and his own.

Read the rest of the extract and answer the associated questions, which are designed to help you consider more closely the nature and conventions, and possible purposes, of reportage writing. Make sure all your points are supported by evidence from the text.

ⓘ The Vietnam War (1964–75) was officially fought between the governments of North Vietnam and South Vietnam. The Soviet Union, China and other communist allies supported the North Vietnamese, while the United States, South Korea, Australia and other anti-communist allies supported the South Vietnamese. In particular, a large number of US military troops were sent to help fight in the conflict.

■ US President John F Kennedy at a press conference about Vietnam in 1961

One day, however, I was returning from a good lunch when I saw that a crowd had formed around the Old Woman, who was wailing and gesticulating. The child was more than usually grey, and there were traces of vomit around her face. People were turning her over, slapping her, trying to force her eyes open. At one point she and the old woman were bundled into a taxi. Then they were taken out again and the slapping was repeated. I went into the hotel and told the girl at reception to call a doctor. 'No,' she replied. 'But the child is sick.' 'If baby go to hospital or doctor' — and here she imitated an injection — 'then baby die.' 'No,' I replied, 'if baby don't go to hospital maybe baby die.' 'No.'

I took the girl out into the street, where the scene had taken on the most grotesque appearance. All the beggars I had ever seen in Saigon seemed to have gathered, and from their filthy garments they were producing pins and sticking them under the child's toenails. 'You see,' I said to the girl, 'no good, number ten. Baby need number-one hospital.' 'No, my grandmother had same thing. She need this — number one.' And the receptionist produced a small phial of eucalyptus oil. 'That's not number one,' I said, 'that's number ten. Number ten thousand,' I added for emphasis. But it was no good insisting or appealing to other members of the crowd. Everybody was adamant that if the child was taken to the hospital, the doctor would kill it with an injection. While I correspondingly became convinced that a moment's delay would cost the child's life.

- What are the different beliefs held about the sick baby by the narrator, and by the hotel receptionist?
- Why does the hotel receptionist believe an injection will kill the baby?
- How is the narrator presented in this section? What kind of a person does he seem to be?

- What differences of belief can you observe between the narrator and the local people?
- What is the narrator's attitude to the scene?
- How do you feel about the narrator at this point? Why?

- The writer continues in this paragraph to illustrate the cultural differences in how the narrator and the local people perceive the situation, and what should be done about it.
- What details in the paragraph show that the narrator feels he is right, and that he should try to take control of the situation?
- What details suggest that he is much less in control than he tries to be?
- How would you describe the tone of the sentence: 'We were travelling through Cholon, the Chinese quarter, on an errand of Western mercy'? Why do you think the writer chooses the term 'Western mercy' at this point?

- What can we tell from this passage about the role that the narrator sees nations such as France and the US playing in the local context of Vietnam?
- What evidence is there in the passage of feelings of superiority on the part of the narrator?

- When the narrator jumps out of the car and seizes the taxi driver's arm, what do you think he is most concerned about at this point? What makes you think that?

Finally, after a long eucalyptus massage and repeated pricking of the fingers and toes had produced no visible results, I seemed to win. If I would pay for taxi and hospital, the woman would come. I pushed my way through the crowd and dragged her towards the taxi – a battered old Renault tied together with string. The baby was wrapped in a tarpaulin and her face covered with a red handkerchief. Every time I tried to remove the handkerchief, from which came the most ominous dry gaspings, the woman replaced it. I directed the taxi-driver to take us to number-one hospital and we set off. But from the start everything went wrong. Within a hundred yards we had to stop for gas. Then a van stalled in front of us, trapping the taxi. Next, to my amazement, we came to what must have been, I thought, the only level-crossing in Saigon, where as it happened a train was expected in the near future. And around here we were hit by the side effects of Typhoon Sarah, which at the time was causing havoc in the northern provinces. We also split a tyre, though this was not noticed till later. Driving on through the cloudburst, the taxi driver seemed strangely unwilling to hurry. So I sat in the back seat keeping one hand on the horn and the other attempting to alleviate the restrictions around the baby's breathing apparatus. I also recall producing a third arm with which to comfort the old woman from time to time and I remember that her shoulder, when my hand rested on it, was very small and very hard. Everything, I said, was going to be number one, okay: number-one hospital, number-one doctor, babysan okay. We were travelling through Cholon, the Chinese quarter, on an errand of Western mercy.

All things considered, it took a long time for it to dawn on me that we were not going to a hospital at all. We even passed a first-aid post without the driver giving it a glance. In my mind there was an image of the sort of thing required: a large cool building dating from French times, recently refurbished by American aid and charity, with some of the best equipment in the East. I could even imagine the **sententious** plaques on the walls. Perhaps there would be a ward named after the former US ambassador.

It was when the old woman began giving directions that I saw I had been duped. We were now threading our way through some modern slums, which looked like the Chinese equivalent of the Isle of Dogs. 'Where is the hospital? This is no hospital,' I said. Yes, yes, the taxi-driver replied, we were going to hospital, number-one doctor. We stopped by a row of shops and the driver got out. I jumped from the car and seized him by the arm, shouting: 'I said number-one hospital. You lie. You cheap charlie. You number-ten-thousand Saigon.' We were surrounded by children, in the pouring rain, the taxi man tugging himself free, and me gripping him by the arm. It was left to the woman, carrying the little bundle of tarpaulin, to find out exactly where the doctor lived. Finally I gave in, and followed her up some steps, then along an open corridor lined with tailors and merchants. At least, I thought, when the baby dies I can't be blamed. And once I had thought that, the thought turned into a wish: A little cough would have done it, a pathetic gurgle, then a silence, and my point about Western medicine would have been proved to my own satisfaction. I should have behaved very well; of course I should have paid for, and gone to, the funeral.

In **retrospect** it was easy to see how the establishment would command confidence: the dark main room with its traditional furnishings, the walls lined with photographs of ancestors in traditional Vietnamese robes, a framed jigsaw of the Italian lakes. And in the back room (it would, of course, have to be a back room), a plump middle-aged lady was massaging the back of another plump, middle-aged lady. They paid hardly any attention when we came in. There was not the slightest element of drama. Indeed, I began to see that I was now the only person who was panicking. When she had finished the massage, the doctor turned her attention to the baby. First she took some ointment from a dirty bowl at her elbow, and rubbed it all over the little grey body. Then from another bowl she produced some pink substance resembling Euthymol toothpaste, with which she proceeded to line the mouth. In a matter of minutes, the child was slightly sick, began to cry, and recovered. I had never been more furious in my life. To complete my humiliation, the doctor refused any payment. She provided the old woman with a prescription wrapped in newspaper, and we left.

We drove to the miserable shelter in which the old woman lived. 'Sit down,' she said, indicating the wooden bed which was the only feature of her home apart from the roof (there were no walls). In any other mood I might have been moved by the fact that the only English she knew beyond the terrible pidgin currency of the beggars was a phrase of hospitality. But I so deeply hated her at that moment that I could only give her a couple of pounds, plus some useless advice about keeping the baby warm and off the pavements, and go.

- How helpful is the narrator being in this scene?
- When he thinks about the baby dying, what do these few sentences suggest is most important to the narrator? How is a reader expected to react to the narrator's wish?
- When considering his behaviour and the funeral, what do the main concerns of the narrator seem to be? What does this sentence show about the type of person he is?

- What impression does the narrator think the 'hospital' probably has on those who visit? What evidence do you see that it should make such an impression?
- Why do you think the word 'traditional' is repeated in the first sentence of this passage?
- The local doctor treats the baby very quickly and refuses payment. In view of this, why do you think the narrator says that 'I had never been more furious in my life'?

- How is the old woman presented in this passage? How might a reader be expected to respond to her at this point?
- Why do you think the narrator says that he 'so deeply hated her at that moment'?

I left the taxi-driver at a garage not far from the Royale, where I also gave him some money toward repairing the split tyre. 'You number one, Saigon,' he said, with a slight note of terror in his voice. The weather had cleared up, and I strolled along past the market stalls…

And I began to think, supposing they were all in it together? Suppose the old woman, the taxi driver, the man whose van stalled, the engine driver — suppose they were all now dividing out the proceeds and having a good laugh at my expense, congratulating the child on the way it had played its role? That evening I would be telling the story to some old Saigon hand when a strange pitying smile would come over his face. 'You went to Cholon did you? Describe the doctor…uhuh… Was there a jigsaw puzzle of the Italian lakes? Well, well, well. So they even used the toothpaste trick. Funny how the oldest gags are still the best….'

Indeed I did have rather that conversation a few days later, with an American girl, a weaver. It began 'You realise, of course, first of all that the taxi driver was the husband of the old woman… But I do not think it was a conspiracy.' Worse, I should rather conclude that the principals involved were quite right not to trust the hospital doctors with a beggar's child. It was for this reason that the hotel receptionist had **countermanded** my orders to the taxi man, I learned afterwards, and many people agreed with her.

When the old woman came on the streets, I hardly recognised either her or the child, who for the first time looked conscious and well. 'Babysan okay now, no sick,' she said, gazing at me with an awful adoring expression, though the hand was not stretched out for money. And when I didn't reply she turned to the child and told it something in the same **unctuous** tones. This performance went on for the rest of my stay: Whenever I was around, the child would be made to look at the kind foreigner who had saved its life. I had indeed wanted to save the child's life, but not in that way, not on the old woman's terms.

I was disgusted, not just at what I saw around me, but at what I saw in myself. I saw how perilously thin was the line between the charitable and the murderous impulse, how strong the force of righteous indignation.

- Earlier in this extract the narrator stated that he had been 'duped'. On the evidence of these final five paragraphs, how likely do you think it is that that is what has happened? Give reasons for your answer.
- What had the hotel receptionist actually done when she 'countermanded my orders to the taxi man'?
- Why do you think it may have been 'quite right not to trust the hospital doctors with a beggar's child'?
- 'Whenever I was around, the child would be made to look at the kind foreigner who had saved its life':
  - How much did the narrator actually do to help the baby, or anyone else involved in the situation?
  - Which words in this sentence are particularly **ironic**?
  - **Irony** can be used to criticize something. What do you think is being criticized in this sentence?

- From the evidence contained in the extract **as a whole**, what reasons might the narrator have at this point for feeling disgusted with himself?
- What may the writer be implying in his comment about why people may want to try to do something 'charitable'?
- Again, thinking about this extract as a whole what do you think the writer may be warning of when he refers to 'the [strong] force of righteous indignation'?
- How sympathetic is the narrator, across the whole extract from Fenton's book? Give reasons for your answer.

ACTIVITY: Travel blogging

Advances in technology have brought many changes in the world in recent times, including in the area of travel. The expansion of air travel has made it possible for far more people to travel far and wide, while communications technology makes it possible to stay permanently connected to everywhere else, wherever we may be.

These factors have led more and more people to travel, and to publish the details of their journeys and experiences. For some, it has become a way of life, and they make their living from professional travel blogging, as in the case of professional travellers such as Matthew Karsten ('Expert Vagabond' – https://expertvagabond.com/), Sankara (www.beontheroad.com/), Meruschka Govender ('MzansiGirl' www.mzansigirl.com/) and Lauren Juliff (www.neverendingfootsteps.com/). Many people, however, like to show and tell others about what they are doing while travelling, even if this is through photos and a bit of text on social media during a short holiday somewhere.

Why do you think people want to blog about their travels? What practical reasons might they have to do so? What might they want to try to show to others about themselves? In what ways might they think it could help others?

List some possible ideas. Write your own ideas first, and then get together with two or three others in your class and share these. Add any others you did not include at first, which your classmates may have had.

Let us imagine you have just started your own travel blog and need to write the introduction. What might you say in it?

Write your introduction, which should be between 500 and 1,000 words in length, and might include the following points (you can use real details about yourself or imagine yourself as an entirely different person, as you prefer):
- **Your background / home context**
- **When, how and why you became interested in travelling**
- **What you really enjoy and are interested in seeing / experiencing on your travels**
- **What you find challenging about travelling**
- **Why you write a travel blog, and what you hope it will achieve**

Assessment opportunities

This activity can be assessed using Criterion C: Producing text and Criterion D: Using language.

ACTIVITY: My first travel blog

One of the questions for bloggers is what to write about. Read this advice:

https://expertvagabond.com/how-to-start-travel-blog/

You are now going to write a travel blog post in which you either:

a   Describe a holiday or travel experience you have had.
b   Introduce readers to '10 / 15 awesome things to do in …' or 'How to visit … on a budget'.

Write 500–1,000 words for your travel blog. Ensure you use the above features in order to write in an informal **register**.

How **biased** will you be? Write a rationale of 300 words to accompany your travel blog post, which identifies and explains how particular aspects of and details in your text may make it more biased in nature.

Assessment opportunities

This activity can be assessed using Criterion C: Producing text and Criterion D: Using language.

What can we learn through travel?

ACTIVITY: First impressions

■ ATL

- ■ Communication skills: Make inferences and draw conclusions; write for different purposes

What do you think the place in the picture is?

1 **Write a description of this place and scene, in about 300–400 words. Think about using the following techniques, and any others you might think of, to make your description more vivid:**

- similes
- metaphors
- adjectives
- sensory imagery
- narrative technique
- use of speech
- use of syntax.

2 **Write a narrative of 500–600 words about something that you think happened in this place.**

◆ Assessment opportunities

In this activity you have practised skills that are assessed using Criterion C: Producing text and Criterion D: Using language.

Travel blogging style – things to consider

Travel blogs are a further example of a non-fiction text, and – as with all texts – it is important to consider the writer and their purpose(s). These texts are often **autobiographical** in nature, since the writer is frequently recounting his or her own experiences or perceptions of places; and will want to present him- or herself, and what is being described or discussed, in certain ways. It is important, therefore, to consider how **objective**, or how **biased**, they may be.

Another thing to consider is the **register** used in travel blogging. The intention is often to present a 'friendly face', and thus blogs tend to be quite informal in nature.

Consider the following extract, which is taken from MzansiGirl's account of a trip to the Kwazulu-Natal coast:

"My second leg of my #GottaluvKZN trip involved a hectic 5 day adventure on the South Coast, KZN. It was so good to be back and rediscover the South Coast with my hosts Tourism Kwazulu-Natal. Being on the South Coast brings back so many memories for me – from childhood holidays with my family, to living there for 18 months when I worked at a beach backpackers.

Besides its chilled family holiday vibe, the KZN South Coast is an awesome adventure destination. I got to explore my adventurous side and challenge my fears ziplining, jumping off a gorge and horse-riding on the beach.

My travel buddies for the week were actor Ntokozo TK Dlamini from SABC1's Uzalo and Ukhozi FM DJ Thembeka Zondo. We discovered that the South Coast is so much more than just a beach destination. Here are my highlights of the trip:

Leopard Rock Lookout at Oribi Gorge

I've been to Oribi Gorge many times, and it never ceases to amaze me. This scenic gorge has some of KZN's most spectacular views, which can be experienced in a variety of ways. For the less adventurous you can drive to one of the lookout points – Leopard Rock Lookout is one of the most spectacular. For the adrenalin junkies, try hiking, ziplining or jumping from the gorge!"

How **biased** do you think the passage is? What particular details make you say that? What features do you see which make the **register** of the piece informal?

Discuss these questions with a classmate, and then with your table group, and write a list of the particular features which you can spot, in the case of each question.

In the case of the **register**, look in particular at vocabulary use, contractions, and narrative voice (is it only first person which can be found for this?).

DISCUSS

Imagine you came across this advertisement for a 'Killing Fields' tour – what would your response to it be? **Discuss** your impressions with a classmate.

DARK TOURISM

'**Dark tourism**' is the term given to visiting sites where something terrible or destructive has happened previously. These tend to be events that have taken place in the recent past, often within living memory of some of those who visit.

Some examples of dark tourism destinations are:

- Auschwitz, Poland
- Chernobyl/Pripyat, Ukraine
- Hiroshima, Japan
- Sarajevo, Bosnia-Herzegovina
- Murambi Technical School, Rwanda
- S21 prison and Choeung Ek, the 'Killing Fields', Phnom Penh, Cambodia.

Tuol Sleng Genocide Museum in Phnom Penh, Cambodia, is a former high school that was turned into a prison and place of torture and death under the rule of the **Khmer Rouge** in Cambodia in the 1970s. Also known as S21, it is today, as the Genocide Museum, one of the most visited tourist sites in Phnom Penh, along with a place just outside of the city called Choeung Ek, or the 'Killing Fields', where those imprisoned in S21 were taken at night and brutally killed.

What kind of place did you think the photograph on page 180 showed? How did you describe it?

In fact the photograph shows the Tuol Sleng Genocide Museum in Phnom Penh, where around 20,000 people are thought to have been imprisoned, almost all of whom died either while in the prison, or at Choeung Ek.

ACTIVITY: Jigsaw research on dark tourism sites

■ ATL

- Collaboration skills: Work collaboratively in teams; give and receive meaningful feedback; help others to succeed
- Information literacy skills: Access information to be informed and inform others; make connections between various sources of information

Get together in a group of six or eight. You are publishers of travel guides and have been tasked with writing a tourist brochure filled with short summaries that give background information on some dark tourism sites. Each summary should be 300–500 words long, and should be largely factual in nature.

Within your group, get into pairs. Each pair should choose one dark tourism site to research and write about. Do not use the example of S21 and Choeung Ek (the 'Killing Fields') in Cambodia, however, as we will be looking more closely at that site shortly.

Think about the following aspects when writing your summary:

- **What are the important points to include about the history of your site?**
- **Is the language formal and the tone objective?**
- **Is the language suitable for a general audience, being not too difficult, but not written as if aimed at children?**

Within your group, swap your draft summaries so that other pairs can review and provide feedback to help make your summary better. You should give feedback on every summary your group has written.

Ask any questions or **discuss** any points further as may be needed, and then revise your summary into its final version.

◆ Assessment opportunities

In this activity you have practised skills that are assessed using Criterion C: Producing text and Criterion D: Using language.

To what extent do the advantages of travel outweigh the downsides?

ACTIVITY: The ethics of dark tourism

■ ATL

- ■ Communication skills: Make inferences and draw conclusions; evaluate evidence and arguments

The following passage is taken from an account given by one of the few survivors of S21, Bou Meng. In the passage, Meng describes the conditions in the room in which he was imprisoned in S21.

Prisoners were shackled in lines, and male and female prisoners were put in different rooms. My room smelled bad. I glanced around and saw approximately 50 other prisoners sleeping on the floor in two lines. All were men. Some looked skinny and weak; some had long beards and moustaches; some looked deathly pale; and some bore scars left from wounds. They looked like ghosts. It seemed to me that all the prisoners were waiting for death. That was hell on earth! (norauk lok-kei).

It became colder and colder. All the prisoners slept on the floor. We did not have blankets to cover us. Mosquitoes bit us continuously. Groaning, snoring, and swatting mosquitoes sounded throughout the room. I tried to sleep, but I could not. I was exhausted. I turned my body very often. I was so starving that my stomach began to growl…

…

There were about four ammunition cans and five plastic bottles in my room. The prisoners defecated in ammunition cans and urinated in plastic bottles. But before we did that we needed to ask permission from the security guards. If we did it without permission, we would receive 20 to 60 lashes of the whip. When those containers were full of excrement and urine, a guard took them out. Sometimes, excrement and urine overflowed onto the floor.

Bou Meng: A survivor from Khmer Rouge Prison S21 (translated by Huy Vannak)

Answer the following questions about the Bou Meng extract:

- **What do you think are the main purposes of this text?**
- **How do you think an audience is intended to respond to it?**
- **What techniques have been used to convey the conditions in the prison more vividly?**

◆ Assessment opportunities

In this activity you have practised skills that are assessed using Criterion A: Analysing.

THINK–PAIR–SHARE

The ethics of visiting places such as S21 and Choeung Ek have long been debated. Think about the following questions, then **discuss** them with a classmate. Share your thoughts with the class. Does everyone agree?

1 Is it 'right' to visit such places at all?
2 Are there different categories of sites that 'should' or 'should not' be visited?
3 How should people behave when they visit such sites?

ACTIVITY: Is it 'right' to visit dark tourism sites?

■ ATL

■ Critical-thinking skills: Consider ideas from multiple perspectives

In pairs, or groups of three or four, **discuss** why each of the following groups of people may want to visit a site such as S21 and Choeung Ek. Copy the table below and add your notes about the kinds of reasons, arguments and justifications there might be for the different kinds of people to visit.

General tourists	
School children	
Relatives of victims	
Residents of the town or city in which a disaster or atrocity took place	
Nationals of a country in which a disaster or atrocity took place	
Other group?	
Other group?	

A *National Geographic* article ('Is Dark Tourism OK?') debates the ethics of visiting such places. The article suggests that there is nothing fundamentally wrong with visiting dark sites, but that the reasons behind a tourist's visit should be considered. Find the full article online then, in your group, answer the following questions:

● Which, if any, dark tourism sites would you like to visit, and why?
● Are there any sites that you feel you would not like to visit? What are those, and why?
● What different motivations do you think people have for visiting dark tourism sites? In answering this you might consider your own answers to the question of whether you would like to visit any dark tourism sites, and why.
● How do you think you would feel after visiting a dark tourism site? Write a **comment** of 100–200 words outlining your thoughts.

◆ Assessment opportunities

In this activity you have practised skills that are assessed using Criterion A: Analysing and Criterion C: Producing text.

The ancient historian Livy once said of history that:

'In history you have a record of the infinite variety of human experience plainly set out for all to see: and in that record you can find for yourself and your country both examples and warnings: fine things to take as models, base things, rotten through and through, to avoid.' – Livy, The History of Rome

The researcher who recorded Bou Meng's account of his life in S21 prison during the times of the Khmer Rouge in Cambodia, Huy Vannak, similarly states in the 'Acknowledgements' section of that book that:

'As a researcher, I have the chance to learn a great deal about the lives of survivors and terror regimes in the 20th century. My studies convince me that we must learn history so that we will not repeat the past.'

DISCUSS

After reading these quotes look back at the 'Is it "right" to visit dark tourism sites?' activity you have just completed. Do the quotes change your thinking in any way? Do they further support the arguments you made? **Discuss** the quotes with your original activity group.

ACTIVITY: Are there sites that 'should' or 'should not' be visited?

■ ATL

■ Critical-thinking skills: Identify obstacles and challenges
■ Creative-thinking skills: Use brainstorming and visual diagrams to generate new ideas and inquiries
■ Transfer skills: Change the context of an inquiry to gain different perspectives

The question of visiting so-called dark tourism sites may not be as straightforward as whether to visit them or not, however. It could be argued that some of the most popular and famous sites in the world are dark tourism sites, though questions about visiting them are rarely raised. Consider, for example, the Colosseum in Rome, site of gladiatorial combat and mass killing and death in the times of Ancient Rome. Meanwhile, the Taj Mahal in India is in fact a tomb, built by a grieving husband following the death of his much-loved wife.

DISCUSS

Is there a difference between visiting, say, the Colosseum in Rome, and visiting S21 and the 'Killing Fields' in Phnom Penh? If so, what is it?

Search online for a list of dark tourism sites. Copy out and complete the table below. In the appropriate columns, add sites that you feel are acceptable and not acceptable to visit. For each site, include your reasoning (for example, perhaps you should not visit owing to ethical reasons, or perhaps health and safety reasons).

In groups of three or four, compare your tables. Together, brainstorm any other sites you can think of that you have not yet covered, and then add these to your table as well.

On a piece of poster paper, use the information from your tables to draw a mind map, as illustrated below, to record the collective opinion of the group. The first layer of the map should list the site, while the second layer will indicate whether these should or should not be visited. The reasons for visiting or not should be included in the third layer of the mind map.

■ Mind map template

Every group should stick their poster paper to the classroom wall. Carry out a gallery walk, and see how far you agreed or disagreed with others in your class on sites that might be visited, and why.

◆ Assessment opportunities

In this activity you have practised skills that are assessed using Criterion B: Organizing.

Sites that it should be fine to visit	Reason(s) why it is fine to visit the site	Sites that should not be visited	Reason(s) why the site should not be visited

ACTIVITY: How should people behave when they visit dark tourism sites?

- Collaboration skills: Build consensus
- Critical-thinking skills: Gather and organize relevant information to formulate an argument

In 2016, the United States Holocaust Museum asked visitors to stop playing the augmented reality game *Pokémon Go* when they were in the museum as they felt it was 'not appropriate in the museum, which is a memorial to the victims of Nazism'.

How do you think visitors should be expected to conduct themselves when at sites where people have suffered and died?

■ Sign for tourists at Tuol Sleng Genocide Museum, Phnom Penh

Imagine that you are managers of a sensitive dark tourism site that tourists wish to visit. Your job is to manage such visits in a way that allows visitors of different kinds to experience visits that are worthwhile, and protects the sensitivity of the site.

1 Decide as a group what type of site you would like to use for this activity.
2 **Discuss** which kinds of people are likely to visit and what challenges or needs may arise as a result of their visiting your site. You might find a table like the one below helpful when making notes.
3 As a group, decide on the behavioural guidelines and expectations you would like to have for your site.
4 Consider how you will make these guidelines and expectations known to all visitors, both before they come to the site, and while they are there.
5 Individually, produce a visitor leaflet containing the behaviour guidelines and expectations for your site. You should use A4-size paper for this, and should decide on the following:
    a the content you will include, which should focus mainly on expected behaviour and advice and guidelines on this
    b how you will organize your content, into different sections, subsections, with headings and subheadings, lists, and so on
    c what images to include for your site
    d the register that would be appropriate for your leaflet: how formal or informal you might be; what would be most appropriate for your site
    e the tone of what you write.

◆ Assessment opportunities

In this activity you have practised skills that are assessed using Criterion B: Organizing, Criterion C: Producing text and Criterion D: Using language.

Types of visitor	Reasons why they are likely to visit	Potential challenges/needs to consider for this group of visitors
General tourists		
School children		
Relatives of victims		
Residents of the town or city in which a disaster or atrocity took place		
Nationals of a country in which a disaster or atrocity took place		
Other group?		
Other group?		

ACTIVITY: Circle of viewpoints

We've looked at the ethics of visiting ('dark tourism') and the factors that these tourists and site operators should consider, but are there other ethical considerations to think about when travelling?

Below are some examples of ethical questions which might be asked in relation to travel:

- **Is it ethical to travel when lots of people can't, due to their relative wealth / poverty?**
- **Is it ethical to travel if it damages the environment? Flights are known to have an impact on climate change, emitting greenhouse gases which contribute to global warming. This can have a disastrous effect on the environment, as in the case of the Great Barrier Reef, on which parts of the coral have died due to the rising temperature of the sea (https://goo.gl/m1ZYXR).**
- **Is it ethical to travel if it damages or changes the local culture? You might find this article of interest – including the comments: https://goo.gl/BVarsP. Venice is increasingly becoming a concern, as this article indicates: https://goo.gl/brBtjg.**
- **However, does travel increase a person's understanding of a culture / people, and so help break down barriers? Does this make the world a better place?**

Can you think of any other travel-related ethical questions which might be asked?

Now get into a group of four. Using the questions above, and any other ethical questions you can think of, you are going to consider the question 'Is it ethical to travel?' from the perspectives of different people who might be involved in or affected by it.

First of all, brainstorm as a group the following questions and write down some notes for each. Divide a piece of poster paper into four and add notes for each one, so that everyone can see them.

- **Who (and what) is affected by travel?**
- **Who is involved?**
- **Who might care?**
- **How might travel be viewed in different places, and at different points in time?**

Think of at least four different viewpoints which might be held by individuals involved in or affected by travel. Use the ethical questions above to work out whom these might be, and try to come up with viewpoints which are as varied as possible.

Then note down ideas which each of your individual viewpoints might hold about the question 'Is it ethical to travel?' Again, use the ethical questions as prompts to work out possible ideas that a particular viewpoint might hold both on potential benefits of travel, and objections to it.

Once you have noted down all of your ideas, each of you should then choose one of the viewpoints you have been making notes on, and ensure each member of the group takes a different viewpoint from everyone else.

Prepare a two- to three-minute speech for your viewpoint, using the following structure:
1. **I am thinking of the topic of travel from the point of view of [the viewpoint you've chosen].**
2. **I think [describe the topic from your viewpoint. Be an actor: take on the character of your viewpoint].**
3. **A question I have from this viewpoint is [ask a question from this viewpoint].**

Be prepared to express and explain a variety of thoughts. Try to ask more than one question that might be raised by someone speaking from your particular viewpoint.

Once you have all prepared the responses for your viewpoint, sit in a circle and present your viewpoints, in character, in turn.

As viewpoint presentations are made, keep a record of the thoughts and questions of each viewpoint, using a table such as the following:

Viewpoint	Thoughts	Question

Once everyone has given their viewpoints, you should have an idea of the range of perspectives that might exist about some of the ethical issues involved in travel. Follow this up by looking at the questions that have been raised, choosing three of these, and discussing them as a group.

Finally, either write a reflection, or record a video reflection, in which you address the following two questions:

- **The ethics of travel: what new ideas do you have about the topic which you didn't have before?**
- **What new questions do you have?**

Language and Literature for the IB MYP 4&5: by Concept

ACTIVITY: The Travelers' Century Club

■ ATL

- ■ Information literacy skills: Present information in a variety of formats and platforms

The 'Travelers' Century Club' is an international society that can be joined by anyone who has visited more than 100 countries. Their slogan is 'World travel – the passport to peace through understanding'.

Research the club online, and make notes to help you answer the following questions:

- ● What types of people are most likely to be interested in joining this club?
- ● What are the advantages of joining a club such as this?
- ● What ethical issues can you see that arise from this?
- ● Would you like to join this society yourself at some time? Why (not)?

Now, imagine you are a member of the club and have been asked to present information about it at an event.

Your audience consists of adults, many of whom are likely to have the means to travel, though some of whom are also likely to have ethical concerns about engaging in mass travel.

Design a ten-minute presentation, which includes the use of a presentation tool such as PowerPoint or Prezi, which you would give to this audience about the club.

Your presentation should focus on how the advantages of travel outweigh the downsides, though you should take care to address both sides of the argument in a balanced manner. Consider what tone might be best to adopt for this event. What rhetorical devices might you include to achieve the kind of presentation you are aiming for?

◆ Assessment opportunities

This activity can be assessed using Criterion C: Producing text and Criterion D: Using language.

SOME SUMMATIVE TASKS TO TRY

Use these tasks to apply and extend your learning in this chapter. These tasks are designed so that you can evaluate your learning at different levels of achievement in the Language and literature criteria.

THIS TASK CAN BE USED TO EVALUATE YOUR LEARNING IN CRITERION B, CRITERION C AND CRITERION D

Task 1: Creative writing – leaving home

Find the lyrics for the Queen song 'Leaving Home Ain't Easy' online. Read the first two verses only to ensure that you generate your own original ideas, then write the story behind the song. Include the following:

- ■ who the narrator is
- ■ whom the narrator is leaving
- ■ why the narrator is leaving home at this point (what do you think has happened which has led to this?)
- ■ what happens following the end of the lyrics.

You should write 500–1,000 words. Remember that to reach highest levels of achievement in Criterion C, you must use extensive relevant details and examples to develop ideas.

Think too about how you might make use of particular stylistic choices, such as imagery and syntax.

Task 2: Analysis of a holiday advertisement

Look at the following image and details of a holiday resort
in Goa, India, which is taken from the website of travel
company *makemytrip.*

Overlooking the Varca Beach, Caravela Beach Resort offers a
fitness centre, conference hall with internet facility, restaurants
and bars.

Nestled on the serene sand of Varca Beach, Caravela Beach
Resort is a 5-star property, spread over 24 acres and has
199 rooms, which are categorized as Garden View, Pool/
Ocean View and Ocean Front, Deluxe Stuides, Family Villa
and Presidential Villa. All rooms have individual controlled
air-conditioner, private bath with shower and bathtub, LCD or
LED televisions, mini bar and tea/coffee maker. Some of the
nearby beaches from this resort are Varca Beach, Sernabatim
Beach and Carmona Beach.

Dabolim International Airport is 30 km and Margao Railway
Station is 10 km from the beach property. For conference,
seminar, meetings and events, it has a spacious conference
hall that offers above 4500 sq ft of indoor space and 7000 sq
ft of outdoor space.

The hall is featured with amenities like internet connectivity
and state-of-the-art audio visual equipment. The resort has
yoga, Ayurveda treatment and fitness centre for recreation.
It also offers activities like water sports, dolphin tours, beach
activities, and indoor and outdoor games.

In-house health club and Ayurvedic centre offers a wide
variety of treatments and traditional massages to pamper the
mind, body and soul and rejuvenate oneself.

This resort is delight for epicureans as it houses several dining
establishments. Surf n Turf dining option Carnaval dishes
out enticing sea-foods and offers international wines. Cafe
Cascada is in-house coffee shop while Lanai Lounge serves
buffet breakfast, lunch and dinner. Poolside restaurant
Castaways offers light snacks and beverages. To savor free
seafood, grills and Chinese cuisines, head to restaurant Beach
Shack. Atrium Bar is always well-stocked with fine selection of
wines and spirits. Island Bar serves cocktails, chilled beer and
other refreshing beverages. Sunset Bar offers cocktails with
spectacular views of the sunset and the beach. Enjoy beach
sports at the Varca Beach or experience thrilling gambling
sessions at the in-house casino – Goa Nugget!

Analyse the persuasive aspects of both the image and the text, and make notes on how any elements of them are trying to appeal to *pathos*, *logos*, or *ethos*. You might like to use a table similar to those used earlier in this chapter, to organize your notes.

Next, write an analysis of the presentation of the resort, including comments on the significance of each of the following:

- the purpose of the text and image
- the intended audience being targeted by the holiday advertisement, and how details within it provide evidence of that
- the context of the resort
- stylistic features, such as use of descriptive language including adjectives, sentence structure such as imperative language, how the advertisement uses appeals to pathos, logos or ethos, and anything else you may find to say.

THIS TASK CAN BE USED TO EVALUATE YOUR LEARNING IN CRITERION B, CRITERION C AND CRITERION D

Task 3: A public presentation on dark tourism

On page 183 you read two quotes (from Livy and from Bou Meng's researcher) that addressed the importance of learning about terrible moments in history.

Use these quotations as the basis for a speech that you have been asked to give at an event organized by the local historical society. The speech, entitled 'What we can learn from our travels', should try to persuade your audience to visit dark tourism sites, and should be 600–1,000 words in length.

Remember that as a persuasive speech it should include techniques such as rhetorical questions, use of the rule of three, and other persuasive devices.

Reflection

In our own journey through this chapter we have considered some of the reasons why people travel, the kinds of learning which may arise from that, and the different ways in which such experiences may be expressed to others. This has led us to explore texts of different kinds that are often used to focus on travel in some way, and the variety of purposes such texts may have, such as to convey personal experiences or to persuade others to travel. Within that we have been able to look at conventions that can be found in particular text types, and at how language might be used for certain effects or may reveal a writer's biases. Hopefully the chapter may also have led you to think more deeply about the kinds of experiences travel might bring, and possible physical, ethical and moral challenges that can arise as a result, along with how we might react or adapt in such instances.

Use this table to reflect on your own learning in this chapter.					
Questions we asked	**Answers we found**	**Any further questions now?**			
Factual:					
Conceptual:					
Debatable:					
Approaches to learning you used in this chapter:	**Description – what new skills did you learn?**	**How well did you master the skills?**			
		Novice	Learner	Practitioner	Expert
Communication skills					
Collaboration skills					
Information literacy skills					
Critical-thinking skills					
Creative-thinking skills					
Transfer skills					
Learner profile attribute(s)	Reflect on the importance of being a risk-taker in this chapter.				
Risk-takers					

8 What do our ethical and moral choices reveal about us?

○ Narrative **structures** can be used to show moral and ethical dilemmas, with people's responses to these **revealing aspects** of their **character** and **identity**.

CONSIDER THESE QUESTIONS:

Factual: What are some of the main narrative features of *Cold Mountain*? What are the intentions and effects of narrative structures? What are moral and ethical dilemmas?

Conceptual: What can the use of violence say about human nature? How might our choices in times when the normal rules do not apply communicate who we are? What can a war film show about the ways in which conflict can affect different people?

Debatable: Can killing someone ever be wholly excused or justified?

Now **share and compare** your thoughts and ideas with your partner, or with the whole class.

○ IN THIS CHAPTER, WE WILL …

■ **Find out** what aspects of film content may be used by a director to affect a viewer's reactions.

■ **Explore** ways in which war can affect different individuals or communities in different ways.

■ **Take action** by considering, taking into account, and being guided by the moral and ethical implications of the choices we make.

■ These Approaches to Learning (ATL) skills will be useful …

■ Communication skills
■ Collaboration skills
■ Information literacy skills
■ Media literacy skills
■ Creative-thinking skills
■ Critical-thinking skills

◆ Assessment opportunities in this chapter:

◆ **Criterion A:** Analysing
◆ **Criterion B:** Organizing
◆ **Criterion C:** Producing text
◆ **Criterion D:** Using language

● We will reflect on this learner profile attribute …

● Principled – explore what is meant by acting with integrity, and with respect for the dignity and rights of others; take responsibility for one's own actions and their consequences.

'We are the choices we
make. And have to make.
We aren't anything else.'
– Patrick Ness, author

KEY WORDS

catalyst
chronological
dramatic tension
episodic
foreboding
graphic
impassive
ominous
premeditated
unwittingly

SEE–THINK–WONDER

1 Watch the following videos, all of which are from a TV series entitled *What would you do?*
   a https://youtu.be/gwNEEChLwSI
   b https://youtu.be/mt1JfmFb6Xg
2 Choose ONE of the videos on which to answer the following questions:
   a What do you see happening in the video? Describe what happens in one or two paragraphs.
   b What does it make you think? Describe in a paragraph your thoughts about how different people respond to the situation they encounter.
   c What does it make you wonder?

DISCUSS

3 What do you think you would have done had you been present in the scene and witnessed this scenario? **Explain** your decision.
4 In groups of four, share your responses to the questions above. Would you change what you have said, after hearing the points of view of others? If you changed your response, edit your paragraphs to incorporate any new viewpoints.
5 Look at the quote from Patrick Ness above. What do you think – or perhaps hope – that your own choice about what you would do says about the kind of person you are?
6 What judgements did you make about other people (not actors) in the video, on the basis of the choices they made in responding to the scene? Choose THREE characters in your video. For each one, write down the choice(s) they made, and then **comment** on what judgements those led you to make about the kind of people they are.

What are moral and ethical dilemmas?

ACTIVITY: What would you do?

■ ATL

- Communication skills: Make inferences and draw conclusions
- Collaboration skills: Encourage others to contribute
- Critical-thinking skills: Gather and organize relevant information to formulate an argument; evaluate evidence and arguments; consider ideas from multiple perspectives

ETHICAL DILEMMAS

Look at the following examples of ethical dilemmas that might arise in school.

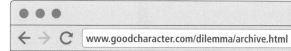

Ethical dilemmas in school

1 Three of Maryam's classmates have created an offensive website that attacks other students. The principal wants to know who did it; Maryam is the only one who knows. Maryam is not sure what she should do in the situation and whether she should lie to the principal, say which of her classmates are behind the website, or do something else.

2 Rajiv sees the same bully torment the same victim every day in the schoolyard, and nobody does anything about it. Rajiv has to decide whether to do something about the situation, or ignore it and mind his own business.

3 A high-achieving but stressed student has used a tutor to produce most of an internal assessment that will be used as part of her final examination grade. That grade will be needed for her to gain entry to university. Her best friend knows about the use of the tutor, but if she reports it to the school, the matter will then have to be reported to the examination board, and the student will be disqualified from the examination and receive no grade. As a result, she will lose her place at university. The student is pleading with her best friend not to report her collusion to the school. What should the friend do?

Source: adapted from www.goodcharacter.com/dilemma/archive.html

Read these two dilemmas in life.

4 Grace has the responsibility of filling a position in her firm. Her friend Maria has applied and is qualified for the role, but someone else has also applied who seems even more qualified. Grace wants, on the one hand, to give the job to Maria but feels guilty about this as she believes that she ought to be impartial. However, she also wonders if loyalty to her friend is in fact more important morally, in the circumstances. What should Grace do?

5 David confides to his friend Paul that he has daubed graffiti on the walls of a local shop, an act that is a criminal offence. Paul promises never to tell anyone about this. However, Paul later discovers that an innocent person has been accused of the crime, and pleads with David to give himself up. David refuses and reminds Paul of his promise. What should Paul do?

Source: adapted from www.friesian.com/valley/dilemmas.htm

1. In pairs, choose one of the three school scenarios. Each of you should then spend five minutes writing notes on what you think should be done by the character facing the ethical dilemma.
2. Share your thoughts with each other. Would either of you change your mind after hearing the other viewpoint?
3. Choose another partner and repeat this exercise with a different school dilemma.
4. Team up with another pair, and share your thoughts on the second dilemma. How far did everyone agree on what those involved should do?
5. Look at ethical dilemmas 4 and 5. Choose one of these scenarios. Imagine you are another friend of Grace, or Paul, according to the scenario you have chosen. You meet up with them informally over coffee where they explain the situation they are in and ask for your advice. In 450–550 words, write the script of the advice you would give, which includes the **justification** for that.

◆ Assessment opportunities

In this activity you have practised skills that are assessed using Criterion C: Producing text and Criterion D: Using language.

How to take notes

1. **Taking notes**
   Your notes should follow the same format: in style (for example, use of abbreviations) and structure (for example, allow space on your page to add later comments or revisions) – this makes it easier to read and search the information you have noted down. Be concise – you should record only the important information, and use bullet points and lists where possible.

2. **Reviewing notes**
   Review and revise the content of your notes afterwards to ensure you understand them, and that there are no errors or ambiguities. Highlight any key information and **identify** any links between different areas or information.

3. **Reflecting on notes**
   Write a brief summary of your notes to establish the key points, ideas and concepts. Include mention of how the information in these notes connects to previously learned information or ideas.

There are a number of different note-taking techniques. Research and **evaluate** the following methods, to help decide which works best for you:

- **Prose/linear note-taking** – information is recorded in the order you hear or read it, with a focus on key words and key details.
- **Sentence method** – every new fact or topic is recorded on a separate line. You must later review and organize your notes to determine key points and best order.

- **Outline note-taking** – notes are organized across the page, from left to right: major points are closest to the left-hand margin, subsequent or less important notes are indented across to the right-hand margin.
- **Visual notes** – such as mind-mapping or spider diagrams (individual key words or short phrases are noted down and connected to the central theme using lines).
- **Flow charts** – major ideas are recorded, with later points connected via arrows and flow lines. This method helps show and maintain key connections between points.
- **Cornell notes** – divide your page into two columns. Record your notes in one column and, afterwards, write any questions you have outstanding in the second column. Then, using just the questions as a prompt, check how well you remember your notes.
- **Charting or using tables** – use a table to order your notes, with different information in different columns and rows. This can help you draw out key information easily.
- **Mapping** – similar to flow charts, this organizes information neatly and works best for people with a visual memory.
- **Audio notes** – can help ensure key information is recorded and can be particularly useful for students with dyslexia. Note-taking software can help convert audio notes into written notes.

A website that might be helpful as a starting point when researching note-taking is **www2.open.ac.uk/students/skillsforstudy/notetaking-techniques.php**.

Film: *Cold Mountain* (2003)

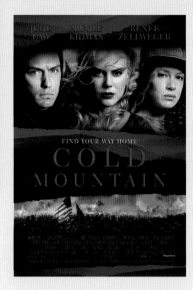

Director: Anthony Minghella

Main cast: Inman (Jude Law), Ada Monroe (Nicole Kidman), Ruby Thewes (Renée Zellweger)

Cold Mountain tells the story of love and devotion, set against the backdrop of the American Civil War, where a wounded soldier, Inman, sets out on a perilous journey back home to Cold Mountain to reunite with his sweetheart, Ada.

The film is based on the novel of the same name by Charles Frazier. *Cold Mountain* presents a context of war, which creates situations in which different individuals or communities may well more readily face significant moral and ethical choices. The novel and film consider, among other things, the question of how war can present different people with ethical and moral choices. It also invites an audience to consider what motivations may lie behind the choices those people (the characters) make, and what that may say about their characters and natures.

In this chapter, we will be looking closely at the film *Cold Mountain*. We suggest you watch the film all the way through before working through this chapter. There will be activities in this chapter where you will need to watch particular scenes again, or watch, stop and pause, as you make notes and have discussions about what you have seen.

REACTIONS

The choices we make and judgements we make of others depend on how we respond to them in both rational and emotional ways. Writers and film directors are well aware of this so try to create situations and scenes that will engage our interest through provoking reactions in us to what we see and hear.

Below is an extract from a blog entry written by 'Charisse', in which she talks about movies that made her cry. Read what she says about a scene from *Cold Mountain*.

Movies That Made Me Bawl My Eyes Out

I never used to cry while watching movies. I used to sit there and make fun of my mom for crying. That was all until I saw *Cold Mountain*. I went to see it in theatres with my mom, and that movie is filled with sad parts. The part that got to me, however, was the scene with Natalie Portman, where the Yankees come and raid her place. It's an awful scene. They tie her to a pole and lay her sick baby on the ground, and the whole time she's crying and asking them to cover up her baby. Suddenly, I just started feeling really bad, and my throat got sore, and I started to cry. Ever since then, I cry over everything!!! It is extremely annoying. I started crying last week at the end of *The Fly*, when Geena Davis killed Brundlefly! I hate crying in front of other people, so it is extremely embarrassing, but ever since I saw *Cold Mountain* there have been tons of movies to make me cry. There are only a select few, however, that made me bawl my eyes out. By bawl my eyes out, I do not mean just a few tears, I mean actually sobbing, and making noise, and obnoxiously crying. Sometimes it's just from one scene, or from the whole movie, but these are the movies that make me bawl my eyes out.

Source: originally published at http://nativeaudiogrrrl.blogspot.co.uk/2011/07/movies-that-made-me-bawl-my-eyes-out.html

ACTIVITY: Movies that made me bawl my eyes out

Think of a film or television programme you have seen that has provoked a strong reaction of some kind in you. It does not have to have made you cry – it could be a reaction of romantic longing, sadness, shock or feelings of outrage of the unfairness of the situation.

Answer the following questions to help you **describe** and **explain** your reaction to the film further.

1 What is the name of the film or TV programme you have chosen?
2 What one word would best **describe** the reaction you felt?
3 What do you think made you react in such a way?

4 Do you think it was intended that anyone watching the film or TV programme would react in such a way? If so, what makes you say that?
5 Was there a particular scene in the film or TV programme that provoked an especially strong reaction in you? **Describe** what happens in it and how you felt when watching it.

Use the answers you gave to the questions to write a blog entry of your own. Your teacher may provide a platform of some kind for sharing those. If that is the case, once you have posted your own blog entry read some of the other blog posts written by your classmates and **comment** on two of them, **explaining** whether what has been said makes you want to watch the film yourself or would put you off doing so.

Audience response words

We will be looking at how audiences might react to various sections of the film and techniques used to bring about audience responses. Use the diagram below when looking for vocabulary to describe possible audience reactions.

Note that this is not an exhaustive list of possible words. Why not build up your own vocabulary list?

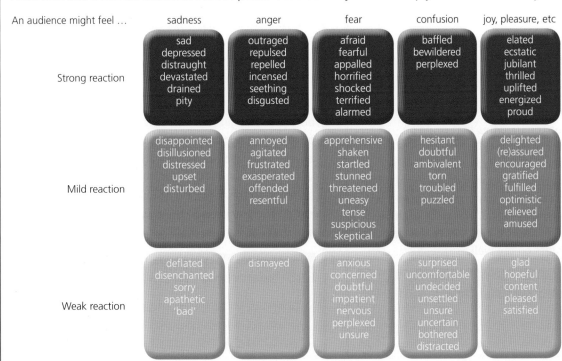

An audience might feel …	sadness	anger	fear	confusion	joy, pleasure, etc
Strong reaction	sad depressed distraught devastated drained pity	outraged repulsed repelled incensed seething disgusted	afraid fearful appalled horrified shocked terrified alarmed	baffled bewildered perplexed	elated ecstatic jubilant thrilled uplifted energized proud
Mild reaction	disappointed disillusioned distressed upset disturbed	annoyed agitated frustrated exasperated offended resentful	apprehensive shaken startled stunned threatened uneasy tense suspicious skeptical	hesitant doubtful ambivalent torn troubled puzzled	delighted (re)assured encouraged gratified fulfilled optimistic relieved amused
Weak reaction	deflated disenchanted sorry apathetic 'bad'	dismayed	anxious concerned doubtful impatient nervous perplexed unsure	surprised uncomfortable undecided unsettled unsure uncertain bothered distracted	glad hopeful content pleased satisfied

What can a war film show about the ways in which conflict can affect different people?

THE ETHICS OF WAR

Humans have been fighting each other since prehistoric times. The ethics of war debates the rights and wrongs of fighting and asks difficult questions like 'Who does war affect? Is it ever right to go to war? Is there a moral way to conduct a war?'

ACTIVITY: How can war affect different individuals or communities in different ways?

■ ATL

- Collaboration skills: Listen actively to other perspectives and ideas; encourage others to contribute

1 In groups of three or four, you will use a T-chart to record particular examples of individuals and communities that could be affected by war in some way.
2 On the left-hand side of the T-chart, list examples of individuals or communities that could be affected by war in some way.
3 On the right-hand side, **explain**, as precisely as possible, how each of the examples you listed might be affected. Do not forget that in some cases it is actually possible for effects of war to be positive.
4 Each group will **present** their ideas to the class. Display the posters on the wall.

◆ Assessment opportunities

In this activity you have practised skills that are assessed using Criterion B: Organizing.

ACTIVITY: How does war affect different people in different ways?

■ ATL

- Communication skills: Take effective notes in class; make effective summary notes for studying

One of our conceptual inquiry questions asks 'What can a war film show about the ways in which conflict can affect different people?' You have already considered that in general terms but we are now going to consider it in relation to the *Cold Mountain*.

First, copy out the table below. From what you remember from your first viewing of *Cold Mountain*, make notes about any individuals or groups of people whom you feel are portrayed as being affected in some way by war.

As you watch the film again, note down the way(s) in which you feel the individuals/groups are being affected. Combine your two sets of notes, expanding, correcting and developing them.

Individual/group affected	Description of how they are affected

Use your combined notes to write an essay, of 500–1,000 words, which shows the ways *Cold Mountain* represents how war can affect different people or communities in different ways.

Make sure you refer to the 'Essay planning' ATL cog before you begin your essay. With the help of that process, and good notes, your final essay should be a well-organized and accurately written analysis that uses examples from the film to illustrate your ideas and opinions on this topic. Do not be afraid to state these – just ensure you provide the evidence to support them, and that you explain them fully and clearly.

◆ Assessment opportunities

In this activity you have practised skills that are assessed using Criterion A: Analysing, Criterion B: Organizing and Criterion D: Using language.

Essay planning

In order to plan your analysis of a topic, it is important to review your notes. You need to:

- decide which points you will use
- decide on the order you will use them in, and
- **outline** how you intend to develop them.

Planning is a crucial stage of the process of producing *quality* writing, so ensure you give sufficient time and thought to it. Here is a process that you can use for planning and writing the essay. To help you in the 'How does war affect different people in different ways?' activity, specific advice for this task has been included in green.

✓ when complete	Process
	Read the task and make sure you understand it thoroughly.
	Review your notes very carefully, at least two times. • Have you included all of the individual people, groups and communities who were shown in the film as being affected by war, and whom you want to discuss in your essay? • Have you made clear and sufficient notes about how each of them is shown to be affected?
	Share your notes with a classmate to ensure you included all of the details needed to understand them yourself, and be able to convey them to a reader in a way that they will understand. Add any further details you may think of during this process, or that your classmate may suggest. • Note that, although it is not as easy to quickly 'skim-watch' a film as it is to skim-read a written text, this stage is important to complete.
	Brainstorm the points you want to use in the essay. You might want to consider using a MIND MAP or FLOW CHART to write these down and begin to develop your ideas. • Key points for this essay should relate to the individuals, groups and communities you are going to talk about.
	For each of your points, jot down ideas as to what you might say about them, in order to develop them. Keep the question/topic in mind and do not be afraid of offering some opinions of your own on this. • The topic for this essay is how war can affect each individual character/group/community). Bear in mind the possibility that some of the effects of war might be positive, rather than negative, for certain parties.
	Think about the ORDER in which you might explore your points in your essay. • Chronologically? Discuss each point or example as it occurs in the film. • By category? For instance, discuss points relating to individuals, followed by points relating to groups of people. • Character by character? Would you begin with Inman, or Ada, and then move through characters in order of their importance? • Might you use some other order? If so, what and why?
	Begin to write the introduction. Ensure you do the following: **1** Use a FORMAL register. **2** Write a thesis statement that signposts clearly the topic of discussion and main points you intend to make in the course of your essay.
	Begin to write the body paragraphs of the essay. Ensure you do the following: **1** Use a FORMAL register. **2** Make each point clearly when you begin to discuss it. **3** Explain points clearly and in as much detail as you can. Use the notes you made on these to help you do this. • Since the essay is about a film, there is less expectation for quotations to be used. You may have noted some, though, and should use them if so.
	After four or five paragraphs, share your work with a classmate to get feedback on your work so far, and to give some feedback on theirs: **1** Have you both explained or commented on everything as fully as you can? (Remember that including 'detail, development and support' are important aspects of Criteria A and B.) **2** Have you/they used language – vocabulary and punctuation, for instance – correctly and effectively? How appropriate (formal) is the **register** you are using (Criterion D)?
	Revise your opening paragraphs in the light of the advice you have been given, and write the rest of the essay.
	Proofread the whole essay, making changes where needed.
	Produce the final version of the essay and hand in by the deadline given to you by your teacher.

What are some of the main narrative features of *Cold Mountain*?

THE SEQUENCE OF EVENTS IN *COLD MOUNTAIN*

[V/O Ada reads letter to Inman] Confederate soldiers await Yankee attack. 0:30–4:56

F/B Ada and father arrive in Cold Mountain; Ada meets Inman. 4:56–9:06

Inman leaves hospital for Cold Mountain. 43:32–44:16

Outside hospital, Inman meets blind man who advises him to leave but warns that men going AWOL are being shot. 41:49–43:32

As letter is read to Inman, Teague is shown entering church to see Ada. Swangers visit farm; Ada hides. Ada's hardships are shown; her letter asks Inman to return. 39:20–41:49

Inman in hospital; Ada's letter with news of father's death is read to him. 38:10 …

Ada and father travel home then sit outside. Ada goes inside; calls father in but he has died. 35:13–38:10

On same day, Ada hears Bosie read a decree that deserters will be hunted down. 44:16–46:06

Ada meets Teague, who asks if everything is alright. 46:06–46:20

Ada eats with Swangers; she thinks she sees a vision of Inman in their well. 46:20–49:05

Ruby arrives to help Ada on the farm and sets out her terms. 49:05–51:34

On journey, Inman meets Pastor Veasey, about to drown a slave woman. Inman stops him. 51:34–54:47

At home in woods, Maddy feeds Inman and treats his wounds. 1:23:52–1:28:46

Ada and Ruby set Sally free. 1:22:48–1:23:52

Inman pulled along in cart by Maddy. 1:22:12–1:22:48

Home Guard arrive at Swanger farm and shoot Esco, then tie up and torture Sally. Her sons run out of barn where they'd been hiding and are shot by Teague and Bosie. 1:19:34–1:22:12

Inman is sole survivor of chain gang. 1:18:19–1:19:34

Ada and Ruby find Stobrod (Ruby's father) on their farm. 1:28:46–1:32:45

Inman leaves Maddy and begins journey again. 1:32:45–1:33:17

Ada wakes to Stobrod and Pangle playing music in thanks for food and clothing. Ruby listens to Ada reading. 1:33:17–1:35:49

Inman pleads for shelter in Sara's cottage; she allows him inside. 1:35:49–1:37:38

Sara prepares food for Inman and provides shelter. 1:37:38–1:40:02

Georgia rushes to farm with news of shootings. Ruby points out musicians' tracks in snow. 1:58:49–2:00:26

Bosie is unimpressed with music; he shoots Stobrod and Teague shoots Pangle. 1:57:35–1:58:49

Stobrod and Pangle play and sing. Georgia, in hiding, watches. 1:56:03–1:57:35

Teague asks musicians to play; Pangle reveals that they are deserters. 1:54:10–1:56:03

Musicians return to camp on mountain. Georgia is ill and, while he is gone, Home Guard arrive. 1:54:10–1:56:03

Ada and Ruby go to look for bodies; they find Stobrod still breathing so they take him to hut. 2:00:26–2:03:03

Ada goes to get food and meets Inman arriving back. She doesn't recognize him initially but then realizes who he is. 2:03:03–2:05:31

Ada takes Inman back to hut; Ruby is upset and talks about her plans for farm. Ada talks about her earlier vision of Inman. 2:05:31–2:07:25

Ruby helps Inman shave; she asks him if he has the right feelings for Ada. 2:07:25–2:08:29

On mountain, Ada and Inman talk. He says he received three letters from her; she says she sent 103. They reminisce; he talks about the effect of the war on him. 2:08:29–2:11:32

V/O Ada speaking to Inman. 2:25:10–2:25:42

Ada in fields with her daughter, trying to save a newborn lamb. 2:24:25–2:25:10

Wintry scene slowly changes to spring and Easter. 2:23:56–2:24:25

Ada and Inman speak; she kisses him as he dies. 2:22:20–2:23:56

Inman appears, staggering towards Ada, before falling as in the well vision. 2:21:55–2:22:20

Ruby and Georgia sit at a loaded table with their baby. Sally and Stobrod also sit, while Ada brings food and Stobrod plays violin. 2:25:42–2:26:46

V/O Ada explains how she looked in Swangers' well again but saw only clouds, clouds, and then the sun. 2:26:46–2:27:14

Key
V/O = voiceover
F/B = flashback
AWOL = absent without leave

Yankees attack but are trapped and shot by Confederate soldiers. 9:06–12:17

Inman picks up injured Confederate soldier and takes him inside to die. 12:17–16:40

F/B Function at Ada's house: Esco Swanger explains that Teague wanted the house now inhabited by Ada and her father. Inman tells Ada he loves her. 16:40–22:30

Confederate army is under threat. Inman is shot in neck while trying to rescue colleague. 22:30–23:56

F/B Ada and Inman meet in church. Inman frees a trapped dove. 23:56–25:24

Inman in hospital. 34:14–35:13

F/B Ada goes to Inman's lodgings; they kiss. Inman goes to join townsmen in war. 30:49–34:14

Inman is carried wounded from battle clutching papers (Ada's letters). 30:22–30:49

F/B News arrives in Cold Mountain community that war has been declared. Inman declares himself 'the law'. 27:32–30:22

F/B Inman visit's Ada's home; they walk and talk with Ada's father. 25:24–27:32

Ruby and Ada at breakfast; they go to work on farm, where Ruby gives Ada a list of jobs. 54:47–56:57

Inman walks through cornfield; group of slaves is trying to escape to north. Out of sight they are attacked; Inman escapes into river to evade dogs. 56:57–59:00

Inman meets Veasey in swamp. 59:00–59:28

Inman and Veasey accept help from girl in boat; she is shot. Inman and Veasey row out of danger. 59:28–1:01:01

Ada and Ruby on farm; then Ada is shown playing piano with Ruby listening. Piano is then carried away having been sold. Ruby talks about father's love of music. 1:01:01–1:05:08

Teague threatens Ada while she makes a scarecrow. 1:16:59–1:18:19

Inman and Veasey dragged along in chain gang; group is attacked by Yankees. Inman persuades prisoners to try to escape: shoot-out between Home Guard, Yankees and prisoners. 1:14:52–1:16:59

Ada and Ruby visit Sally but, strangely, she doesn't let them in. 1:13:07–1:14:52

Junior takes Inman and Veasey home and gets them drunk before handing them over to the Home Guard. 1:08:00–1:13:07

Inman and Veasey meet Junior, trying to pull a dead cow from a stream. 1:05:08–1:08:00

Ada, Ruby and Sally at Christmas party; Stobrod, Pangle and Georgia play music. 1:40:02–1:40:37

Sara invites Inman to sleep next to her; he turns down her advances and says he loves someone else. 1:40:37–1:43:41

Ruby watches Georgia sing; Ada places a bangle on her wrist. 1:43:41–1:44:51

Musicians leave farm; Ruby tells them not to sleep on farm. Ada tells Ruby and Sally that she loves them. 1:44:51–1:46:47

Inman leaves cottage quickly as three Yankees arrive. They take Sara's baby and force her to tell them where they can get food. 1:46:47–1:49:14

Inman walks through snowy landscape. 1:52:07–1:54:10

Musicians leave farm the morning after party, leaving footprints in snow. 1:51:35–1:52:07

While Yankee undresses, he explains that he hasn't eaten in a long time. As he is leaving, Sara shoots him dead. 1:50:25–1:51:35

Inman kills second Yankee and threatens the third; he orders him to undress. 1:49:49–1:50:25

Sara reveals where her hog is. A Yankee takes her inside to rape her; Inman is waiting inside and kills soldier. 1:49:14–1:49:49

Ruby interrupts Ada and Inman, saying she is disturbed by their talking. She says she will go to sleep with Stobrod. 2:11:32–2:11:58

Ada and Inman go to Ruby's hut. Ruby is shown lying next door, crying. 2:11:58–2:12:37

In hut, Ada and Inman discuss marriage and perform their own marriage ceremony. 2:12:37–2:14:23

Ada and Inman spend night together. 2:14:23–2:15:43

Ada and Ruby set off for farm; Inman asks Ruby if he can live on farm. 2:15:43–2:17:35

Ada runs up path in a scene similar to the vision in the well. 2:21:42–2:21:55

Bosie is dead. It becomes clear that Inman has been shot too. 2:21:16–2:21:42

Ada and Ruby hear shots; Ada screams and runs towards shots. 2:21:00–2:21:16

Inman rides after Bosie. After a shouted conversation, they shoot at each other simultaneously. 2:19:54–2:21:00

Stobrod rides down. Teague goes to kill him but Ruby shoots at Teague to stop him. Bosie rides away during shoot-out and Teague is shot dead by Inman. 2:18:55–2:19:54

On way to farm, Teague and Bosie stop Ada and Ruby, and tell them they have caught Georgia on farm. They threaten Ada and Ruby. 2:17:35–2:18:55

What are the intentions and effects of narrative structures?

TYPES OF PLOT STRUCTURE

Texts such as novels, short stories and, indeed, films can use different types of plot and narrative devices for particular effects. Some of the most prominent found in the film version of *Cold Mountain* are **cyclical structural techniques**, **parallel plotlines**, **flashbacks**, foreshadowing and **framing**.

❶ Types of plot structure

- **Cycles of time/cyclical structure** show the passing of time.
- **Parallel plots** are where the narrative switches from one plot to another, with the two plots usually linked by a common character or similar theme.
- **Flashbacks** are scenes in a film, novel, and so on, which are set in another time from the main story.
- **Foreshadowing** is where hints or clues are given about something that will happen later on in the narrative. It is used to raise a reader's expectations, or *anticipation*, about what is to happen.
- **Framing** is where interlinking stories provide an overall 'frame' or pattern that surrounds the narrative. In *Cold Mountain,* Inman and Ada's stories create an overall pattern of separation–reunion–separation–reunion– separation, which 'frames' the overall narrative of the film.
- **Episodic plot** is where the plot is broken into divisible episodes.

ACTIVITY: The narrative structure of *Cold Mountain*

■ ATL

■ Communication skills: Organize and depict information logically

Look at the timeline on pages 198–199 that details the sequence of events taking place throughout *Cold Mountain*. From the diagram, **identify** all of the structural elements of the narrative that you can (for example, cycles of time, parallel plots, flashbacks, foreshadowing, framing and episodic plot). How do you think these narrative elements help the story? Can you see any patterns in the way these features are used?

EXTENSION

As you can see from the timeline, a good way of representing a sequence of events is by a concept map or flow diagram. Choose a film that presents a moral or ethical dilemma (some suggestions are given below) and record the sequence of events for all or part of your chosen film's narrative. What narrative elements can you **identify**?

Share your analysis with a classmate who examined a different film from you. Do your films use similar techniques? Why (not)? Does the age or genre of the film affect how it has been filmed?

Suggested films:

Never Let Me Go   *12 Angry Men*

Saving Private Ryan   *Changing Lanes*

Lions for Lambs   *Crash* (2004)

The Truman Show   *Hotel Rwanda*

◆ Assessment opportunities

In this activity you have practised skills that are assessed using Criterion A: Analysing and Criterion B: Organizing.

Cycles of time/cyclical structure

In *Cold Mountain*, this is shown most clearly in the use of the seasons, showing the passing of time and often also symbolizing the nature of events taking place within them – more optimistic and pleasant events tend to take place in sunshine, while harsher events often occur within a wintry landscape.

The most obvious contrast of this kind occurs at the end of the film, where the scenes showing the shootings of the musicians and deaths of Pangle, Teague, Bosie and Inman all take place in a snowy setting, symbolizing the bleakness of the events, and the human coldness and lack of human feeling in so many of these characters. This includes Inman, whose experiences have turned him into a killer himself, as shown most vividly in his very deliberate and cold-blooded killing of Teague, who is completely defenceless at the time Inman kills him. We will look more closely at this scene in an activity later in the chapter.

The final scene, taking place in the bright sunshine of spring, and full of symbols of new life and abundance (the lambs, the young children, the shots of fruit on the trees, the spread of food, and so on), is – in complete contrast – full of human warmth and love, and strongly suggests new and hopeful beginnings.

The use of nature to reflect events and feelings and actions of humans within them represents a technique called **pathetic fallacy**, which is used constantly throughout the film. One such scene, which again suggests strongly the theme of the cycle of time, is that of the death of Ada's father, Reverend Monroe. The weather as he and Ada sit outside becomes colder and breezier, and when Ada goes inside to play the piano, a storm ominously blows in. When she goes to find her father, he has died.

The cyclical structure of the film thus shows us the cyclical nature of time – how life and time carry on through everything, and how all things pass, both the best of times and the worst of times. Thus we began by being shown the best of times, when Ada and Inman fell in love (again in scenes full of sunshine), through flashbacks Inman has during the worst of times in the war that followed. Those worst times also pass, however, and the film finishes amid scenes of human love in the sunshine once more.

Parallel plots

The two protagonists, Ada and Inman, are separated by war, and their stories as they come back together are told using a parallel plot device, with the narrative of the film switching from one to the other.

Much of Ada's story in the beginning is told in flashback, until the point at which Inman is shown on the Carolina coast, and Ada enters a shop to try to sell her father's watch for food. At this point, for the first time the stories of the two protagonists are told synchronously, that is, they are happening at the same time. The respective plots allow both characters to go on a human journey of development and evolution, before they meet again.

ACTIVITY: The parallel plot

■ ATL

- Media literacy skills: Make informed choices about personal viewing experiences; communicate information and ideas effectively using a variety of media and formats

This activity will help you to become more familiar with the events of the film overall, and of the parallel plots in particular.

Look at the sequence of events on pages 198–199. Find the box with the timing 38:10 (which states 'Inman in hospital; Ada's letter with news of father's death is read to him.').

Ada has written many letters to Inman about what has been happening at home in Cold Mountain, without knowing if he has received any of them. Not only has Inman received many but also they form a catalyst for his decision to desert and try to return to Ada. We can see this from the scene in which Inman is carried wounded from the battlefield, clutching the letters tightly. When he is placed injured on a train, a man runs to hand him the letters he has, we are told, been worrying about; then we see the impact Ada's letter containing news of her father's death has on him when it is read to him.

Communication between the two is thus of great importance; today it would be a great deal easier. Now look at the sequence of events for the remainder of the film (pages 198–199).

First, colour-code the events involving Ada in red, and the other events taking place in the course of Inman's journey in blue.

Imagine these two characters were able to communicate with each other during this period by using Twitter, and sent a series of tweets to let the other know what was happening. Choose THREE of the scenes described in the shaded boxes for Ada, and THREE for Inman, and for each box write a tweet that summarizes the event in no more than 140 characters.

◆ Assessment opportunities

In this activity you have practised skills that are assessed using Criterion A: Analysing, Criterion B: Organizing, Criterion C: Producing text and Criterion D: Using language.

Flashback

The events of the film in chronological terms begin when Inman and his fellow soldiers are shown in their trench just before the large explosion carried out by their enemies. The director uses flashbacks to show events that have taken place before the action of the film itself begins. Such flashbacks occur when, for instance, Inman has been stunned (such as when his trench is blown up at the start of the film) or injured. One flashback, when Inman is in hospital, is generated by a different technique, namely the use of a letter read out to him by an unnamed female visitor.

Both Inman and Ada focus often on their memories, which form a significant plot **catalyst**, motivating some of their most important decisions and actions. For instance, Inman's determination to return to Cold Mountain, and Ada's decision and determination not to leave from there. The flashbacks thus have several functions:

- As a plot catalyst, motivating Inman's actions in returning to Cold Mountain and Ada.
- Filling in important background information, especially about Ada's and Inman's love story, and other characters such as Ada's father, and Teague.
- Allowing us to see the cycles of time, through the contrast they show between happier times in Cold Mountain before the war, and the situation during the war.

Foreshadowing

The film makes a great deal of use of symbolism, in particular as a device for foreshadowing, where a director or author provides a clue as to something that will happen later on.

Ways of foreshadowing

There are various ways in which foreshadowing might be achieved in a film. Some of those ways are through:

- a character's actions, which may mirror in some way actions they may take later
- dialogue, which reveals information suggesting something may happen later
- a character's physical appearance, which may suggest how that character may be anticipated to act
- a prop, which has symbolic significance
- costume, which may suggest subsequent actions, events, and so on
- music, which evokes a mood and suggests how things may be as they move forwards
- lighting and colours evoked
- aspects of setting that may symbolize the future.

Purposes of foreshadowing

There are a number of reasons why directors and writers use foreshadowing, including:

- In inviting an audience to look ahead, foreshadowing most commonly increases an audience's sense of anticipation.
- Often, foreshadowing serves to create an ominous mood, and a sense of **foreboding**, if it seems that something bad may happen in the future.
- Foreshadowing can also increase an audience's awareness of a character, and hint at some of their ethical or moral standpoints.

ACTIVITY: Foreshadowing

■ ATL

■ Information literacy skills: Use critical-literacy skills to analyse and interpret media communications

Let us look more at some of the ways in which foreshadowing helps suggest the ethics and nature of characters in *Cold Mountain*, as well as increasing dramatic tension. The timings given for each example indicate where in the film the particular scene occurs.

Timings	Description of scene in which foreshadowing occurs
16:40–22:30	During a function at Ada's house, given by her father to thank everyone for their efforts in building the new church, Teague rudely walks across Ada's father, Reverend Monroe, as he makes a speech. Esco Swanger explains that Teague's grandfather had once owned all of Cold Mountain, and Teague wanted the house that Ada and her father have acquired instead. This is the first appearance in the film of Teague, who is a large man with a thick dark beard. He is – as usual in the film – dressed all in black.
23:56–25:24	Ada and Inman meet in the church, where they find a dove that is unable to get out. Inman manages to catch it and takes it outside to set it free.
35:13–38:10	Ada and her father are sitting at a table outside their home. Ada tells her father to keep warm against the cold, while her father asks her to play the piano. As Ada goes inside and does so, the weather worsens and she calls her father in.
46:20–49:05	When Ada has a meal with Sally and Esco Swanger, she looks down their well and thinks she sees a vision of Inman.
1:08–1:13	Junior takes Inman and Veasey back home for a meal. They approach and enter the house, greeted by female members of Junior's family.
1:51–1:52	Following the Christmas party, the musicians disobey Ruby and spend the night at the farm. Snow falls. The musicians are shown departing over the bridge in the snow the morning after the party. They leave footprints in the snow as they depart.
2:03–2:05	In a snowy landscape, Ada goes off to shoot a bird for food. While out on the path she sees Inman arriving back. He is dressed all in black and she does not initially recognize him.
2:17–2:18	On their way back to the farm, Ada and Ruby are stopped by Teague and Bosie, who inform the girls that they have captured Georgia on the farm. Teague and Bosie threaten Ada and Ruby, and Teague shows them the black and red coat that Ruby had made and which Pangle was wearing when he was killed by Teague.

Read the descriptions of the scenes in the second column (and, if possible, watch them again). In groups of three or four, complete the blank sections of the table, ensuring you **explain** what is being foreshadowed in a particular scene, what techniques the director is using to create foreshadowing, and what the purpose of it appears to be. The first one has been done for you as an example.

What is being foreshadowed?	The means by which foreshadowing is introduced	The purpose of the use of foreshadowing
• Teague's action of walking across Rev Monroe shows that he is an aggressive man who wants to show that he is more powerful than anyone else, and has no concern for anyone else at all – or even perhaps that he wants to spoil any love and joy that others might want to enjoy at a particular time, as at this celebratory event. This foreshadows his highly destructive and cruel actions as the leader of the Home Guard. • The revelation that his grandfather once owned all of Cold Mountain, and that Teague had wanted Ada's and her father's house before they purchased it, suggests that he is likely to resent Ada and her father, and may try to take back the house, or take out his resentment on the Monroes later on in the film. • Teague's appearance as a large and overbearing man is an intimidating one. • Teague's black costume hints at the morality of his character – he is in the film an evil man without morals, who likes to find excuses to kill.	• A character's actions • Dialogue • Physical appearance • Costume	• To reveal character, and the ethics of the character. • To reveal information which – since it has been mentioned – suggests something may happen later. It thus serves to increase anticipation and tension. • To increase tension and create an ominous mood. • To suggest character and the morality of the character.
	• Use of setting, especially the weather	
	• Use of music • Use of lighting and colours	
	• Props – Teague's gun, his neck scarf, and the coat Pangle was wearing when he was shot by Teague • Colours	

◆ Assessment opportunities

In this activity you have practised skills that are assessed using Criterion A: Analysing.

Framing

The film is framed by an overall pattern in the cases of Inman and Ada of separation–union–separation–reunion–separation. This again reflects the cycles and passing of time, and perhaps the role of fate in one's life, along with themes such as the importance of human relationships over isolation and the human desire to overcome isolation and achieve union.

Episodic plot

Inman's journey is 'episodic' – broken into divisible episodes. As such it parallels the classical story of Odysseus's journey home from the Trojan War, in Homer's *Odyssey*, particularly as the episodes involve Inman, like Odysseus, undergoing a variety of trials. As such the plot is a classical **allusion**, along with several individual episodes within it, such as the scene at Junior's house where Inman is tempted by a woman, which reflects the story of Odysseus's encounter with the Sirens in the Greek myth. Meanwhile his efforts to pull along dead companions chained together is an allusion to the myth of Sisyphus, who was sentenced to push a heavy rock up a hill for eternity, only to see it each time roll all the way back down to the bottom.

A classical allusion is 'a reference to a particular event or character in classical works of literature, such as ancient Roman or Greek works' (**www.wisegeek.com/what-is-classical-allusion.htm**).

Allusions are often made to *The Odyssey* in other works, especially where a protagonist undertakes a journey of some kind, and meets various challenges and trials along the way. *Cold Mountain* is one such work that makes a number of allusions to *The Odyssey*.

ⓘ *The Iliad* and *The Odyssey*

The Iliad and *The Odyssey* are two epic poems by Homer that tell the story of the Trojan War fought between the Greeks and the Trojans (the *Iliad*), and then of Odysseus's journey back home from the war. The poems are thought to have been composed – quite possibly orally, rather than in written form – around the end of the eighth century BCE.

The Odyssey is an epic poem made up of no fewer than 24 books – although these are more like chapters in length.

EXTENSION: CLASSICAL ALLUSIONS – *THE ODYSSEY*

Research the story of **Odysseus** by reading about it here: www.shmoop.com/odyssey/book-i-summary.html, or search for other sources that summarize his journey.

Choose one of the books between 1 and 24, and **create** a storyboard of what you think are the six to eight most important points to make about that book.

Once complete, **identify** any parallels you can between the Classical myth of Odysseus and what happens to Inman in *Cold Mountain*.

Creating storyboards

Storyboards are a further form of visual note-taking, and can help you in things such as the following:

- selecting important ideas, processes and sequences
- keeping track of those ideas, processes or sequences
- summarizing them
- visualizing them.

Choosing what to include in the storyboard compels you to evaluate and be selective over what is important. When you are looking at events in literature, selecting and visualizing events can help you understand more fully what is happening. It can also help you better remember incidents (and their order – necessary if something like a timeline, or the elements of a 'cause and effect' plot, is important).

Once you have completed a storyboard, you can do other things with it – such as cutting up the individual frames and trying to reorder them in a different way to see how that may appear, or adding written information on the back of a frame, and then testing yourself on what is being represented in it by looking at the illustration and details and providing a commentary, written or oral, on that. Storyboards can help students who may find some difficulty in expressing themselves in the language of instruction to show their learning and understanding in a way that depends less on that language. They help your teacher to see how much you have understood of what you have been reading, exploring, and so on.

An example of what your storyboard might look like once it has been completed can be seen here: **https://goo.gl/z27h9s**.

▼ Links to: Arts

Have you learned about storyboarding in your media and drama classes? How important are storyboards for films, actors and directors?

As we have seen, various structural techniques can be used to create various effects, including motivating the development of character and helping to reveal that. We see how characters are placed in situations within the narrative in which they are able, and at times have to, make moral and ethical choices that reveal their nature. This mirrors what happens in real life, and brings us back to the quotation by Patrick Ness at the beginning of the chapter: 'We are the choices we make. And have to make. We aren't anything else.'

So let us now consider some of the characters in the film and the choices they have to make, along with how these contribute to their characterization. In this way we can look at what the film has to say about moral and ethical choices, and their role in helping to make us who we are as human beings.

ACTIVITY: Dynamic characterization

ATL

- Information literacy skills: Use critical-literacy skills to analyse and interpret media communications
- Critical-thinking skills: Interpret data

Inman and Ada are the two main characters, or protagonists, in the film, with Ruby also playing a major role. All three are dynamic characters, which means they undergo changes and evolve as the film – and their personal (and in Inman's case physical) journeys – develop.

The use of narrative structures such as the parallel plots, framing of union–separation, and cycles of time enable us as viewers to compare them at earlier and later points, and see the ways in which their characters evolve and develop. This can be seen in the comparisons we are invited to make between Ada and Inman, and Ada and Ruby.

The use of *parallel plots* allows us to see the two protagonists at the start of their relationship; and to compare them with that when they are reunited; something that helps to show the substantial changes that both characters have undergone. Such changes are, meanwhile, further emphasized by some of the film techniques employed in these scenes.

Let us look at and **compare** the two scenes showing Inman and Ada when they first meet at the beginning of their story (04:56–09:06), prior to the war, and as they are reunited when Inman arrives on the path to the hut in which Ada and Ruby are staying.

What impressions are given of Inman and Ada respectively, in this scene that shows their first meeting?

In making points about this, we need to **interpret** the data we see and hear. That data includes:
- **what the characters say, and their actions and appearances**
- **techniques used and choices made by the director, such as the use of** *costume* (including colour), *props* and aspects of the *setting*.

Possible interpretations of Inman, on the basis of the data presented in the scene, are given as an example in the table opposite. Feel free to add any further observations of your own on the detail relating to Inman in this scene.

Inman in the first conversation with Ada	Inman – possible interpretations
Actions:	
• Is hammering wooden planks to make the roof of the church	• Works hard, tough as can do physical work in the hot sun
• Keeps looking at Ada from the church roof	• Interested in Ada
• Takes off hat when greets Ada	• Polite and well-mannered
Words:	
• 'I work wood. I mostly work wood.'	• A man of few words, as commented by others in the scene. Straight and to the point when he speaks, and seems to have little to say that might be very profound. Seems to have little wider experience of anything. However, he says he 'works wood', and then seems about to say something else and stops, before adding that he 'mostly' works wood' – hints at a more mysterious, hidden side to him
• Agrees after hesitation to clear a field	• Suggests his interest in Ada, as he seems to agree in order to please her
• Gives his name as 'WP Inman' and then says that repeating it doesn't make it any better	• Seems self-conscious about his name – possibly wants to impress Ada, when of a lower status? Not saying what the 'WP' stands for again hints at a more mysterious side to him
• Formal/polite in how he addresses Ada	• Suggests a decent man, respectful of others
Appearance:	
• Young and handsome, no beard	• He is innocent and inexperienced.
Costume:	
• Wears light-coloured work clothes	• Represent his status as a local worker. Light colours may also represent his inexperience and innocence at this point – later he only wears dark clothes
Setting:	
• Is working on building the new church	• Symbolically associated with something holy, or more morally upright
• Is on the roof	• Again may suggest moral uprightness at this point
• Sunny day	• *Pathetic fallacy* – suggests a pleasant, warm, hopeful time
Props:	
• Hammer and nails	• Show he is a hard worker

Now, copy out a blank version of the table and complete the table, but this time you should observe Ada during her conversation with Inman, and make notes on your observations and interpretations for her.

In pairs, complete the same exercise again but use the scene in which Inman returns to Cold Mountain and meets Ada once more (2:03–2:05). One of you should observe Inman and the other Ada. Compare your notes once complete.

◆ Assessment opportunities

In this activity you have practised skills that are assessed using Criterion A: Analysing and Criterion D: Using language.

What can the use of violence say about human nature?

ACTIVITY: Why use scenes of violence?

ATL

- Communication skills: Take effective notes in class; make effective summary notes for studying
- Media literacy skills: Make informed choices about personal viewing experiences; understand the impact of media representations and modes of presentation

Our **conceptual** question asked, 'What can the use of violence say about human nature?'

A further scene following closely on from when Inman returns to Cold Mountain and meets Ada once more, and which reveals how these two characters have changed, is that in which Teague is forced from his horse and killed. This is one of a number of scenes of violence in the film that raise moral and ethical questions. We will look at that scene in more depth, but before we do so, let us consider the wider context of scenes of violence in the film, along with their purposes and presentation.

Writing a scene analysis

When analysing a scene it is important to **identify** key points and moments, explain why you think they are important, and then **justify** and support your reasoning with evidence. The following breakdown of the analysis process will help you when you do your own analysis. The *Cold Mountain* example used in the breakdown is the scene showing the execution of the musician deserters (Stobrod and Pangle) by Teague and Bosie.

Scene summary:

It is useful to begin an analysis with a brief summary of the scene or extract that is being explored. How a writer says something will link to what the writer is saying, and so it is important to have an idea of the latter from the start. It also helps, when exploring detail in a text, to have a picture in mind of what is taking place overall, and you can create that if you first write a brief summary (not a long description, narrative or paraphrase, note!) of the content of the extract.

To do this, you could try writing three to five bullet point statements which include the most important points about what a passage is saying. You can then combine these into a prose summary.

Those points might consider, and cover, the following:

- What actions take place in the scene
- Characters, particularly those who seem to be important
- The setting, which may be important in some way.

Keep in mind that whatever you see in a scene – actions, characters, setting – are there because the director has chosen to include them, and they are therefore likely to be significant in some way. Writing a summary to begin with helps in noting what is actually in a scene. You can then start to think about why it may have been included.

Statements on how viewers might react to the scene:

Analysis of a text involves considering **audience** and **purpose** – how a director or writer might try to persuade their audience to react in a particular way, and why they may be trying to do that.

A viewer might, for instance, be invited to feel different emotions towards characters, which may shape their impressions of those characters. It may also shape their views on a particular topic, or **theme** which the text is about – such as a theme of war, for instance.

In analysing a text, there is a need to suggest emotions which it seems an audience is being invited to feel through what is presented. The following are some

Look at some of the scenes of violence in the film, and explore the reasons for why the director included them.

a   **The battle scene (09:12–14:23); the clip is also available at** https://youtube.com/watch?v=x5fbYJMEyes
b   **Torture of mother (Sally Swanger) –** https://youtu.be/YIzeMI8Uxjo
c   **Yankee soldiers stealing food from a widow –** https://youtu.be/ozDgVHAZ7lI
d   **Shooting of the musician deserters –** https://youtu.be/fHZ4kgOzpyU
e   **Killing of Teague (0:00–2:10) –** https://youtu.be/Qvpj4IARWMw
f   **Deaths of Inman and Bosie (02:10–4:26) –** https://youtu.be/Qvpj4IARWMw

Note: as the same video extract contains both e) the killing of Teague and f) the deaths of Inman and Bosie, use only from 2:10 to 4:26 if you wish to do f) for this activity.

Note: Scenes c–e are considered in detail in other activities and should not be chosen for this activity.

One purpose of such scenes in a film is to elicit particular responses in a viewer. Scenes of violence are especially designed to provoke certain reactions.

Choose one of the three permitted scenes (a, b or f), from the list above, and then write a prose analysis of the scene.

1   **Describe** the scene in three to five sentences.
2   **State** how you would expect most viewers to react to the scene.
3   **Identify** and **list** some specific aspects of the scene a viewer is actually reacting to.
4   Next to each aspect noted, **explain** why you think each aspect evokes such a response/responses.

examples of possible emotions a viewer may feel on watching this particular scene of *Cold Mountain*. You can, if you wish, refer to the list of words for emotion given on page 195 of this book.

Viewers might feel <u>hopeful</u> at first that Stobrod and Pangle will escape, when Teague is not sure if they are the deserters he is looking for, and then when he seems to be moved by the music.

Viewers may be <u>fearful</u> when seeing how Bosie has no feelings at all, and <u>appalled</u> at his coldness towards killing the two musicians.

Finally, viewers are likely to feel <u>pity</u> and <u>sadness</u> for Stobrod and Pangle when it becomes clear they are going to be shot, and are completely defenceless. They may well be <u>shocked</u> by the graphic depiction of the shooting of the musicians, and <u>repulsed</u> and <u>outraged</u> by the act.

Some specific aspects of the scene a viewer is actually reacting to:

It is also very important to consider what exactly an audience is reacting to in a text, which leads them to experience a particular emotion. These are the choices, and techniques, which a director or writer is using with the purpose of trying to evoke emotion of some kind.

Use of the following elements can all help to evoke emotion of some kind in a viewer of a film:

- Setting
- Costume
- Camera angles, such as close-ups of facial expressions
- Particular words or dialogue
- Particular actions

Below are some suggestions as to how some of these things may be being used in this scene from *Cold Mountain*, in order to evoke particular emotions in a viewer:

Setting – the darkness helps to create an <u>ominous</u> scene and suggests that something evil is going to happen. The snow suggests (<u>symbolism</u>) the coldness of what Teague and the Home Guard have come to do in the scene, and the lack of human warmth or feeling.

Costume – all of the Home Guard are dressed in black, as if wearing funeral clothes. Stobrod and Pangle are also wearing dark-coloured clothes that contain red, as if <u>foreshadowing</u> that their blood will be spilt in the scene.

Actions – the actual shooting happens very quickly, perhaps more quickly than we expect, and therefore comes as something of a shock. Pangle's act of smiling shows his innocence and unawareness, and makes the shooting all the more tragic and shocking.

ACTIVITY: Your reaction to a violent scene

ATL

- Communication skills: Give and receive meaningful feedback
- Information literacy skills: Present information in a variety of formats and platforms

You are now going to take your prose analysis from the 'Why use scenes of violence?' activity and turn it, and any other notes you took from the scene, into a short speech. The speech should **explore** your personal responses to the scene and your reasons for those responses. It should also include explanations of the literary and other techniques used by the director.

1 **Find one or two classmates who chose the same scene as you in the 'Why use scenes of violence?' activity. Together, discuss the reactions you had and how these were elicited by the film. You should also discuss any vocabulary you think might be used in articulating emotions or other responses experienced by a viewer. Take notes of any key points made during this discussion that might be useful to your own presentation.**
2 **Using your previous prose analysis and notes from your discussion, prepare a speech of three to five minutes on your chosen scene. Use the notes about oral presentation skills, above, to help you.**
3 **Find two or three classmates who looked at a scene different from the one you did and get into a group. Present your speech to each other on your different scenes and provide feedback, on both the content of the speech and its presentation.**

◆ Assessment opportunities

In this activity you have practised skills that are assessed using Criterion A: Analysing and Criterion D: Using language.

Oral presentation skills

When preparing for an oral presentation, bear the advice below in mind to help you write, prepare and present the best presentation you can.

- Show knowledge and understanding of the topic/content
  - When planning your speech **identify** your key points and **outline** how you intend to develop each one. Plan the order and structure of your speech, and decide how to present and deliver your points in a way appropriate for the activity and topic.

ACTIVITY: The death of Teague

ATL

- Media literacy skills: Understand the impact of media representations and modes of presentation

Now let us look at the scene that shows the death of Teague (around 2:17–2:20). As a class, watch the scene once again then, individually, **identify** some of the techniques the director uses and **explain** the reasons why.

Teague death scene: **https://youtu.be/Qvpj4lARWMw**

Think back to some of the techniques we saw used in the reunion scene between Ada and Inman (the second scene we examined in the 'Dynamic characterization' activity). Have any of these same techniques been used again?

◆ Assessment opportunities

In this activity you have practised skills that are assessed using Criterion A: Analysing.

- Show thorough appreciation of the aspect discussed
  - Consider multiple perspectives on the subject and, when planning, make sure you are addressing the question that has been asked (and not the question you want to answer!).
- Use appropriate strategies to engage an audience
  - Will you use visual aids? Audio prompts? Will you interact with the audience?
  - Your tone, register, body language and eye contact all impact how well your presentation will be received by your audience. For Criterion D, remember to take into account these aspects of oral communication: pronunciation, intonation, tone, pitch, inflection, pace, pausing, voice control, volume, projection, body language, gesture, and eye contact.
- Deliver the presentation in a manner and register that is appropriate to the task and audience
  - What level of understanding does your audience have on the subject? Should you explain things in detail, or as a reminder only? Is this a formal presentation (with formal vocabulary and register?), or a more relaxed presentation?

There is a lot of excellent advice online about how to best give an oral presentation. The website below is a good starting point, but what else can you find?

https://goo.gl/WQwV8V

ACTIVITY: A different angle on Teague's death scene

ATL

- Critical-thinking skills: Revise understanding based on new information and evidence; interpret data

In Teague's death scene there is a distinct use of a film-specific technique – camera shots and angles – to help show how these characters have changed.

A number of storyboard stills from this scene have been reproduced below. Look at each image and read its associated comments. For each still, consider the use of the camera and answer the questions posed.

Watch the scene again and try to **identify** any other camera angles used. For new and repeated camera angles you should state which angle has been used and – more importantly – why. What is the purpose or benefit of the chosen angle to the scene?

	**Timing: 2:18:54** This still shows a camera **long shot**, with the camera filming downwards from a **high angle** behind Teague's shoulder and across a distance. What effects do you think the director was trying to achieve through such a camera shot? This is also known as a **point-of-view** shot. Whose point of view are we being shown?
	**Timings: 2:18:33–2:18:46** The camera is not always still – while movement of a camera cannot be seen in a still, at this point in the film if you watch the sequence you will see that it is **panning** across the scene, echoing how Ada and Ruby are being surrounded and encircled by the Home Guard. In what ways is this shot also similar to the one used of Teague above?
	**Timing: 2:19:01** This is called a **mid shot**, which focuses more closely on two of the characters in the same scene. What does changing to this type of shot enable the director to do, which was not so possible in the previous **point-of-view** shot? What is the **angle** of the camera for this shot? Why do you think this was chosen?

	**Timing: 2:18:59** Here is another **mid shot**, but what angle is the camera at this time? How does it differ from the angle used in the shot of Ada and Ruby? Why has the director used this angle for this particular shot, do you think?
	**Timing: 2:20:04** Now that we have looked at a few camera shots and angles, and why they are used, what can you say about the use of the camera in this shot?
	**Timing: 2:20:03** And what about this one?
	**Timing: 2:20:08** Where is the camera in this shot? What is the effect of that on the impression a viewer might have of Inman here?
	**Timing: 2:20:09** This shot is called a **close-up** shot. Why do you think the director has chosen to use it with Teague at this particular point?
	**Timing: 2:20:11** What can you say about the use of the camera and angles in this shot?
	**Timing: 2:20:12** This **close-up** shot is used when Inman goes to Teague to take his gun. Why do you think the director has used this **close-up** here?
	**Timing: 2:20:14** What kind of camera shot and angle are being used in this still? To what effect?

◆ Assessment opportunities

In this activity you have practised skills that are assessed using Criterion A: Analysing and Criterion D: Using language.

Language and Literature for the IB MYP 4&5: *by Concept*

Ruby is the third dynamic character. Her character is used to counterpoint that of Ada. Their parallel storylines enable the viewer to compare and contrast them throughout the film, which helps show how both change as a result of their situation.

Ruby and Ada very much contrast each other when they first meet. This scene is where Ruby first appears in the film, arriving to help Ada at her homestead (timings: 53:05–54:53). You can watch the scene again in this short clip: **https://youtu.be/jmpuAz59EbQ**.

Using a Venn diagram, make notes on differences between Ruby and Ada that you identify in this scene, and – in the middle section – any similarities you see.

Ruby and Ada begin almost as opposite characters when they first meet, but gradually develop to each take on the attributes of the other. Their journey also has a parallel structure, though once Ruby has entered the film they are almost always seen together, allowing us to compare and contrast them and to notice those changes. If you or your teacher wishes, you can learn more about their journey as dynamic characters in the digital material that accompanies this chapter.

Here for the moment, though, we will look at the entry of Ruby from the perspective of the MYP eAssessments. This particular scene was used in the very first eAssessment for MYP English Language and Literature in May 2015.

PRACTISING eASSESSMENTS

In the eAssessment, this scene formed part of a task along with another text – a passage from a short story called *The Drover's Wife*.

- The task involved **analysing** a passage from *The Drover's Wife*, reproduced below, and answering a set of questions (1a–c).
- This was then followed by the scene of Ruby's entrance in *Cold Mountain,* and some questions on that. The format of this part of the eAssessment is to use two texts, one written and one visual, and to ask questions on each text individually (1d–e).
- After this, students have to **compare** a literary aspect that is present in both texts. In the case of these two texts, that aspect was the presentation of the female characters (1f).

Get together in a group of four, and **discuss** what you might answer for each of the questions listed in Task 1 and Task 2.

The Drover's Wife

She thinks how she fought a flood during her husband's absence. She stood for hours in the drenching downpour, and dug an overflow gutter to save the dam across the creek. But she could not save it. There are things that a bushwoman cannot do. Next morning the dam was broken, and her heart was nearly broken too, for she thought how her husband would feel when he came home and saw the result of years of labour swept away. She cried then.

She also fought the pleuro-pneumonia – dosed and bled the few remaining cattle, and wept again when her two best cows died.

Again, she fought a mad bullock that besieged the house for a day. She made bullets and fired at him through cracks in the slabs with an old shot-gun. He was dead in the morning. She skinned him and got seventeen-and-sixpence for the hide.

She also fights the crows and eagles that have designs on her chickens. Her plan of campaign is very original. The children cry "Crows, mother!" and she rushes out and aims a broomstick at the birds as though it were a gun, and says "Bung!" The crows leave in a hurry; they are cunning, but a woman's cunning is greater.

Occasionally a bushman in the horrors, or a villainous-looking sundowner, comes and nearly scares the life out of her. She generally tells the suspicious-looking stranger that her husband and two sons are at work below the dam, or over at the yard, for he always cunningly inquires for the boss.

Only last week a gallows-faced swagman – having satisfied himself that there were no men on the place – threw his swag down on the veranda, and demanded tucker. She gave him something to eat; then he expressed the intention of staying for the night. It was sundown then. She got a batten from the sofa, loosened the dog, and confronted the stranger, holding the batten in one hand and the dog's collar with the other. "Now you go!" she said. He looked at her and at the dog, said "All right, mum," in a cringing tone and left.

Extract from Henry Lawson's *The Drover's Wife*

THIS TASK CAN BE USED TO EVALUATE YOUR LEARNING IN CRITERION A

Task 1: Analysing *The Drover's Wife*

1 a From paragraphs 1 and 2, **identify** two things that the bushwoman could not do.   [2 marks]

   b From paragraphs 3, 4 and 5, **summarize** how the bushwoman protects and provides for her family. Use your own words.   [4 marks]

   c From paragraph 6, **interpret** how the writer's use of language makes the bushwoman seem in control/powerful. Support your answer with reference to the text.   [4 marks]

THIS TASK CAN BE USED TO EVALUATE YOUR LEARNING IN CRITERION A AND CRITERION D

Task 2: Analysing *Cold Mountain* and *The Drover's Wife*

1 d 'Ada's behaviour is timid in this scene.' **Justify** this statement by making one comment about Ada's:
   - use of body language or facial expression [1 mark]
   - use of intonation [1 mark]
   - use of language (what she says) [1 mark]

> **Hint**
> Criterion A: Analysing (i) Analyse the content, context, language, structure, technique and style of a text.

   e 'Them cows wants milking. If that letter ain't urgent them cows is, is what I'm saying.' (Ruby Thewes) From the quotation above, what could the audience **interpret** about Ruby's character and why? [2 marks]

> **Hint**
> Criterion A: Analysing (ii) Analyse the effects of the creator's choices on an audience

   f **Compare and contrast** how the writer and filmmaker present the female characters in Texts 1 and 2. Make detailed reference to **both texts** in your answer. *For Text 2, you should focus on what is said, the use of body language, facial expressions and intonation.*   [35 marks]

Can killing ever be excused or justified?

ACTIVITY: Another ethical dilemma in *Cold Mountain*

To help you practise formulating arguments and presenting effectively, let us look at one of the most memorable moral and ethical dilemmas in *Cold Mountain*, which occurs when Sara shoots the Yankee soldier. Watch the clip of this scene once again (timings: 1:46:47–1:51:38): **https://youtu.be/ozDgVHAZ7lI**.

Was Sara justified in shooting the soldier?

Copy out the T-chart below and use it to write arguments both for and against this question. Add rows as necessary.

It was right for Sara to shoot the soldier because …	Sara was not justified in shooting the soldier because …

Assessment opportunities

In this activity you have practised skills that are assessed using Criterion A: Analysing.

ACTIVITY: Closing arguments

Sara is in court being prosecuted for shooting the soldier. Choose ONE side of the argument and decide whether you want to prosecute her or defend her.

Write the closing arguments for Sara's case, which will be in favour of the viewpoint you are arguing. An example of a closing argument can be seen here: **https://youtu.be/qnM8OTnF7Bw**.

Your argument must be three to four minutes long. Watch the video clip of the scene in the film as many times as needed in order to collect the evidence, which will form the basis of your argument.

- **Draft out your argument. You could use the structure suggested in this website: https://mocktrialblog.com/2011/09/14/mock-trial-closing-arguments-for-prosecution/, or search the internet for alternative mock trial structures.**
- **Outline the structure of this to begin with, and keep this outline very brief but precise.**
- **Avoid generalities. Focus your comments on what you think are the main points illustrated by this scene, and state these clearly and systematically.**
- **Practise delivering your speech as if to a jury. Video yourself on a smartphone or tablet, and watch your performance back, looking at aspects of communication, such as facial expression, gestures, eye contact and body language, as well as listening to what you say. Revise what you say and your delivery as much as may be needed.**

Pair up with a classmate and deliver your closing arguments to each other. You should video each other's speeches, and then assess and provide feedback on your partner's speech.

Your teacher may pick one or two of the videos so that everyone can look at what makes an effective argument, and how feedback might be given.

Assessment opportunities

In this activity you have practised skills that are assessed using Criterion C: Producing text and Criterion D: Using language.

A SUMMATIVE TASK TO TRY

Use this task to apply and extend your learning in this chapter. The task is designed so that you can evaluate your learning at different levels of achievement in the Language and literature criteria.

THIS TASK CAN BE USED TO EVALUATE YOUR LEARNING IN CRITERION C AND CRITERION D

Task 1: Presentation

Now that we have looked closely at some of the moral and ethical issues encountered in *Cold Mountain,* here is a summative assessment task for you to try on this topic.

It is designed to place you in a 'real life' context by asking you to take on a role in a particular situation. In the course of playing that role you will be addressing the statement of inquiry: 'Narrative structures can be used to show moral and ethical dilemmas, and how people's connections and responses to these reveal much about their character, identity and nature.'

Create a presentation for parents of how *Cold Mountain* is used in the English language and literature course to help students engage with moral and ethical questions. In your presentation you should also consider how literary, visual and stylistic features have been used.

The steps for this task use the GRASPS task design prompts:

Goal

The goal is to show your understanding of how aspects of narrative structure can be used to show moral and ethical dilemmas, and how responses to those reveal aspects of human nature.

Role

You are the head of the Language and Literature department at your school, and you have been asked, as part of a parent event, to show parents how the school is providing 'moral and ethical education' as the school states it will do on its website. You need to give a presentation on how *Cold Mountain* is used in your course to encourage students to consider moral and ethical issues.

Audience

The audience consists of parents who are keen to see that students are being asked to consider moral and ethical issues as part of the education they are receiving from the school.

Situation

The school's website quotes Nord and Haynes, two experts on moral education within schools, in stating that the school will 'provide students with the intellectual resources that enable them to make informed and responsible judgments about difficult matters of moral importance', and that moral education 'is appropriately integrated into all courses'.

The situation you find yourself in is illustrating to parents how the use of *Cold Mountain* within the English Language and Literature course provides various examples of moral and ethical situations, and how analysis of the literary devices used in these helps inform possible moral and ethical judgements that might be made about them.

Product, performance and purpose

You will **create** and perform a presentation that includes both speech and media, and illustrates to your audience examples of how ethical and moral situations are shown in *Cold Mountain*, and how various literary devices are used to communicate further ideas about those.

Standards and criteria for success

Your presentation needs to be five minutes long, involve at least one digital media tool, and use three or four specific examples in the film of how moral and ethical issues arise, and how literary and visual devices used with those might shape an audience's responses to the characters involved and the choices made.

■ Information literacy skills: Access information to be informed and inform others

! This unit should have given you a lot of opportunity to think about how ethical and moral dilemmas can arise, and what the choices we make in response to those may say about us. It has also illustrated how, as the quotation by Patrick Ness at the start of the chapter states, and as the narrative of Inman in *Cold Mountain* shows, we sometimes have to make certain choices, which serve to shape who we are.

! One area in which moral and ethical choices arise for students in school is that of academic honesty. The school must have a policy on this, but the policy may be in language that is quite difficult for students in the first year of the MYP to understand.

! You might, therefore, **design** a leaflet or videocast for students in that grade level, which **explains** in language more accessible for them five different types of academic malpractice that students in a school might be tempted to engage in.

! In your leaflet or videocast:

   ◆ **Research** and **describe** each type of malpractice.

   ◆ **Evaluate** and **explain** the consequences of academic malpractice, both in terms of school sanctions, and of wider implications such as how different people might see and feel about us.

! Ensure that you reference on your leaflet any documents used, such as the school's academic honesty policy, using your school's designated referencing and citation system, or a recognized system.

Reflection

In this chapter we have explored different elements of structure that may be part of the narrative of a film, and some of the purposes of those. We have looked in particular at how such elements might be used to help present moral and ethical dilemmas, and at the choices that might be made by characters in response to those. We have also considered the use of other filmic and literary features, which may be used to help shape an audience's response. We have, finally, considered some moral and ethical issues.

Use this table to reflect on your own learning in this chapter.		
Questions we asked	**Answers we found**	**Any further questions now?**
Factual:		
Conceptual:		
Debatable:		

Approaches to learning you used in this chapter	Description – what new skills did you learn?	How well did you master the skills?			
		Novice	Learner	Practitioner	Expert
Communication skills					
Collaboration skills					
Information literacy skills					
Media literacy skills					
Critical-thinking skills					
Creative-thinking skills					

Learner profile attribute(s)	Reflect on the importance of being principled in this chapter.
Principled	

9 Should we always be able to say what we want, when we like?

○ The **rights and responsibilities** of **communication** are important to consider, particularly in terms of the **point of view** being expressed, the **purpose** of expressing it and the **audience** to which it is expressed.

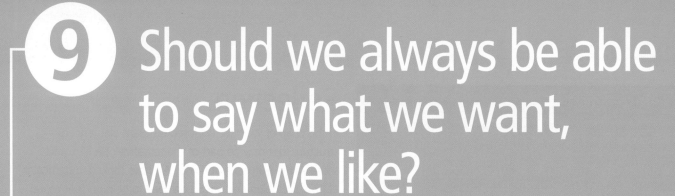

CONSIDER THESE QUESTIONS:

Factual: What is 'freedom of expression'? In what ways can communication both help and cause harm in different situations?

Conceptual: How can rights and responsibilities be balanced? What represents responsible communication or use of freedom of expression in different situations?

Debatable: Should we always be allowed to say whatever we think and feel? How far should freedom of speech be restricted? Is it ever okay to withhold some of the truth? Which is more important – an individual's right to free speech or the well-being or wider interests of others or a community?

Now **share and compare** your thoughts and ideas with your partner, or with the whole class.

■ Who tells us what to do? Who should be able to tell us what to do?

○ IN THIS CHAPTER, WE WILL …

■ **Find out** different ways in which communication might both help and harm in different situations; what constitutes propaganda, why it might be used, and ways in which it may be identified.

■ **Explore** situations in which communication might have an impact, and the possible ways in which communication of different kinds might impact on others, along with the rights people should have in regard to communication, and the responsibilities that may need to be considered.

■ **Take action** by analysing situations and exercising responsible communication based on ethical decision-making.

■ Communication skills
■ Collaboration skills
■ Information literacy skills
■ Media literacy skills
■ Critical-thinking skills
■ Creative-thinking skills
■ Transfer skills

KEY WORDS

advocate	desensitization	policy
ambiguous	disaffection	propaganda
ambivalent	frailty	sentiment
consensus	integrity	
credulity	ostracize	

We will reflect on this learner profile attribute …

● Thinkers – develop as a thinker through various activities involving analysing complex issues and what 'responsible action' might look like in responding to those; exercise initiative in making reasoned, ethical decisions.

Assessment opportunities in this chapter:

◆ **Criterion A:** Analysing
◆ **Criterion B:** Organizing
◆ **Criterion C:** Producing text
◆ **Criterion D:** Using language

ACTIVITY: Freedom of expression – when should it be allowed?

■ ATL

■ Collaboration: Listen actively to other perspectives and ideas; negotiate effectively; encourage others to contribute; make fair and equitable decisions; build consensus
■ Communication skills: Use intercultural understanding to interpret communication; negotiate ideas and knowledge with peers

In a group of three or four look at the following situations, which raise questions of whether people should have the right to express whatever they wish.

Copy out and complete the table below and, for each of the situations, consider and **discuss** the possible consequences for and against, as well as your decision (and your reasons for that decision).

For each scenario you might like to research the situation online – there are a number of articles and forum discussions for each that can help your thoughts and discussions on each issue.

◆ Assessment opportunities

In this activity you have practised skills that are assessed using Criterion B: Organizing.

Situation	Possible consequences of allowing it	Possible consequences of not allowing it	Decision on whether to allow it or ban it	Reasons for your final decision
Wearing whatever one likes in school				
Having a tattoo in school				
Swearing, using obscene language				
Posting whatever one likes on social media				
Saying whatever one likes about someone else, regardless of whether it is true or has any evidence to support it				
Holding protest marches				
Wearing religious symbols in a workplace				
Sharing state secrets				
Shouting 'Fire!' in a crowded theatre, when this is not true				

The *Universal Declaration of Human Rights*

In 1948, the United Nations set out fundamental human rights in a document called the *Universal Declaration of Human Rights*. The document was drafted by representatives with different legal and cultural backgrounds from across the world, and consisted of 30 articles that listed the rights that all human beings, wherever they might be, should have. It has been translated into more than 500 languages.

■ Universal Declaration of Human Rights

Article 19 of the *Universal Declaration of Human Rights* states that 'Everyone has the right to freedom of opinion and expression; this right includes freedom to hold opinions without interference and to seek, receive and impart information and ideas through any media and regardless of frontiers.'

Is this always possible? Can free speech be allowed in every context?

DISCUSS

In small groups, think about and **discuss** the following questions. You may like to use some of the ideas from the previous activity:

- **What examples of situations can you think of in which it might be difficult to allow people to exercise the right of freedom of expression?**
- **Are there any examples of situations in which people should always be stopped from exercising this right?**

One famous example, often used to show that limits should be placed on freedom of expression, is the act of falsely shouting 'Fire!' in a public theatre – something you looked at in the 'Freedom of expression – when should it be allowed?' activity. This situation was examined by the US courts and, in 1919, a judge named Oliver Wendell Holmes Jnr stated that:

> *'The most stringent protection of free speech would not protect a man falsely shouting fire in a theater and causing a panic.'*

Source: www.law.cornell.edu/supremecourt/text/249/47

The judge was arguing that, when unnecessary danger and damage has been caused, a person cannot be protected from being held responsible for the consequences of their action (shouting 'Fire!') by claiming the right of free speech.

The European Union also has a *European Convention on Human Rights,* in which Article 10 states that:

> *'Everyone has the right to freedom of expression. This right shall include freedom to hold opinions and to receive and impart information and ideas without interference by public authority and regardless of frontiers.'*

Source: http://fra.europa.eu/en/charterpedia/article/11-freedom-expression-and-information

This is followed, however, by a further statement that the right of freedom of expression 'carries with it duties and responsibilities', and may be subject to factors such as:
- national security
- public safety
- prevention of disorder.

In other words, the EU and the US both agree that the right to freedom of expression is not an absolute right; and in certain contexts, such as the above, the responsible thing to do may be to limit it.

ACTIVITY: Freedom of expression

Rights and responsibilities can often come into conflict in issues involving freedom of expression. Questions of where, when and how freedom of expression should be limited, and to what extent, are debated a great deal.

Differing opinions on this subject are reflected in the following quotations. Read through these, and with a partner, note down:

- **how much freedom of expression each speaker thinks there should be**
- **whether their arguments are for limiting or not limiting freedom of expression.**

Once you have written your notes, as a pair, choose one of the quotations and together prepare and present a two-minute speech that explains:

- **what the quotation says**
- **what your own opinions of it are**
- **why you hold that/those opinions.**

'… social media make it easy for anyone to publish anything to a potentially global audience. This is a huge boost for freedom of speech, and has led to a vast increase in the volume of material published. But when words and pictures move so rapidly across borders, conflict often results. Different nations have different notions of what may and may not be said.' – The Economist

Source: **www.economist.com/international/ 2016/06/04/the-muzzle-grows-tighter**

'To uphold the right to gratuitously offend, without any sense of responsibility that should accompany freedom of expression, is childish, even dangerous.' – Sharif Nashashibi, Al Jazeera

Source: **www.aljazeera.com/indepth/opinion/2015/01/islam-free-speech-what-so-funny-201511345039925211.html**

'It was a shocking thing to say and I knew it was a shocking thing to say. But no one has the right to live without being shocked. No one has the right to spend their life without being offended. Nobody has to read this book. Nobody has to pick it up. Nobody has to open it. And if you open it and read it, you don't have to like it. And if you read it and you dislike it, you don't have to remain silent about it. You can write to me, you can complain about it, you can write to the publisher, you can write to the papers, you can write your own book. You can do all those things, but there your rights stop. No one has the right to stop me writing this book. No one has the right to stop it being published, or sold, or bought, or read.' – Philip Pullman

Source: **www.goodreads.com/quotes/tag/freedom-of-speech**

'You can't pick and choose which types of freedom you want to defend. You must defend all of it or be against all of it.' – Scott Howard Phillips

Source: **goo.gl/Ps1PRd**

'You're free to say whatever you want but you're not free of the impact of your words. People think that saying "It's free speech" means that they will be free of any consequences.' – poster quote, author unknown

CONNECT–EXTEND–CHALLENGE

Now we have looked more at freedom of expression, and some of the issues that arise with this, record some of your thinking about this topic in a table with three columns.

In the first column, titled 'Connect', note down how the ideas and information you have looked at are CONNECTED to what you already knew.

In the second column, titled 'Extend', make a note of any new ideas you have found which EXTENDED or pushed your thinking in some new directions.

In the third column, titled 'Challenge', record your ideas on what is still CHALLENGING or confusing to you about issues connected to freedom of expression. What questions, wonderings or puzzles do you now have about this topic?

Schools, business and other institutions often have principles, rules or guidelines on how to act and behave when you are there – these are often known as policies. Some policies might involve questions of freedom of expression; for example, your school might have policies on the following:

- the use of social media, either inside the school, outside the school, or both
- what you should wear – a school dress code or uniform
- language (profanity) and talking (for example, criticism of teachers) around the school.

Since policies apply to everyone within a school community, they are often created by committees that contain representatives from each part of the community, such as teachers, students, school leadership and parents.

ACTIVITY: Making school policy

ATL

- Collaboration skills: Listen actively to other perspectives and ideas; negotiate effectively; practise empathy; manage and resolve conflict, and work collaboratively in teams; build consensus
- Communication skills: Use intercultural understanding to interpret communication; negotiate ideas and knowledge with peers
- Transfer skills: Change the context of an inquiry to gain different perspectives

! Imagine your school wants to draw up a new 'Freedom of expression' policy that, in particular, deals with social media use, school dress and 'school talk'.

1 In a group of four, choose one of the three areas to look at – or your teacher may select one for your group.

2 Assign each member of your group one of the following roles which might influence or be affected by the policies under discussion: a student; a teacher; the school principal or head; a parent.

3 Individually consider (and make notes on) your chosen area from the perspective of the role you are playing:
  ◆ What guidelines would you like to see, as a student/teacher/principal/parent?
  ◆ What might be the benefits and disadvantages of any potential rules or guidelines?

4 In your group, hold a working group meeting in which each of you *still in role* puts forward your own thoughts and reasons for those, and states what you think should go into the policy. Can your group arrive at a consensus on that?

5 As a class, **discuss** each of the three areas before deciding on a final policy for each area.

◆ Assessment opportunities

In this activity you have practised skills that are assessed using Criterion C: Producing text and Criterion D: Using language

FREEDOM OF EXPRESSION IN TIMES OF WAR AND CONFLICT

During the First World War, the US operated a draft – meaning that people had to undertake mandatory military service if they were selected to do so. One man produced, printed and distributed posters that urged people to refuse to serve in the military, even if they were selected. He was accused of illegally attempting to obstruct the draft. The accused man argued, however, that he had a right to distribute the posters because they represented his right to freedom of expression, which was protected under the **First Amendment of the US Constitution**.

This is a good example of the conflict that can arise between someone's right to freedom of expression, and other responsibilities that may exist, such as protecting national security.

■ Young men registering for military conscription, New York City, June 5, 1917

DISCUSS

What are your views on how much freedom of expression people should have during times of war and conflict? What do you think should have happened in this case? What might have happened if people had refused to undertake military service when ordered to do so in a time of war?

After you have discussed this, you can research the case – **Schenck v. United States** – further if you wish. Do you recognize the name of the judge?

National security and times of war and conflict raise particular questions about the limits that may or should be placed on freedom of expression. During times of war, what rights and responsibilities might different people have in terms of what they may communicate, their purpose in doing so and who they communicate it to?

THINK–PAIR–SHARE

Copy out the table below and, in it, make notes on what rights and responsibilities each individual/group might have in terms of communication during a time of war. What might each say, to whom, and why? What might they not be permitted to say, to whom, and why?

Individual/group	Rights	Responsibilities
Soldiers		
Generals, commanders		
Government		
Members of the public		
Journalists (including photojournalists)		
Writers – novelists, poets, etc		

Now **discuss** your ideas with a partner. Add any further points or ideas your partner had but which you did not include in your own notes.

Join together with another pair to form a group of four. **Discuss** once again the notes you made for each individual or group. Once more, add anything further to your own notes if any other good ideas are mentioned in the discussion.

As a group, **discuss** whether you feel any of the people in the list should have their communications, and the subjects of their communications, restricted. If so, what and why?

ACTIVITY: 'Careless talk costs lives'

Posters have been used by countries and governments for many years to convey persuasive messages to their citizens, including telling them during wartime to be careful over communication.

In pairs, look at the three example posters and, for each, make notes about the persuasive techniques – looked at previously in Chapters 6 and 7 – that are being used. You should also consider the following techniques when thinking about the effects the posters have on their audience. Remember, you should always ask yourself: *What is there and why has it been chosen to be included?*

Written techniques:
- **Tone of the poster**
- **Narrative voice**
- **Stylistic devices**
- **Emotions/feelings being evoked**
- **Imagery**

Visual techniques:
- **Significance of the chosen images**
- **Significance of the chosen characters, as well as their style and their actions**
- **Symbols**
- **Where does the eye fall first on the poster? What is important about that?**
- **Font / typeface**

THE EXPLANATION GAME

ATL

- Media literacy skills: Understand the impact of media representations and modes of presentation

In pairs, search for **British First World War posters** online and pick two or more posters that you did not look at in the 'Careless talk costs lives' activity. For each poster, take it in turns to complete the sentence prompt 'I notice that …'

Join together with another pair and examine the purpose behind the posters your pairs have chosen, and the messages they are trying to convey.

Once someone has identified a detail, the group as a whole should then **discuss** possible answers to the question of 'Why is it that way?'.

Write two or three paragraphs for each poster explaining the purpose and message you think that poster is trying to convey to a reader, and how the visual and written features used are helping to convey that message.

Once you have drafted your paragraphs, share them with a partner, and provide feedback on each other's paragraphs. Use the ladder of feedback protocol:
- **CLARIFY with your partner any questions you have about the work.**
- **VALUE your partner's work by commenting on what is good about what he or she has written.**
- **CONCERNS about any aspect of the work should then be raised with your partner.**
- **SUGGEST to your partner what he or she might do to improve the work.**

▼ Links to: Art

Research wartime posters from different eras and countries. Who are the artists behind the posters? Are there any significant differences in the style or design of the posters? One good comparison is between Russian and UK or US posters; some examples can be found online:

https://goo.gl/fmRxnP

https://goo.gl/zefHj9

CENSORSHIP – RESPONSIBLE PRACTICE OR DENIAL OF RIGHTS?

ℹ Censorship

Censorship is the act of forbidding or limiting information on something, or the access to it. Censored information is often considered to be in some way unacceptable (for example, it might be offensive, harmful or sensitive). Governments, organizations and individuals can all engage in censorship. You can also self-censor – this is when you stop yourself saying or doing something depending on who is listening or watching you.

Censorship occurs in everyday life – for example, the film industry decides who can, and who cannot, watch films of different kinds (via the age rating system). It is also used in more extreme situations: for example, by governments in times of war or when national security is perceived to be threatened.

The question of what may be communicated during wartime, and the different ways you might view the decisions made on that, are illustrated by the two posters at the start of this chapter (page 220), which are based on the same poster design.

9   Should we always be able to say what we want, when we like?

227

First World War

Also known as the 'Great War', the First World War began in 1914 with the assassination of Archduke Franz Ferdinand. The two main sides in the conflict were the Allied Powers (France, Russia, Britain and, later on, the USA) and the Central Powers (Germany, Austria–Hungary, and the Ottoman Empire). More than 70 million military personnel fought in the war and most of the fighting took place in two locations – the Western and Eastern fronts in Europe. The war ended on 11 November 1918 with the surrender of Germany and the signing of the Treaty of Versailles. More than 17 million people died during the conflict.

■ Trench warfare in the First World War

Censorship and control of information took place to a large degree in the course of the First World War. However, some writers turned to writing novels and poetry to try to convey the reality of what happened there. Some of this, such as some of Siegfried Sassoon's poetry, was published while the war was still taking place, and led to a great deal of debate about his 'patriotism' in writing and publishing the poems. Other works, such as the novel *All Quiet on the Western Front*, were written and published by writers looking back on the events of the war.

We will shortly be looking at *All Quiet on the Western Front*, as well as other texts and poems written by (and about) soldiers who served in the First World War and on the Western Front. To better understand the context of these texts, we will first investigate some of the background to the First World War.

ACTIVITY: Research the Great War

■ ATL

- Information literacy skills: Access information to be informed and to inform others
- Media literacy skills: Seek a range of perspectives from multiple and varied sources

In this activity you are going to research one aspect of the First World War and then share some of the facts you find with the rest of the class.

1 Your teacher will assign you one of the following questions to research online or in your library.
   - Why/how did the First World War start?
   - Why/how did the First World War end?
   - What was life in the trenches like for soldiers?
   - What was the Western Front?
   - What was the Treaty of Versailles?
   - What was the legacy and aftermath of the First World War?
2 Use one of the note-taking methods you learned in Chapter 8 to note down key information on your topic as you research.
3 Choose five of the most interesting or important facts you have found then share these with your class.

Some resources you might use during your research are:
- **An interactive documentary on *First World War: The story of a global conflict*. In seven short videos ten historians from around the world explain different aspects of the war. Available in eight different languages, it is an excellent introduction to the topic of the First World War: https://goo.gl/XKJLcC**
- **A timeline detailing key events of the war: www.historyonthenet.com/world-war-one-timeline/**
- **A short video outlining the key events of the war using rap and actors: www.youtube.com/watch?v=Nj43X-VBEPE**

◆ Assessment opportunities

In this activity you have practised skills that are assessed using Criterion A: Analysing and Criterion B: Organizing.

LIMITING COMMUNICATION IN THE FIRST WORLD WAR

The following newspaper extract talks about the limits that were placed on journalists who were reporting on what was happening during the First World War. The article was written on the 100th anniversary of the start of the war. As you read, think about your responses to the discussion you had for the 'Censorship in the First World War' activity (page 229). Do you still feel that same way? Why (not)?

First world war: how state and press kept truth off the front page

(published 27 July 2014) – Roy Greenslade

On this, the 100th anniversary of the day the first world war began, it is **sobering** to look back at the way that conflict was so badly reported. The catalogue of journalistic misdeeds is a matter of record: the willingness to publish propaganda as fact, the apparently tame acceptance of censorship and the failure to hold power to account. But a sweeping condemnation of the press coverage is unjust because journalists, as ever, were prevented from informing the public by three powerful forces – the government, the military and their own proprietors [owners of their newspapers].

…

[Censorship] was imposed from the opening of hostilities and, although gradually relaxed, it remained sufficiently strict to constrain reporters from obtaining information or, should they manage to get it, from publishing it. … The Defence of the Realm Act, enacted four days after hostilities began, gave the authorities power to **stifle** criticism of the war effort. One of its regulations stated: "No person shall by word of mouth or in writing spread reports likely to cause **disaffection** or alarm among any of His Majesty's forces or among the civilian population." Its aim was to prevent publication of anything that could be interpreted as undermining the morale of the British people.

…

… censorship ensured that all sorts of facts were hidden from the readers of British newspapers … even the bloodiest defeat in British history, at the Somme in 1916 – in which Allied troop casualties numbered 600,000 – went largely unreported. The battle's disastrous first day was reported as a victory … Only later did the public learn of the high casualty toll and the horrific nature of trench warfare, such as the use of poison gas and the effects of **shell shock**. With these appalling conditions in mind, it was no wonder that Lloyd George [the British Prime Minister at the time] confided to Scott in December 1917: "If people really knew [the truth], the war would be stopped tomorrow. But of course they don't know, and can't know." He was speaking after listening to Gibbs's description – at a private meeting – of the reality on the western front. He conceded that the censors "wouldn't pass the truth".

www.theguardian.com/media/2014/jul/27/first-world-war-state-press-reporting

ACTIVITY: Wartime reporting

1 What does the article writer say were the three main failures of journalists during the war?
2 What does the writer mean by 'a sweeping condemnation of the press coverage is unjust'?
3 Who were involved in censoring journalists during the First World War?
4 What was the aim of the Defence of the Realm Act?
5 Did this aim justify the censoring of information that reached the general public from the war front? Give reasons for your answer.
6 Why do you think the British Prime Minister, Lloyd George, said that the British people 'can't know' about the reality of the war?
7 Return to the questions you discussed in the 'Censorship in the First World War' activity. Answer the questions again, but this time *in relation to the article you have just read*. Make notes on your answers and use details from the article to illustrate and support the points you make.

◆ Assessment opportunities

In this activity you have practised skills that are assessed using Criterion A: Analysing.

ACTIVITY: Writing a newspaper editorial

A newspaper opinion article is a column, often written by the editor, which takes a particular position on an issue and argues for that position. The column generally reflects the position of the newspaper and its staff in general, and so does not usually have a byline.

As a newspaper editor during the First World War you are faced with a number of reporting restrictions. You decide you do not care about the censors, however, and write a column revealing your newspaper's opinion on the idea that newspapers should, in times of war, present news and information in particular ways, such as keeping back information or bad news, and/or emphasizing 'good' news. Your column should be 500 words long, and when writing it you should follow the process outlined in the ATL cog 'Writing a newspaper opinion column' on pages 230–231.

◆ Assessment opportunities

In this activity you have practised skills that are assessed using Criterion C: Producing text and Criterion D: Using language.

Writing a newspaper opinion column

Use the following process when writing a newspaper opinion column:

1 Choose the topic of your column and the position (for or against) that you will be arguing.
2 Gather the information and facts you will be using. Research further if needed.
3 Plan out the key points you wish to make. Opinion columns are short, so make sure you do not pick more points than you can properly address in the space you have.
4 Start the column by making your opinion on the subject clear.
5 Explain why, objectively, the issue is important.
6 Give the opposite view to your own first; include quotations and facts.
7 **Refute** the view you have just given by exposing the flaws in the argument.
8 Develop your own case using facts, details, figures and quotations as evidence.

ACTIVITY: Waiting in the trenches

The conditions for soldiers living in the trenches of the Western Front were very tough. Watch this short video on this subject now: **https://youtu.be/FvYIIuxh2kY**.

Task 1

Imagine you are a soldier living in one of these trenches. Close your eyes. What are the first five things you notice, or become aware of? Without sight, use all your other senses: hearing, smell, touch, taste.

Write down your five things then expand each point into a descriptive paragraph of the experience, as in the following example.

Sensory note: *Hearing someone walking through the mud*

Descriptive writing: *The mud. Never ending mud. A river of mud. It gives way beneath my boot, with a belch of satisfaction. Then it sucks and pulls, and heaves against my tired legs, groaning with the effort. Off-balance, I drop my knife. It is instantly gobbled up. I put my hand into the mud, a sliding, slimy mass which immediately escapes from my grasp, wherever my fingers stray. The knife glints, like buried treasure, amidst the brown and grey sludge which seeks to bury it – and which would like to bury me too.*

Use a range of literary techniques to make your description vivid for a reader – the example uses metaphor, personification, onomatopoeia, alliteration, assonance and simile (among others). If needed, turn back to Chapter 4 for more examples of literary devices you might use.

Use as many literary techniques as possible in your descriptive writing in order to make the description vivid and immediate for a reader.

After you have written one or two paragraphs, swap these with a partner and provide feedback on each other's writing. Revise your descriptive piece based on the feedback. Repeat this process for the rest of your descriptive paragraphs. Remember to include transitions between the different points you make.

Task 2

Make a list of the literary devices you have used in your descriptive passage and, for each device, add notes on the effect it is intended to create.

Turn your list into a continuous prose analysis of your passage, which examines and explains how the techniques you used helped to convey meaning and impact.

9 Acknowledge any good points the opposing view has. This makes your argument seem rational and well thought out.
10 Conclude your column by restating your opening remark in a way that grabs the reader's attention.
11 Keep your column to 500 words; make every word count.
12 Note that an editorial opinion column never uses 'I'.

Adapted from:
www.geneseo.edu/~bennett/EdWrite.htm

The following short video and article provide more information on what newspaper editorials are, and what they contain:

Video:
www.youtube.com/watch?v=fvOgOWD-rPM

Article:
www.geneseo.edu/~bennett/EdWrite.htm

ACTIVITY: War poetry – writing commentary

Having written your own piece of prose describing the experience of being in a trench, we will look now at a poem that describes the experiences of soldiers in the First World War.

> Bent double, like old beggars under sacks,
> Knock-kneed, coughing like hags, we cursed
>   through sludge,
> Till on the haunting flares we turned our backs
> And towards our distant rest began to trudge.
> Men marched asleep. Many had lost their boots
> But limped on, blood-shod. All went lame; all
>   blind;
> Drunk with fatigue; deaf even to the hoots
> Of tired, outstripped Five-Nines that dropped
>   behind.

These lines are the first verse of a poem entitled 'Dulce et Decorum Est', one of the most famous First World War poems, written by one of its most famous poets, Wilfred Owen, who was himself a serving officer in the war. Thought to have been written between 8 October 1917 and March 1918, the poem as a whole narrates a gas attack at the Front. It describes some of the realities of trench warfare, such as the use of poison gas and the terrible nature of 'shell shock'. You can look up war-specific vocabulary (such as 'flares', 'hoots', 'Five-Nines') here: www.warpoetry.co.uk/owen1.html.

Write an analysis or commentary between 500 and 600 words in length that examines this first verse of the poem. Your commentary should **identify** the main ideas and purposes of the lines, and **explore** the aspects of style and technique used by the poet to convey these. What message is the poet trying to convey? What techniques is he using to put this across as powerfully as possible?

In Chapter 4 an ATL cog on 'How to write about a poem' gives the full process for writing a commentary on poetry. Refer to this if needed before writing your commentary.

EXTENSION

Find the complete 'Dulce et Decorum Est' online and expand your analysis, writing a commentary on the entire poem that is 1,000–1,500 words long. Alternatively, you might search for other, more recent wartime poems online – for example, poetry from soldiers who served in Afghanistan from 2001: www.warpoetry.co.uk/Afghanistan_War_Poetry.html. **Compare and contrast** your chosen poem with Owen's First World War poem.

ACTIVITY: What makes you say that?

ATL

■ Critical-thinking skills: Gather and organize relevant information to formulate an argument; draw reasonable conclusions and generalizations

Read the following poem. What is being compared to a 'game'?

Who's for the Game?

Who's for the game, the biggest that's played,
The red crashing game of a fight?
Who'll grip and tackle the job unafraid?
And who thinks he'd rather sit tight?
Who'll toe the line for the signal to 'Go!'?
Who'll give his country a hand?
Who wants a turn to himself in the show?
And who wants a seat in the stand?
Who knows it won't be a picnic – not much –
Yet eagerly shoulders a gun?
Who would much rather come back with a crutch
Than lie low and be out of the fun?
Come along, lads –
But you'll come on all right –
For there's only one course to pursue,
Your country is up to her neck in a fight,
And she's looking and calling for you.

Jessie Pope

In small groups, answer the following questions about the poem, using a visible thinking routine called 'What makes you say that?'

When responding to a question, each group member should also give some evidence or reasoning to support their point – use the prompt *'What do you see that makes you say that?'* to do this.

● **What do you think the poem is about?**
● **What is being compared to a 'game'?**
● **Who is being addressed by the speaker of the poem?**
● **What tone is adopted in the poem?**

Following this, your group members should each consider the broader prompt question: 'What's going on?'

Each group member should suggest a response to the prompt question. For every observation that is made, they should also answer *'What do you see that makes you say that?'* Go round the group twice at least, and carry on until no one has any further comments or suggestions to add.

Focus on the content of the poem, but do not forget to **comment** on any stylistic features you can see.

Hopefully, you noticed in this exercise that war is being compared to a game. Is this an appropriate comparison? Why (not)? **Discuss** these questions as a group.

◆ Assessment opportunities

In this activity you have practised skills that are assessed using Criterion A: Analysing.

As you will have noticed from 'Dulce et Decorum Est', Wilfred Owen – along with contemporaries like Siegfried Sassoon and Robert Graves – used poetry as a means to express experiences of the war. They were highly critical of the things they saw happening.

Not all poets saw things the same way, however. 'Who's for the Game' was written by Jessie Pope, a poet who strongly supported the war. Pope's poetry urged people to join up to the war effort and was widely published in popular newspapers.

Towards the end of 'Dulce et Decorum Est' Owen directly addresses 'My friend', and accuses him or her of enthusiastically promoting to children the claim that 'Dulce et Decorum est / Pro patria mori' – 'it is sweet and right to die for one's country'.

> My friend, you would not tell with such high **zest**
> To children **ardent** for some desperate glory,
> The old Lie; Dulce et Decorum est
> Pro patria mori.

Instead of the 'glory' that is being promoted, Owen's poem is intended to show what the reality of war looks like, which is anything but 'sweet' and 'right'. This is a claim that he directly calls a 'Lie', emphasizing this word further through use of a capital letter, and by juxtaposing the short phrase 'The old Lie' with the saying 'Dulce et Decorum est'.

DISCUSS

Consider the above verse from 'Dulce et Decorum Est', then **discuss** the following questions briefly as a group:
- **What is the tone used when the speaker says, 'My friend'?**
- **Who might the speaker (and Owen) be addressing as 'My friend'?**

In fact, Owen originally dedicated the poem, ironically, to Jessie Pope, in response to her popular and unquestioningly patriotic poetry. He later erased the dedication and may have intended the term 'friend' to be ambiguous. This allows it to be applied to a number of people who supported the war – such as the general public, or other poets whose poetry tried to convince readers that joining up for war was a patriotic course of action.

These poets and their poems offer very different views on the war. Though Owen wrote from direct experience, Pope, as a woman, did not (*could not,* since women were not allowed to fight at the Front in the war). Many members of the public held the same view as Pope, however, and this was partly owing to the fact that many of the things they knew about the war were influenced by the propaganda material they read, saw or were told. Think back to the posters we examined in the 'Careless talk costs lives' activity. These are a good example of wartime propaganda and exemplified the use of written and visual communication techniques employed to help sway a reader's opinion.

Propaganda

The broadcasting or publication of information, ideas and opinions in an effort to influence people's views on a subject is known as propaganda. Often the published information is biased, or only shows one side of an argument. During wartime, propaganda has been used to try to persuade people to join the war effort in different ways: signing up for the military, rationing and growing your own food, keeping a look out for suspicious activity, and more.

ACTIVITY: Who would you vote for?

■ ATL

■ Communication skills: Use intercultural understanding to interpret communication; use a variety of speaking techniques to communicate with a variety of audiences
■ Information literacy skills: Access information to be informed and inform others; make connections between various sources of information

We have looked previously in this chapter at some propaganda of the First World War, which formed part of the context in which poets such as Owen and others, including Jessie Pope, were writing. We will now look further into the contrasting points of view being expressed, and also examine the context in more detail.

Before we begin, read the following two articles:

www.bbc.co.uk/guides/z38rq6f *(read sections 1–5 only)*

www.bbc.co.uk/news/magazine-32298697

1 **Using the information in these articles, and the poetry of Owen and Pope, prepare a two-minute speech in response to the following prompt:**
    If Wilfred Owen and Jessie Pope had both stood for election as prime minister during the First World War, who do you think would have made the best prime minister during that period of war? Why?

    Your thinking on this might address topics such as the following:
    ● what you think the country may have needed at the time
    ● the views of the respective poets about the war
    ● the possible impact on people of those views

    ● evidence from their poems (feel free to look at more poems written by either – or both, poets)
    ● evidence found in the articles you have read.
2 **Once you have chosen the poet you think will make the best prime minister, determine the points you will include when arguing their case. For this short speech you should pick three or four key points to use, so that you have enough time to argue these sufficiently well. You can find guidance on giving speeches and presentation on pages 212–213.**
3 **Make notes on how you might develop each point, and the details and evidence you could bring in for each from the poetry and articles.**
4 **Draft your speech, including an attention-grabbing introduction and conclusion.**
5 **Rehearse your speech – you could use a smartphone, tablet, webcam, and so on to record yourself, which will enable you to review yourself more thoroughly.**
6 **Once your speech has been prepared, get into a group of four. Each of you will take it in turns to give your speech to the group as a whole.**
7 **Each group member should assess each speech, using the guidance referred to above.**
8 **Together, decide which speech you as a group most prefer; that speech should then be given to the class as a whole. You may want to, or your teacher might ask you to, similarly assess these also; or you may want to listen to the speeches at this stage and enjoy and think about their qualities individually.**

◆ Assessment opportunities

In this activity you have practised skills that are assessed using Criterion C: Producing text and Criterion D: Using language.

All Quiet on the Western Front by Erich Remarque

Erich Maria Remarque was **conscripted** to fight for the German army in the First World War. He served at the Western Front until wounded by shrapnel, spending the remainder of the war in a military hospital. *All Quiet on the Western Front* was written in 1927 and graphically shows the extreme situations that soldiers at the Front faced during the war – dealing continually with death, destruction, and physical and mental stresses. The book was published in 1929, and can now be read in more than 45 different languages. In 1930, it was adapted into an Oscar-winning film.

■ Erich Maria Remarque

NOVELS AND WAR

Poetry was not the only literary medium used to present views, ideas and information about the First World War. One solider, who fought on the German side, wrote a famous novel based on his experiences. Talking later about writing the book, he said:

> 'It was through … deliberate acts of self-analysis that I found my way back to my war experiences. I could observe a similar phenomenon in many of my friends and acquaintances. The shadow of war hung over us, especially when we tried to shut our minds to it. The very day this thought struck me, I put pen to paper, without much in the way of prior thought.'

The novel he wrote was *All Quiet on the Western Front*.

We will be looking at one or two particular extracts from *All Quiet on the Western Front* in this chapter, and it is important to have an overview of the novel as a whole for this.

There are a number of methods you can use to gain an overview of a novel, detailed below. Begin by using the reading schedule method, outlined in the ATL cog on pages 238–40, but also research and explore further methods if you think they might work better for you.

- **Reading schedule** – prose summary notes detailing key events for each chapter, sometimes also includes key quotes – see the ATL cog.
- **Facts chart** – for each chapter list ten factual statements about things that take place, or are narrated, within the chapters being looked at.

- **Key events map** – note down the main points or events of each book chapter in the form of a diagram – a flow chart usually works well.
- **Literary Text Infographic** – infographics convey information about a topic visually, with some use of text. They are often organized around themes and characters rather than chapter by chapter. See this example, from a novel entitled *The Things They Carried*: **www.columnfivemedia.com/work-items/the-things-they-carried**.

JOINING UP

Having experienced the brutal reality of fighting in the trenches, Wilfred Owen criticized those like Jessie Pope who blindly encouraged men to join up and fight. Much propaganda existed, however, urging people to do just this.

All Quiet on the Western Front looks at how young German men came to join up and fight for their army. In the passage on page 237 the narrator, Paul Bäumer, describes the role of the soldiers' old schoolmaster, Kantorek, in convincing the men to sign up, serve in the army and fight in the war. Other individuals also pressure the young men to sign up – people whom the narrator suggests should have known better.

As you read this extract from Chapter 1, think about the inquiry question: What represents responsible communication or use of freedom of expression in different situations?

During drill-time Kantorek gave us long lectures until the whole of our class went, under his shepherding, to the District Commandant and volunteered. I can see him now, as he used to glare at us through his spectacles and say in a moving voice: "Won't you join up, Comrades?"

These teachers always carry their feelings ready in their waistcoat pockets, and trot them out by the hour. But we didn't think of that then.

There was, indeed, one of us who hesitated and did not want to fall into line. That was Joseph Behm, a plump, homely fellow. But he did allow himself to be persuaded, otherwise he would have been **ostracised**. And perhaps more of us thought as he did, but no one could very well stand out, because at that time even one's parents were ready with the word "coward"; no one had the vaguest idea what we were in for. The wisest were just the poor and simple people. They knew the war to be a misfortune, whereas those who were better off, and should have been able to see more clearly what the consequences would be, were beside themselves with joy.

Katczinsky said that was a result of their upbringing. It made them stupid. And what Kat said, he had thought about.

Strange to say, Behm was one of the first to fall. He got hit in the eye during an attack, and we left him lying for dead. We couldn't bring him with us, because we had to come back helterskelter. In the afternoon suddenly we heard him call, and saw him crawling about in No Man's Land. He had only been knocked unconscious. Because he could not see, and was mad with pain, he failed to keep under cover, and so was shot down before anyone could go and fetch him in.

Naturally we couldn't blame Kantorek for this. Where would the world be if one brought every man to book? There were thousands of Kantoreks, all of whom were convinced that they were acting for the best – in a way that cost them nothing.

And that is why they let us down so badly.

For us lads of eighteen they ought to have been mediators and guides to the world of maturity, the world of work, of duty, of culture, of progress – to the future. We often made fun of them and played jokes on them, but in our hearts we trusted them. The idea of authority, which they represented, was associated in our minds with a greater insight and a more humane wisdom. But the first death we saw shattered this belief. We had to recognise that our generation was more to be trusted than theirs. They surpassed us only in phrases and in cleverness. The first bombardment showed us our mistake, and under it the world as they had taught it to us broke in pieces.

While they continued to write and talk, we saw the wounded and dying. While they taught that duty to one's country is the greatest thing, we already knew that death-throes are stronger. But for all that we were no mutineers, no deserters, no cowards – they were very free with all these expressions. We loved our country as much as they; we went courageously into every action; but also we distinguished the false from true, we had suddenly learned to see. And we saw that there was nothing of their world left. We were all at once terribly alone; and alone we must see it through.

All Quiet on the Western Front – Chapter 1

9   Should we always be able to say what we want, when we like?

237

Reading schedule

A reading schedule helps you digest a book chapter by chapter, and making summary notes can help you better understand the events and relationships within a text.

- Draw out a table like the one below, with a line for each chapter.
- When you have read a chapter tick it off in the 'Read?' column, then, in the third column, write five or six sentences that you think **summarize** the most important events/aspects of that chapter.

- Aim to read one chapter at a time, making notes as you go. Try also to set aside some time to read each day as reading a little and often will help you finish the book quickly and make it more manageable.

The example below is from *All Quiet on the Western Front*. Complete the rest of the schedule as you read through the book.

Chapter	Read?	Summary of important events
1	✓	• The soldiers have just eaten as the novel begins, and are full and satisfied – they have had extra rations because half of their company were killed in fighting the previous day. • Main characters introduced – Kropp, Müller, Leer, Tjaden, Haie Westhus, Detering, Kaczinsky (leader of the group), and the narrator Paul Bäumer. • Description of the men's use of latrines for social time and activities show how desensitized they have become due to their experiences in the war. • Kantorek's persuasion of the men to join up as soldiers described in flashback and criticized by the narrator, Bäumer. • The men visit badly wounded Kemmerich in hospital, and bribe a medical orderly to give Kemmerich some morphine. • Bäumer knows Kemmerich will die of his injuries, and Müller is keen to get Kemmerich's boots before they are stolen when he dies.
2		
3		
4		

You might also add two further columns to your table (or start a new, identical table – see below). In one column you should **identify** and write down what you feel to be the most important three to five quotations in the chapter. In the final column you should explain why you have chosen each quotation.

Chapter	Read?	Quotes	Reason for choice of quotes
1	✓	We are at rest five miles behind the front. Yesterday we were relieved, and now our bellies are full of beef and haricot beans. We are satisfied and at peace. Each man has another mess-tin full for the evening; and, what is more, there is a double ration of sausage and bread. That puts a man in fine trim. We have not had such luck as this for a long time.	These are the opening lines of the novel. The impression given is of things being very positive. In reality, the 'luck' the men have had, and reason for why there is so much food available, is that only 80 men from the whole company of 150 returned from the front the previous day, with the others all having been killed or injured in a sudden attack at that time. The novel mostly uses the first-person narration of a soldier involved in all events, and so it is his perceptions which the reader gets to know. Discovering that what the narrator perceives in this quotation as 'such luck as this' is in fact referring to the deaths of so many fellow soldiers is quite a shocking revelation which shows how the values and perceptions of these young men have been warped by their experiences – death has become so common that it is a lot less important than pragmatic considerations such as having enough to eat.

Chapter	Read?	Quotes	Reason for choice of quotes
		At the head of the queue of course were the hungriest – little Albert Kropp, the clearest thinker among us and therefore only a lance-corporal; Müller, who still carries his school textbooks with him, dreams of examinations, and during a bombardment mutters propositions in physics; Leer, who wears a full beard and has a preference for the girls from officers' brothels. He swears that they are obliged by an army order to wear silk chemises and to bathe before entertaining guests of the rank of captain and upwards. And as the fourth, myself, Paul Bäumer. All four are nineteen years of age, and all four joined up from the same class as volunteers for the war.	This quote introduces the individuals within the group of soldiers which the novel will focus on. It also introduces some themes: • Criticism of those in charge of the war – 'the clearest thinker among us and therefore only a lance-corporal' • Reminders of how young the men are who are experiencing the events of the novel – boys who left school to join the war – 'who still carries his school textbooks with him, dreams of examinations, and during a bombardment mutters propositions in physics'; 'All four are nineteen years of age, and all four joined up from the same class as volunteers for the war'. The contrast between what they should be doing (school), and what they are doing (the war) is constantly drawn in the novel.
		And perhaps more of us thought as he did, but no one could very well stand out, because at that time even one's parents were ready with the word "coward"; no one had the vaguest idea what we were in for.	This quote shows the pressures that were placed on young men, even school boys, to join up – everyone, including their parents, would have accused them of being cowards if they had not done so. Ignorance was another factor as no one really knew how bad things would be.
		There were thousands of Kantoreks, all of whom were convinced that they were acting for the best – in a way that cost them nothing. And that is why they let us down so badly. For us lads of eighteen they ought to have been mediators and guides to the world of maturity, the world of work, of duty, of culture, of progress – to the future. We often made fun of them and played jokes on them, but in our hearts we trusted them. The idea of authority, which they represented, was associated in our minds with a greater insight and a more humane wisdom.	Kantorek was the boys' teacher at school, who took the boys to the recruiting office to join up. He represents many of the older people who were keen to encourage boys to join up when they would not be doing so, or be directly involved, in the war themselves. They were assumed to have greater wisdom and experience, and were looked up to and trusted by boys such as Paul and his fellow soldiers for that reason. The realities of the war the men have found themselves in has taught them that, in fact, those older authority figures whom they trusted in fact had no such wisdom and insight, and have effectively betrayed the young men they were keen to encourage to sign up.
		While they continued to write and talk, we saw the wounded and dying. While they taught that duty to one's country is the greatest thing, we already knew that death-throes are stronger. But for all that we were no mutineers, no deserters, no cowards – they were very free with all these expressions. We loved our country as much as they; we went courageously into every action; but also we distinguished the false from true, we had suddenly learned to see. And we saw that there was nothing of their world left. We were all at once terribly alone; and alone we must see it through.	Paul continues to criticize those authority figures who let the boys down so badly. He uses contrast to show: • the emptiness of their patriotic rhetoric when compared with reality • how in fact it is the soldiers who have the insight and wisdom • the untrustworthiness of people they ought to have been able to trust. Aspects of sentence structure are used to emphasize these contrasts, such as: • balanced sentence phrasing containing elements relating to 'they' and 'we' • repetition of phrases such as 'While they… we…' • asyndeton and repetition of 'no' in 'no mutineers, no deserters, no cowards', which helps convey the strength of feeling and bitterness of the narrator at their betrayal. The increased repetition of 'we' towards the end shows the focus turning entirely to the soldiers and the situation they are in. They are actually the only ones who know the reality of that situation, and they must face it now alone.

Chapter	Read?	Quotes	Reason for choice of quotes
		Death is working through from within. It already has command in the eyes. Here lies our comrade, Kemmerich, who a little while ago was roasting horse flesh with us and squatting in the shell-holes. He it is still and yet it is not he any longer. His features have become uncertain and faint, like a photographic plate from which two pictures have been taken. Even his voice sounds like ashes.	The section of the chapter is a vivid description of Kemmerich dying. Imagery and use of detail make this a vivid portrayal of death. • **Personification** of death, almost as an enemy soldier itself – 'it already has command in the eyes'. • **Simile** – 'His features have become uncertain and faint, like a photographic plate from which two pictures have been taken' – which suggests how Kemmerich is fading away in front of them, and foreshadows how he will soon be nothing more than a memory or image in the mind. This simile may also suggest an x-ray image, which shows someone's skeleton – again, an image of death. • **Simile** – 'Even his voice sounds like ashes' – foreshadowing Kemmerich's death as ashes are a symbol of death. • **Sensory imagery** – the description contains references both to images and sound. • **Connotative language** – 'Here lies', used to introduce Kemmerich in the hospital, is a phrase commonly found on gravestones showing who is buried in a particular grave. This again foreshadows Kemmerich's death. • **Contrast** – 'Kemmerich, who a little while ago was roasting horse flesh with us and squatting in the shell-holes' – Kemmerich's horrible situation is emphasized by the comparison with what he was doing just a short time before.
2			
3			

You can use this schedule yourself, or as part of a group.

• Divide a book's chapters equally between the group. Each person should make notes on their assigned chapters, using the above tables, before sharing and combining their summaries with the rest of the group.

• You might create a single group table for the book and share it within the group via Google documents. Each group member should fill in their relevant sections. Comments, quotations or additional events and information could be added to each section by the other group members. Make sure any additions are clearly marked if you do this – perhaps use a different colour of text.

ACTIVITY: Joining up for the Western Front

■ ATL

- ■ Communication skills: Make inferences and draw conclusions
- ■ Critical-thinking skills: Gather and organize relevant information to formulate an argument

Having read the Chapter 1 extract from *All Quiet on the Western Front* on page 237, answer the following questions in small groups.

1 What persuaded the boys to sign up to join the army? What would have happened to anyone who refused to join up?
2 What persuasive techniques did Kantorek use with the boys?
3 Bäumer draws a contrast between richer and poorer people. Why do you think richer people were 'beside themselves with joy'?
4 In what ways do you think people like Kantorek thought that 'they were acting for the best'? Why did it cost such people 'nothing'?
5 What does Bäumer mean when he says 'And that is why they let us down so badly.'? How were Bäumer and the young soldiers being let down?
6 What, according to Bäumer, should teachers do? What kind of relationship does Bäumer think should exist between teachers and students?
7 In the final two paragraphs of the passage, Bäumer draws a number of contrasts between the young soldiers and Kantorek, and people like him.
   Copy out and complete the table on the right, detailing any contrasts you see.

The young soldiers	Kantorek and people like him
Trusted their teachers – thought they had more insight and wisdom	Turned out not be trustworthy – they did not know and did not convey to the boys the realities of the war, and death it would bring
Knew the realities of war	Knew only 'phrases' and 'cleverness'

8 How does the use of sentence structure in the following sentences of the final paragraph help to show the contrasts between the experience of the young soldiers, and that of the group of people like Kantorek?

> While they continued to write and talk, we saw the wounded and dying. While they taught that duty to one's country is the greatest thing, we already knew that death-throes are stronger. But for all that we were no mutineers, no deserters, no cowards – they were very free with all these expressions. We loved our country as much as they; we went courageously into every action; but also we distinguished the false from true, we had suddenly learned to see. And we saw that there was nothing of their world left. We were all at once terribly alone; and alone we must see it through.

9 What other stylistic techniques are used in the final paragraph, and what is the effect in each case?

◆ Assessment opportunities

In this activity you have practised skills that are assessed using Criterion A: Analysing.

COMPARE AND CONTRAST WRITING

Literature often involves the comparison of texts that focus on similar themes. Some of the issues raised in the previous passage from *All Quiet on the Western Front* are also examined in the passage on page 242 from *The Sorrow of War*, a novel by Bao Ninh.

Both extracts explore how people who will not be fighting think about the idea of going to war. While *All Quiet on the Western Front* shows active encouragement of young men doing this, *The Sorrow of War* depicts a character cautioning against it.

The Sorrow of War by Bao Ninh

Originally written in Vietnamese in 1990, *The Sorrow of War* is written in a stream of consciousness style and recounts events surrounding Kien, a North Vietnamese soldier fighting in the Vietnam War (1955–75). The author, Bao Ninh, fought in the Vietnamese war himself, serving in the Glorious 27th Youth Brigade.

The entire scene reflected his stepfather's extreme poverty. On a dusty family altar his mother's photo rested in a frame with broken glass. The bed in the same room was limp and bedraggled. A writing table was a mess of books, papers and glasses. The atmosphere was depressing. Yet in sharp contrast his stepfather lived in a style which belied his conditions. His thinning white hair was neatly combed back, disguising some scars, his beard was well shaven and tidy, and his clothes were clean and pressed.

He treated Kien warmly and politely and with the correct intimacy for the occasion, making him hot tea and inviting him to smoke and generally feel at home.

Kien noticed that his eyes were blurred and his scraggy and frail old hands trembled.

He looked over to Kien and said gently, 'So, you're off to the war? Not that I can prevent you. I'm old, you are young. I couldn't stop you if I wanted to. I just want you to understand me when I say that a human being's duty on this earth is to live, not to kill,' he said. 'Taste all manner of life.

Try everything. Be curious and inquire for yourself. Don't turn your back on life.'

Kien was surprised by the integrity of his stepfather's words and he listened intently.

'I want you to guard against all those who demand that you die just to prove something. It is not that I advise you to respect your life more than anything else, but for you not to die uselessly for the needs of others. You are all we have left, your mother, your father and me. I hope you live through the war and return home to Hanoi, for you still have many years ahead of you. Many years of joy and happiness to experience. Who else but you can experience your life?'

Surprised, and far from agreeing with him, Kien nevertheless trusted his stepfather's word, feeling an affinity with his sentiments. He saw in the old man a wise multi-faceted intelligence with a warm romantic heart that seemed to belong to another era, a sentimental era with all its sweet dreams and heightened awareness, alien to Kien, but attractive nonetheless.

The Sorrow of War

Comparing and contrasting literary texts

Follow the method below when comparing and contrasting texts. This type of analysis and note-taking should generate the ideas, details and notes needed to undertake comprehensive and focused comparative writing.

1 Make notes on possible themes found in each extract. Can you find passages or words within the text that support each theme?
2 How does each text treat the themes you have identified? What similarities or differences can you **identify**? For instance, what does one author include, when the other does not? What does one author emphasize, when the other does not? Why?
3 How are the similarities or differences presented in each text? How are literary aspects used to put the themes or messages across? Consider for example:
    a Use of narrative voice
    b Use of character
    c Use of relationships between characters
    d Use of aspects of style.
4 Structure your notes into an outline for your essay. Include all the key points you want to make, any evidence you have to support your points, and the order these points will be examined in.
5 Using quotations is a good way of supporting your argument. Some tips can be found here: **https://writing.wisc.edu/Handbook/QuoLiterature.html**
6 There are two common ways to structure writing that compares and contrasts:
    a Going through individual points of comparison one at a time, and considering each point in relation to each text. This is known as the 'point-by-point' method.
    b Talking about the texts one at a time, and making all points in relation to one, and then moving on

to make all of the points in relation to the other. This is sometimes known as the 'all of one/all of the other' method.

Some people feel that the point-by-point method makes the comparison and contrast more clear throughout the writing, and is better suited to when there are a lot of individual points being made. Note that the points that are being compared and contrasted – and their order of discussion – do not change, whatever structure is chosen.

7 Draft a thesis paragraph – this should set out at the beginning of your essay what you intend to show or argue. It should refer to points of both comparison and of contrast.
8 When comparing and contrasting, you should use some of these transitional words:
    a (Showing similarities) similarly, in the same way, in a similar way, similar to, likewise, just as, alike, compared with, not only … but also, same as, resemble, both.
    b (Showing difference) in contrast (with this), on the other hand, as opposed to, however, unlike, whereas, differs, different from, but not, on the contrary, instead of, less than, more than.
9 Do you know what a topic sentence is? How might it focus your writing?
10 Write your essay. Remember to get feedback on your writing as you go, so that you can redraft and improve your essay to the best that you can.
11 There is a lot of help available online for how to structure **compare and contrast** writing. Go to **www.slideshare.net** and search for **'compare and contrast writing'** or **'compare and contrast essay'**. Choose at least three slide presentations to look through for ideas and guidance on this.

Under pressure

Both *All Quiet on the Western Front* and *The Sorrow of War* refer to the external pressures placed on young men to join up: In *All Quiet on the Western Front* men are 'ostracised … because at that time even one's parents were ready with the word "coward"', while in *The Sorrow of War,* Kien's stepfather tells him that 'I want you to guard against all those who demand that you die just to prove something'.

We saw earlier too how patriotic poems, such as those written by Jessie Pope and **ubiquitous** propaganda posters also urged young men to join the war.

The consequences of this external pressure was well captured by *All Quiet on the Western Front* when Joseph Behm, who 'did not want to fall into line … did allow himself to be persuaded' owing to the pressure placed on him by others. Behm became 'one of the first to fall' during the fighting, his death a direct result of the pressure he faced to enlist. It is no accident that Remarque portrays Behm as shot in the eye, abandoned on the battlefield and 'mad with pain' before he dies – these painful details further emphasize the point he is making.

As we have seen, Wilfred Owen was critical of those who pressured men to fight without fully understanding the consequences of their actions. In 'Dulce et Decorum Est' Owen shows his readers the true consequences of sending men to fight; his graphic description of a gas attack demonstrates the grim reality of patriotic fervour:

> And watch the white eyes writhing in his face,
> His hanging face, like a devil's sick of sin;
> If you could hear, at every jolt, the blood
> Come gargling from the froth-corrupted lungs,
> Obscene as cancer, bitter as the cud
> Of vile, incurable sores on innocent tongues,

ACTIVITY: Comparing and contrasting literary texts

You will now **compare and contrast** the two extracts from *All Quiet on the Western Front* and *The Sorrow of War*, focusing on the themes presented by each.

To start, you should note down all possible themes of the passages you can find. Some themes from one, or both, of the passages are listed below – can you **identify** sentences or words within each text that support these themes? What other themes can you **identify**?

- **Teacher–student relationship**
- **Attitudes to joining up for war**
- **Effect of war on soldiers**
- **Poor vs rich attitudes**
- **Patriotism and duty to one's country**
- **Value of life**
- **War seen as negative**

When writing your essay comparing and contrasting these two texts you should follow the method outlined in the ATL cog on 'Comparing and contrasting literary texts'. Your essay should be 500–800 words.

◆ Assessment opportunities

In this activity you have practised skills that are assessed using Criterion A: Analysing, Criterion B: Organizing and Criterion D: Using language.

Prose commentary

A prose commentary involves close analysis of a text, which means looking at the **main ideas** a writer is trying to convey, and **how he/she does this**.

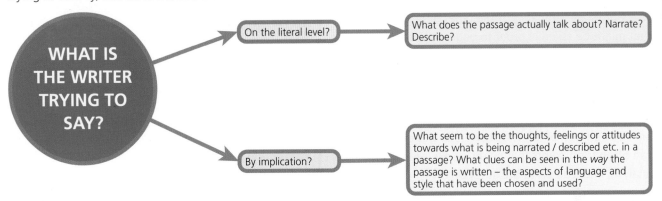

WHAT IS THE WRITER TRYING TO SAY?

On the literal level? → What does the passage actually talk about? Narrate? Describe?

By implication? → What seem to be the thoughts, feelings or attitudes towards what is being narrated / described etc. in a passage? What clues can be seen in the *way* the passage is written – the aspects of language and style that have been chosen and used?

Where do we hear the words from?

Remember there is a **speaker** between the writer and the words, and ourselves as readers. The speaker may or may not be representing what the writer him/herself thinks or feels. We **must** consider the role of the speaker in the presentation of the story, in trying to get at the writer's intentions.

Approaching the writing of a commentary:

1 Look closely at what each paragraph is focusing on – jot down what this is at the side.
    *Noting this will lead you to look at what the text is actually saying at different times, and should begin to suggest to you some **main ideas** of the text.*

2 Jot down some main elements of what is being presented in the passage:
    a Is a character or characters being presented?
    b Is a relationship between characters being described?
    c Is setting or a scene being described?
    d Are lots of events being described, or a sequence of them? WHAT things are going on?

If you can identify some main elements, ask some further questions about how they are being used or presented. For example:

• Is a character being presented?

   ○ What impressions are being presented of that/ those character(s)? What does the writer's attitude towards the character seem to be? Critical? Approving? Are there elements of both, meaning the character is ambiguous or ambivalent in his / her presentation?

• Is a relationship between two (or more) characters being described?

   ○ How does each character seem to feel about the other? Is one person dominating?

   ○ (Look out for other types of 'relationship', such as that of a human with the environment.)

   ○ What conflicts are shown in the passage?

• Is setting or a scene being described?

   ○ Is it appealing, hostile, or bits of both? How might this affect any characters present?

   ○ Is the scene presented very vivid? Are there appeals to the senses?

   ○ How might the scene or setting relate to anything else happening in the narrative?

• Are lots of events being described, or a sequence of them? WHAT things are going on?

   ○ What stages of action take place?

   ○ Does one thing lead to another?

   ○ Does the narration seem to be 'dramatic' or 'climactic' in some way? Where? Why?

➤

These are some examples of the types of questions that might be asked in order to begin 'interrogating' or exploring a passage of prose, and analysing what it is saying, and how it is saying it.

Meanwhile, a general question that might be asked about any of the above elements is 'What impressions am I being given of it?' The answers to this question can often form points that might be explored in an analysis, and lead on to the question of:

'Why am I getting these impressions? What specific details of the text are helping to convey them to me?'

Identifying specific details in turn should lead to consideration of how those particular details are actually working each time to help convey particular impressions a reader gains. Exploring such details will involve addressing literary features.

How to write up a point

There is a particular order for doing this:

> State the POINT clearly at the beginning.

> Bring in EVIDENCE from the text (usually by quoting) which you think contains an example of that point – ILLUSTRATES it.

> – EXPLAIN how the evidence shows the point you are making. Often something is actually implied in words or phrases, and it is important to identify such words and phrases, say what they are implying, and explain how.
> – Pick out any specific words in a quote which you think are especially important, and explain how / why they are important – i.e. how they are working to help convey the impression you are being given.
> – If they are examples of specific literary features, name them ('this simile', etc), and explain their significance – their purpose and effect.

ACTIVITY: Debate

■ ATL

- Critical-thinking skills: Evaluate evidence and arguments; develop contrary or opposing arguments
- Collaboration skills: Delegate and share responsibility for decision-making; listen actively to other perspectives and ideas; exercise leadership and take on a variety of roles within groups
- Communication skills: Use a variety of speaking techniques to communicate with a variety of audiences; negotiate ideas and knowledge with peers and teachers; interpret and use effectively modes of non-verbal communication

What are your own views on writers such as Owen and Remarque presenting war in the shocking ways that they do? Do you think they, and others, have a right to do this in a time of war for a nation? Or are they acting irresponsibly by publishing such things at such a time?

As a class, debate the following proposition:

> This house believes that poets and novelists who write in ways such as Owen, Sassoon and Remarque during times of war are irresponsible in **undermining** support for a crucial national cause.

The class should split into two sides in order to conduct the debate: one side will argue in favour of the proposition, and the other side will oppose it.

There are many different ways to conduct a debate, and you should decide which format your debate will take. Do this by researching **debate formats** and exploring note-taking materials online, using the below links as a starting point:

https://taniasanti.files.wordpress.com/2013/03/debates.pdf

www.esu.org/our-work/esuresources

◆ Assessment opportunities

In this activity you have practised skills that are assessed using Criterion A: Analysing, Criterion B: Organizing, Criterion C: Producing text and Criterion D: Using language.

FREEDOM OF EXPRESSION – WHAT DO WE THINK NOW?

During a THINK–PAIR–SHARE earlier in this chapter (page 225), you considered the rights and responsibilities you felt different individuals and groups in society should have in times of war.

You completed the table below at that time, adding notes on your thoughts and discussions. Review your notes and, now that we have looked more closely into questions of rights and responsibilities of some of these individuals, make any changes or additions that might reflect your thinking at this point.

Individual/group	Rights	Responsibilities
Soldiers		
Generals, commanders		
Government		
Members of the public		
Journalists (including photojournalists)		
Writers – novelists, poets, etc		

In a group of four or five, **discuss** your opinions on this now. How far do you all agree or disagree? Why?

Would you change any of your views further following this discussion?

Two or three people from each group should then go to other groups, while two new people should join yours. Once again, **discuss** how far you agree or disagree in your opinions on the rights and responsibilities that should exist.

Finally, think through your own context, and what you think your own rights and responsibilities are with regard to freedom of expression. Where might you be able to exercise those? Where should you be able to exercise them? Where might you choose not to do so?

Fill in some thoughts on this in the following table:

Freedom of expression – me …	
Rights	**Responsibilities**

SOME SUMMATIVE TASKS TO TRY

Use these tasks to apply and extend your learning in this chapter. These tasks are designed so that you can evaluate your learning at different levels of achievement in the Language and literature criteria.

THIS TASK CAN BE USED TO EVALUATE YOUR LEARNING IN CRITERION A, CRITERION B AND CRITERION D

Task 1: Poetry commentary

Find Carol Ann Duffy's poem '**War Photographer**' online. After you have read it, write a commentary on the poem that identifies the main ideas and purposes of the text, and also explores the style and techniques used by the poet to convey these. Your analysis should be between 500 and 1,000 words in length.

THIS TASK CAN BE USED TO EVALUATE YOUR LEARNING IN CRITERION A, CRITERION B AND CRITERION D

Task 2: Prose commentary

Read the passage on page 248 from *All Quiet on the Western Front* and write a commentary that explores how the writer makes the scene vivid and immediate. **Identify** the author's main ideas, and **analyse** the aspects of style and technique used to convey these. Also comment on why the author chose to write the scene in this way. Your commentary should be between 500 and 1,000 words in length.

The shell hole is gaping in front of me. I fix my eyes on it, grasping at it almost physically, I have to get to it in one jump.

Then I feel a blow in the face, and a hand grabs me by the shoulder – has the dead man come back to life? The hand shakes me, I turn my head, and in a flash of light that lasts only a second I find myself looking into Katczinsky's face. His mouth is wide open and he is bellowing, but I can't hear anything; he shakes me and comes closer; the noise ebbs for a moment and I can make out his voice: 'Gas – gaaas – gaaaas – pass it on!'

I pull out my gas-mask case … Someone is lying a little way away from me. All I can think of is that I've got to tell him: 'Gaaas … gaas.'

I shout, crawl across to him, hit at him with the gas-mask case but he doesn't notice – it I do it again, and then again – he only ducks – it is one of the new recruits – I look despairingly at Kat, who has his mask on already – I tear mine out of the case, my helmet is knocked aside as I get the mask over my face, I reach the man and his gas-mask case is by my hand, so I get hold of the mask and shove it over his head – he grabs it, I let go, and with a sudden jolt I am lying in the shell hole.

The dull thud of the gas shells is mixed in with the sharp noise of the high explosives. In between the explosions a bell rings the warning, gongs and metal rattles spread the word – Gas – gas – gaas –

There is a noise as someone drops behind me, once, twice. I wipe the window of my gas-mask clear of condensation. It is Kat, Kropp and somebody else. There are four of us lying here, tensed and waiting, breathing as shallowly as we can.

The first few minutes with the mask tell you whether you will live or die. Is it airtight? I know the terrible sights from the field hospital, soldiers who have been gassed, choking for days on end as they spew up their burned-out lungs, bit by bit.

I breathe carefully, with my mouth pressed against the mouthpiece. By now the gas is snaking over the ground and sinking into all the hollows. It insinuates itself into our shell hole wriggling its way in like a broad, soft jellyfish. I give Kat a nudge: it is better to crawl out and lie up on top rather than here, where the gas concentrates itself the most. But we can't. A second hail of shellfire starts. It's as if it is not the guns that are roaring; it's as if the very earth is raging.

All Quiet on the Western Front – Chapter 4

THIS TASK CAN BE USED TO EVALUATE YOUR LEARNING IN CRITERION A, CRITERION B AND CRITERION D

Task 3: Video analysis – feature article

Blackadder Goes Forth is a British comedy series set in the First World War. A character in the series, General Melchett, is used to satirize, and criticize, military leadership during the war: **www.youtube.com/watch?v=rblfKREj50o**.

An educational organization has asked you to write a feature article for their website which provides a link to the video above, and explains how it contains criticisms of generals in the First World War. The article will be a resource for middle-years students, and should **identify**:

- Why the educational organization chose this video to be used

- the specific aspects of the character of General Melchett that are presented and criticized
- how such criticism is achieved – for instance, does that happen through:
  - □ his own words
  - □ his actions
  - □ the words of others (You should note particularly the role of the character of Blackadder himself as a commentator in this regard.)
  - □ his appearance
  - □ other methods, such as the use of props?

Within your article you should use specific quotations and details from the video to illustrate any points you make, ensure the register and choice of language are suitable for students within MYP grade levels, and you should properly cite all outside sources, including the video, in accordance with the referencing tool used/advised by your school or class teacher.

Task 4: Letter from a poet

Imagine you are Wilfred Owen, or another First World War poet of your choice. You have written a number of poems based on the war and are now keen to have them published so that the general public will better understand what war is really like. You decide to write a letter to a publisher that explains the purpose behind your poems, and persuades the publisher to publish your work.

Using only the poems of Owen, or your chosen poet, as the basis for the explanations and arguments you will be making, write a letter to a publisher. In the letter you, as the poet, should explain:

- some of the specific purposes you had in writing the poems
- how your poems achieve those purposes, using evidence from the poems to support your points
- why you think it is important for your poems to be published. Think about the persuasive techniques you might use here to convince this publisher to take on your poems.

Your letter should be between 500 and 1,000 words.

Reflection

We have explored what rights may exist in communicating what we want, and whether and how far such rights might be restricted. We have considered what can be involved in communicating responsibly, and the role of censorship, including self-censorship, focusing on literature of war, and also how different genres of writing can be used to communicate the realities of such situations. In doing this we have compared and contrasted some texts, and looked at the conventions of these texts. We have also noted ways of summarizing longer texts to gain an overview of their content and structure.

Use this table to reflect on your own learning in this chapter.						
Questions we asked	**Answers we found**	**Any further questions now?**				
Factual:						
Conceptual:						
Debatable:						
Approaches to learning you used in this chapter:	**Description – what new skills did you learn?**	**How well did you master the skills?**				
		Novice	**Learner**	**Practitioner**	**Expert**	
Communication skills						
Collaboration skills						
Information literacy skills						
Media literacy skills						
Critical-thinking skills						
Creative-thinking skills						
Transfer skills						
Learner profile attribute(s)	Reflect on the importance of being a thinker for your learning in this chapter.					
Thinkers						

10 What do healthy relationships look like?

○ **Context** can influence the ways in which people **connect** with each other, and the **nature of the relationships** they form.

CONSIDER THESE QUESTIONS:

Factual: What kinds of close relationships do people have with others?

Conceptual: How might context play a role in influencing the nature of relationships? How might issues of truth and deception impact on relationships? What makes a relationship 'healthy'? How great is the role of perception in a healthy relationship? How important is personal responsibility in promoting and sustaining healthy relationships?

Debatable: How far are perceptions of a healthy relationship contextual? How dependent are relationships on universal factors?

Now **share and compare** your thoughts and ideas with your partner, or with the whole class.

ACCOUNTABILITY
- Accepting responsibility, behaviours and attitudes
- Admitting mistakes (or being wrong)

TRUST
- Accepting each other's word
- Giving the benefit of the doubt

SAFETY
- Refusing to intimidate or manipulate
- Respecting physical space
- Expressing self non-violently and honestly

RESPECT

COOPERATION
- Asking, not expecting
- Accepting change
- Making decisions together
- Being willing to compromise
- Seeking mutually satisfying resolutions to conflict

HONESTY
- Communicating openly and truthfully

SUPPORT
- Supporting each other's choices
- Being understanding
- Offering encouragement
- Listening non-judgementally
- Valuing opinions

■ Foundations of a healthy relationship

○ IN THIS CHAPTER, WE WILL …

■ **Find out** through considering relationships presented particularly in Shakespeare's writing, different ways in which close relationships might be perceived as 'healthy', and what factors may be involved in that.

■ **Explore** the ways in which personal responsibility may play a role in promoting and sustaining healthy relationships.

■ **Take action** by evaluating our own close relationships and what may make or keep them healthy, and engaging and taking personal responsibility in those relationships accordingly.

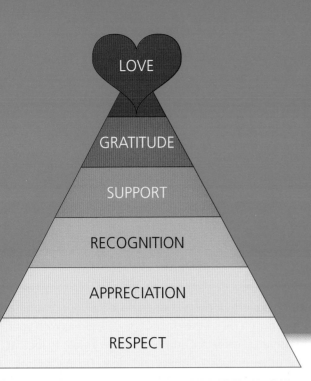

LOVE

GRATITUDE

SUPPORT

RECOGNITION

APPRECIATION

RESPECT

■ These Approaches to Learning (ATL) skills will be useful …

- Communication skills
- Collaboration skills
- Creative-thinking skills
- Critical-thinking skills
- Reflection skills
- Transfer skills
- Information literacy skills
- Media literacy skills

● We will reflect on this learner profile attribute …

- Caring – explore further what it means to be caring in the context of relationships with others, and the roles of empathy, compassion and respect in those. The chapter will look at how such approaches help to make a difference in the lives of both ourselves and others closest to us, and help to build sensitive, supportive and positive relationships.

KEY WORDS

anticipation	perception
appearance	reality
context	relationship
deception	romantic
justified	shame
misunderstanding	social expectations

◆ Assessment opportunities in this chapter:

- **Criterion A:** Analysing
- **Criterion B:** Organizing
- **Criterion C:** Producing text
- **Criterion D:** Using language

THINK–PAIR–SHARE

Read, consider and then make notes on the following questions:

1 **What are the four or five closest relationships you have with others, for example parents, siblings, grandparents, aunts, uncles, cousins, friends, boyfriend/girlfriend and so on?**
2 **What are some main characteristics of a relationship that you would describe as healthy? Write down a list of as many as you can think of.**
3 **From your list of characteristics, what do you think are the five most important? List these in order of priority, with the most important characteristic at the top.**

In pairs, once you have completed your notes, share your thoughts with your partner. How close were the two of you in your thinking? Having seen your partner's ideas, would you change any of yours? Join with another pair now, and share once again.

What is a healthy relationship?

ACTIVITY: A healthy relationship

■ ATL

- Communication skills: Organize and depict information logically
- Collaboration skills: Build consensus

In the same groups of four from the previous THINK–PAIR–SHARE activity, look at the two graphics at the start of this chapter. These diagrams contain ideas on what healthy relationships look like and involve. You can find more informative graphics on this topic online by searching for **healthy relationship diagrams**.

Using the two opening graphics, and your own research, your group will now **create** a graphic that details the key characteristics of a healthy relationship. First, decide on the following:

- **the categories, factors or criteria you would use to define relationships that are healthy**
- **descriptors or details of any behaviours, actions or signs that suggest what each category may look like in practice**
- **a format for a graphic. Is it a wheel? A list? Something different?**

Using a piece of poster paper, produce your graphic and then post it on to the classroom wall, along with your classmates' efforts. Carry out a gallery walk to look at the other groups' graphics and ideas. Do any factors appear on every list?

In your group, copy the table below. Write any recurring factors you spotted, or – if there are none that appear on every poster – the most common factors, in the left-hand column of the table.

In the middle column add the descriptors that were included for each factor across the different posters.

Look closely at the factors and descriptors you have listed. Decide as a group whether you feel each of these factors need to be present for a relationship to be considered healthy. In the right-hand column write down your decision along with your reasoning.

An example is given for you.

Common factors in a relationship that is healthy	Indicators for each factor	Always necessary or not in a healthy relationship? Why (not)?
Support for each other (**mutual** support)	• Encouraging each other's choices • Valuing each other's opinions • Reassuring each other in times of difficulty or challenge • Being present when support is needed	Always necessary. If two people in a relationship do not encourage each other or value each other, their relationship may involve arguments, they may well feel they cannot trust each other, and may feel they have to deal with things on their own. This would not be a healthy relationship, and if people deal with things on their own, they are not acting within a relationship to begin with.

MUCH ADO ABOUT NOTHING

The main text we will be looking at in this chapter is William Shakespeare's *Much Ado About Nothing*, a play that focuses a great deal on relationships.

It may be helpful before beginning to study the play more closely to gain an overview of what happens in it. Shakespeare's plays often have a lot of things going on at once, between a large number of characters, while his use of language can also provide a challenge at times.

Remember that, as a play, *Much Ado About Nothing* was meant to be watched rather than read. Your school may have a version of the play you can watch but, if not, several performances of the play can be found on YouTube by using the search term **Much Ado About Nothing full play**.

A 1993 version of the play, starring Denzel Washington, Keanu Reeves and Michael Keaton, can be found at the following link: **https://youtu.be/K5qQRepozGU**.

Summaries of the play may also be useful. A number of these can be found online by searching **Much Ado About Nothing summary**. A video summary, based on the 1993 film, can be found here: **https://youtu.be/9-AGIUNsGgA**.

Features of *Much Ado About Nothing*

As is characteristic of Shakespeare's plays, *Much Ado About Nothing* comprises five acts, and is written using three forms of writing. The decisions Shakespeare made of when and how to use each type of writing can help inform the audience about certain aspects of the play, such as character and relationships. The three types of writing used are **prose**, **blank verse** and **rhymed verse**, and we will look at each of these in more detail below.

Prose

Prose is the writing of ordinary speech and everyday life. Shakespeare's plays on the whole are written in blank verse, but *Much Ado About Nothing* is an exception to this, since it is mainly written using prose.

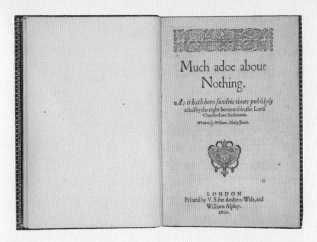

Much Ado About Nothing

Written by William Shakespeare around 1598, and first performed in 1612, *Much Ado About Nothing* is a comedy set in Messina, a port on the island of Sicily. The play is about love and relationships, looking in particular at the courtship of Hero and Claudio, and the marriage of Benedick and Beatrice. Much of the action takes place in and around the household of Leonato, Hero's father, and the play thus also explores their father–daughter relationship. Relationships between friends are also depicted.

It is often stated that Shakespeare used prose for lower status characters and poetry for those of higher social classes. While this is often the case, it is not a set rule. You must look carefully at what style is being used and think about the possible reasons for that; this is particularly the case with *Much Ado About Nothing* where so much prose is used, including, quite frequently, by characters of a higher social class.

Prose is often used in Shakespeare's plays in the following instances:

- as the usual speech of characters from a lower social class
- where a character of a higher social status wants to engage in light-hearted conversation or speech
- where the more refined and **highbrow** form of poetry may not be appropriate for the subject being spoken of at the time
- for devices such as letters
- where a character is mad, or pretending to be.

Blank verse

Shakespeare wrote mostly in blank verse in his plays (with *Much Ado About Nothing* an exception to that). Some of the features by which blank verse can be recognized in Shakespeare plays are:

- each line begins with a capital letter
- it does not rhyme
- it is written in **iambic pentameter** – lines with ten syllables and a particular stress pattern.

Blank verse is often used by Shakespeare:

- as the usual speech of characters of a higher status
- where more elevated themes are the focus of speech, such as love
- where song forms a part of the script.

Iambic pentameter

A line written in iambic pentameter consists of one short (or unstressed) syllable followed by one long (or stressed) syllable. This is sometimes represented as follows:

    x / x / x / x / x /

Each pair of syllables is known as a '**foot**' and the stressed–unstressed pattern of these means that each foot has a beat that is sometimes described as 'da DUM'. This can be heard when the line is spoken.

A further explanation of iambic pentameter can be read here: **www.shmoop.com/literature-glossary/iambic-pentameter.html**.

ℹ️

Shakespeare's language

Shakespeare wrote his plays during the late 1500s and early 1600s, and language has changed a lot since then. To better understand his writing, you may find the following British Council worksheet on the language of Shakespeare helpful: **https://goo.gl/o5nrEY**.

Rhymed verse

Rhymed verse is less common in Shakespeare's plays. When used, it usually utilizes **rhyming couplets**, where the final words of two successive lines of verse rhyme with one another. Rhymed verse tends to be found in:

- songs or chants
- poetry, including sonnets, about love
- at the climax to a scene, or a more noticeable conclusion (rhyming couplets can be used to emphasize the concluding line of an exchange).

ACTIVITY: Identify the form

 ATL

- Communication skills: Read critically and for comprehension
- Critical-thinking skills: Gather and organize relevant information to formulate an argument

Practise recognizing each form of writing by looking at the extracts on page 255, all taken from *Much Ado About Nothing*. For each extract indicate whether Shakespeare has used prose, blank verse, or rhymed verse. In each case, see if you can **identify** *why* he might have used that particular form of writing. (This may be difficult with passages taken out of context, spoken by characters you may be unfamiliar with, so just try your best.)

 Assessment opportunities

In this activity you have practised skills that are assessed using Criterion A: Analysing.

BEATRICE: What fire is in mine ears? Can this be true?

Stand I condemn'd for pride and scorn so much?

Contempt, farewell! and maiden pride, adieu!

No glory lives behind the back of such.

And, Benedick, love on; I will requite thee,

Taming my wild heart to thy loving hand:

If thou dost love, my kindness shall incite thee

To bind our loves up in a holy band;

For others say thou dost deserve, and I

Believe it better than reportingly.

■ Extract 1

DON JOHN: The word is too good to paint out her wickedness; I could say she were worse: think you of a worse title, and I will fit her to it. Wonder not till further warrant: go but with me to-night, you shall see her chamber-window entered, even the night before her wedding-day: if you love her then, to-morrow wed her; but it would better fit your honour to change your mind.

■ Extract 2

LEONATO: I cannot bid you bid my daughter live;

That were impossible: but, I pray you both,

Possess the people in Messina here

How innocent she died; and if your love

Can labour ought in sad invention,

Hang her an epitaph upon her tomb

And sing it to her bones, sing it to-night:

To-morrow morning come you to my house,

And since you could not be my son-in-law,

Be yet my nephew: my brother hath a daughter,

Almost the copy of my child that's dead,

And she alone is heir to both of us:

Give her the right you should have given her cousin,

And so dies my revenge.

■ Extract 3

BENEDICK: She told me, not thinking I had been myself [not knowing it was me she was speaking to], that I was the prince's jester, that I was duller than a great thaw; huddling jest upon jest with such impossible conveyance upon me that I stood like a man at a mark [like a target man], with a whole army shooting at me. She speaks poniards [daggers], and every word stabs: if her breath were as terrible as her terminations, there were no living near her; she would infect to the north star.

■ Extract 4

CLAUDIO: Friendship is constant in all other things

Save in the office and affairs of love:

Therefore, all hearts in love use their own tongues;

Let every eye negotiate for itself

And trust no agent; for beauty is a witch

Against whose charms faith melteth into blood.

This is an accident of hourly proof,

Which I mistrusted not. Farewell, therefore, Hero!

■ Extract 5

BORACHIO: Sweet prince, let me go no farther to mine answer: do you hear me, and let this count kill me. I have deceived even your very eyes: what your wisdoms could not discover, these shallow fools have brought to light: who in the night overheard me confessing to this man how Don John your brother incensed me to slander the Lady Hero, how you were brought into the orchard and saw me court Margaret in Hero's garments, how you disgraced her, when you should marry her: my villainy they have upon record; which I had rather seal with my death than repeat over to my shame. The lady is dead upon mine and my master's false accusation; and, briefly, I desire nothing but the reward of a villain.

■ Extract 6

Now let us begin to look in detail at *Much Ado About Nothing* and, in particular, **explore** the concept and context of connections and relationships. As we do this, we will also look more closely at how Shakespeare wrote his play and the techniques he used to help convey ideas about these topics to his audience.

ACTIVITY: The art of opening a literary work

■ ATL

- Creative-thinking skills: Consider multiple alternatives, including those that might be unlikely or impossible
- Media literacy skills: Understand the impact of media representations and modes of presentation

What should a writer try to do when writing the first scene of a piece of literature such as a play or novel? What might an audience need to know? What might they find interesting? In a group of four, brainstorm ideas on this and record them in a table like the one below.

What functions should an opening scene perform?
•
•
•
•
•

One reason people carry on watching or reading a play is that their curiosity has been raised about something they have seen, heard or read. Below are the opening lines of *Much Ado About Nothing*. What questions might be provoked by these lines, which might help raise the curiosity of an audience?

ACT I

SCENE I. Before LEONATO'S house.

Enter LEONATO, HERO and BEATRICE, with a Messenger

LEONATO: I learn in this letter that Don Pedro of Arragon comes this night to Messina.

MESSENGER: He is very near by this: he was not three leagues off when I left him.

LEONATO: How many gentlemen have you lost in this action?

◆ Assessment opportunities

In this activity you have practised skills that are assessed using Criterion A: Analysing.

The Globe

The Globe was built in 1599 by Shakespeare's playing company, the **Lord Chamberlain's Men**. Situated on the bank of the Thames, London, the theatre accidentally burned down 14 years after it opened (during a play a theatrical cannon misfired and set fire to the wood and thatch building). After being rebuilt, the theatre closed for good in 1642. In 1997, an authentic replica of the original theatre was constructed and today you can visit and watch Shakespearean plays performed in a setting very similar to the original.

Find out more about the Globe at the following links, or do your own research online:

- **www.shakespeare-online.com/theatre/ triptotheglobe.html** – a written account of a visit to the Globe, from the perspective of a member of the audience in Shakespeare's time.
- **https://youtu.be/b9uDK3xsLYk** – a 20-minute documentary that gives a more in-depth look at the theatre.
- **https://youtu.be/T3PIhGgtWTs** – a scene from the film *Shakespeare in Love* giving an idea of what performing a play at the Globe in Shakespeare's time would have been like.

Many of Shakespeare's plays were first performed in London at a venue called the Globe theatre. The theatre was open to the weather and, throughout the play, vendors moved among the crowd selling food and drink. There could be quite a bit of noise and movement therefore and, in the face of all this disruption, Shakespeare had the task of attracting (and then keeping!) the attention of his audience.

ACTIVITY: Capturing an audience's interest

■ ATL

- Communication skills: Read critically and for comprehension; make inferences and draw conclusions

The opening lines from *Much Ado About Nothing* are reproduced in full on the following two pages. Read them and, individually, try to **identify** aspects of the opening that have been designed to capture the interest and raise the curiosity of the audience. Note down any passages, ideas or techniques that may have been included for this purpose. Once you have finished, share your ideas in groups of three or four.

The ATL cog 'How to begin a play' (page 260) details the different functions of a play's opening scene; it might be helpful to consider these when examining the opening of *Much Ado About Nothing*.

◆ Assessment opportunities

In this activity you have practised skills that are assessed using Criterion A: Analysing.

SCENE I. Before LEONATO'S house.

Enter LEONATO, HERO and BEATRICE, with a Messenger

LEONATO: I learn in this letter that Don Pedro of Arragon comes this night to Messina.

MESSENGER: He is very near by this: he was not three leagues off when I left him.

LEONATO: How many gentlemen have you lost in this action?

MESSENGER: But few of any sort, and none of name.

LEONATO: A victory is twice itself when the achiever brings home full numbers. I find here that Don Peter hath bestowed much honour on a young Florentine called Claudio.

MESSENGER: Much deserved on his part and equally remembered by Don Pedro: he hath borne himself beyond the promise of his age, doing, in the figure of a lamb, the feats of a lion: he hath indeed better bettered expectation than you must expect of me to tell you how.

LEONATO: He hath an uncle here in Messina will be very much glad of it.

MESSENGER: I have already delivered him letters, and there appears much joy in him; even so much that joy could not show itself modest enough without a badge of bitterness.

LEONATO: Did he break out into tears?

MESSENGER: In great measure.

LEONATO: A kind overflow of kindness: there are no faces truer than those that are so washed. How much better is it to weep at joy than to joy at weeping!

BEATRICE: I pray you, is Signior Mountanto returned from the wars or no?

MESSENGER: I know none of that name, lady: there was none such in the army of any sort.

LEONATO: What is he that you ask for, niece?

HERO: My cousin means Signior Benedick of Padua.

MESSENGER: O, he's returned; and as pleasant as ever he was.

BEATRICE: He set up his bills here in Messina and challenged Cupid at the flight; and my uncle's fool, reading the challenge, subscribed for Cupid, and challenged him at the bird-bolt. I pray you, how many hath he killed and eaten in these wars? But how many hath he killed? for indeed I promised to eat all of his killing.

LEONATO: Faith, niece, you tax Signior Benedick too much; but he'll be meet with you, I doubt it not.

MESSENGER: He hath done good service, lady, in these wars.

BEATRICE: You had musty victual, and he hath holp to eat it: he is a very valiant trencherman; he hath an excellent stomach.

MESSENGER: And a good soldier too, lady.

BEATRICE: And a good soldier to a lady: but what is he to a lord?

MESSENGER: A lord to a lord, a man to a man; stuffed with all honourable virtues.

BEATRICE: It is so, indeed; he is no less than a stuffed man: but for the stuffing — well, we are all mortal.

LEONATO: You must not, sir, mistake my niece. There is a kind of merry war betwixt Signior Benedick and her: they never meet but there's a skirmish of wit between them.

BEATRICE: Alas! He gets nothing by that. In our last conflict four of his five wits went halting off, and now is the whole man governed with one: so that if he have wit enough to keep himself warm, let him bear it for a difference between himself and his horse; for it is all the wealth that he hath left, to be known a reasonable creature. Who is his companion now? He hath every month a new sworn brother.

MESSENGER: Is't possible?

BEATRICE: Very easily possible: he wears his faith but as the fashion of his hat; it ever changes with the next block.

MESSENGER: I see, lady, the gentleman is not in your books.

BEATRICE: No; an he were, I would burn my study. But, I pray you, who is his companion? Is there no young squarer now that will make a voyage with him to the devil?

MESSENGER: He is most in the company of the right noble Claudio.

BEATRICE: O Lord, he will hang upon him like a disease: he is sooner caught than the pestilence, and the taker runs presently mad. God help the noble Claudio! If he have caught the Benedick, it will cost him a thousand pound ere a' be cured.

MESSENGER: I will hold friends with you, lady.

BEATRICE: Do, good friend.

LEONATO: You will never run mad, niece.

BEATRICE: No, not till a hot January.

MESSENGER: Don Pedro is approached.

How to begin a play

One of the main functions the opening of a play should perform is to raise the interest of an audience and persuade them to read or watch on. There are a number of other functions, however, and the diagram below indicates some of those that might also appear in the opening scene.

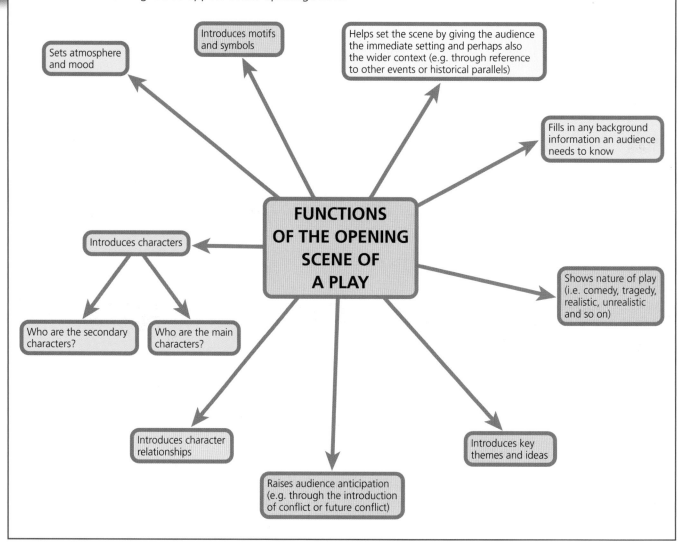

ACTIVITY: Relationships as an opening 'hook'

ATL

- Communication skills: Read critically and for comprehension; make inferences and draw conclusions

One function of a play's opening may be to introduce one or more important character relationships, and to use these to gain the attention and interest of an audience. Anticipation can also be raised, with the audience imagining what will happen in (or to) that relationship. This is true of the literary examples included below. For each example try to answer the following questions, making notes in the right-hand column of a copy of the table below.

- **What does each example suggest about the nature of the relationship being introduced?**
- **What questions could be posed to raise anticipation in a reader or audience?**
- **Do you think any of the examples portray relationships that you would define as healthy? Which ones, and why?**
- **Why do the others not seem to be healthy relationships?**

She waited, Kate Croy, for her father to come in, but he kept her unconsciously, and there were moments at which she showed herself, in the glass over the mantel, a face positively pale with the irritation that had brought her to the point of going away without sight of him.	*The Wings of the Dove* – Henry James
Like most people I lived for a long time with my mother and father. My father liked to watch the wrestling, my mother liked to wrestle: it didn't matter what. She was in the white corner and that was that.	*Oranges are not the Only Fruit* – Jeanette Winterson
All happy families are alike; each unhappy family is unhappy in its own way.	*Anna Karenina* – Leo Tolstoy
It's a funny thing about mothers and fathers. Even when their own child is the most disgusting little blister you could ever imagine, they still think that he or she is wonderful.	*Matilda* – Roald Dahl
Amergo Bonasera sat in New York Criminal Court Number 3 and waited for justice; vengeance on the men who had so cruelly hurt his daughter, who had tried to dishonor her.	*The Godfather* – Mario Puzo

◆ Assessment opportunities

In this activity you have practised skills that are assessed using Criterion A: Analysing.

Relationships in the opening of *Much Ado About Nothing*

One of the functions of the opening of *Much Ado About Nothing*, which you may well have noticed, was to introduce what will be a very important relationship in the play as a whole – that of Beatrice and Benedick. Though Benedick does not actually appear at this point, Beatrice's reactions to the Messenger's reports on the battle tell us something about her relationship with Benedick.

DISCUSS

Read through the opening scene again. What kind of relationship seems to exist between Benedick and Beatrice? What evidence is there to support your view? Make notes on your impressions of that relationship, using the prompts on the right as your starting point. **Discuss** your thoughts with a partner.

On the evidence of this passage, I would describe the relationship between Beatrice and Benedick as … because …

The particular details from the text that show this …

My expectations for this relationship as the play progresses are that …

How far are perceptions of a healthy relationship contextual?

ACTIVITY: What's in a relationship?

ATL

- Critical-thinking skills: Draw reasonable conclusions and generalizations
- Critical-thinking skills: Gather and organize relevant information to formulate an argument

To help you investigate how a relationship is presented in literature, whenever you read a passage that reveals a relationship you have not seen before, make sure to bear in mind the questions from the discussion activity on page 261.

You should also consider what literary devices are being used, and what they suggest about the nature of the relationship between the characters. Read the following quotes about Benedick and Beatrice and, for each one, note the literary device being used and what it suggests about the relationship.

◆ Assessment opportunities

In this activity you have practised skills that are assessed using Criterion A: Analysing.

BEATRICE: And a good soldier to a lady: but what is he to a lord?	
LEONATO: There is a kind of merry war betwixt Signior Benedick and her: they never meet but there's a skirmish of wit between them.	
BEATRICE: He wears his faith but as the fashion of his hat; it ever changes with the next block.	
MESSENGER: I see, lady, the gentleman is not in your books. **BEATRICE:** No; an he were, I would burn my study.	
BEATRICE: O Lord, he will hang upon him like a disease: he is sooner caught than the pestilence, and the taker runs presently mad … If he have caught the Benedick, it will cost him a thousand pound ere a' be cured.	*(Remember that if an image is repeated in different forms, as with the simile and metaphors of disease and illness used by Beatrice of Benedick here, it can be termed an* **extended metaphor**.*)*

ANTICIPATION

In the introduction Beatrice makes it clear that she does not like Benedick, despite the Messenger suggesting that he is a brave soldier. Leonato also describes their relationship as a 'kind of merry war', with 'merry' also suggesting that there is some humour in how they relate to each other. This all raises the audience's anticipation and leaves them eager to find out several things, such as:

- What will happen when Benedick arrives? How will Beatrice act towards him in person?
- How will Benedick act in return? What are his perceptions of the relationship between them?
- What kind of character is Benedick? Two different perspectives of him are presented by Beatrice and the Messenger.
- Why does Beatrice feel so strongly about Benedick that she feels a desire to make such comments to a Messenger – somebody she does not know? What has happened between them in the past to create these feelings?

HUMOUR

The relationship between Beatrice and Benedick also raises the interest of an audience through its use of humour. Much of the humour results from Beatrice's quick-wittedness – she can immediately use what someone has said and turn it into a clever, and quite often amusing, response.

Beatrice takes the Messenger's words and turns them into something that insults Benedick. At times she uses a technique known as 'damning with faint praise', where someone appears at first to be praising someone or something, but then follows it quickly by saying something which shows they are really being critical or insulting. Modern examples of this include remarks such as 'I'm impressed; I've never met such a small mind inside such a big head before'; or 'Some day you'll go far – and I really hope you stay there.'

DISCUSS

Are Beatrice's insults harmless **wit**, or bullying? How would you feel or react if you were on the receiving end of similar comments? Do you think you would always react in the same way? Would your reaction change depending on who was speaking, and your relationship with that person? **Discuss** your responses to these questions now with a classmate.

Despite insulting Benedick to others when he is not there to respond or defend himself – a rather cruel and hurtful thing to do – our first impression of Beatrice remains positive. This is because Beatrice, as a character in the sense of a literary device, is an important source of humour for the play, and Shakespeare takes care not to risk **undermining** that by turning the audience against her.

He does this by making it clear that Beatrice's quick-witted insults of Benedick are something she commonly does; and that he is very capable of doing the same back to her – and always does so ('they never meet but there's a skirmish of wit between them'). This game of insults appears to be just that – a game!

Later in the play (Act 2 Scene 1), however, when Don Pedro comments that Beatrice has 'lost the heart of Signior Benedick', she replies that 'he lent it me awhile; and I gave him use for it, a double heart for his single one: marry, once before he won it of me with false dice' (lines 209–13). Beatrice may be suggesting here that the two were previously in a relationship, which ended when Beatrice felt she was betrayed in some way by Benedick ('he won it of me with false dice'). Her remark 'a double heart for his single one' meanwhile suggests that she feels she committed herself much more fully to the relationship than Benedick. How does knowing this affect your view of Beatrice's comments, and the couple's interactions, in Act 1?

ACTIVITY: Relationships – a meeting of minds?

■ ATL

- Critical-thinking skills: Gather and observe relevant information to formulate an argument

Despite the insults, exchanges between Beatrice and Benedick appear to show that the pair share a number of similarities, which might suggest that they are in fact well-matched for each other.

One exchange is reproduced below, and begins when Benedick appears to be making a joke about Hero possibly not being the real daughter of Leonato, though it seems the others are walking away and do not hear him. Beatrice notices this and begins to mock him because nobody 'marks' – takes any notice – of him and what he is saying.

What similarities do you see between Benedick and Beatrice in this passage? Work in pairs to read through the passage. Make notes about any points you find.

BENEDICK: If Signior Leonato be her father, she would not have his head on her shoulders for all Messina, as like him as she is.

BEATRICE: I wonder that you will still be talking, Signior Benedick: nobody marks you.

BENEDICK: What, my dear Lady Disdain! are you yet living?

BEATRICE: Is it possible disdain should die while she hath such meet food to feed it as Signior Benedick? Courtesy itself must convert to disdain, if you come in her presence.

BENEDICK: Then is courtesy a turncoat. But it is certain I am loved of all ladies, only you excepted: and I would I could find in my heart that I had not a hard heart; for, truly, I love none.

BEATRICE: A dear happiness to women: they would else have been troubled with a pernicious suitor. I thank God and my cold blood, I am of your humour for that: I had rather hear my dog bark at a crow than a man swear he loves me.

BENEDICK: God keep your ladyship still in that mind! so some gentleman or other shall 'scape a predestinate scratched face.

BEATRICE: Scratching could not make it worse, an 'twere such a face as yours were.

BENEDICK: Well, you are a rare parrot-teacher.

BEATRICE: A bird of my tongue is better than a beast of yours.

BENEDICK: I would my horse had the speed of your tongue, and so good a continuer. But keep your way, i' God's name; I have done.

BEATRICE: You always end with a jade's trick: I know you of old.

◆ Assessment opportunities

In this activity you have practised skills that are assessed using Criterion A: Analysing.

This is not the only example in a Shakespeare play where an exchange between two characters seems to suggest that they are well matched for each other. Another famous instance occurs in *Romeo and Juliet* (Act 1 Scene 5), when the two lovers meet for the very first time. What similarities might be observed between them, and what features of their conversation may suggest that they are well matched?

Language and Literature for the IB MYP 4&5: *by Concept*

In the left-hand column below is the original passage from the play, which shows their first meeting. To help your understanding of the passage, the right-hand column is a modern rewording of the original text (source: *No Fear Shakespeare* **http://nfs.sparknotes.com/romeojuliet/ page_66.html**).

DISCUSS

In groups of two or three, **discuss** and respond to the following questions on the sonnet:

- What aspects of the *Romeo and Juliet* passage suggest that these characters are well matched for each other? Can you **identify** any stylistic or literary devices that support your thinking? Does Shakespeare use similar or different devices in this passage and the conversation between Beatrice and Benedick?
- What form of writing does Shakespeare use in the passage with Beatrice and Benedick? How does it differ from the *Romeo and Juliet* passage? Why do you think that Shakespeare chose the form that he did in each case?

ROMEO: *(taking JULIET's hand)* If I profane with my unworthiest hand

This holy shrine, the gentle sin is this:

My lips, two blushing pilgrims, ready stand

To smooth that rough touch with a tender kiss.

JULIET: Good pilgrim, you do wrong your hand too much,

Which mannerly devotion shows in this,

For saints have hands that pilgrims' hands do touch,

And palm to palm is holy palmers' kiss.

ROMEO: Have not saints lips, and holy palmers too?

JULIET: Ay, pilgrim, lips that they must use in prayer.

ROMEO: O, then, dear saint, let lips do what hands do.

They pray; grant thou, lest faith turn to despair.

JULIET: Saints do not move, though grant for prayers' sake.

ROMEO: Then move not, while my prayer's effect I take.

Kisses her

ROMEO: *(taking JULIET's hand)* Your hand is like a holy place that my hand is unworthy to visit. If you're offended by the touch of my hand, my two lips are standing here like blushing pilgrims, ready to make things better with a kiss.

JULIET: Good pilgrim, you don't give your hand enough credit. By holding my hand you show polite devotion. After all, pilgrims touch the hands of statues of saints. Holding one palm against another is like a kiss.

ROMEO: Don't saints and pilgrims have lips too?

JULIET: Yes, pilgrim — they have lips that they're supposed to pray with.

ROMEO: Well then, saint, let lips do what hands do. I'm praying for you to kiss me. Please grant my prayer so my faith doesn't turn to despair.

JULIET: Saints don't move, even when they grant prayers.

ROMEO: Then don't move while I act out my prayer.

Kisses her

Sonnets

A sonnet is a particular form of poetry, most commonly associated with the themes of love. It usually contains the following features:

- Rhymed verse is used throughout, with a rhyme-scheme of ABAB CDCD EFEF GG (these are known as **Shakespearean sonnets**).
- There are 14 lines in the passage.
- These lines are all iambic pentameter.

While the Shakespearean sonnet is the most famous form of this rhyme, another well-known example is the '**Italian**' (or '**Petrarchan**') **sonnet**. This sonnet follows a different rhyme-scheme: ABBA ABBA CDE CDE.

The sonnet form may be used and varied by poets in order to serve their purposes. You can read more about this at websites such as: **https://literarydevices.net/sonnet/**. You can read all of Shakespeare's sonnets here: **www.shakespeares-sonnets.com/**.

SONNETS

The exchange between *Romeo and Juliet* is a famous example of a sonnet.

Shakespeare uses the sonnet form here in a number of ways to help convey meaning, such as the following:

- Since the fourteenth century the sonnet has been well known as a form of poetry used to describe and declare love. By using this form here, Shakespeare is suggesting that love exists (or will exist) between Romeo and Juliet from the first moment they meet.
- The form of the sonnet is also perhaps used to suggest the compatibility of Romeo and Juliet – the lines are split fairly equally between them, with each taking four lines with self-contained rhyme to begin with, but then moving into single lines that complete the rhyming pattern started by the other. This is a feature that may suggest like-mindedness, for instance, and two people on the same wavelength.
- The idea of like-mindedness and compatibility is further suggested by their shared use of religious imagery. Romeo raises the image of his lips being like pilgrims (suggesting that his lips, in moving towards her, will be embarking on a holy journey). In her responses Juliet continues and develops this imagery; in fact, she uses it to tease him by telling him that pilgrims kiss the statues of saints by putting their palms to those of the statues, rather than using their lips.

The overall suggestion is that these two characters who have just met are very much on that same wavelength and extremely comfortable with each other, being able immediately to pick up on the other's thoughts and form of speech in the sonnet and continue with those in the same way.

ACTIVITY: Dating – *Much Ado About Nothing* style ...

ATL

- Communication skills: Make inferences and draw conclusions
- Critical-thinking skills: Draw reasonable conclusions and generalizations

Within *Much Ado About Nothing* the relationship between Benedick and Beatrice is not the only 'romantic' relationship we see. The following passage reveals Claudio's desire to marry Hero:

```
CLAUDIO: My liege, your highness now may do me good.
DON PEDRO: My love is thine to teach: teach it but how,
And thou shalt see how apt it is to learn
Any hard lesson that may do thee good.
CLAUDIO: Hath Leonato any son, my lord?              5
DON PEDRO: No child but Hero; she's his only heir.
Dost thou affect her, Claudio?
CLAUDIO: O, my lord,
When you went onward on this ended action,
I look'd upon her with a soldier's eye,
That liked, but had a rougher task in hand      10
Than to drive liking to the name of love:
But now I am return'd and that war-thoughts
Have left their places vacant, in their rooms
```

Come thronging soft and delicate desires,

All prompting me how fair young Hero is, 15

Saying, I liked her ere I went to wars.

DON PEDRO: Thou wilt be like a lover presently

And tire the hearer with a book of words.

If thou dost love fair Hero, cherish it,

And I will break with her and with her father, 20

And thou shalt have her. Was't not to this end

That thou began'st to twist so fine a story?

CLAUDIO: How sweetly you do minister to love,

That know love's grief by his complexion!

But lest my liking might too sudden seem, 25

I would have salved it with a longer treatise.

DON PEDRO: What need the bridge much broader than the flood?

The fairest grant is the necessity.

Look, what will serve is fit: 'tis once, thou lovest,

And I will fit thee with the remedy. 30

I know we shall have revelling to-night:

I will assume thy part in some disguise

And tell fair Hero I am Claudio,

And in her bosom I'll unclasp my heart

And take her hearing prisoner with the force 35

And strong encounter of my amorous tale:

Then after to her father will I break;

And the conclusion is, she shall be thine.

In practise let us put it presently.

Exeunt

Either on your own or with a partner, answer the following questions about what is happening in this passage:

1 When Claudio first asks for help (in love, as we soon discover), what is the first question he asks? Why do you think he asks this?
2 In lines 7–16, what explanation does Claudio give for his apparently quite sudden interest in Hero at this point in time?
3 What does Don Pedro tell us in lines 19–22 about the process through which a man such as Claudio might get to marry a lady such as Hero?
4 What does Claudio seem to be concerned about in lines 25–26?
5 Has Hero spoken to either Don Pedro or Claudio at this point?

Don Pedro wants to help his friend, and says that if Claudio says he loves someone, then he, Don Pedro, will be happy to do whatever will help him obtain his love: '*Look, what will serve is fit: 'tis once, thou lovest, / And I will fit thee with the remedy.*'

In lines 31–39, Don Pedro outlines a plan by which he will **woo** Hero, or try to gain her love on behalf of Claudio. Don Pedro plans to go to the party and, while wearing a mask, pretend to Hero that he *is* Claudio, in order to try to persuade her to agree to marry Claudio. In light of this, answer the following questions:

6 Do you feel any possible problems might arise from Don Pedro's plan?
7 Can you say anything about the imagery used in lines 35–38? Remember that Don Pedro has just returned from a war. How might it make Hero appear?
8 What are your feelings about Don Pedro, and the plan he reveals here?
9 Prior to this scene, Don Pedro, Claudio and Benedick speak together in prose verse. Once Benedick leaves and the other two men are alone, however, they speak in blank verse. Can you suggest any reasons for this change?

Much Ado About Nothing has much to say about how reality can be quite different from how things first appear. Appearance vs reality, as well as deception, are important themes in the play, and Shakespeare gives repeated examples of both throughout to help convey this to his audience. Don Pedro's deception of Hero is one good example, and we shall look at both of these themes in more detail later in the chapter.

◆ Assessment opportunities

In this activity you have practised skills that are assessed using Criterion A: Analysing.

In Act 2 Scene 1, Don Pedro puts his plan to woo Hero for Claudio into action. The following steps illustrate how Hero reaches a point during the evening of being committed to marriage to Claudio – the same day that he first expressed an interest in her – and before she has actually spoken to him:

Before the party begins, Leonato has mistakenly gained the idea that Don Pedro will in fact be wooing his daughter, Hero.	Just before the party, in Act 2 Scene 1, Leonato tells Hero: 'Daughter, remember what I told you: if the prince do solicit you in that kind, you know your answer'.	Don Pedro describes more of the 'dating' process when he gives Claudio the good news about Hero, later in the party: 'here, Claudio, I have wooed in thy name, and fair Hero is won; I have broke with her father, and his good will obtained: name the day of marriage…'

The prince and Count Claudio walking in a thick-pleached alley in mine orchard, were thus much overheard by a man of mine: the prince discovered to Claudio that he loved my niece your daughter, and meant to acknowledge it this night in a dance, and if he found her accordant, he meant to take the present time by the top, and instantly break with you of it. – *Antonio*

Although Antonio mentions overhearing Don Pedro say that he will see if Hero is 'accordant' – in agreement with – the idea of marrying him, we know that he has received his information from a servant, and that the information is unreliable. We do not know if Don Pedro asks Hero if she agrees to marrying Claudio, since we are not shown what he actually says to her in that conversation. This appears to be the only possible time Hero might have been consulted about the marriage. Meanwhile, Hero's father has told her what to say if Don Pedro asks to marry her ('You know your answer'), so we cannot be sure she was in any position to give her own answer to such a question in any case.

ACTIVITY: Dating then, dating now

■ ATL

- Transfer skills: Change the context of an inquiry in order to gain a different perspective

In your own words write a paragraph describing the process of dating within the context of the society shown in *Much Ado About Nothing*. Are there certain expectations that surprised you?

Now, write a second paragraph in which you describe your own experiences or understanding of romance and dating in your own context (that is, the present day). How do these differ from those you have seen in Shakespeare's play?

◆ Assessment opportunities

In this activity you have practised skills that are assessed using Criterion C: Producing text.

ACTIVITY: The dating game

Having looked at Hero and the context in which she comes to be engaged to marry Claudio, let us look more at our own contexts with regard to dating expectations and **protocols** that we might experience ourselves.

1   In a group, draw two concentric circles on to a piece of poster paper (like the diagram on the right – but do not divide the outer circle into sections just yet).

2   In the inner circle, write down any social expectations you feel you have in a dating relationship; for example, what are you expected to say, do and so on? You will be sharing your diagram with the rest of the class afterwards so do not add anything you may not want everyone else to see.

3   Together with your group, think about which individuals within your own life and context might have particular expectations of you when it comes to dating and relationships; for example, your family, friends, or figures of authority (teachers, religious leaders, legal figures, etc).

4   Divide the outer circle so that there is one section for every person you listed in point 3. In each section add notes on *what* expectations you feel they have of you, and how you should act and behave in the context of a dating relationship.

5   Which two people do you think have the *most* influence over how you act and behave in dating relationships? Why are they so influential? Indicate these two and add notes on why you have chosen them.

6   Display your diagrams on the classroom wall and carry out a gallery walk with the rest of your class. Make notes on the following:
    ● How similar or different are the expectations of yourself and your classmates?
    ● Who are the people who seem to most influence dating expectations and practices? Do any cultural patterns seem to be present?
    ● How far do parents influence dating expectations and practices?

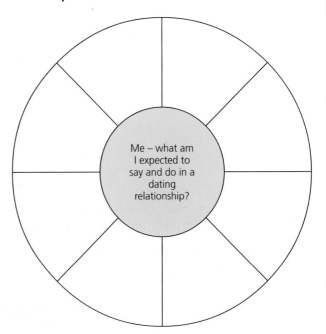

Me – what am I expected to say and do in a dating relationship?

How dependent are relationships on universal factors?

ACTIVITY: Romance around the world

ATL

- Critical-thinking skills: Gather and organize relevant information to formulate an argument
- Creative-thinking skills: Practise flexible thinking – develop multiple opposing, contradictory and complementary arguments; create original works and ideas; use existing works and ideas in new ways

The article opposite discusses different dating customs around the world. What are some of the advantages and disadvantages of the different dating protocols? Copy and complete the table below by choosing five examples from five different countries. Note the advantages and disadvantages in the appropriate columns and consider whether each practice is likely to lead to a healthy or unhealthy relationship. Note your conclusion (and reasoning!) for this in the final column.

Country	Possible advantages?	Possible disadvantages?	Likely to lead to a healthy/ unhealthy relationship?
1			
2			
3			
4			
5			

EXTENSION

Choose one country from your list of five and imagine you are dating someone there. Research dating and romance within the country further, then write a diary in which you reflect on your experiences of dating. Make sure to include any important aspects of the dating customs and practices of your chosen country and context. You should write four or five entries and each one should address a different aspect of the dating experience. You might consider:

- Are your diary entries spread over a week? A month? A year?
- Is your dating relationship a healthy or unhealthy one? Does the experience change over the period of the diary?
- Is this a diary for your eyes only? Or to be shared? Think how this might affect your choice of register and vocabulary.

www.healthguidance.org/entry/15127/1/Dating-Customs-Around-the-World.html

Dating Customs Around the World

BY COLLEEN CRAWFORD | DATING |

Having a relationship with someone is important in all cultures, however the process of dating is different according to countries. Thus, culture affects the way people date, suggesting various kinds of dates from heavily supervised meetings to evenings spent at the movies. Dating is seen as both a complex and simple matter, the difference between the Western world and other civilizations making it very intriguing as some dating rituals are extremely liberal, some are less free of constraints, while others are cut down to old fashioned gatherings, or are even illegal.

Dating Customs on Various Continents

Dating in Australia for example is illustrated by teens going out in large groups without really forming couples until they reach 18 or 19 years of age. Here, it is not the boys who often make the first step of asking girls to go on a date with them, rather the girls take this part and they also take the responsibility of paying for the date. The most common dating places preferred by couples are dinner parties, barbecues, or the beach.

Dating in Europe is again, sort of a group event. In Finland for example, groups as large as thirty teens take part in an event together, such as going to the movies. Slumber parties are preferred by the young living in Italy, as well as Switzerland. At such parties, teens gather at someone's home and remain over night after the party has come to an end. Many Spanish teens join groups or clubs that bring people together connected by common interests, be it camping or cycling. The dating part however is done one-to-one, both sides asking each other out and splitting the expenses associated with a particular evening.

Russians are very fond of dancing places, most dates taking place at dance parties, balls or at clubs where the young ones have meals and chat in groups. In small towns of Russia, teens get together in certain areas downtown, such as around fountains. A particular dating custom is set in Kiev, where women do not like to shake hands for they perceive it as a rather unfeminine gesture. This is strongly connected to the fact that women do not hold hands with men when being on a date, but instead they hold onto their arms.

In the United Kingdom, teens do rarely have the courage to ask someone on a date by themselves, so such interactions usually take place in groups, where people are being supported by their friends into making this gesture or they rely on alcohol to acquire the confidence to admit they like someone.

Dating is extremely strict in Middle East since most dates are in fact supervised gatherings arranged by parents for the purpose of the young meeting one another before marriage. In Afghanistan, opportunities to meet are rare since young people don't get the chance to go on a date, but they are introduced to each other by their families after their matrimonial union is already settled. Schools are separate for boys and girls in this country, and they are even forbidden to go outside past a certain hour, for girls the curfew time is at 7:00 P.M., whilst the boys curfew is at 11:00 P.M.

In Iran, people are even stricter as dating is completely illegal. Teens spend their life separated until they reach the appropriate age set for marriage. Afterwards, their families make the introductions and on rare occasions, the event is followed by a period of courtship.

In Central and South America, teens are not allowed to date until they are at least 15 years old. Dating takes place in large groups, hence it is a common occurrence for teens to go out together in local clubs, to eat and chat, or to go dancing at weekend dance parties.

As far as Africa is concerned, in many parts of this continent dates are very strict because parents arrange their sons' and daughters' marriages, and even if couples are allowed to date, they are well aware of the fact that their families have already chosen a partner for them and they cannot break out from the relationship-to-be even if they do not approve of their partner after a few dates.

In most Asian countries young people do not leave the house they grew up in until they are married. Newlyweds live with their partner's parents for a while until they get a place for themselves.

In Japan and Korea, dating doesn't usually begin before college, when boys alone do the asking and accept the cost of the date. Most high school students don't go on dates, nor to parties, but choose to spend their time studying. In China, some parents still arrange their sons' and daughters' marriages, but most young people are free to choose their partner by themselves, dating beginning sometime around the age of 20. Chinese people get married a lot faster than couples from other countries, most dates never reaching a number higher than one or two.

As people can see, differences in dating customs are highly influenced by religion and parental control, but in America, dating is rather conventional and movie-like. The term "date" makes more sense when talking about American people as teens from U.S.A live in a much more relaxed society where they can be themselves and behave unconstrained by their parents or religious traditions. Dates, as seen with young people in America, are a way of testing a potential partner before making an actual commitment and to determine whether a particular person is compatible with them or not. Teens in America start dating really early, even before high school, and they usually go to see a movie or have a drink/meal at the local diner.

◆ Assessment opportunities

In this activity you have practised skills that are assessed using Criterion C: Producing text and Criterion D: Using language.

How might issues of truth and deception impact on relationships?

The article from the 'Romance around the world' activity continues to talk about another, rather more recent, form of dating – that of internet or online dating.

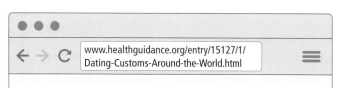

Online Dating

Dating people online has become an extremely popular custom that has developed as more and more people have figured out the advantages of using the internet as a way of finding love. People of all ages submit to dating online, teens and grownups alike searching for that special person by setting up accounts on online dating sites and browsing through other people's profiles. On dating websites, singles are provided the opportunity of learning a few things about various potential partners, making their decision of contacting them based on dating profile descriptions and photos.

Out of the many countries where people practise online dating, the United Kingdom is perhaps the most keen on online dating since most English people prefer to browse on the internet in order to find dates instead of trying to meet other persons in bars, clubs, parks or at parties.

Dating may vary across the globe, countries being known for peculiar and outrageous dating traditions, yet as time passes, people develop new dating customs, such as dating with the help of the internet. Although this form of dating is mostly practised in the Western civilization, no one can tell for sure what other customs will emerge as the world changes, and whether strict dating will come against some people's right of choosing whatever partner they see fit for themselves.

DISCUSS

Would you consider online dating? What might be some advantages and disadvantages of this? Turn to a partner now and **discuss** your thoughts on these two questions.

THINK–PAIR–SHARE

How healthy do you think an online relationship can be?

On a scale of 1 to 10 (with 10 being a very healthy relationship, and 1 being very unhealthy) choose a number from the scale that represents how healthy you think an online relationship might be. Write this number down and, beneath it, give your reasons why.

Now share your number and reasons with a partner. Are they similar?

If there is time, share your numbers and reasons with the rest of your class. Do other classmates have different views from you? Can your class come to an agreement about an appropriate level?

DISCUSS

In what ways might an online relationship be both healthy and unhealthy? Use your earlier work from the start of this chapter on healthy and unhealthy relationships to consider this question.

ACTIVITY: What is deception?

■ ATL

- Collaboration skills: Build consensus
- Information literacy skills: Access information to be informed and to inform others

We mentioned previously that deception is an important theme in *Much Ado About Nothing*, and that Don Pedro's wooing of Hero in Act 2 Scene 1 was a good example of this.

Don Pedro wears a mask to pretend to be somebody else (when wooing Hero on Claudio's behalf). While *Much Ado About Nothing* is a comedy, and there may be an assumption that an audience should perceive this deception as a 'good' thing as it helps kindle the relationship between Claudio and Hero, we might also wonder about the possible ethics and dangers of a situation in which someone poses as a different person in a process of establishing a dating relationship.

What do you understand by the term 'deception'? Without looking up the word, **discuss** its meaning in a group of three or four, and come to a consensus on a definition.

Share your group's definition with the rest of the class – if possible by writing out and putting it where it can be seen by everyone (such as on the wall, or on a Googledoc or wiki, for instance). Look at the other groups' definitions. Can you come up with a class definition, which is agreed upon by all?

EXTENSION

Look up the definitions of 'deception' and 'deceive' in several different dictionaries – either online or in your library. Do the definitions vary at all? What are the key similarities between them? Which is the closest to your class version?

Dictionary definitions of 'deception' and 'deceive' tend to share some common factors:

- They involve someone being led to think something is true when it is not.
- They are intentional acts, carried out consciously and deliberately on the part of the person deceiving.
- Some – though not all – of the definitions state that deception is carried out for personal gain or advantage of some kind.

Bearing in mind the definitions you found surrounding 'deception', as well as the above points, reread the passage in which Don Pedro reveals his plan to woo Hero for Claudio. How far does Don Pedro's plan fit the definition of 'deception'?

With everyone's faces covered at the masked party, Hero has no way of knowing who it is that she is speaking to. With internet dating there is a similar issue – we cannot know who is *really* sitting at the keyboard on the other side of the conversation and speaking with us about forming a relationship. Hero thinks for a time that she is speaking to someone different from the person actually talking to her, and online dating carries the potential danger of something similar taking place. In fact, the anonymity provided by online dating is increasingly being taken advantage of by fraudsters who carry out online dating scams; that is, a deliberate attempt to deceive someone and, usually, obtain money from them.

ACTIVITY: Fake love

■ ATL

- Communication skills: Read a variety of sources for information and pleasure; make inferences and draw conclusions
- Creative-thinking skills: Create original works and ideas; use existing works and ideas in new ways

There are numerous examples of dating scams online, and many instances have been written about by journalists, charities and bloggers. Search online for **online dating scam story** and read four or five stories. Now, answer these questions:

- **What factors lead people to try online dating?**
- **Do all scams follow similar steps? Can you outline them?**
- **How do scammers use emotional appeals to persuade their targets to give money?**
- **How much sympathy do you have for people deceived by dating scams? Explain your answer.**

EXTENSION

Imagine you are an online dating scammer. Write a first-person account of between 500 and 1,000 words describing the 'relationship' from your point of view. Consider and include the following points in your account:

- How and why did you become involved in 'work' of this kind?
- What techniques do you use in order to scam somebody, and why do you think these techniques work?
- What are your thoughts and feelings about the person you are scamming? Do your feelings ever change?
- How do you feel about the scam once it has finished, looking back on what has happened?

◆ Assessment opportunities

In this activity you have practised skills that are assessed using Criterion B: Organizing, Criterion C: Producing text and Criterion D: Using language.

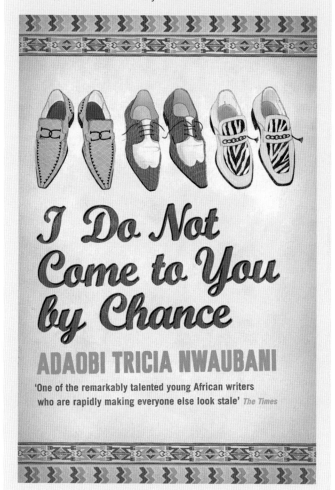

❶ *I Do Not Come To You By Chance* – Adaobi Tricia Nwaubani

Adaobi Tricia Nwaubani is a Nigerian novelist who published *I Do Not Come To You By Chance* in 2009. Set in Nigeria, the book's protagonist, Kingsley, becomes embroiled in the criminal world of Nigerian email scams when tragedy strikes his family and he is in need of money. These scams are known as '419' scams, which is a reference to the section of the Nigerian Criminal Code that deals with fraud.

I Do Not Come To You By Chance won the 2010 Commonwealth Writers' Prize for Best First Book (Africa), as well as a Betty Trask First Book award.

'One of the remarkably talented young African writers who are rapidly making everyone else look stale' *The Times*

ACTIVITY: Love fraudsters

- Communication skills: Read critically and for comprehension
- Critical-thinking skills: Gather and organize relevant information to formulate an argument

The following text, from *I Do Not Come To You By Chance* by Adaobi Tricia Nwaubani, is written from the point of view of a scammer, and describes the experience of scamming someone who has been online to look for a relationship.

In this passage, a Nigerian scammer called Wizard has been posing as an American woman named 'Suzie', and has tricked an American man into an online relationship.

We rushed over to Wizard's desk. The words he typed onto the screen sent everybody quaking with laughter.

'Oh lollipop,' he had written, 'am really scared, hun. Am really scared that I ain't gonna see you again no more, my darl. These people are really threatening me. You know how wild these Africans can be.'

My laughter became loudest of all.

Wizard had been conducting several online relationships with randy foreigners he met in chatrooms. His romance with this particular American had been going on for six weeks. When their loooove blossomed to the point where the man proposed to 'Suzie' that she travel from East Windsor, New Jersey to visit him in Salt Lake City, Utah or vice versa, she informed him that she was just on her way to Nigeria on a business trip. She was a make-up artist, you see, and had an offer to transform girls strutting down the catwalk for an AIDS charity in Lagos. She had arrived in Lagos two days before, and had her American passport stolen in a taxi. Now, she had no way of cashing her traveller's cheques and the proprietor of the hotel was threatening arrest.

'Oh babe,' the man replied, 'what you gonna do now? Ain't there no way of taking it to the police?'

'Sugar pie, all they gonna want is bribes,' Wizard replied. 'Hun, I'm gonna really need your help right now. I wanna see if you can show me that you really love me and that what we share is real. Can you do me a real big favour?'

Wizard must have been watching a lot of American movies. His gonna-wanna American-speak was quite fluent.

'Sure, babe,' the man wrote. 'Anything I can do to help.'

'Honeybunch, I wanna send the traveller's cheques to you to pay into your bank account. Can you do that and send me the cash?'

Wizard broke off typing and turned quickly to us. 'How much should I write? Is $2000 OK?'

'That's too small,' Ogbonna said. 'Double it.'

'Yes, double it,' we **concurred** [agreed].

Wizard resumed.

'What I've got in cheques is about $4000. Honey, I gotta have some help real quick. Can you be the one to help me out here?'

Suzie went on to explain to her beau that the cheques would arrive within three days; she would send them by DHL. He should deposit the cheques as soon as he received them, and then send her the cash by Western Union. Since her own passport had been stolen, she would send him the name of one of her colleagues at the charity event so that he could send the Western Union in the colleague's name. The lover boy, swept away by the current of true love, wasted no time in responding.

'Anything for you, sweetie. I ain't got that much in my cheque account right now but I could get some from my credit card and replace once I've cashed the cheques.'

All of us screamed the special scream. Wizard had made a hit.

It would take about eight days for the bank to process the documents, before the man realized that the cheques that had been paid into his account were fakes. I looked in a corner of the chat box and saw the photograph of the bearded, **voluminous** [large] **Caucasian** [white person]. Then I looked in Wizard's own box and saw the photograph of the trim, buxom blond who had no resemblance whatsoever to the V-shaped eighteen-year-old clicking away at the keyboard. My heart went out to the lonely man, but Wizard was untroubled.

'Thanks, honeysuckle,' he wrote. 'I knew I could really count on you. Please get it done ASAP cos I ain't got nothing left on me no more.'

'Sure, Suz,' the man replied. 'By the way, babe, you gotta take good care of yourself and watch out, OK? Maybe I should've warned you when you said you were going. I saw on CNN sometime that the folks in Nigeria are real dangerous.'

'No problem, love,' Wizard replied. 'I've learnt my lesson and I'm gonna take real good care of myself from now.'

'I love you babe,' the man wrote. 'I really can't wait to meet you.'

'Me, too,' Wizard replied. 'I promise we're gonna have a swell time and you're not gonna wanna let me go.'

I Do Not Come To You By Chance – Adaobi Tricia Nwaubani

Answer the following questions about the extract from *I Do Not Come To You By Chance*:

1 **What are your impressions of and feelings about the actions of the scammers in this passage?**
2 **Can you identify any literary and/or persuasive techniques being used by Wizard?**
3 **What role does language play in this scam?**
4 **How might language be used in an online environment to help make a scam successful? Why would it be much more difficult to do something similar in a face-to-face situation?**
5 **Find an example of irony within the dialogue.**

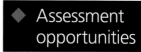

◆ Assessment
  opportunities

In this activity you have practised skills that are assessed using Criterion A: Analysing.

Language and Literature for the IB MYP 4&5: *by Concept*

ACTIVITY: Fiction and non-fiction texts

■ ATL

■ Critical-thinking skills: Gather and organize relevant information to formulate an argument; evaluate evidence and arguments

You have now read both fiction and non-fiction accounts of online dating scams. The online dating scam stories that you found and read are non-fiction texts, whereas *I Do Not Come To You By Chance* is a novel – a work of fiction. What aspects of style and features do you see in each type of text? Copy the table on the right and make notes on each of the aspects listed in column one, for both types of text.

	Non-fiction – news report	Fiction – novel
Narrative perspective – narrative voice?		
Tone		
Formal/informal register		
Formal structural features (i.e. as use of headings and subheadings)		
Use of paragraphing		
Use of direct speech		
Any other features		

◆ Assessment opportunities

In this activity you have practised skills that are assessed using Criterion A: Analysing.

ACTIVITY: Reporting a scam

■ ATL

■ Creative-thinking skills: Create original works and ideas; use existing works and ideas in new ways

Having looked at the different features of fiction and non-fiction texts, you are going to try turning the fictional account from *I Do Not Come To You By Chance* into a news report.

Imagine you are a news reporter who has been speaking with the American man scammed by 'Suzie'. You are speaking with him after he finally discovered that he was being scammed. Write an account of at least 400 words, and up to 800, describing the American man's experience, written in the style of the online reports and articles you first found when researching online dating scams (page 274). You might want to look back at Chapter 1 and Chapter 6 to remind yourself of the key features of a news report. Include the following points:

● **Open with an introductory section that gives an overview of what happened to the American man. What comments, information and details might you include?**
● **Describe how the scam worked, including how the American became involved.**
● **How did the man realize he was being scammed? What happened after the scam was discovered?**

● The tone and register for a news report should be relatively formal and objective.
● As with the news reports you looked at previously, your report should also contain a number of direct quotations from the man who was scammed.

EXTENSION

In an effort to warn others about the scam, the American man calls a local radio phone-in in order to tell the DJ and the listeners his story.

With a partner, write the script of what the American says to the radio station. One of you should take the part of the American man, and the other should play the DJ. During phone-ins, radio DJs often play the role of **devil's advocate**, and so might try to present a counterargument to the American man's story.

Once finished, record your scene and, if there is time, share it with the rest of your class.

◆ Assessment opportunities

In this activity you have practised skills that are assessed Criterion C: Producing text and Criterion D: Using language.

How great is the role of perception in a healthy relationship?

APPEARANCE AND REALITY

Throughout *Much Ado About Nothing* the theme of deception is often intertwined with the theme of appearance vs reality.

Another example of this is when Don John schemes to upset the marriage of Hero and Claudio. Don John was recently defeated in battle by Don Pedro (his half-brother) and Claudio, and now seeks revenge on them.

As the following passage outlines, Don John's companion, Borachio, comes to him with a plan to deceive Claudio and Don Pedro into believing they have witnessed Hero being unfaithful to him. What appears to Claudio as evidence of Hero's unfaithfulness is in fact a trick. The reality is that he has mistaken another woman for Hero.

ACTIVITY: The path to misunderstanding

■ ATL

■ Creative-thinking skills: Use brainstorming and visual diagrams to generate new ideas and inquiries; consider multiple alternatives, including those that might be unlikely or impossible

The key scenes leading up to Claudio's misunderstanding are detailed below. Reread them now and, in small groups, brainstorm some of the reasons why Claudio and Don Pedro came to believe that Hero had been unfaithful prior to her and Claudio's wedding.

You might use free diagramming software, such as: https://bubbl.us/ to help you plan out the events leading up to the misunderstanding.

Key scenes:
● **Act 2 Scene 2 (Borachio's plan)**

Much Ado About Nothing	No Fear Shakespeare
BORACHIO: Go, then; find me a meet hour to draw Don Pedro and the Count Claudio alone, tell them that you know that Hero loves me; intend a kind of zeal both to the prince and Claudio (as in love of your brother's honour, who hath made this match, and his friend's reputation, who is thus like to be cozened [tricked] with the semblance of a maid) that you have discovered thus. They will scarcely believe this without trial: offer them instances; which shall bear no less likelihood than to see me at her chamber-window, hear me call Margaret Hero, hear Margaret term me Claudio*; and bring them to see this the very night before the intended wedding, for in the meantime I will so fashion the matter that Hero shall be absent, and there shall appear such seeming truth of Hero's disloyalty that jealousy shall be called assurance and all the preparation overthrown.	**BORACHIO:** Find a time to speak with Don Pedro and Claudio alone. Tell them you know that Hero loves me. Pretend to be very concerned about both the Prince, who has compromised his honour by making the match, and Claudio, whose reputation will be ruined by this woman who's pretending to be a virgin. Of course, they won't believe you without proof. Tell them you've seen the two of us at Hero's bedroom window, and then bring them to see for themselves on the night before the wedding. I'll arrange it so that Hero is away for the night, so what they'll actually see is Margaret and me at the window, calling each other 'Hero' and 'Claudio'*. It'll be such blatant evidence of Hero's disloyalty that Claudio's jealousy will quickly turn to certainty, and the wedding will be instantly called off.
Act 2 Scene 2	

*Shakespeare may have made an error here, because if Margaret was mistaken for Hero being unfaithful with someone else, it would not be Claudio, and she would presumably be calling the man she was with by *his* name, and not using Claudio's. In some versions of the play,* therefore, you may find that the name 'Claudio' at this point has been replaced by the editor with 'Borachio'.

In passages such as this Shakespeare uses language to emphasize the deception being proposed.

- Act 3 Scene 2, where Don John comes to speak with Claudio and Don Pedro
- Act 3 Scene 3, where Borachio and Conrade discuss what has happened after Don John took Don Pedro and Claudio to see what they thought was Hero being unfaithful
- Act 3 Scene 5, where Dogberry and Verges go to see Leonato to report their arrest of Borachio and Conrade.

> Misunderstanding – Claudio thinks Hero has been unfaithful. How did this situation arise?

> Leonato does not listen properly to Dogberry and sends him away when Dogberry is trying to give him information that would alert him to what Don John has done.

> Don John states that he is a 'plain-dealing villain' and deliberately tries to trick Claudio and Don Pedro to stop the marriage between Claudio and Hero from taking place.

◆ Assessment opportunities

In this activity you have practised skills that are assessed using Criterion A: Analysing and Criterion B: Organizing.

THINK–PAIR–SHARE

What details in Borachio's account might suggest that Claudio and Don Pedro should have thought more critically about their sources of information and how reliable those may have been? After you have identified some instances, share these with a classmate. Have they found any that you missed?

Do you see any other patterns of language being used in this section, which might emphasize other themes in the play?

How many references can you find in Shakespeare's text to things not quite being as they seem, or things being made to appear different from the reality?

As a result of Don John's deception, in Act 4 Scene 1 Claudio humiliates and shames Hero at their wedding. In front of the entire wedding party he accuses Hero of cheating on him and then abandons her at the altar.

The deception of Claudio and Don Pedro, like that of Hero, and those defrauded by online dating scams, is due to an inability to distinguish between reality and appearance. One way this might be done, however, is to carry out research into situations we encounter. By doing this we are better prepared and so more able to work out who is telling us what, and whether we should believe them (or not!).

In Act 3 Scene 3, after Borachio has successfully carried out the deception of Claudio, he boasts about it to Conrade:

Much Ado About Nothing	No Fear Shakespeare
BORACHIO: Know that I have tonight wooed Margaret, the Lady Hero's gentlewoman, by the name of Hero. She leans me out at her mistress' chamber window, bids me a thousand times good night. I tell this tale vilely. I should first tell thee how the Prince, Claudio and my master, planted and placed and possessed by my master Don John, saw afar off in the orchard this amiable encounter.	**BORACHIO:** But I will tell you that I seduced Margaret, the Lady Hero's waiting woman, tonight. I called her 'Hero' the whole time. She leaned out of her mistress's bedroom window and told me good night a thousand times – but I am telling this story poorly. I should backtrack and begin with how my master, Don John, arranged for the Prince, Claudio, and himself to witness this friendly encounter from the orchard.
CONRADE: And thought they Margaret was Hero?	**CONRADE:** And they thought Margaret was Hero?
BORACHIO: Two of them did, the Prince and Claudio, but the devil my master knew she was Margaret; and partly by his oaths, which first possessed them, partly by the dark night, which did deceive them, but chiefly by my villainy, which did confirm any slander that Don John had made, away went Claudio enraged, swore he would meet her as he was appointed next morning at the temple, and there, before the whole congregation, shame her with what he saw o'ernight and send her home again without a husband.	**BORACHIO:** The Prince and Claudio did, but the devil, my master, knew that it was Margaret. They believed the charade partially because of my master's testimony – which first caused them to doubt Hero – and partially because of how dark and deceiving the night was, but mostly because of my villainous actions, which confirmed Don John's slander. Claudio went away enraged, swearing that he'd meet Hero at the temple as planned and there, before the entire congregation, shame her with what he'd discovered and send her home without a husband.

Act 3 Scene 3

Later in *Much Ado About Nothing*, Don Pedro strongly claims to Leonato that:

> '… *on my honour she was charged with nothing*
>
> *But what was true, and very full of proof.*'

The reality, however, is that Don Pedro's **research methodology** was poor; he did not properly use the evidence he had, nor test that evidence, nor consider the reliability of his sources. All of this leads him consequently to draw conclusions that were far from true. All of these elements should, however, form part of a research process.

What might Don Pedro have done if he had used better research methodology? Perhaps more things such as the following:

■ **Use his evidence better** – Don Pedro needs to think more about the evidence he has discovered, and what it means. He does not try to analyse, for instance, how likely it is that Hero has acted in the way she has been accused of, given who she is, and the timing – the night before her wedding. Nor does he seem to consider that there may be other possible explanations for what he has seen. Nor does he consider asking anyone else about it, to see if there are other suggestions for what may have taken place.

■ **Test his evidence** – it does not seem to occur to Don Pedro to speak with anyone about what he has seen, including Hero and Borachio themselves. Nor does he try to check if anyone else knows about Hero's whereabouts during the evening, or try to confirm that she really was where he thinks she was.

ACTIVITY: The research process

■ ATL

- ■ Reflection skills: Identify strengths and weaknesses of research learning strategies

'Research' is one of the five approaches to learning skills in the MYP. It is in turn divided between 'Information literacy skills' and 'Media literacy skills'. Some of the information literacy skills are listed in the table opposite.

Claudio, Don Pedro and Leonato all misunderstand the situation regarding Hero. In groups of three, each choose a different one of these characters and use the table to **evaluate** how your character performs in each skill. In the right-hand column you should **explain** what he does or does not do in respect of each skill, along with what he might have done and what difference that may have made.

■ **Consider the reliability of his sources** – Don Pedro is being shown what he thinks is a scene of Hero being unfaithful, by his half-brother Don John, who was very recently his enemy in battle and whom he knows has reason to resent him. Don John has actively come to find him to show him the scene he witnesses (or thinks he does). He never seems to question at all, however, whether there may be anything untrustworthy about any of the situation which his half-brother takes him to see, nor whether he should unquestioningly trust Don John. Nor does he consider at all whether there may be more trustworthy sources – such as Beatrice, who knows Hero extremely well – whom he could seek out and speak to.

Research is something you are likely to do throughout school and, later, at college or university. In the MYP you will have already done some research, and subjects such as individuals and societies, sciences and so on may well also require you to use research processes and skills in the projects you undertake. Research is an important skill so let us look further at the research process now.

My character:	
ATL information literacy skills	**Evaluation of my character's performance in each skill**
Finding, interpreting, judging and creating information	
Collect, record and verify data	
Access information to be informed and inform others	
Make connections between various sources of information	
Understand the benefits and limitations of personal sensory learning preferences when accessing, processing and recalling information (*i.e. how much can and should we trust our senses?*)	
Collect and **analyse** data to **identify** solutions and make informed decisions	
Evaluate and **select** information sources [and digital tools] based on their appropriateness to specific tasks	
Identify primary and secondary sources	

◆ Assessment opportunities

In this activity you have practised skills that are assessed using Criterion A: Analysing.

How to research

The processes used in research may vary according to what is being researched, and how a researcher may wish to go about his or her research. Nonetheless, it is well worth being aware of some of the stages involved in the basic process of research, as shown in the following diagram:

DEFINE TASK	IDENTIFY OPTIONS	SELECT SOURCES	ANALYSE CONTENT	PRESENT FINDINGS
What is your assignment, problem or question?	What kinds of information do you need and where do you look?	How do you search for them and which do you choose?	What did you discover and what does it mean?	How do you organize and communicate what you learned?

EVALUATE
Is your research process leading to relevant and useful results?

Research sources

Primary sources – sources that have a direct or first-hand connection with whatever is being researched.

Examples: Eyewitness accounts, data from experiments, audio and video recordings, photographs, interviews, surveys.

Secondary sources – sources that describe, evaluate, comment and interpret primary sources, but do not themselves have a direct or first-hand link to what is being researched.

Examples: Book and film reviews, literary criticism, some newspaper articles, broader journal review articles.

You can read more about the difference between sources here: **https://libguides.ithaca.edu/research101/primary**.

ACTIVITY: Finding the source

The misunderstanding over Hero that is made by Claudio, Don Pedro and Leonato is due in part to their use (or misuse) of sources.

Reproduce the following table and, in it, list the possible sources that one or more of the three characters may have used. Complete the remaining columns and, in the fourth column, note how reliable each source is: Are they accurate? Can they be trusted? Why? An example has been started for you.

Having completed the table, think about which sources Claudio, Don Pedro and Leonato did not use, and which they might have used. Would these have given them important information? Did any of the characters consider the reliability of their sources?

◆ Assessment opportunities

In this activity you have practised skills that are assessed using Criterion A: Analysing and Criterion B: Organizing.

Possible source	Primary or secondary?	Used or not?	Reliability factor?	Why?
Interviews	Primary	No	Depends on reliability of interviewee – could be anything from highly reliable to entirely unreliable. What motivations might they have for saying what they would say? What biases might they hold?	Depends on individual character and motivation: – Don John is actively trying to deceive the three men and thus has an interest in trying to 'prove' something which he knows himself is not true. Interview data from him is likely to be highly unreliable. – Beatrice? – Hero? – Borachio? – Anyone else?

ACTIVITY: Using online sources

With the wealth of information available to us on the internet, we now have far more content and sources available to us than people did in the time of *Much Ado About Nothing*.

Have you heard about the substance 'dihydrogen monoxide', sometimes known as DHMO? If not, it is now easy to look this up online. We might first go to the website: **www.dhmo.org/**, which contains a great deal of information about the substance, and also has a detailed 'Frequently Asked Questions' section (**www.dhmo.org/facts.html**).

Having now read about DHMO, answer the following questions:
● **What are your initial thoughts about DHMO?**
● **What are the three most important points that you think the article makes?**
● **How dangerous is DHMO? Do you think it should be banned? Or restricted?**
● **What is your response to the claim in the article that 'In fact, DHMO is often very available to students of all ages within the assumed safe confines of school buildings. None of the school administrators with which we spoke could say for certain how much of the substance is in use within their very hallways'?**

◆ Assessment opportunities

In this activity you have practised skills that are assessed using Criterion A: Analysing.

Language and Literature for the IB MYP 4&5: *by Concept*

While you were on the website **www.dhmo.org**, did you notice anything odd? Did you look up more information on dihydrogen monoxide elsewhere? You may remember this website from the *Sciences for the IB MYP 3: by Concept*, Chapter 6.

If you did that, you may have discovered that this website is in fact another example of deceptive information – **www.dhmo.org** is a hoax website; that is, a website that has been created in order to be deliberately misleading. This website is actually talking about the familiar substance of 'dihydrogen' = hydrogen (for which the chemical symbol is 'H'), × 2 (di), along with 1 (mono) part of oxide (O). Put these together – H × 2 + O – and we have 'H_2O', better known, of course, as water. The website is actually all about water, which the website creator tries to persuade readers is a highly dangerous substance!

If you look again at some of the information on the website, you may now notice how much of what is said there is actually true. It is, though, phrased in a way that gives a misleading impression. Like Beatrice talking of Benedick in the first scene of the play, loaded language and selective comments have been chosen in an effort to create a particular impression of the topic being discussed. Here all of them are negative in order to create an overall impression of dihydrogen monoxide as a dangerous, alarming and threatening substance. As with Beatrice's comments about Benedick, the writer also uses a language technique known as **omission** to try to manipulate the impression a reader forms of the topic under discussion.

! Carrying out internet research

■ ATL

- Information literacy skills: Access information to be informed and inform others; make connections between various sources of information; present information in a variety of formats and platforms; evaluate and select information sources and digital tools based on their appropriateness to specific tasks; use critical-literacy skills to analyse and interpret media communications

! In the twenty-first century we may have more sources available to us than Don Pedro, Claudio and Leonato had, but (as those scammed when dating online found out) it is just as important that we **evaluate** online sources carefully.

! What could you do to avoid being taken in by internet sources and websites that may not be all that they seem? In groups of four or five, complete the following steps and **create** a brochure to help students with online research.

- ◆ Individually, use the search phrase How to research on the internet for students, and spend 20 minutes looking through some of the sites listed.

- ◆ Decide on the three that you think provide the clearest and most effective advice for students aged 14–16.

- ◆ Gather in your group now and share your findings with each other. Then **select** the three sites your group finds the most helpful and informative.

- ◆ Collate the information from those sites and use it to plan the content of a brochure entitled '[Name of your school]'s guide to effective internet research'.

- ◆ Individually, write up the full version of the brochure, using the group plan that you created.

! Your final brochure should contain 500–800 words, section headings and subheadings as may be needed, and images that illustrate what you are saying in the brochure.

! Web pages such as **www.printplace.com/articles/key-brochure-design-elements** can provide further information on the elements that need to go into a brochure, or search brochure writing for students in Google Images for more formats and examples.

◆ Assessment opportunities

In this activity you have practised skills that are assessed using Criterion B: Organizing, Criterion C: Producing text and Criterion D: Using language.

How important is personal responsibility in promoting and sustaining healthy relationships?

ACT 4 SCENE 1 – THE WEDDING: CLAUDIO PUBLICLY SHAMES HERO

This is a very dramatic scene in the play. Read through the scene again up to the point at which Don Pedro, Don John and Claudio leave.

THINK–PAIR–SHARE

The deception of Claudio and Don Pedro (as well as their failure to research the facts) has severe consequences. The public shaming of Hero by Claudio at their wedding in Act 4 Scene 1 is very dramatic and leaves the audience with a number of questions.

Read through the scene again, up to the point at which Don Pedro, Don John and Claudio leave, then make notes on the following questions:

- **Why do you think Claudio waited until the wedding to accuse Hero of sleeping with someone else?**
- **Could Claudio have dealt with things in any different ways? What might he have done instead?**
- **What personal responsibility did Claudio have towards Hero in this situation? How far does the fact that he has been deceived by Don John absolve him of blame for his actions in this scene and what he does to Hero?**
- **What do you think of Claudio at this point?**

Once you have finished writing your own notes on these, turn to a partner and **discuss** your responses. Are you in agreement? As a class, **discuss** the issue of personal responsibility in this situation in more detail.

MAKING A CRISIS INTO A DRAMA …

Whatever you may think of Claudio, you should bear in mind Shakespeare's desire to create moments of high drama on the stage. *Much Ado About Nothing* was written to be performed and moments that might command an audience's attention, keep their interest and impress them with spectacle were important. Claudio's behaviour in this scene may possibly be as much the result of dramatic or performance considerations as decisions about his characterization. You might also remember how Borachio raised the anticipation of an audience earlier in the play by foreshadowing what Claudio was going to do when he thought he had seen Hero being unfaithful:

> *'away went Claudio enraged, swore he would meet her as he was appointed next morning at the temple, and there, before the whole congregation, shame her with what he saw o'ernight and send her home again without a husband.'*
>
> (Act 3 Scene 3)

The consequences of Don John's deception, and the subsequent shaming of Hero, are so great that it is no exaggeration to say that they could have led to the death of Hero. Indeed, when Hero's family pretend that Hero has died of shock and grief (in order to hide her from the outrage and – believing Hero to be innocent of what she is accused – so that the truth of the situation can come to light), her death is readily believed by everyone in the play. Even without the possibility of death, it is likely that the shaming of Hero would have resulted in her being unable to marry in the future, nor be seen in public again.

Amid the shock and confusion of Claudio's accusations at the wedding, it is Friar Francis who, convinced that there has been some mistake, comes up with the plan for what to do next:

FRIAR FRANCIS: Call me a fool;

Trust not my reading nor my observations,

Which with experimental seal doth warrant

The tenor of my book; trust not my age,

My reverence, calling, nor divinity,

If this sweet lady lie not guiltless here

Under some biting error.

Act 4 Scene 1

Friar Francis therefore suggests a plan:

FRIAR FRANCIS: Pause awhile,

And let my counsel sway you in this case.

Your daughter here the princes left for dead:

Let her awhile be secretly kept in,

And publish it that she is dead indeed; 5

Maintain a mourning ostentation

And on your family's old monument

Hang mournful epitaphs and do all rites

That appertain unto a burial.

LEONATO: What shall become of this? What
will this do? 10

FRIAR FRANCIS: Marry, this well carried
shall on her behalf

Change slander to remorse; that is some good:

But not for that dream I on this strange
course,

But on this travail look for greater birth.

She dying, as it must so be maintain'd, 15

Upon the instant that she was accused,

Shall be lamented, pitied and excused

Of every hearer: for it so falls out

That what we have we prize not to the worth

Whiles we enjoy it, but being lack'd and
lost, 20

Why, then we rack the value, then we find

The virtue that possession would not show us

Whiles it was ours. So will it fare with
Claudio:

When he shall hear she died upon his words,

The idea of her life shall sweetly creep 25

Into his study of imagination,

And every lovely organ of her life

Shall come apparell'd in more precious habit,

More moving-delicate and full of life,

Into the eye and prospect of his soul, 30

Than when she lived indeed; then shall he
mourn,

If ever love had interest in his liver,

And wish he had not so accused her,

No, though he thought his accusation true.

Let this be so, and doubt not but success 35

Will fashion the event in better shape

Than I can lay it down in likelihood.

But if all aim but this be levell'd false,

The supposition of the lady's death

Will quench the wonder of her infamy: 40

And if it sort not well, you may conceal her,

As best befits her wounded reputation,

In some reclusive and religious life,

Out of all eyes, tongues, minds and injuries.

Act 4 Scene 1

How might issues of truth and deception impact on relationships?

ACTIVITY: The death of Hero

 ATL

■ Critical-thinking skills: Gather and organize relevant information to formulate an argument; consider ideas from multiple perspectives

Friar Francis's suggestion is that, as a result of what has happened to her at the wedding, they all pretend that Hero has died.

With a partner, **discuss** the following questions:

1 **What reasons does he give for suggesting that they do this?**
2 **How does he think it will affect:**
   a Claudio?   **b people generally?**
3 **Do you think the Friar and the others who agree to this plan are justified in carrying out the pretence that someone is dead, when they are not? What reasons do you have for your view on this?**
4 **How might cultural factors relating to the context in which these characters live contribute to their feeling a need to take measures such as these, after what has happened? Think about perceptions of such things as reputation, honour and so on.**
5 **Friar Francis tells Hero:**

   'Come, lady, die to live, this wedding day

   Perhaps is but prolonged: have patience and endure.'

   The assumption is that if things go well with the plan, Hero may be able to marry Claudio after all.
      After all that has happened, should she do so:
   a in your personal opinion? Why (not)?
   b within the cultural context in which she lives? Why (not)?
6 **How far does Friar Francis's plan fit the definitions of deception you looked at previously (page 273)?**

◆ **Assessment opportunities**

In this activity you have practised skills that are assessed using Criterion A: Analysing.

ACTIVITY: Is deception always wrong?

■ **ATL**

■ Critical-thinking skills: Evaluate evidence and arguments; consider ideas from multiple perspectives

We have seen how negative the impact of deception can be, but is it sometimes possible for the wrong action to be taken for the right reason?

What did you think about the Friar's plan? Was it justified? Looking back once more to Don Pedro's seduction of Hero in Act 2 Scene 1, was it done for the right reasons? Would the plan, and Don Pedro's lie to Hero, have been justified once Hero agreed to marry Claudio?

Both plans raise the question of whether deception, and the lies which are inevitably involved, can be justified in certain contexts. Now, consider the following scenarios – are there any in which lying and deception are justified, do you think?

Try this activity on your own to begin with and then compare your answers with a partner, and then a further couple, to see how far you agree.

1 **During a visit to your grandmother, she spends a long time cooking a meal for you. However, it contains a number of ingredients that you do not like. What would you say to her?**

2 You hide your friend's smartphone as a joke but they become extremely upset about losing it (and would be extremely angry to find that you had hidden it). You decide that they need to have it back. How would you return it to them? Would you say anything to them? If so, what?

3 You see your friend shoplifting a chocolate bar. The shopkeeper suddenly asks you: 'Did you see that person just take something and put it in their bag?' What do you reply?

4 Your boss wants you to work some extra hours. You think it is unfair that you have been asked this. What do you reply?

5 You have to complete a very important piece of school coursework and have not left enough time for it. There seem to be some items on the internet that you could copy and paste quite quickly, though. What do you do?

- Which, if any, of the above did you think you might tell a lie about and deceive someone else?
- Why was that the case for each instance?
- Did the instances in which you would tell a lie have anything in common?

Some of the above are examples of possible 'white lies' (look up the term if you do not know it). Is it okay to tell such lies and practise deception of this kind? Has your perspective on this changed? **Discuss** this in groups and, if possible, as a class.

ACTIVITY: Judging deceptions

ATL

- Critical-thinking skills: Gather and organize relevant information to formulate an argument; consider ideas from multiple perspectives

In groups of three or four, consider the deceptions listed below that take place in *Much Ado About Nothing*. How many of them do you think are justified? Copy the table below and add any further deceptions you can **identify** to the two left-hand columns. In the two right-hand columns, note possible arguments for and against each deception. Remember to consider the context in which the deception takes place.

Act and scene	Nature of deception	Arguments for the deception being justified	Arguments for the deception not being justified
2:1	Don Pedro pretends to be Claudio at the masked dance, in order to woo Hero for Claudio.		
2:1	Don John tells Claudio that Don Pedro has deceived him and wooed Hero for himself.		
5:1	Leonato tells Claudio he has a niece whom Claudio should marry the next day, to make up for what happened to Hero.		

ACTIVITY: Deception within a relationship

■ ATL

- Critical-thinking skills: Consider ideas from multiple perspectives
- Creative-thinking skills: Consider multiple alternatives, including those that might be unlikely or impossible

When you have finished reading the whole play, carry out these activities.

In what way(s) does deception play a role in the relationships between the following characters in *Much Ado About Nothing*? What impact does the deception have?

- **Does it undermine the relationship? How?**
- **Does it help the relationship? How?**

Characters	Deception(s)	Effect of deception(s) on their relationship
Claudio and Hero		
Leonato and Hero		
Benedick and Beatrice		
Don Pedro and Don John		

◆ Assessment opportunities

In this activity you have practised skills that are assessed using Criterion A: Analysing.

ACTIVITY: The gossip columnist

■ ATL

- Creative-thinking skills: Create original works and ideas; use existing works and ideas in new ways

When Claudio, Don Pedro and Leonato are deceived into believing Hero has been unfaithful, a major source of their information comes from **gossip**.

Imagine you are a gossip columnist in Messina. You have been asked to write a magazine feature article on the relationships between the individuals at Claudio's wedding (that is, the key characters of *Much Ado About Nothing*). You have 800–1,000 words in which to do this.

Begin by **outlining** your thoughts on what constitutes a healthy relationship, then **discuss** each character's relationship in turn and judge whether they are healthy or unhealthy. Make sure to include evidence from the play to support each conclusion. You might also **comment** on how you think the relationship will turn out in the end, and **identify** who is responsible for any problems between couples.

The ATL cog on 'Writing a gossip column' gives further guidance on how you might style a column.

◆ Assessment opportunities

In this activity you have practised skills that are assessed Criterion C: Producing text and Criterion D: Using language.

Writing a gossip column

Gossip columns are opinionated, and often quite subjective and biased towards or against the people they are writing about.

- What attitudes might a column display towards different people?
- What literary techniques will be used to show those attitudes? (For example, tone, register, word choice, sentence use, grammar, rhetorical questions and so on.)

A gossip column should grab and hold the attention of its readers.

- What eye-catching headline might they use?
- How would they use subheadings? Or images?
- What interest-grabbing wordplay could they use for the headings and captions?

In Act 5, Hero is **exonerated** when Borachio is caught and confesses the deception in which he, Don John and Conrade took part.

Claudio and Don Pedro respond to this realization, in Act 5 Scene 1, with the comments in the table below. **Explain** what kind of imagery each of them uses in their respective lines, and why Shakespeare might have chosen that particular image in each case.

	Image used	Comments on image used
DON PEDRO: Runs not this speech like iron through your blood?		
CLAUDIO: I have drunk poison whiles he utters it.		

Claudio tells Leonato that he will do whatever Leonato wishes in order to make up for his mistake ('*Impose me to what penance your invention/ Can lay upon my sin*') and Leonato – aware that Hero is alive – responds with one final deception.

ACTIVITY: Writing for your audience

■ ATL

- Communication skills: Use appropriate forms of writing for different purposes and audiences

In pairs, imagine you are publishing a series of books called *Simple Shakespeare,* which paraphrases Shakespeare plays into more modern and less complex language. Working together, paraphrase Leonato's speech to Claudio into normal, present day, prose. You have previously seen examples of this technique from *No Fear Shakespeare*, and you might remind yourself how this is done by using this link (but do not look at Act 5 Scene 1!): **http://nfs.sparknotes.com/muchado.**

LEONATO: I cannot bid you bid my daughter live;

That were impossible: but, I pray you both,

Possess the people in Messina here

How innocent she died; and if your love

Can labour ought in sad invention,

Hang her an epitaph upon her tomb

And sing it to her bones, sing it to-night:

To-morrow morning come you to my house,

And since you could not be my son-in-law,

Be yet my nephew: my brother hath a daughter,

Almost the copy of my child that's dead,

And she alone is heir to both of us:

Give her the right you should have given her cousin,

And so dies my revenge.

◆ Assessment opportunities

In this activity you have practised skills that are assessed using Criterion C: Producing text and Criterion D: Using language.

CULTURAL CONTEXT AND CHOICES

In order to atone for his treatment of Hero, Claudio agrees to Leonato's wishes and goes to church, ready to marry the woman he believes is Hero's cousin. The final deception is exposed, however, when the veiled woman reveals herself to be Hero. Claudio is overwhelmed with joy and the two marry.

Despite all that happens to Hero in Act 4, we still see Hero marrying Claudio, regardless of how he treated her at what should have been their wedding the first time around.

Part of the reason for this may be cultural: Hero may need to marry Claudio to prove to the world that she really is innocent and pure, and thus to ensure that the reputation of Leonato and the family remains intact.

Part of the reason may be dramatic: Shakespeare's comedies tended to have conventional happy endings and he therefore needed to create one for *Much Ado*. Happy endings on television or in film nowadays often focus on weddings, and the promise of living 'happily ever after', and the same is true of Shakespeare's characters.

Are the couple likely to live 'happily ever after' following all that has happened, however?

ACTIVITY: Read all about it!

ATL

- Creative-thinking skills: Create original works and ideas; use existing works and ideas in new ways

The local newspaper, the *Messina Messenger,* hears about the marriage of Claudio and Hero once it finally takes place. The editor wants to write an opinion piece explaining his or her views on:

- **whether Hero should have married Claudio after his actions at the ceremony when they were first due to be married**
- **whether it is a good thing or not that they do eventually get together and marry**
- **whether their marriage might be expected to be a happy and successful one.**

As the editor of the *Messina Messenger,* write that opinion article, ensuring you **explain** your views on each of these points. You may find it helpful to refer to the ATL cog on writing a newspaper column on pages 230–231.

◆ Assessment opportunities

In this activity you have practised skills that are assessed using Criterion C: Producing text and Criterion D: Using language.

DISCUSS

Following their reconciliation, Claudio and Hero produce love poems that Beatrice and Benedick have written to one another, and Beatrice and Benedick also finally get together and marry.

Think about these questions individually, then **discuss** your thoughts with a partner:

- **How much choice does Beatrice have about whom she marries?**
- **What do we see in the play about the dating processes between Beatrice and Benedick?**
- **How does their romance differ from Claudio and Hero's? What reasons do you think there are for the differences in the situations of Hero and Beatrice?**
- **Do you think Beatrice and Benedick will have a successful (happy and healthy) marriage? Why (not)?**

ACTIVITY: Two relationships, both alike in … health?

At the start of this chapter you worked in groups of four to **create** a graphic that detailed the key characteristics of a healthy relationship ('A healthy relationship' activity, page 252).

If possible, return to these original groups now and use the graphic you produced at the time to **evaluate** both Hero's relationship with Claudio and Beatrice's relationship with Benedick. Alternatively, form new groups and decide which group member's graphic you will use for this activity.

In what ways are the relationships healthy? In what ways are they unhealthy? Copy the table below and make notes in the appropriate columns. Where possible, use evidence from the play to support your conclusions.

	Healthy	Unhealthy
Hero and Claudio		
Beatrice and Benedick		

◆ Assessment opportunities

In this activity you have practised skills that are assessed using Criterion A: Analysing.

ACTIVITY: Couples counselling

Stay in the same group as the previous activity. Imagine both Hero and Claudio, and Beatrice and Benedick, have decided to seek out some pre-marriage guidance from a marriage guidance counselling agency.

Use the results of your previous analysis to role-play these pre-marriage meetings:

- **Guidance councillors:**
  **What healthy relationship criteria indicate some less healthy aspects to the relationship? What advice will you give the characters about these? Which aspects are more positive, and how might the characters build on those in the future?
  How or why might the characters need to display empathy, compassion and respect in their relationships – perhaps more so than they have done before?**
- **Couples:**
  What questions might you have after your experiences of dating, getting together and reaching a point where it has been decided you will marry?

Two group members should take on the role of marriage guidance counsellors, while the other two play the couple being counselled. Once you have role-played this for one couple, swap roles and do the same for the remaining couple. You should also swap parts so that everyone has the opportunity to play both a marriage guidance counsellor and a character.

Once finished, as a group review the points that were made about healthy or unhealthy aspects of the relationship of the characters and the advice given. Do you all agree on what they are? Was anything missed out? Was the advice given appropriate/helpful/ sufficiently detailed?

Finally, look again at your criteria listed on the graphic detailing healthy relationships. Would you change any of this now? Add anything? Take anything out? Add any extra detail, or phrase anything differently?

◆ Assessment opportunities

In this activity you have practised skills that are assessed using Criterion D: Using language.

SOME SUMMATIVE TASKS TO TRY

Use these tasks to apply and extend your learning in this chapter. These tasks are designed so that you can evaluate your learning at different levels of achievement in the Language and literature criteria.

THIS TASK CAN BE USED TO EVALUATE YOUR LEARNING IN CRITERION B, CRITERION C AND CRITERION D

Task 1: Benedick's diary

You are Benedick after you have left Beatrice in Act 4 Scene 1. Write your diary for the day, explaining your feelings at different times, according to the various things that have happened that day. Ensure you include:

- Claudio's shaming of Hero at the wedding altar
- your profession of love to Beatrice
- Beatrice's challenge to you to kill Claudio, and your acceptance of that.

You might find the ATL on diary writing (page 39) useful.

THIS TASK CAN BE USED TO EVALUATE YOUR LEARNING IN CRITERION A, CRITERION B AND CRITERION D

Task 2: Literature essay

Answer the question 'How are stories about other places and times about me?' using *Much Ado About Nothing*.

- To do this, choose some aspects of the play that are relevant to you and your own experiences and context – these are often themes such as relationships, deception and so on.
- During your essay you might **identify** two or three key points to talk about in depth. When discussing these points you should be detailed and critical (analytical and evaluative) in your writing, and **comment** on specific literary features.
- For example, Claudio's use of more formal poetry at times during his relationship with Hero might be compared to how we sometimes change our use of language in order to reflect our feelings at particular times. Here, particular parts of the play have been identified for discussion, as well as a specific literary feature to **comment** on.
- Finally, do not forget to **explain** in your essay that the place and time in the 'story' of *Much Ado About Nothing* are both similar to, and different from, your own.
- Your essay should be 500–800 words in length.

Take action

! The relationships you have with your friends can vary wildly. Read the following article about 'toxic' friendships: www.verywell.com/toxic-friends-to-avoid-460645. Your group's task, for an audience of students in the MYP 1–3 year groups, is as follows:

1 **Create a short drama that illustrates the nature of each friend type. During this you should explain or narrate the key points about the friend types you are presenting.**

2 **Following the drama, give a five-minute presentation on some actions you might take to deal with such friends. Could anything be done to help friends exhibiting such 'toxic' behaviour?**

! Use your presentations to develop awareness about the different types of relationships among MYP 1–3 level students, and what might be done in response to such behaviours. The students might in turn form into groups of three and devise further dramatic skits and narrations themselves on this, to show their own understanding and awareness.

Reflection

In this chapter we have explored the nature of relationships and the factors that may contribute to making them healthy or unhealthy – along with how different contexts and cultural factors may influence perspectives on them. We have considered different ways in which relationships can be formed, including modern opportunities offered by the internet; the potential that exists for people's desire for relationships to be used for deception, and the importance of research in establishing successful and healthy relationships. For all of this, we have used examples of relationships presented in texts, and looked at techniques that can be used by writers to convey ideas about these relationships, as well as looking more closely at what the skills of research – an ATL category – actually involve.

Use this table to reflect on your own learning in this chapter.

Questions we asked	Answers we found	Any further questions now?			
Factual:					
Conceptual:					
Debatable:					
Approaches to learning you used in this chapter	Description – what new skills did you learn?	How well did you master the skills?			
		Novice	Learner	Practitioner	Expert
Communication skills					
Collaboration skills					
Creative-thinking skills					
Critical-thinking skills					
Reflection skills					
Transfer skills					
Information literacy skills					
Media literacy skills					
Learner profile attribute(s)	Reflect on the importance of being caring for your learning in this chapter.				
Caring					

11 How do we deal with a double-edged sword?

○ Different **perspectives** across different texts show how **innovation** brings both **opportunity** and **risk**, along with **consequences** and **responsibilities**.

■ Are these double-edged swords?

CONSIDER THESE QUESTIONS:

Factual: What is a 'double-edged sword'? What kinds of innovations bring both opportunity and risk? What opportunities can invention bring? How can texts show different points of view?

Conceptual: What are some different points of view and perspectives about invention? What does 'taking responsibility' mean in the context of a life- or world-changing innovation? What and who is responsible for an innovation? What are the consequences of innovation?

Debatable: How far can the consequences of an innovation be controlled? Can something that has been invented ever be 'un-invented'?

Now **share and compare** your thoughts and ideas with your partner, or with the whole class.

○─ IN THIS CHAPTER, WE WILL ... ───

■ **Find out** about the kinds of things which represent 'innovations', and the kinds of opportunities and risks they can bring.

■ **Explore** the responsibility that comes with life-changing innovations, and the different ways and groups who might take responsibility.

■ **Take action** by considering and evaluating risks and opportunities, and possible consequences, and by taking responsibility for our own actions when we seek to innovate and create.

■ These Approaches to Learning (ATL) skills will be useful ...

■ Communication skills
■ Collaboration skills
■ Creative-thinking skills
■ Critical-thinking skills
■ Information literacy skills

◆ Assessment opportunities in this chapter:

◆ **Criterion A:** Analysing
◆ **Criterion B:** Organizing
◆ **Criterion C:** Producing text
◆ **Criterion D:** Using language

● We will reflect on this learner profile attribute …

● Principled – develop skills involved in being principled through various activities that involve considering how to act with integrity and honesty, along with possible consequences of our actions and those of others in the world, and responsibilities which could and should be taken for those by ourselves and others.

KEY WORDS

atomic power	potential
discovery	radiation
invention	report
patent	responsibility
perspective	risk

ACTIVITY: A double-edged sword

■ ATL

■ Critical-thinking skills: Consider ideas from multiple perspectives

Think about the phrase 'a double-edged sword'. What do you think it means?

Each of the following quotations is about something that can be described as a double-edged sword. After reading through each quote, write down your thoughts on what a double-edged sword means.

Share your thoughts with a partner, and then get into a group of four. In your group, decide on a definition of a double-edged sword then, together, **discuss** how the objects represented by the images on these pages might represent a double-edged sword.

Individually, make up your own quotation(s). You should begin your quotation with: 'x is a double-edged sword', then continue on to explain how your example can be both positive and negative.

> Security is a double-edged sword: while a fence sure protects the fenced; it also imprisons the protected. – Mokokoma Mokhonoana

> Love is a double-edged sword, it can conquer your happiness but one wrong swing and it can also cause you misery. – Anon

> Like a double-edged sword, our greatest strengths are often also our weaknesses. For me, that has always been caring too much and feeling too intensely. It's allowed me to understand and deeply connect to people, but has also been the cause of a lot of heartache. For everything there is a price. – Yasmin Mogahed

> Technology is always a two-edged sword. It will bring in many benefits, but also many disasters. – Alan Moore

◆ Assessment opportunities

In this activity you have practised skills that are assessed using Criterion A: Analysing and Criterion D: Using language.

What opportunities can invention bring?

ACTIVITY: Scientific and technical innovation – the joys of progress

ATL

- Communication skills: Use a variety of speaking techniques to communicate with a variety of audiences
- Collaboration skills: Listen actively to other perspectives and ideas

Look at this infographic showing 60 life-changing products invented over the past 60 years: http://explore.which.co.uk/60products.

DISCUSS

Looking at the list, which product do you think you would miss the most if it did not exist? Why? In pairs, **discuss** your choice. Did your partner choose something else? What are the reasons for your partner's choice?

1 Write a one-minute speech explaining your choice of product and the reasons behind it.
2 With your class, walk individually and randomly around the classroom until your teacher tells you to stop. Pair up with the classmate closest to you and deliver your speeches to each other.
3 Spend one minute giving feedback on your partner's choice of product and speech. What other ideas or points might you each have included in talking about your choice of product?
4 Revise your speech based on the feedback you have received.
5 Repeat steps 2–4 again two more times.
6 Gather in groups of four or five. Each member should give their speech to the group.

7 Having heard a number of arguments for different products, decide now whether you want to stick with your original choice or change to a different product.
8 In your group, write each member's name, their final product choice and their reasons for choosing it onto a piece of poster paper.
9 Display your completed group chart on the wall of the classroom and hold a gallery walk.
10 Which products were chosen more than once by members of the class? As a class, **discuss** possible reasons for the popularity of that product. Might age, gender or nationality have been factors in any of the more popular choices? Are there any other common factors?

EXTENSION

Which product do you think your parents, or another older relative, would choose, and for what reason(s)? How would they explain their choices? Write a one-minute speech for each parent/relative you have chosen, in the voice of that parent/relative each time, explaining their choice and why they have made it.

Now, if you have the opportunity, ask them directly! Did you predict their choice and reasons?

Assessment opportunities

In this activity you have practised skills that are assessed using Criterion C: Producing text and Criterion D: Using language.

ACTIVITY: Newspaper feature article

■ ATL

- Communication skills: Read critically and for comprehension
- Information literacy skills: Use critical-literacy skills to analyse and interpret media communications

Read this article in the Daily Mail by Jan Moir about innovations over the last 60 years: https://goo.gl/X8C8Kj. The newspaper article contains one journalist's reflections on the 60-product infographic we looked at in the previous activity.

As you know from earlier chapters, a newspaper feature article differs from a news report in a number of ways. In particular, it is more subjective and may contain the personal views and reflections of its writer. The language and register may also be more informal and perhaps **colloquial**.

Read the article from 'Little things that were actually big things' to the paragraph about digital hearing aids. Look for the features highlighted below.

- **Use of incomplete sentences helps to give a more conversational feel to the text.**
- **Note the irony in the comment at the end of the second paragraph in this section.**
- **The non-sentence and exclamation at the start of the third paragraph in this section provide insight into the personal feelings of the writer about doing the laundry. This is further emphasized through the use of hyperbole and alliteration (the hard 'b' helping to convey the effort used in this task) and through the use of personification.**
- **The use of zoomorphism helps convey the writer's perception of the machine as a monster. Use of hyperbole in the following simile further exaggerates this point.**
- **Note the contrasting descriptions of doing the laundry. The onomatopoeia of 'swishes' in the fifth paragraph contrasts with the previous alliteration.**
- **Alliteration and epic language highlights and foreshadows the importance of this invention.**
- **Personal pronouns and contractions create a personal, more informal register.**
- **Informal vocabulary.**
- **The mild expletive in the fifth paragraph creates a colloquial tone.**

THINK–PAIR–SHARE

The bullet points above identify and comment on some aspects of the text's style.

Review the rest of the section of the article and then make your own notes **identifying** and **explaining** any aspects of style that you recognize. Questions to consider might include these:

- **What impressions are given by the writer of the different inventions?**
- **Is it a positive or negative picture that is presented for each? What makes you say that?**
- **What specific literary techniques have been used in the description each time?**

Once you have finished your own notes, get into a pair and share them with your partner.

Now, join with another pair and, in your group of four, share your thoughts and ideas on the text once again.

ACTIVITY: eAssessment-type questions

■ ATL

- Critical-thinking skills: Gather and organize relevant information to formulate an argument
- Communication skills: Paraphrase accurately and concisely

1 a Using the information in the first two paragraphs only ('Little things ...' and 'The laundry!'), state two points about how new inventions made life easier for people. **[2 marks]**
   b From paragraphs 3, 4 and 5 ('Sopping wet ...' to 'Oh, my absolutely lovely ...'), summarize the ways in which household tasks used to be more difficult and unpleasant before the invention of modern appliances. **[4 marks]**
   c From paragraph 6 ('Apart from those ...'), interpret how the writer's use of language makes the washing machine seem like a strong ally in a time of difficulty. Support your answer with reference to the text. **[4 marks]**

◆ Assessment opportunities

In this activity you have practised skills that are assessed using Criterion A: Analysing.

ACTIVITY: Longer literary response questions

■ ATL

- Critical-thinking skills: Gather and organize relevant information to formulate an argument; draw reasonable conclusions and generalizations

Read the following questions, then choose **one** question and write 500–600 words in answer to it:

a What is the overall point of view of the writer of this article about products that have been invented over the past 60 years?
   Think about: What techniques does she use to convey that point of view?
b How would you describe the tone of this article? What techniques are used to create this tone?
   Think about: The use of humour, register, sentence structure, language (including epic colloquialisms, epic language and hyperbole), diction choices.

◆ Assessment opportunities

In this activity you have practised skills that are assessed using Criterion A: Analysing and Criterion D: Using language.

What are some different points of view and perspectives about invention?

As you will have come to realize, the writer of the newspaper article you have just reviewed feels (on the whole) extremely positive about the impact that inventions and innovations have had on lives over the past 60 years. Not everyone might feel this way, however.

The poem 'My Blue Heaven' is one text with a different, less positive, perspective on invention and innovation. In the poem, the speaker becomes aware of a dreadful smell, and they begin to consider what it could be. They realize the smell is coming from the 'Blue Factory', which manufactures blue dye, an ingredient used in washing detergent.

ⓘ Bluing

When white clothes are regularly laundered they will turn slightly yellow over time. 'Bluing' is the practice of adding a small amount of blue dye to clothes when they are being washed. The human eye perceives the tiny amount of blue, and this makes the fabric appear whiter.

The invention and mass production of washing machines meant that factories were also required to mass-produce the blue dye used in detergent. The use of chemicals in, and the other side effects of, this process make it a good example of a double-edged sword.

My Blue Heaven

I thought it was a Glue Factory –
a whiff of boiled bones
and the **knackers yard**

excreted in the **lee** of the **fells**.
The smell of desperate **exhumations**   5
briefly fills the car

I was wrong, the wind flicking
the **plosive** back into the throat
it's the Blue Factory

staining the air, staining   10
the village **beck**, leaving
its **cobalt** drift of talcum

on window-sill and ledge
tinting the grey-green slate
with hints of early Picasso.   15

The factory chimney steams
like a pencil designing fumes.
All this to manufacture Blue:

that stuff to make the sheets gleam
bright in a glossy commercial.   20
the stuff they use to justify

the suburbs aerial madness.
As the **ferro-cyanic** stench
recedes, I wonder what

strange manufacturer   25
makes all the distant stuff
that gives some inflated clouds

their whiter than cotton whiteness?
What heavenly smell, pray,
lies behind all that?   30

Rodney Pybus

ACTIVITY: Writing about the Blue Factory

Imagine you are the speaker in the poem. Choose one of the following written tasks to complete:

1 Write a diary

Write a diary entry for the day, describing the experiences you had of driving close to the 'Blue Factory', and your thoughts and feelings about it.

Think about the format and content of a diary. You might refer to the ATL cog on diary writing (page 39), or there are a number of resources online you could investigate: www.tes.com/teaching-resource/how-to-write-a-diary-entry-6219883.

Your diary entry should be 500–600 words.

2 Write a letter to a newspaper

You decide to write an extended letter to the editor of your local newspaper, complaining about the impact this factory is having on the local environment.

Use the details of the poem to compose your letter, and remember: this letter is your opinion and you are trying to be persuasive.

Your letter will use much of the same structure and stylistic techniques that a journalist would when writing an opinion column (see the ATL cog on pages 230–31). You might also look back at the ATL cogs on letter writing in Chapter 2 (page 46), and on some of the persuasive writing techniques outlined in Chapter 4.

Your letter should be 500–1,000 words.

EXTENSION

Write a 200–300 word rationale in which you explain the nature and purpose of your writing. You should provide information on the text's audience, the context in which it has been written (you are playing the role of the poem's narrator, what is your context?), and explain what aspects of style you used and for what reasons.

◆ Assessment opportunities

In this activity you have practised skills that are assessed using Criterion A: Analysing, Criterion C: Producing text and Criterion D: Using language.

ACTIVITY: Speed learning

'The sword of science is double-edged. Its awesome power forces on all of us, including politicians, a new responsibility – more attention to the long-term consequences of technology …'
– Carl Sagan, *The Demon-Haunted World: Science as a Candle in the Dark*

Let us consider further how science (and scientific inventions) might, as Sagan suggests, be double-edged.

Use brainstorming, or another visual diagram, to write down a number of scientific or technical innovations – try to come up with things you have not yet looked at. For each innovation include examples of any benefits they have brought to the world, and also any problems they have created. Can you think of short-term and long-term benefits or problems?

All students should now arrange their chairs in two rows, facing each other.

Sit and, using your notes, speak to the classmate you are facing for 60 seconds about the ways in which science and technology have benefited humanity. Following this, your partner will speak for 60 seconds about some possible downsides, or concerns, about scientific or technical innovations.

Use a graphic organizer, such as the example below, to note down all the points your partner makes.

All students should now move a seat along to the left or right, so that everyone is facing a new partner.

With your new partner, carry out the exercise once again, this time swapping topics so that if you talked about some pros of scientific innovation the first time, you will talk about the cons the second time around.

Repeat the exercise a further two or three times.

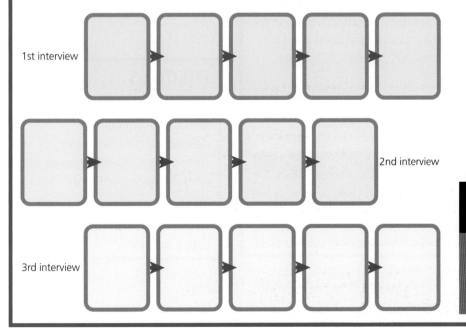

1st interview

2nd interview

3rd interview

ACTIVITY: A biography of Sir Isaac Newton

ATL

- Communication skills: Use appropriate forms of writing for different purposes and audiences
- Information literacy skills: Create references and citations, use footnotes/endnotes and construct a bibliography according to recognized conventions

Sir Isaac Newton's Law of Motion is an idea we will look at more over the course of this chapter, and one which very much summarizes the double-edged sword nature of innovation we have already begun to look at.

Write a 500–1,000 word biography of Sir Isaac Newton. Begin by researching three or four useful sources of information, which must include at least one example of each of the following:
- **a web page**
- **a video**
- **hard-copy written information; for instance, from a book such as an encyclopaedia, or a journal or magazine you may have come across.**

You should include at least one image of Newton and, as well as describing the man himself, your biography should focus in particular on some of Newton's more significant achievements.

As your biography is drawing on other sources of information, you must cite and reference those appropriately, and include a bibliography or reference list or works used list. Look at the ATL cog on 'Citing and referencing' opposite for how to do this.

You might also refer to the ATL cog in Chapter 1 (page 19) to remind yourself of some of the main features of biographical writing.

Assessment opportunities

In this activity you have practised skills that are assessed using Criterion B: Organizing, Criterion C: Producing text and Criterion D: Using language.

Sir Isaac Newton

Sir Isaac Newton was an English mathematician and natural philosopher. Born in 1642, Newton studied at the University of Cambridge and became famous for his scientific work, and several scientific discoveries. Among those were the Laws of Motion, one of which states that 'To every action there is always opposed an equal reaction'.

DISCUSS

When speaking of his discoveries, Sir Isaac Newton famously claimed that *'If I have seen further it is by standing on ye [the] sho[u]lders of Giants'*.

What do you think Newton's statement means? **Discuss** this with a partner.

Citing and referencing

There are a number of common citation and reference systems used by schools and institutions. These are:

- MLA (The Modern Language Association)
- APA (The American Psychological Association)
- CMS (The Chicago Manual of Style) – often abbreviated to 'Chicago'
- Harvard.

Whichever one you use, you need to be consistent in using that system, as referencing and citation styles are different in the different systems.

The two main aspects you need to consider are:

- In-text citation
  Specific mention of a source, made throughout the course of your text.
- Referencing of sources
  A list of all books, websites and other references cited, included at the end of your work.

A useful resource about research citation styles can be found here: **https://owl.purdue.edu/owl/research_and_citation/resources.html**

You might need to cite or reference a source in something other than a written piece of work. Find out how to do this here: **www.ibo.org/globalassets/digital-tookit/brochures/effective-citing-and-referencing-en.pdf**.

Online referencing tools

There are lots of small details to remember in formatting references and citations correctly, whichever system is used for this. Modern technology has made things easier, however, through the development of online tools. Some well-known tools are:

- EasyBib – **www.easybib.com/**
- Citation Machine – **www.citationmachine.net/**
- Harvard Generator – **www.harvardgenerator.com/**

Other well-known online tools are used more widely by universities and colleges, and researchers. Two of the best known are:

- Mendeley – **www.mendeley.com/**
- EndNote – **http://endnote.com/**

DISCUSS

Watch the following example of an airline safety video: **https://youtube.com/watch?v=fSGaRVOLPfg**.

How is the video trying to convey a clear message to passengers on a flight? Do you find it an interesting video? What makes you say that? **Discuss** your answers in groups of two or four.

Citing and referencing are based on strict formats and protocols, which need to be known and used exactly as stated. In some ways they might be compared to an airline safety video, where strict wording, formats and protocols are used at the start of a flight.

ACTIVITY: How to cite and reference

To try to persuade passengers to watch safety videos (and listen to the message), some airlines try hard to make their videos both clear and interesting.

How interesting are the following airline safety videos? By yourself, give each a score out of 10, with 1 being not interesting at all and 10 indicating that you could not take your eyes off the video.

1 LATAM: www.youtube.com/watch?v=lJ6dV5-amJI
2 Turkish Airlines: www.youtube.com/watch?v=9NqSg4dSBvI
3 Air New Zealand: www.youtube.com/watch?v=qOw44VFNk8Y
4 Singapore Airlines: www.youtube.com/watch?v=25brQSPMORg
5 Virgin America: www.youtube.com/watch?v=DtyfiPlHsIg

Note how the messages are the same in each case, often down to the same wording. Despite this, the airlines were able to present formulaic information in an interesting and appealing way.

Get into groups of four or five. Your task is to present information on how to cite and reference accurately and correctly, in an interesting and entertaining way, within a maximum of three minutes. You will do this by making a **parody** of an airline safety video.

1 **As a group, brainstorm some possible ideas as to how you might present citing and referencing information.**
2 **After you have decided, write a script and assign roles for the video.**
3 **When writing your script and planning your presentation, keep in mind the features and possible limitations of the setting in which you will give your presentation.**
4 **Draw up a list of any props you may need – again, this needs to be realistic for your context.**
5 **Learn script lines and rehearse as needed. You may need or want to arrange to do this at a time out of class.**
6 **Present at the appointed time.**

EXTENSION

Give feedback on each other's presentations using the instructions suggested for oral presentations by the 'readwritethink' International Reading Association: **www.readwritethink.org/files/resources/printouts/30700_rubric.pdf**.

Discovering radioactivity

In 1895 Wilhelm Conrad Röntgen discovered a new type of ray that could penetrate objects, including human body tissue (something he tested on his wife's hand!). He called his discovery, which had been largely accidental and that he did not fully understand, 'X-radiation'.

Röntgen's discovery came to the notice of a physicist named Henri Becquerel in 1896 in Paris. Becquerel conducted his own X-radiation experiments and, in what is again believed to have been an accidental discovery, realized that the chemical element uranium emits radiation.

Two years later, again in Paris, Marie and Pierre Curie began to study the rays Becquerel had discovered that were emitted by uranium. They found a way of measuring the intensity of radioactivity, and also identified some other radioactive elements – polonium, thorium and radium. It was Marie Curie who first coined the term 'radioactivity'.

Learn more by searching **discovery of radioactivity** or visiting these websites:

https://science.howstuffworks.com/innovation/inventions/who-invented-the-x-ray.htm

www.aps.org/publications/apsnews/200803/physicshistory.cfm

You can read more about radiation in *Physics for the IB MYP 4&5*, Chapter 11.

■ Wilhelm Conrad Röntgen

■ Henri Becquerel

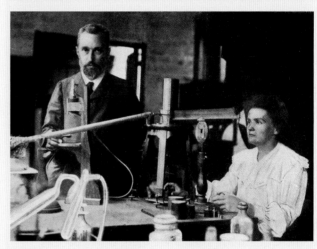
■ Marie and Pierre Curie

Two of the most significant examples of scientific discovery – and potential double-edged swords – were the discoveries of radiation and radioactivity.

The history of these discoveries illustrates the Newton quotation about 'standing on the shoulders of giants' extremely well. One scientist (Röntgen) makes a discovery (X-radiation), which is then taken by another scientist (Becquerel) who develops it further (uranium emits radiation), before more scientists (Pierre and Marie Curie) advance it further still (able to measure emitted radiation and identify other chemical elements that emit radiation).

Following these discoveries, radiation was used to identify injuries inside the human body – commonly known as 'x-rays'. It was also soon being used to try to treat and cure illnesses, such as cancer. In 1896 a physician named Émil Grubbé attempted to treat a woman with breast cancer using x-rays. Read the following account of Grubbé's x-ray treatment: **www.pbs.org/newshour/health/emil-grubbe-first-use-radiation-treat-breast-cancer**.

Having understood how Röntgen achieved his discovery, Grubbé was able to reproduce Röntgen's work in part because Röntgen refused to patent processes and inventions related to his discovery. This meant that Grubbé and others could use Röntgen's work and try to develop it further.

Patents

Patents are a way of protecting intellectual property. An invention may take a lot of time and money to produce or discover. A patent gives the inventor the exclusive right to use or license their invention. This means that someone else cannot copy that invention and use or sell it for themselves, unless they are given (or pay for) permission from the patent holder.

What and who is responsible for an innovation?

Like Röntgen, the Curies also refused to patent methods and inventions related to their work on radiation. Nowadays, however, medical inventions *are* usually patented. Research and development (R&D) into new drugs tends to be carried out by large pharmaceutical (drug) companies, and those new drugs are then patented to prevent individuals or other competing companies from copying them.

However, when a new drug is invented the company that holds the patent to the drug can also set its price. In order to make a profit, the company, which is the only source of the new drug, often sells the medication at a very high price. As a result, many people who could benefit from a drug, and many national health systems, cannot afford to buy it.

Sometimes a drug might be affordable in one country, but costs too much in another. This has happened in the case of HIV drugs in Africa, where many people died from the disease even though a drug had been developed which could have prevented that. You can find out more about antiretroviral drugs by visiting the following website: www.unaids.org

Drug companies argue, however, that it costs a huge amount of money to research, develop and safely bring a drug to the point of being used by humans. For every successful drug produced there can also be many more potential drugs that prove unsuccessful. The R&D cost of these drugs also has to be paid for. Without high prices, drug companies could not afford to research and develop new drugs. Companies also argue that, without financial profits, there is no incentive for anyone to continue to research and develop drugs. Combined, this means that new drugs will take much longer to be developed and introduced, and used by those who need them.

ACTIVITY: Perspectives on patents

A television debate has been arranged which is to focus on the issues surrounding patents on drugs. Taking part in the debate will be:

- **a patient in need of life-saving drugs, which he or she cannot afford**
- **an executive of one of the large drug companies**
- **a doctor, or worker in a national health system**
- **a government minister from the Ministry of Health, who has the power to grant or refuse patents to drug companies that want to sell new drugs in her or his country.**

In a group of four, decide who will take on which role in the debate.

To prepare for your own role, research your position by reading through the arguments contained on this web page: **http://debatewise.org/debates/2307-patents-on-life-saving-drugs-should-be-bypassed/#no6.**

You should make notes on two things:

- **the arguments that are most relevant to your own position**
- **at least five questions that you might ask other participants in the debate.**

You might also find this article to be of interest: **https://debatewise.org/debates/2307-patents-on-life-saving-drugs-should-be-bypassed/.**

Finally, look through your notes and points, and come up with a belief statement – a single statement that **summarizes** your point of view.

Once you have finished your debate, hold a debrief discussion as a group. Who had the strongest arguments and may have 'won'? What suggestions can you each make to individuals in the group that might have made their arguments more convincing?

If there is time you might hold a 'super-debate', with a member from each group joining a debate on this subject in front of the class.

How to debate

1. During a debate, each person speaking has a set time (for example, two minutes) in which to present their point of view on a topic. Debaters speak in turn, one after the other.

2. When speaking, you should begin by relating your belief statement, followed by the main points that you think **justify** it.

3. Once everyone has spoken, there is a question and answer session (for example, for ten minutes). Panellists can use questions they had previously prepared, or might ask any new questions they think of as a result of listening to someone else's opening speech.

4. Debates are often overseen by a discussion moderator. The moderator makes sure everyone gets to speak, and that the audience can hear what is being said. Your teacher might like to take this role.

ACTIVITY: If I ruled the world …

■ ATL

■ Creative-thinking skills: Make guesses, ask 'what if' questions and generate testable hypotheses; consider multiple alternatives, including those that might be unlikely or impossible

Have you ever asked yourself the question, 'What would I do if I ruled the world'? Thomas Friedman is a three-time Pulitzer-prize winning journalist who asked himself this question and came up with six edicts. You can read them here: **https://goo.gl/tiJ8mZ**.

What would your six edicts be? Write them down and then share them with two or three classmates. How similar or different were your choices?

◆ Assessment opportunities

In this activity you have practised skills that are assessed using Criterion C: Producing text and Criterion D: Using language.

COMPASS POINTS

Wilhelm Conrad Röntgen, Émil Grubbé and Marie and Pierre Curie all explored radiation with a view to advancing medical science (and, therefore, the health and welfare of human beings). They looked for the benefits of radiation, but, as we saw in the cases of Grubbé and the Curies, they also began to realize the potential harmfulness of radiation.

Imagine you are the first scientist to discover the power of radiation to destroy. You still do not fully understand it, but you realize it is a potentially harmful force. How do you feel about your discovery? What would you do with this discovery? How would you use it? Who would you share it with?

Use the Visible Thinking 'Compass points' to help you **organize** some of your thoughts.

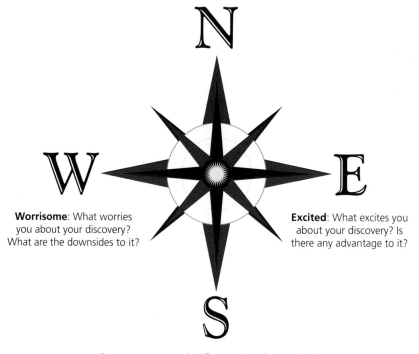

Need to know: What else do you need to know or find out about this discovery? What additional information would help you to evaluate things?

Worrisome: What worries you about your discovery? What are the downsides to it?

Excited: What excites you about your discovery? Is there any advantage to it?

Stance or suggestion for moving forward: What options are there for how to move forward with your discovery? Which one might you choose, and why?

HG Wells

An English writer born in 1866, HG Wells is sometimes called the 'father of science fiction'. His most famous works include *The Time Machine* (1895), *The Invisible Man* (1897) and *The War of the Worlds* (1898).

■ Herbert George Wells

ACTIVITY: Tweet diary

We learn that Holsten writes a diary about his experiences, but today it might be more common for people to use social media to record and share their experiences.

With Twitter, people can write 'tweets' of 280 characters. What might Holsten have said if he had written a series of tweets about his experience discovering radiation, and of the following 24 hours as described in the extract from the novel?

Write down a series of ten tweets that Holsten might have written over this period.

◆ Assessment opportunities

In this activity you have practised skills that are assessed using Criterion C: Producing text and Criterion D: Using language.

ACTIVITY: The 'march of human progress' – the discovery of atomic energy

HG Wells' *The World Set Free* is a fictional account of a man, Holsten, discovering atomic energy, and his realization that it could lead to 'worlds of limitless power'. The selected passages on page 310 are drawn from the opening chapter of the book.

1　What kind of text is this? What makes you say that?
2　How does Holsten feel about his discovery of radioactivity? What details are given in this section of the text that makes you say that? List all of the details that show how Holsten is feeling.
3　What would you choose as the most important sentence in the opening paragraph? Why?
4　In the final two passages, what are we told that Holsten is afraid of?
5　**Identify** two possibilities that Holsten considers while thinking about whether he can stop his discovery becoming known.
6　State the reason why he thinks it would be pointless to burn his papers.
7　Holsten wonders if 'some secret association of wise men should take care of his work and hand it on from generation to generation until the world was riper for its practical application'. Should there be such an association in the world, which should take care of potentially very dangerous discoveries? Why (not)?

EXTENSION

Note down your thoughts on Question 7 then **organize** them into a one-minute speech that expresses your views on this. After preparing the speech, practise until you are confident. In small groups, present your speeches to each other.

◆ Assessment opportunities

In this activity you have practised skills that are assessed using Criterion A: Analysing, Criterion C: Producing text and Criterion D: Using language.

CHAPTER THE FIRST
THE NEW SOURCE OF ENERGY

The problem which was already being **mooted** by such scientific men as Ramsay, Rutherford, and Soddy, in the very beginning of the twentieth century, the problem of inducing radioactivity in the heavier elements and so tapping the internal energy of atoms, was solved by a wonderful combination of induction, intuition, and luck by Holsten so soon as the year 1933. From the first detection of radioactivity to its first **subjugation** to human purpose measured little more than a quarter of a century. For twenty years after that, indeed, minor difficulties prevented any striking practical application of his success, but the essential thing was done, this new boundary in the march of human progress was crossed, in that year. He set up atomic disintegration in a minute particle of **bismuth**; it exploded with great violence into a heavy gas of extreme radioactivity, which disintegrated in its turn in the course of seven days, and it was only after another year's work that he was able to show practically that the last result of this rapid release of energy was gold. But the thing was done – at the cost of a blistered chest and an injured finger, and from the moment when the invisible speck of bismuth flashed into riving and rending energy, Holsten knew that he had opened a way for mankind, however narrow and dark it might still be, to worlds of limitless power. He recorded as much in the strange diary biography he left the world, a diary that was up to that particular moment a mass of speculations and calculations, and which suddenly became for a space an amazingly minute and human record of sensations and emotions that all humanity might understand.

He gives, in broken phrases and often single words, it is true, but none the less vividly for that, a record of the twenty-four hours following the demonstration of the correctness of his intricate tracery of computations and guesses. 'I thought I should not sleep,' he writes – the words he omitted are supplied in brackets – (on account of) 'pain in (the) hand and chest and (the) wonder of what I had done ... Slept like a child.'

… [*Holsten, feeling 'strange and disconcerted the next morning', decides to go out, and is walking across London*] … Young Holsten's face was white. He walked with that uneasy **affectation** of ease that marks an overstrained nervous system and an under-exercised body. He hesitated at the White Stone Pond whether to go to the left of it or the right, and again at the fork of the roads. He kept shifting his stick in his hand, and every now and then he would get in the way of people on the footpath or be jostled by them because of the uncertainty of his movements. He felt, he confesses, 'inadequate to ordinary existence.' He seemed to himself to be something inhuman and mischievous. All the people about him looked fairly prosperous, fairly happy, fairly well adapted to the lives they had to lead – a week of work and a Sunday of best clothes and mild **promenading** – and he had launched something that would disorganise the entire fabric that held their contentments and ambitions and satisfactions together.

…

In the evening Holsten went out again. He walked to Saint Paul's Cathedral, and stood for a time near the door listening to the evening service. The candles upon the altar reminded him in some odd way of the fireflies at Fiesole. Then he walked back through the evening lights to Westminster. He was oppressed, he was indeed scared, by his sense of the immense consequences of his discovery. He had a vague idea that night that he ought not to publish his results, that they were premature, that some secret association of wise men should take care of his work and hand it on from generation to generation until the world was riper for its practical application. He felt that nobody in all the thousands of people he passed had really awakened to the fact of change, they trusted the world for what it was, not to alter too rapidly, to respect their trusts, their assurances, their habits, their little accustomed traffics and hard-won positions.

…

'It has begun,' he writes in the diary in which these things are recorded. 'It is not for me to reach out to consequences I cannot foresee. I am a part, not a whole; I am a little instrument in the armoury of Change. If I were to burn all these papers, before a score of years had passed, some other man would be doing this …

How can different texts show different points of view?

FICTION AND NON-FICTION TEXTS

The World Set Free is, we need to remember, a work of fiction. In it HG Wells narrates how the character Holsten discovers atomic power in 1933, and describes its **capacity** to be used both to aid mankind and to create bombs for use in war; all of which would later come true in real life. Wells himself in fact wrote this story in 1913, however – 20 years before the fictional world of Holsten, which he creates in the story. Though this story may sound like a historical account, all of his narrative about atomic power was actually largely guesswork on his part.

DISCUSS

Do the extracts sound to you as if they are taken from a fictional work? Could they be mistaken for a non-fiction, perhaps biographical, work? What differences are there between these two types of text?

ACTIVITY: Elements of fiction

ATL

- Critical-thinking skills: Gather and organize relevant information to formulate an argument; recognize unstated assumptions and bias; interpret data; evaluate evidence and arguments
- Communication skills: Read critically and for comprehension; make inferences and draw conclusions; use and interpret a range of discipline-specific terms and symbols

1 The key elements of fiction are noted here. For each, make notes about how these are used and/or presented in the extract from *The World Set Free.* We have looked at these elements in detail before (Chapter 5), so look back at this now if you need a reminder.

- Character
- Setting
- Plot
- Theme
- Narrative voice
- Dialogue
- Conflict
- Style

2 This element framework can guide your approach to critical interpretation of fictional texts, whether these are unseen or previously familiar. Write a 500–1,000 word commentary on some or all of the extract from *The World Set Free* on page 310. Detailed notes on how to tackle a written commentary are given in Chapter 9 (page 245), although it is a process largely based on brainstorming points, making notes and identifying aspects of technique.

◆ Assessment opportunities

In this activity you have practised skills that are assessed using Criterion A: Analysing, Criterion B: Organizing and Criterion D: Using language.

▼ Links to: History

J Robert Oppenheimer is credited as the 'father' of the atomic bomb, having led the development of the bomb during the **Manhattan Project**.

How did Oppenheimer feel about the project and the atomic bomb? The bomb was invented during the Second World War. Do you think the circumstances around the invention of the bomb affected his view? Did everyone feel the same way as Oppenheimer?

Atomic bombs

In 1945, atomic bombs developed by the Manhattan Project were dropped by the US air force onto the Japanese cities of Hiroshima and Nagasaki. In Hiroshima alone between 90,000 and 166,000 people died due to injury or radiation. About 70 per cent of the city's buildings were destroyed. These were the first, and so far only, times nuclear weapons have been used during war.

ACTIVITY: Elements of non-fiction

■ ATL

- Critical-thinking skills: Gather and organize relevant information to formulate an argument
- Communication skills: Read critically and for comprehension; make inferences and draw conclusions; organize and depict information logically

Like fiction, non-fiction texts also contain particular elements to consider. You are to **create** a framework that might be followed when a student has to critically **interpret** a non-fiction text.

First, search **How to read non-fiction texts** and research these elements now. Some examples are:

http://octavius.vibygym.dk/analyse-af-non-fiction.html

www.classroomnook.com/2017/02/teaching-nonfiction.html

In groups of four, combine your research (and the elements you have identified) in a table. Did you **identify** any of the following elements? If not, research and add these now:

- **Audience**
- **Purpose**
- **Bias**
- **Stylistic features**

As a group, **discuss** which elements you feel should be included in a non-fiction framework, and any further notes that might be given with each. Decide on a single final table or framework for approaching non-fiction texts that might be used by everyone.

As with fictional texts, this type of framework can guide your approach to critical interpretation of non-fiction texts.

EXTENSION

The non-fiction article below looks at predictions made by HG Wells. Use your non-fiction elements framework to write an analysis of it. Begin by making notes on how each of the elements relates to, appears, or is used in the text. Then, use these notes to write and structure your overall analysis of the text. Write 500–1,000 words.

https://qz.com/806857/a-british-sci-fi-writer-made-a-series-of-utopian-predictions-100-years-ago-and-was-right-about-nearly-all-of-them/

◆ Assessment opportunities

In this activity you have practised skills that are assessed using Criterion A: Analysing and Criterion D: Using language.

ACTIVITY: Differences between fiction and non-fiction

■ ATL

- Communication skills: Organize and depict information logically

Return to your previous groups of four. Use a Venn diagram to compare the elements of fiction and non-fiction. Which elements are found in both text-types?

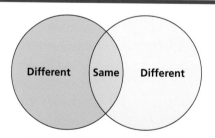

Different | Same | Different

◆ Assessment opportunities

In this activity you have practised skills that are assessed using Criterion B: Organizing.

What are the consequences of innovation?

ACTIVITY: *Enola Gay*

■ ATL

- Communication skills: Read critically and for comprehension
- Critical-thinking skills: Gather and organize relevant information to formulate an argument

The aeroplane that carried the atomic bomb and dropped it over Hiroshima was called *Enola Gay*. The pilot that day, Colonel Paul Tibbets, named the plane after his mother. The bomb itself was nicknamed 'Little Boy'.

A song entitled 'Enola Gay' was written and performed by a group called Orchestral Manoeuvres in the Dark during the 1980s. Watch the music video and find the lyrics online: **https://youtu.be/-vMBp6iUJzk.**

Answer the following questions:

1 What are the 'games' being referred to in the lyrics? What figure of speech is being used? Why was the word 'games' used here?
2 *'We got your message on the radio, conditions normal and you're coming home'* – Who is the speaker of these lines? Why are these lines ironic in the context?
3 *'Enola Gay, is mother proud of little boy today'* – What are the two meanings of this line?
4 What is the 'kiss' that is referred to? What imagery is being used? Why is it 'never ever gonna fade away'?

◆ Assessment opportunities

In this activity you have practised skills that are assessed using Criterion A: Analysing.

ACTIVITY: The power of poetry

■ ATL

- Communication skills: Read critically and for comprehension; use and interpret a range of discipline-specific terms and symbols; use a variety of organizers for academic writing tasks

The poem 'August 6' (on page 314) is named for the date the atomic bomb was dropped on Hiroshima. Written by Sankichi Tōge, a Japanese poet who survived the atomic bombing of Hiroshima, the poem presents a graphic description of the explosion of the atomic bomb and its immediate impact.

How does the poem make you feel? What is the poem trying to argue?

Make some initial notes on these two questions then get into a group of four to six. Do you have similar feelings as your group? Did you, or can you, agree as a group on what the poem is trying to argue?

Divide a piece of poster paper into six equal sections, and assign each section to a different group member. The sections should have the following headings: Words, Perspective, Tone, Techniques, Sound and Context. On the poster paper, each person should write notes on the stylistic technique or element that headlines their section.

As a group, move anticlockwise around the paper so that you are now looking at a new section. Read the notes your classmate made, then add any further notes you think appropriate. Continue in this way until each 'station' has had notes added by at least three members of the group.

Display all of the sheets on the classroom wall, and carry out a gallery walk of the whole class.

Return to your own poster paper, and add anything further that you have learned from or observed in other groups' posters.

◆ Assessment opportunities

In this activity you have practised skills that are assessed using Criterion A: Analysing, Criterion B: Organizing and Criterion D: Using language.

August 6

can we forget that flash?
suddenly 30,000 in the streets disappeared
in the crushed depths of darkness
the shrieks of 50,000 died out
when the swirling yellow smoke thinned   5
buildings split, bridges collapsed
packed trains rested singed
and a shoreless accumulation of rubble and embers – Hiroshima
before long, a line of naked bodies walking in groups, crying
with skin hanging down like rags   10
hands on chests
stamping on crumbled brain matter
burnt clothing covering hips
corpses lie on the parade ground like stone images of Jizo, dispersed in all
directions   15
on the banks of the river, lying one on top of another, a group that had crawled to
a tethered raft
also gradually transformed into corpses beneath the sun's scorching rays
and in the light of the flames that pierced the evening sky
the place where mother and younger brother were pinned under   20
alive
also was engulfed in flames
and when the morning sun shone on a group of high-school girls
who had fled and were lying
on the floor of the armory, in excrement   25
their bellies swollen, one eye crushed, half their bodies raw flesh
with skin ripped
off, hairless, impossible to tell who was who
all had stopped moving
in a stagnant, offensive smell   30
the only sound the wings of flies buzzing around metal basins
city of 300,000
can we forget that silence?
in that stillness
the powerful appeal   35
of the white eye sockets of the wives and children who did not
return home
that tore apart our hearts
can it be forgotten?!

Sankichi Tōge, translated by Karen Thornber

www.pbs.org/newshour/features/hiroshima-poems/

Language and Literature for the IB MYP 4&5: *by Concept*

ACTIVITY: Who's responsible?

■ ATL

- ■ Creative-thinking skills: Practise flexible thinking – develop multiple opposing contradictory and complementary arguments

Who was responsible for the decision to drop the atomic bomb on Japan during the Second World War? Should they have been?

In groups of four or five, assign each group member one of the groups or institutions below. Individually, research your assigned group and decide whether you think they *were* responsible, *should* have been responsible, or *should not* have been responsible for the decision to drop an atomic bomb.

- **The US government**
- **The pilot and crew of the *Enola Gay***
- **The Allies (UK, USA, USSR, France)**
- **The League of Nations**
- **Someone else …**

Use your research notes to prepare a two-minute speech that **outlines** your position. After everyone in the group has spoken, decide together if there is one group or institution responsible for the bombing. Is there more than one? Can you agree?

◆ Assessment opportunities

In this activity you have practised skills that are assessed using Criterion A: Analysing, Criterion C: Producing text and Criterion D: Using language.

DISCUSS

Discuss the rhetorical techniques used in the Martin Amis extract. What is the effect of each one? How would you describe the tone used in the extract? What makes you say that?

NUCLEAR FEARS

In 1987, Martin Amis wrote a non-fiction essay about his fear of nuclear weapons, titled 'Thinkability'.

> What is the only provocation that could bring about the use of nuclear weapons? Nuclear weapons. What is the priority target for nuclear weapons? Nuclear weapons. What is the only established defence against nuclear weapons? Nuclear weapons. How do we prevent the use of nuclear weapons? By threatening to use nuclear weapons. And we can't get rid of nuclear weapons, because of nuclear weapons. The intransigence [refusal to change a view or position], it seems, is a function of the weapons themselves. Nuclear weapons can kill a human being a dozen times over in a dozen different ways; and before death – like certain spiders, like the headlights of cars – they seem to paralyse.

NUCLEAR ENERGY

As we have seen, radiation is a double-edged sword – used both for life-saving medical treatments and in the production of nuclear bombs. Nuclear energy is produced at nuclear power plants, and is considered a possible answer to the world's energy and pollution problems. It also brings many risks, however, including the risk of accidents.

There are a number of non-fiction blogs online that examine the advantages and risks of nuclear power. One blog post is linked below, or you might search for **blog advantages risks of nuclear power** and find your own: **http://sitn.hms. harvard.edu/flash/2016/reconsidering-risks-nuclear-power/**.

Choose the article you think best explores the opportunities and risks of nuclear power. In pairs, share your articles with each other. **Select** one of the articles and, together, **discuss** what each paragraph is saying. For each paragraph you should write one sentence, phrase or question that summarizes it. Now, arrange these phrases in a list. This will

ACTIVITY: Un-inventing technology

■ ATL

- Critical-thinking skills: Consider ideas from multiple perspectives; evaluate and manage risk

Amis continues in *Thinkability* to express his disapproval of the fact that nuclear weapons, now invented, cannot be un-invented.

The magazine *New Scientist* once asked readers what they would like to un-invent, if they had the chance. Some of the responses included:
- **mobile phones**
- **life-support machines**
- **the personal computer**
- **cars**
- **television**
- **the combustion engine**
- **cigarettes**
- **plastic grocery bags.**

For each suggestion, write a reason why it should be un-invented, and a reason why it should remain. Afterwards, think about what you might want to un-invent, then write a paragraph explaining your object and giving your reasons. You should be as persuasive as possible, so think about what stylistic and literary techniques you might use.

◆ Assessment opportunities

In this activity you have practised skills that are assessed using Criterion C: Producing text and Criterion D: Using language.

quickly give you an overview of what the text is saying and its structure.

You have read a lot about both the potential risks and benefits of nuclear power, and you can find out more about these in *Physics for the IB MYP 4&5: by Concept*, Chapters 11 and 12. This might be helpful in approaching the next activity, in which you will need to take on the role of someone who has to make a decision about whether to allow a nuclear power plant to be built locally, and in making that decision must consider all of the possible risks and benefits such a plant may bring with it.

ACTIVITY: Should we build a nuclear power plant?

- Collaboration skills: Listen actively to other perspectives and ideas; build consensus
- Critical-thinking skills: Gather and organize relevant information to formulate an argument
- Creative-thinking skills: Use brainstorming and visual diagrams to generate new ideas and inquiries

A town council needs to decide whether to allow the building of a nuclear power plant in the council's district.

In groups of four to six, imagine you are the town council. You should brainstorm some of the arguments for and against using nuclear power.

As a town council you can use a strategy called an 'options diamond' to interrogate the possibility of a nuclear power plant being built locally. The 'Options diamond' ATL cog below shows how this works.

You can also use question stems to help you **identify** and consider key points and options surrounding the construction of a nuclear power plant. Some example stems are below (there are more in Chapter 1 on page 5).

- Why ...?
- Is it true that ...?
- How might things change if ...?
- What information might be useful?
- What is the purpose of ...?
- What are some of the problems of ...?
- What is the value of ...?
- How would you feel if ...?
- What do you think could/will happen ...?
- Can you see a possible solution to ...?

As a group, decide on the nuclear power plant option you prefer, and indicate this clearly on your options diamond chart.

Each group should display their completed chart at different points of the classroom, spaced far enough apart for groups to gather round and **explore** them.

Hold a gallery walk. As you read the other groups' charts, note down any points you think are good, and which you had not made yourself.

Once you have looked at all of the other charts, return to your own chart and add any of the new ideas you noted down.

Options diamond

The process for developing an **options diamond** is detailed below. The question of building a nuclear power plant locally is used as an example:

- Draw a large diamond in the middle of a piece of poster paper.
- In the centre of the diamond, write 'Building a nuclear power plant options'.
- At the left-hand point of the diamond, write one or two main points in favour of allowing the building of the nuclear power plant.

- At the right-hand point of the diamond, write one or two main points against allowing the building of the nuclear power plant.
- Add to each diamond point possible advantages and disadvantages of the decision.
- Then add in individual circles around each any possible solutions to problems caused.
- Continue to think through possible options relating to building a nuclear power plant locally, including compromise options.

You can find out more about how to use the options diamond here: **https://goo.gl/hfCLsi**.

Combine opposites

Main points in favour of building a nuclear power plant

Main points against building a nuclear power plant

Reject any proposal to build a nuclear power plant

Cheaper and more plentiful fuel, with less pollution. Safer to produce than many other types of fuel. Increased employment.

Nuclear power plant policy opposites (trade-offs)

Nuclear power perceived as dangerous. Fears of long-term risks to health of those living locally. Impact on visitors to town/tourism?

Build a nuclear power plant regardless of concerns

Carry out a complete risk assessment and drop the project if risks are identified which seem too great

Compromise between opposites

ACTIVITY: Report writing

The town council must now write a report summarizing the possible options, stating which option has been chosen by the council and giving the reasons for that choice.

Write a mini-report, which should be between 800 and 1,000 words.

The structure of a report is outlined in the ATL cog on 'Report writing', and some links to further resources are also there. For this report, remember:

● **who you are writing for (the people of the town)**
● **what the purpose of the report is (informing the people of the town of the council's discussions about the possibility of allowing a nuclear power plant to be built in the local area)**
● **what the focus of the report should be (the options available and discussed, and the council's decision on that with the reasons for it).**

Your report should be individually written, rather than as a group. As it is an individual task, you can choose whichever nuclear power plant option you personally prefer, regardless of what your group decided in the 'Should we build a nuclear power plant?' activity. Bear in mind, however, that there may have been more discussion, and more notes available, on the group's final choice.

Report writing

Report writing is an academic writing task commonly assigned to students. Unlike an essay (which is often discursive and focused on demonstrating what you think about a topic), a report is written to communicate the results or findings of a project. Owing to this, a report is generally more concise, and more formally structured, than an essay. When writing a report, remember:

● who you are writing for
● what the purpose of the report is
● what the focus of the report should be.

The main elements of a report are listed below:

● Cover page
● Contents page
● Investigating
● Planning
● Taking action
● Reflecting
● Bibliography
● Appendices

There are many online resources explaining these elements further. Some links are below, or you could try searching online for **university guidelines for writing a report**.

https://www2.le.ac.uk/offices/ld/resources/writing/writing-resources/reports

https://library.leeds.ac.uk/info/14011/writing/114/report_writing

SOME SUMMATIVE TASKS TO TRY

Use these tasks to apply and extend your learning in this chapter. These tasks are designed so that you can evaluate your learning at different levels of achievement in the Language and literature criteria.

Task 1: Discursive writing

'Technology is always a two-edged sword. It will bring in many benefits, but also many disasters.' – Alan Moore

In what ways has technology brought both benefits and disasters? **Identify** one technological invention (that you have not yet discussed) and write a 500–1,000 word essay that presents both sides of the issue. Support your points with justifications, examples, and/or reasons. Conclude the essay by stating your own opinion in the final paragraph.

Task 2: Magazine feature article

You may remember in *The World Set Free*, one character, upon discovering atomic energy *'… had a vague idea that night that he ought not to publish his results, that they were premature, that some secret association of wise men should take care of his work and hand it on from generation to generation until the world was riper for its practical application.'*

Write a magazine opinion piece in which you argue that governments should (or should not!) keep information about potential dangers to the world – such as the sighting of a UFO, or a dangerous discovery – secret from the general population.

Your article should try to persuade the reader, so remember to acknowledge counter-arguments and use any persuasive literary techniques when appropriate.

The text should be in a formal register, although given that this writing is expressing a personal opinion, aspects of your personal voice may also be evident in it.

You should write between 500 and 1,000 words, although the work should be closer to 1,000 words in order to contain the range of points and details that are needed for highest levels of achievement in the assessment criteria.

Task 3: Commentary – poetry

Esther Pang Hui Min's poem 'Technology' (page 320) offers another perspective on the double-edged nature of technology. **Analyse** the poem using the skills you have learned in previous chapters (refer to ATL cogs on page 243 if required). Some guiding questions are suggested below, which you may use if you wish to, but you do not have to.

Write between 500 and 1,000 words.

Guiding questions:

- What is the speaker's attitude towards technology, and what evidence can you find for that?
- What stylistic devices are used to convey the points of view expressed in the poem?
- How does the poet make use of contrast in various ways throughout the poem?

Task 4: Comparative writing

Find and read online the following two texts, which both talk about the dropping of the atomic bomb on Hiroshima.

Analyse, **compare and contrast** these texts. Include comments on the similarities and differences between the texts and the significance of context, audience, purpose and formal and stylistic features.

- *Reunion of the Enola Gay* by Henry Allen: **https://goo.gl/b399F9**
- Extract from *Aerial Photograph Before the Atomic Bomb* by Toi Derricotte: **www.pbs.org/newshour/features/hiroshima-poems/** – from 'Everything / looked green … ' to the end of the poem.

Technology

In a world without technology,
can you imagine how it would be?
To not have any lights.
We'll probably stay home at night.

In a world without technology,
we'll lose forms of connectivity.
We'll not have wifi or 3G,
distance will be as it should be.

However, without technology,
We won't have people far away,
because we can only walk on foot.
Most will live at home for good.

Without technology,
perhaps there'll be more sincerity,
where more people would be seen,
not looking at their phone screens.

Instead they'll stop and listen,
giving undivided attention,
to the people by their side.

Perhaps without technology,
we would have to do things
    manually.
Life may be tough physically.

But with technology,
is our life really that easy?
Is the world really as it should be?
Are people living in harmony?

Or is there more strife?
More people losing their lives?
Or is there more pain,
more people dying in vain?

What about pollution?
Isn't it part of our contribution?

All the fuels and carbon,
it'll soon bring us to extinction.

Our earth today is now diseased,
life on earth is not at peace.
We can deny all this,

And this is the utter irony,
while it gives us mass connection,

It reduces engagement,
attention and perhaps even
    compassion.
'Across the globe, millions reported
    dying',
ends up being desensitizing.

Technology's connectivity,
leaves us more detached than we
    should be.

Esther Pang Hui Min

Take action

! In the course of this chapter we have been looking at how innovations are frequently 'double-edged swords', which, while representing progress of some kind that can help significantly in the world, also bring with them dangers and downsides. Some of the latter can be on a very great scale.

! Meanwhile, taking 'action' can mean a number of different things. You are probably aware that it often means taking some kind of **direct action**, or **indirect action** such as raising money to donate to a cause.

! However, we need to be informed about something in order to know what action – direct or indirect – to take, and how to do so effectively. **Research** is therefore also an important type of action which can be taken.

! And sometimes the action we can take may be to urge others to do something, or do it differently. This type of action is known as **advocacy**, and it is also an important kind of action.

! Action which you take over the MYP as a whole should include all four kinds at different times: research, advocacy, indirect action, and direct action.

! This section focuses on two different scenarios which involve research and advocacy as the types of action you might take in some situations.

1 Energy conservation

! The first scenario focuses on energy conservation – an important consideration for the world as sources from which some types of energy are derived are finite, which means that they will only last a certain amount of time. It is thought, for instance, that some of the fossil fuels used in producing energy may run out in about 50 years.

! This means that there is a need to think of other possible sources of energy, and is a reason why nuclear power and other alternative sources of energy are considered so seriously and used, despite concerns about possible dangers.

➤

! Most energy which we use every day still comes from fossil fuels, however, and in order to make them last longer there is a need to conserve energy where possible. Where in your school might you do this? You are going to research knowledge and ideas on this, and then engage in advocacy of different kinds to try to persuade different members of the school community to conserve energy in the school wherever possible.

Research

! Get into a group of three or four. Each of you should use the search terms 'energy saving tips for school' and 'how can we save energy in school?' to find websites which provide information on this topic.

! Each member of the group should ensure he or she looks at three different websites on this, and writes down a bullet point list of ideas and tips to be used to pass on to others. Ensure you all make careful note of the website details and addresses so that you can cite and reference them properly at the end.

! Once everyone has made their notes from the websites, come together as a group and share the ideas that you all have.

! Use the table below to decide on which pieces of information, advice and tips might be best suited for different audiences within your school community. Some of these might be the same for everyone, and some might be especially relevant to particular people or groups, so think carefully about who could do what, as you complete the table:

Fellow MYP students	
Primary school students	
Older students in your school	
Teachers	
Parents	
Members of your school's leadership team, who might be able to tell everyone else in the school to do things if they think your ideas are good ones	
Any other group in the school, such as those who help to maintain it	

! Decide on a full and final list which fits your own school context best, and which you will be using in creating a product or products to use in advocating conservation of energy to your school community.

Advocating

! Once you have the information you need, you can decide on how best to use it within your own school context. You may, for instance create the following products:

◆ a presentation for a meeting or assembly, using PowerPoint, Prezi or something similar. Your presentation will depend on your audience, and so think carefully about tips and advice for those, use of images and language, and so on, as they may be different for parents than for primary students, for instance.

◆ two or three different posters to put up around the school. Again, audience is an important consideration. Where might posters be placed, and who might see them there? What would be helpful to include in them? How can they be made to look appealing and to draw people's attention?

◆ a web page to add to the school's website. Once more it will be important to think about who the main audience(s) might be for this, and to design the layout, information and language accordingly. In the case of a web page anyone from outside the school may be able to access it, unless it is on a restricted access part of the site.

◆ as part of an assembly or meeting presentation, or to include on a web page – or even just to be used as a standalone in classes, you might want to create an informational video, filmed around the school.

◆ a brochure or handout might also be considered, so that any audience can take away ideas and remind themselves of them afterwards. Electronic versions of these can also be emailed to parents and students, as a more environmentally friendly way of distributing such reminders.

! You may have other ideas for products, which is fine. And of course the above can be combined in any way. Which audiences you might be able to present to in the different ways, and which of the above products might be most possible and effective, will depend very much on your own school context. It might be good to try to create two of the products, and to reach out to two different audiences, if you can do so. You might also plan some research to try to investigate how effective your campaign, and the different products you have created, have been, after a certain period.

➤

2 Social action

! The second looks further at the possible consequences when technology goes wrong. We have seen in the chapter dangers associated with the technology used in nuclear power plants, but others exist with other types of energy-related production. The following link, for instance, provides a list of the largest oil spills to have taken place, which can create immense environmental damage, as was the case where technology failure led to the Deepwater Horizon disaster which you may have heard about, and which is one of the disasters included in the article: www.telegraph.co.uk/news/worldnews/australiaandthepacific/newzealand/8812598/10-largest-oil-spills-in-history.html

! A disaster involving the production of pesticides, meanwhile, took place in Bhopal in India in 1984, where a leak of poisonous gas from a factory in the city was estimated to have caused up to 10,000 deaths. Many more people living in and around the city were affected with illness, while limited hospital facilities at the time made the situation extremely difficult to deal with.

! Even 30 years after the disaster, victims were still waiting for compensation, and court cases were still continuing to try to establish who was responsible for what happened.

! Sometimes where people see a situation which they perceive to be unjust, they feel it may help to start or sign a petition, or to start writing letters expressing their views, suggesting solutions, and so on. If lots of people do this, it can help to bring the issue to public attention and put pressure on others involved to do something about the situation.

! Imagine you felt the situation was unfair for some of the victims, and wanted to write a letter to express your views on this, and suggest what could and should be done. This is again an example of advocacy, and to do this you again need to research information about the event and current situation in order to write an informed 'social action' letter.

Research

! Look at the following videos and websites, which will give you an idea of the background and issues facing some of the people who were caught up in the Bhopal explosion:

Videos

◆ India's Bhopal Gas Disaster explained: www.youtube.com/watch?v=bxdm3JIN3IM (1 min 7 secs)

◆ Seismic Seconds Part 1: www.youtube.com/watch?v=p0aGBPdpMTM (9 mins 25 secs)

◆ Seismic Seconds Part 2: www.youtube.com/watch?v=-FYvWTO70FE (9 mins 20 secs)

◆ Seismic Seconds Part 3: www.youtube.com/watch?v=aSZ9fuRzers (5 mins 2 secs)

Websites

◆ https://goo.gl/mUvaZm

◆ http://blogs.worldbank.org/voices/remembering-bhopal-30-years-later

◆ http://news.bbc.co.uk/2/hi/south_asia/8726671.stm

◆ www.theguardian.com/environment/2009/dec/04/bhopal-25-years-indra-sinha

! You may like to find more yourself to look at, but these should give a good idea of what the disaster was, along with who was affected and how.

! As you look through your sources, write down any details which you particularly notice for some reason, for instance, that they cause you to feel certain emotions such as shock, anger, sadness, and so on. You might like to capture these in the following table:

Detail from source (quote or paraphrase)	Emotion(s) evoked, and why

Advocacy

! Now that you know something about what happened at Bhopal, you are going to write a formal letter to an editor of a newspaper expressing your views on what you have read.

1 **Either choose one of the websites given above, or find another which carries news of the Bhopal disaster. You can look at more websites by searching on the phrase Bhopal disaster newspaper article.**

2 **Decide on the particular article that you want to respond to with a letter to the editor of the newspaper.**

3 **Look at the following three web pages, which each give a step-by-step guide on how to write a letter to a newspaper editor. Read through all of the details on each:**

◇ **https://ctb.ku.edu/en/table-of-contents/advocacy/direct-action/letters-to-editor/main**

- ◇ www.wikihow.com/Write-Letters-to-the-Editor
- ◇ www.treatmentadvocacycenter.org/storage/documents/writingalettertotheeditor.pdf

4   Note on the web pages the suggestions for the different possible purposes which readers may have for writing a letter to a newspaper editor:

- ◆ You are angry about an issue and you want the readers to know about it.
- ◆ You want to publicly congratulate or support something or someone in your community.
- ◆ You want to correct information in an article.
- ◆ You want to suggest an idea to others.
- ◆ You want to influence public opinion or persuade others to take action.
- ◆ You want to influence policymakers or elected officials.
- ◆ You want to publicise a certain organization's work in connection with a current news issue.

Look at the notes you made in your research on Bhopal, and the details you particularly noted. What are the most important ones, and why? Your answers to those questions are likely to indicate what you are most interested in about this event. You can decide what will be the main purpose of your own letter, based on what you have found most notable and important, in relation to the Bhopal disaster.

5   **Follow each step outlined in the web page guides to writing a letter to the editor of the newspaper which you chose earlier in this process. As advised there, you should not write more than 300 words.**

!   If a group of you do this, you should peer review each others' letters once everyone has completed a draft of theirs, before revising and refining the letters as may be needed.

!   This particular activity has hopefully shown you how to use what can be a powerful tool for advocacy – writing a formal letter to a newspaper editor which is informed and has a clear purpose, and is effective; and which may therefore help bring about awareness of some kind, or even contribute towards change. You might follow this up by identifying a local, or even school, issue, and writing – and sending – a 'social action' letter to an editor on that, and seeing if it is published.

!   If not, you should have the learning and awareness about social action letters to try again – whenever may be needed.

Reflection

In this chapter we have looked at various innovations, mainly scientific and technological, and how these have had the potential to change lives, both for better and for worse. As such they are examples of what is known as a 'double-edged sword' – something that can at the same time bring both positive and negative effects or consequences. We have thus explored both opportunities that innovations bring, and the dangers that may be associated with them; along with what responsibilities different individuals, organizations, governments and so on may have in managing these – particularly as innovations cannot be un-invented afterwards. Finally, we have considered particular innovations that are especially important within our own lives, and how we might engage with these in a responsible way. All of this has allowed us to consider how to read, interpret and create different kinds of writing (both fiction and non-fiction) and to examine too how to cite and reference – a very important aspect of academic honesty, and of understanding authentic authorship – both our own work and that of others.

Use this table to reflect on your own learning in this chapter.					
Questions we asked	**Answers we found**	**Any further questions now?**			
Factual:					
Conceptual:					
Debatable:					
Approaches to learning you used in this chapter	**Description – what new skills did you learn?**	**How well did you master the skills?**			
		Novice	Learner	Practitioner	Expert
Communication skills					
Collaboration skills					
Creative-thinking skills					
Critical-thinking skills					
Information literacy skills					
Learner profile attribute(s)	Reflect on the importance of being principled for your learning in this chapter.				
Principled					

12 What am I responsible for?

○ Ideas about personal responsibility presented in a cultural **context** can lead readers to examine the impact of their actions on **those around them**.

KEY WORDS

atmosphere	intervene
connotations	intriguing
contrast	revelation

CONSIDER THESE QUESTIONS:

Factual: What is 'personal responsibility'? What can be involved in taking 'personal responsibility'? What kinds of things might we take responsibility for? What is loyalty?

Conceptual: How can events and choices shape us? How can a cultural context influence our understanding of personal responsibility?

Debatable: To what extent is it possible to atone for past mistakes? Is there a cultural influence in decision-making?

Now **share and compare** your thoughts and ideas with your partner, or with the whole class.

○ IN THIS CHAPTER, WE WILL …

■ **Find out** what kinds of things taking responsibility for something can involve.

■ **Explore** how our choices and decisions can influence what happens in our lives and the kinds of people we are.

■ **Take action** by evaluating our own responsibilities and how we might face up to those in life.

■ These Approaches to Learning (ATL) skills will be useful …

- Communication skills
- Collaboration skills
- Organization skills
- Reflection skills
- Information literacy skills
- Critical-thinking skills
- Creative-thinking skills

◆ Assessment opportunities in this chapter:

- ◆ **Criterion A:** Analysing
- ◆ **Criterion B:** Organizing
- ◆ **Criterion C:** Producing text
- ◆ **Criterion D:** Using language

● We will reflect on this learner profile attribute …

- Reflective – develop skills of reflection through various activities which involve thoughtfully considering the world and our own ideas and experience; work to understand strengths and weaknesses and how these may support personal learning and development.

Never regret anything that has happened in your life. It cannot be changed, undone or forgotten. So take it as a lesson and move on.

The beauty of life is, while we cannot undo what is done, we can see it, understand it, learn from it and change so that every new moment is spent not in regret, guilt, fear or anger, but in wisdom, understanding and love.
– Jennifer Edwards

The worst feeling is regretting not having done something when you had the chance.

THERE'S ALWAYS THAT ONE STUPID MISTAKE THAT CHANGES EVERYTHING.

We all make mistakes, have struggles, and even regret things in our past. But you are not your struggles, and you are here now with the power to shape your day and your future.
– Steve Maraboli

One of the most difficult things to think about in life is one's regrets. Something will happen to you and you will do the wrong things, and for years afterwards you will wish you had done something different.
— Lemony Snicket

I regret nothing in my life even if my past was full of hurt, I look back and smile, because it made me who I am today.

ACTIVITY: Je ne regrette rien? (Do I regret anything?)

ATL

- Collaboration skills: Take responsibility for one's own actions

The title of this activity is taken from the title of a famous song called 'Non, Je Ne Regrette Rien', by French singer **Edith Piaf**. You can watch her performing the song here: **https://youtu.be/rzy2wZSg5ZM**.

Find an English language translation of the song's lyrics online and, after reading them through, think of three or four things that you have done in your own life, which you now regret. Use the table below to record any thoughts and notes you have for each regret.

Which of the quotations above best represent your own attitude to regret? Choose one and, in pairs, explain to each other the reason for your choices.

◆ Assessment opportunities

This activity can be assessed using Criterion A: Analysing.

	What did you say or do that you now regret?	Why do you regret it now?	In what way(s) was what you did a 'learning curve'? What did you learn from it that you put into practice now, as a result?	Is there anything you could do at this point to take personal responsibility for putting it right? If so, what? If not, why not?
1				
2				
3				
4				

What is 'personal responsibility'?

ACTIVITY: Are you responsible?

In 2016, a telephone box was placed in different locations around Fife, Scotland. The telephone was called and, when passers-by answered it, they were asked 20 questions about themselves. You can watch a video of the phone calls here: https://youtu.be/KMWt3k-3YJo.

Some of the personal responsibility questions asked were:

1 **What would you stand up and fight for?**
2 **What do you save for?**
3 **When did you last cry?**
4 **Tell me something good about you.**
5 **What are your bad habits?**
6 **How do other people react to your bad habits?**
7 **Describe a moment when you wish you had spoken up or spoken out.**
8 **Do you believe in true love?**
9 **Give some advice to all of us.**
10 **Name five people you love and tell me why.**

In pairs, ask each other the questions about personal responsibility. The person responding each time should be recorded on video, which might be by using a smartphone, iPad, camera, and so on.

In groups of four, watch each other's videos and write a group definition for 'personal responsibility', then list what you feel people should take personal responsibility for.

Display each group's poster on the wall, and take a gallery walk to look at the other groups' ideas on this.

As a class, with the help of your teacher, you might come up with a final definition and list.

ACTIVITY: Personal responsibility in different social and cultural contexts

You may have found that the responses to the questions about personal responsibility in the 'Are you responsible?' activity were very varied. One reason for this is that our ideas about what we should take responsibility for, and how we should do that, are influenced by our own contexts. This can lead to different understandings and expectations of what 'taking responsibility' means in particular situations.

Look at the following categories then choose four that you feel the strongest sense of responsibility towards. Number these from 1 to 4, with 1 being most responsibility and 4 being least responsibility.

Self	Family	Friends
School	Clubs	Neighbourhood
Religious community	Ethnic community	Country
Humankind		

Next, draw four concentric circles then add to them the four categories you chose. Number 1 should be in the middle, moving outwards to number 4.

In each ring add at least one example of how you show personal responsibility for that category. If needed, you might **discuss** in groups or as a class beforehand what some examples of demonstrating personal responsibility in each case may be.

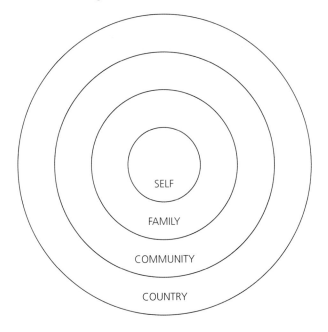

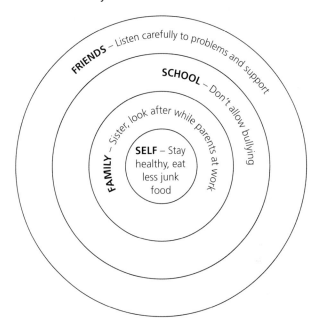

Get into groups and compare your diagrams. Which categories were chosen as priorities? Why? Share your group discussion with the rest of the class and then, as a class, **discuss** how social and/or cultural factors may lead to different ideas about what 'personal responsibility' might actually mean in practice.

ACTIVITY: What other choices might social and cultural contexts affect?

ATL

■ Critical-thinking skills: Consider ideas from multiple perspectives

Consider the scenarios, which are often associated with personal responsibility choices, listed in the table below.

Drinking alcohol	Taking exams	Bullying	Leading a team
Making a mistake	Being with people whom you perceive to be of a different social class	Food choices	College and career choices

For each category, write a comment on an individual sticky note about what it means to you to take personal responsibility in each area. These comments should be anonymous. While you are doing this your teacher will write out each table heading on separate pieces of poster paper and display these on the classroom walls. Stick your anonymous sticky note comments under each correct heading.

As a class, **discuss** what differences there are in how people see personal responsibility in each of these areas.

How can events and choices shape us?

■ ATL

- Creative-thinking skills: Consider multiple alternatives, including those that might be unlikely or impossible
- Critical-thinking skills: Draw reasonable conclusions and generalizations

Read the opening paragraph of *The Kite Runner*. It uses a first-person narrator. What else do we learn about the narrator in this opening? **Identify** some specific details from this text in the table opposite, and explain what each one tells us about the narrator and his life. A couple of examples are given for you:

THE KITE RUNNER

The **protagonist** of *The Kite Runner*, Amir, is deeply troubled by an incident that took place at a kite-fighting competition in Kabul when he was a boy. He has never been able to escape how he acted in response to the incident, and the guilt it makes him feel.

Amir grew up Kabul but, when it was invaded by the Russian army, Amir and his father Baba escape to the United States. Later Kabul is invaded again, this time by the **Taliban**. The novel opens with an adult Amir, at his home in San Francisco, telling the reader that 'it's wrong what they say about the past, I've learned, about how you can bury it. Because the past claws its way out'. However, he has just at this point received a phone call, telling him that 'There is a way to be good again'.

The Kite Runner divides into three sections overall, and we shall look at these sections in turn. The first section introduces us to the major themes of the novel, as listed by Hosseini in his foreword. It also shows us the main characters, as well as the relationships between them, which are where these themes often arise in the novel.

ℹ *The Kite Runner* is a novel set mainly in Afghanistan in the years before, during and after the coming of the Taliban. It centres on the story of the narrator and protagonist Amir, son of a wealthy father, whose mother died while giving birth to him. Amir's best friend is Hassan, the son (as he thinks) of his father's servant, and a boy who is devoted to Amir. The novel's title reflects a common pastime in Kabul of flying kites, with 'kite runners' being those who chase and retrieve kites that have landed. Hassan is Amir's kite runner, and is an expert at this.

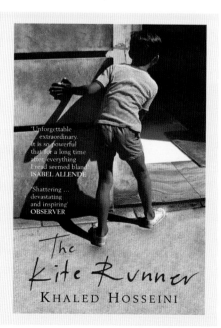

'Unforgettable ... extraordinary. It is so powerful that for a long time after, everything I read seemed bland'
ISABEL ALLENDE

'Shattering ... devastating and inspiring'
OBSERVER

The Kite Runner
KHALED HOSSEINI

Text detail	What it may tell us about the narrator and his life
'December 2001'; 'the age of twelve'; 'in the winter of 1975'	The dates given tell us that the narrator is 38 (possibly 37) years old.
'I remember the precise moment …'	Whatever happened on that day in 1975 was clearly something very significant to the narrator, as the precise moment has stayed with him ever since.

If you would like to hear the author reading Chapter 1 of the novel, an audio recording of this can be found here: https://soundcloud.com/simonschuster/kite-runner-audio-by-khaled.

THINK–PAIR–SHARE

With a partner, share the details that you chose from the paragraph, and your ideas about those. Each of you should add any additional details and points that you think are important to your own table, if you missed them out.

Then share your details and ideas in larger groups, again adding anything further to your own table that you omitted but think may be important.

◆ Assessment opportunities

This activity can be assessed using Criterion D: Using language.

ACTIVITY: Themes of *The Kite Runner*

■ ATL

■ Critical-thinking skills: Gather and organize relevant information to formulate an argument

The author, Khaled Hosseini, has spoken of his 'astonishment … at the reception this book has received worldwide since its publication'. He attributes this to some of the 'universal … human experiences' that the book explores – 'shame, guilt, regret, friendship, love, forgiveness, atonement' – things that affect everyone at different times in their lives. In this comment Hosseini lists some of the main themes of the novel. These are important ideas in the book, and so let us consider first of all what they mean.

1 **Discuss** in small groups what each of the terms in the table means, and give an example of each one. Next, in pairs, try to **identify** each of these themes in Chapter 1. Make sure to support your arguments by noting examples of where they are referenced.

Term	Meaning	Example	Chapter 1 reference
Shame			
Guilt			
Regret			
Friendship			
Love			
Forgiveness			
Atonement			

2 A further theme in the novel is introduced in the very first sentence – 'I became what I am today at the age of twelve …'; it is then referred to several times more in the chapter. Can you tell what it is from the opening, and following, sentences?

> Looking back now, I realize I have been peeking into that deserted alley for the last twenty-six years.

> I knew it wasn't just Rahim Khan on the line. It was my past of unatoned sins.

> … the winter of 1975 came along and changed everything. And made me what I am today.

The theme being referred to in all of these quotations is that of how the past affects and shapes us and our lives in the present. The idea also implies that our present lives will affect our future lives, and the people we become then too.

ACTIVITY: Who am I?

What kinds of events or experiences in our lives do you think might influence what happens to us later, and affect the kind of people we become? Use a mind map to generate ideas about memories then write down in a table some of the most significant events, experiences and people in your own life so far. Aim for at least 20 items and, in each case, explain how you think you were affected, and why. During this activity, you might think about the ideas shown on the mind map below.

The mind map below should help you to think of a range of events, experiences and people who have had some impact on you, and shaped who you are.

Event/experience	How and why it influenced me

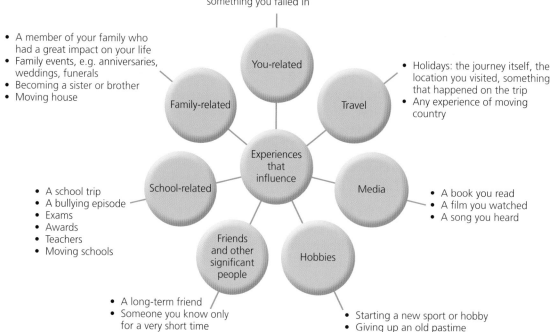

ACTIVITY: What makes me, me?

Ronit Baras is a self-help coach who talks about events in life as being like 'asteroids':

'Although we may be unaware of these "little" events, they have a great influence over us and switch us from one path to another. Think about it as if you were flying through an asteroid field. Every asteroid in your path (event in your life) affects you in one of three ways:

1 *Has no impact, so you just keep going*
2 *Becomes part of who you are and increases your mass (energy, motivation), so you keep going in the same direction, but smaller obstacles no longer matter*
3 *Changes your direction*

If you understand that every event in life falls under one of these categories, you will agree we tend to ignore the ones that have no impact on the direction we take and notice more of the other two – the ones that give us a boost and the ones that change our direction.'

We are looking at events that have an impact on you, or change your direction. Review the list you made in the 'Who am I?' activity, then copy the table below, adding items from your list to the column in which they best fit. The items in the right-hand column represent the most significant life events.

Becomes part of who you are and increases your mass (energy, motivation), so you keep going in the same direction, but smaller obstacles no longer matter	Significant life events which change the direction of your life

ACTIVITY: Learning from life

ATL

- Creative-thinking skills: Use brainstorming and visual diagrams to generate new ideas and perspectives

An Open University student (Alan) represented the most significant events of his life in the following timeline:

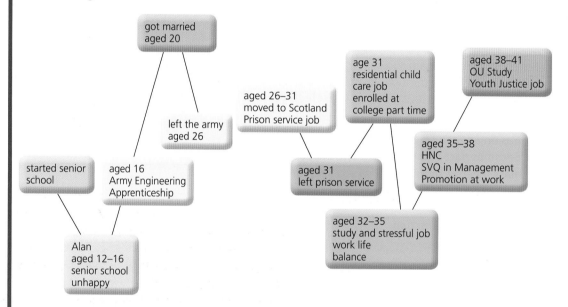

Alan also recorded an audio commentary to accompany his timeline. Another student, Ying, did the same. Read both these timelines, and listen to the audio commentaries here: https://goo.gl/7qCQHa. Transcripts for each commentary are available on the web page.

Create your own timeline and recorded commentary, as Alan and Ying did. To do this, follow these steps:

1 Choose the ten most significant events from the list you created in the 'Who am I?' activity. Do not use any that you would prefer not to share with the class as a whole.
2 On a piece of poster paper, order these ten events chronologically to create a timeline like the diagram above.

3   After creating their timelines, Alan and Ying added any learning that they felt they had gained from the experiences they had included. With these 'learning points' added, Alan's timeline now looked as follows:

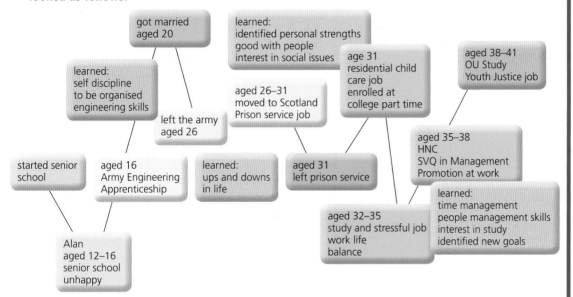

On your own timeline poster add 'learning points' to at least five of your significant events.

4   Listen again to the students' audio commentaries. Write a transcript for a spoken commentary on your own timeline, *which explains what the significant events in your life have been, and what you have learned from them.* The commentary should be two to three minutes in length.

5   Practise your commentary as much as you need to, and then record it so that you can play it back to others, for instance, by using your smartphone, or an iPad or other tablet.

6   Get into a group of four, then swap your posters and audio recordings with each other. Individually, read and listen to each of your other group members' timelines.

7   Once you have seen every member's timeline poster and listened to their audio, **discuss** as a group how similar or different were the life events that each of you came up with. What learning did you take from these?

Once you have completed your posters, you might, as guided by your teacher, display them on the walls of the classroom, with the transcript of your commentary attached. As a class you might then carry out a gallery walk in order for everyone to share their work with the class as a whole.

As the timelines show, rather than a single event impacting you as a person, in the real world it is very common for your life to be filled with lots of smaller (but still very significant) events that change and shape the person you are.

◆ Assessment opportunities

In this activity you have practised skills that are assessed using Criterion B: Organizing, Criterion C: Producing text and Criterion D: Using language.

PAST ACTIONS, FUTURE CONSEQUENCES

A particular technique used by Hosseini throughout the novel, which helps convey an idea of actions having future consequences or of the past being strongly linked to the present and future, is that of foreshadowing.

In *The Kite Runner* the narrator does not tell the reader at this point what happened in 1975, but does give clues about the nature of this particular event.

In the opening paragraph of *The Kite Runner,* the narrator suggests that something very significant happened one day in 1975, but does not say *what* it was that happened, only that it took place in 'winter', on a 'frigid overcast day'. A reader's anticipation is thus raised in expectation of finding out what happened that was so important; and such references foreshadow that event being revealed at some point.

Hosseini foreshadows both events that have already taken place *and* events that are still to take place. This occurs most obviously when the narrator mentions 'my past of unatoned sins' – this foreshadowing the revelation of what he has already done, while also – together with the words spoken by Rahim Khan on the telephone: 'There is a way to be good again', hinting at what will happen in the future.

The foreshadowing used here suggests very clearly the theme of past actions being strongly linked to what happens in the present and future.

ACTIVITY: Literary technique – foreshadowing

■ ATL

- Creative-thinking skills: Make guesses, ask 'what if' questions and generate testable hypotheses
- Communication skills: Read critically and for comprehension; make inferences and draw conclusions

Work in pairs to write notes that help you answer these questions. Share your work in a larger group, or with the class as a whole.

1. What questions are raised by the sentence '*There is a way to be good again*'? These questions will tell you what answers you are hoping to find out as the novel continues.
2. Seasons of the year are often used symbolically in literature to suggest the nature of something. What do you think each season might be used to represent? What is each associated with?
3. What do the details 'winter', 'on a frigid overcast day' and 'frozen creek' hint to us about the nature of the event that the narrator talks about at the beginning of Chapter 1?

ⓘ Symbols and symbolism

Symbols are images, ideas and words that represent something other than what they are. In doing so they help a reader to understand an idea or a thing. For example, a dove is a symbol of peace; the Sun can be a symbol of happiness and joy.

ACTIVITY: The role of parents

■ ATL

■ Creative-thinking skills: Consider multiple alternatives, including those that might be unlikely or impossible

As you may have already discovered yourselves, tensions can arise between parents and their children over the question of how much influence parents should have in their children's lives. This question arises in *The Kite Runner* also.

Find a sheet of paper and, without putting your name on it, draw out the table below. Number the boxes from 1 to 6.

1	2
3	4
5	6

Each box relates to one of the questions below. On your own, think about the questions then write your answers down in the appropriate boxes:

1 'Of course, marrying a poet was one thing, but fathering a son who preferred burying his face in poetry books to hunting … well, that wasn't how Baba had envisioned it, I suppose. Real men didn't read poetry – and God forbid they should ever write it! Real men – real boys – played soccer just as Baba had when he had been young. Now that was something to be passionate about.' **(Chapter 3)**
   What is it that you think your parents most value about you? What makes them proud of you?
2 **What kinds of things do you think would make them proud of you in the future?**
3 **What would your parents like you to do as a profession or job in the future?**

4 **What do you think your parents would say if you told them that you wanted to be a writer, painter or an actor?**
5 **In Chapter 3, Baba complains to Rahim Khan about Amir that:**
   '… he's always buried in those books or shuffling around the house like he's lost in some dream.'

   'And?'

   'I wasn't like that.' Baba sounded frustrated, almost angry.

   Rahim Khan laughed. 'Children aren't coloring books. You don't get to fill them in with your favorite colors.'

   (Chapter 3)
      Amir tells the reader elsewhere that his father has tried to force him to be interested in football and other sports, which he is not.
      How much do you think parents should have a role in deciding what their children are interested in, or what they do, in life?
6 **Do children have any responsibilities to their parents in terms of meeting their hopes and dreams? What are those, if so?**

Cut up your piece of paper so that the six boxes are now separate pieces of paper. Your teacher will have numbered six tables in the classroom from 1 to 6. Place each of your individual responses on the relevant tables.

Go around and read the set of responses from the whole class for each question. Then **discuss** as a class:
● **How similar or different are the responses each time?**
● **What reasons may there be for any differences?**
● **Are any particular cultural and/or social expectations a factor in how different people in the class have responded to the questions?**

You might consider also if you would like to put these questions to your own parents and see what their own answers might be!

ACTIVITY: Fatherhood

In *The Kite Runner* both Amir and Hassan lose their mothers at birth, so the novel concentrates largely on their relationships with their fathers. We also see a number of other father–son relationships: Assef and his father at Amir's birthday party; Kamal and his father when they take part in the same journey away from Kabul as Baba and Amir. Later in the novel we are also given a picture of Hassan as a father to Sohrab, and Amir ultimately takes on that role as a part of his act of redemption.

What do you think are the main responsibilities of a father? In groups of three or four, decide on a list of between eight and ten responsibilities and list them in a table such as the one below.

Responsibilities of a father	Baba	Ali

Beside each of the items on your list, **evaluate** how well Baba and Ali meet that particular responsibility. Make sure to include any evidence from Chapters 1–9 of the novel that support your views of Baba and Ali. You might consider dividing up the chapters between each member of the group, and assigning individual responsibility for collecting evidence from particular chapters.

Using the evidence you have found, write a short comparison of the presentation of Baba and Ali as fathers in the first section of the novel. You should write 400–500 words.

- **Begin by identifying three or four points of comparison between the two men, which you can discuss in relation to both.**
- **Identify** also the particular quotations that may help in supporting each of these points.
- **It may help to use a tool such as a T-chart or other graphic organizer to organize your points and evidence beforehand.**

Organization is always important in a comparative essay. Search online for help in structuring your essay, thinking about transitions and ensuring you include all of the elements of comparative writing.

◆ Assessment opportunities

In this activity you have practised skills that are assessed using Criterion A: Analysing, Criterion B: Organizing and Criterion D: Using language.

WHAT MAKES YOU SAY THAT?

Sometimes, up in those trees, I talked Hassan into firing walnuts with his slingshot at the neighbour's one-eyed German shepherd. Hassan never wanted to, but if I asked, really asked, he wouldn't deny me. Hassan never denied me anything. And he was deadly with his slingshot. Hassan's father, Ali, used to catch us and get mad, or as mad as someone as gentle as Ali could ever get. He would wag his finger and wave us down from the tree. He would take the mirror and tell us what his mother had told him, that the devil shone mirrors too, shone them to distract Muslims during prayer. 'And he laughs while he does it,' he always added, scowling at his son.

'Yes, Father,' Hassan would mumble, looking down at his feet. But he never told on me. Never told that the mirror, like shooting walnuts at the neighbour's dog, was always my idea.

(Chapter 2)

This passage is one of the earliest in the novel that touches on the relationship between Amir and Hassan. From the passage, what do we know about Amir's and Hassan's roles in their relationship?

In pairs, use the visible thinking strategy 'What makes you say that?' to make claims about Amir and Hassan's relationship, and **justify** them. For example:
- **Claim 1: What do you know?**
- **Claim 2: What do you see or know that makes you say that?**

Make as many claims as you can.

◆ Assessment opportunities

In this activity you have practised skills that are assessed using Criterion A: Analysing.

ACTIVITY: Friends will be friends?

In 2007, a film was made of *The Kite Runner.* Find the trailer for the film online, or follow this link: https://youtu.be/sLtavGjAOJY.

The trailer begins by announcing 'Two friends', referring to Amir and Hassan, and continues along the same theme. Are Amir and Hassan friends? Why (not)?

- **Carry out an internet search using the search term** characteristics of friendship.
- **After looking through some of the search results, decide on your own 'top ten characteristics of friendship'.**
- **Now compare your ten chosen characteristics with a classmate's. Are they the same? Together, discuss the reasons behind each of your choices.**

◆ Assessment opportunities

In this activity you have practised skills that are assessed using Criterion A: Analysing.

FROM THE DIRECTOR OF MONSTER'S BALL AND FINDING NEVERLAND

The Kite Runner

A MARC FORSTER FILM

"There is a way to be good again."

COMING SOON
www.kiterunnermovie.com

ACTIVITY: Amir and Hassan

In a group of four, find quotations that show the nature of Amir's and Hassan's relationship. Each group member should take one quotation and make a claim to the rest of the group about what it shows about the nature of their relationship. Ensure you explain your claim, including quoting specific detail(s) that support it.

Having looked more at some details of the relationship between Amir and Hassan, use your criteria for 'friendship' from the 'Friends will be friends?' activity, and measure Amir and Hassan against those.

To what degree might Amir and Hassan be considered 'real friends'?

EXTENSION

With your group, look through chapters 1–9 of *The Kite Runner* and **identify** other passages that give you, the reader, more detail about Amir and Hassan's relationship. Does this further evidence change your view of the boys' relationship?

◆ Assessment opportunities

In this activity you have practised skills that are assessed using Criterion A: Analysing.

How can a cultural context influence our understanding of personal responsibility?

FRIENDSHIP AND SOCIAL STATUS

The social status of Amir and Hassan is described by Amir in Chapter 4: 'In the end, I was a Pashtun and he was a Hazara. I was **Sunni** and he was **Shi'a**, and nothing was ever going to change that. Nothing.'

ℹ

The Pashtuns and the Hazaras

The Pashtuns are the largest ethnic group in Afghanistan, while the Hazaras are much smaller in number. Pashtuns enjoy a position of importance and affluence, while Hazaras are generally much poorer and are considered to be at the bottom of the social hierarchy. The two groups have been in conflict for many hundreds of years, primarily due to religious differences.

DISCUSS

In small groups, gather and discuss the following questions:

- **How much does social status matter in your own circle of friends?**
- **How much *should* social status matter when it comes to friendship?**
- **How far does social status affect the nature of the friendship of Amir and Hassan?**
- **How far can it excuse the kind of 'friendship' that Amir displays towards Hassan?**

The differences between Amir and Hassan as friends are shown through **parallel scenes**, when the two boys encounter the bully Assef and his friends in Chapter 5, and again in Chapter 7.

Amir narrates how 'Years later, I learned an English word for the creature that Assef was … "**sociopath**"'. While the boys do not know what a sociopath is, they do understand that Assef is a powerful, cruel and dangerous bully. Read the scene from Chapter 5 now.

ACTIVITY: Mini character essay

■ ATL

- Communication skills: Draw reasonable conclusions and generalizations

- **Identify** and list significant details about Hassan in the narration of the Chapter 5 scene.
- Use this to write a 500–600 word analysis of how he is presented in the scene.
- Explain how you think the author wished his readers to respond to Hassan, and what the evidence is for your claims.

◆ Assessment opportunities

This activity can be assessed using Criterion A: Analysing and Criterion D: Using language.

CREATIVE QUESTIONS

Bullying and bystanders

Brainstorm a list of questions you have, or which you think others might have, about the topic of bullying. You can do this on your own, or as part of a group.

Next, watch the beginning of *Walking on the Moon* (1999), up to the point at which the opening credits appear (about 1:50): https://youtu.be/zgQcQbS5U7I.

How would you explain the behaviour and actions of the bystanders in this scene?

Look over your list of questions again and transform them into questions that invite more exploration of the topic. They may begin with prompts such as:
- **What would it be like if …?**
- **How would it be different if …?**
- **Suppose that …?**
- **What would change if …?**
- **How would it look differently if …?**

Now look at your questions again: do some of them imply or refer to someone taking responsibility in some way? The table below lists some individuals who you might think should take responsibility if they witnessed bullying. List what responsibilities you feel each person may have.

Bullies	Victims	Bystanders	Parents?	Teachers?

DISCUSS

Discuss the following questions among your group:
- **Have you ever been a bystander when bullying happened? If so, what did you do? What do you think you should have done?**
- **If you were preparing advice to give to younger students in the school about what to do as a bystander if they witness bullying taking place, what would that advice be?**

EXTENSION

Look at the linked web page below, or search 'bullying bystander', and **explore** the topic of bystanders in bullying situations: http://eyesonbullying.org/bystander.html. After reading through the page, write a response to each of the following question stems, about bystanders in bullying situations:
- 'I used to think …'
- 'Now I think …'

What can be involved in taking 'personal responsibility'?

Anti-Bullying Alliance

- Logo of the Anti-Bullying Alliance

! Read the following document, on bystanders and bullying, which contains a lot more detail about this topic, including more about the research which has been carried out on it: **https://goo.gl/z1rytL.**

! Using what you have learned about bystanders in bullying situations in this chapter, in groups of three or four, do one of the following:

1 **Create** a play, dialogue, series of scenes or something similar that illustrates important points about bystanders and bullying, and which could be performed to a younger audience of students.

2 **Create** an advice leaflet aimed at younger students, which contains important points about bystanders and bullying.

! Whichever option you choose, the following are some possible ideas on what to include:

- the different ways in which bystanders can act when they witness bullying of some kind

- the different ways in which 'helpful' bystanders can **intervene**, and what advice you might give on how to act in different kinds of situations (for instance, is it always safe to intervene directly?)

- the possible effects of not intervening on bystanders

- what research shows about the impact of bystanders intervening in some way.

! Feel free also to look around more of the site **www.eyesonbullying.org,** or to use more websites on this topic – there is a lot of information and advice online for you to find!

THINK–PAIR–SHARE

Much of what has been discussed in this section of the chapter has been connected with relationships, and responsibilities of people within those. 'Loyalty' was mentioned by Hosseini as one of the themes of the work and, in the novel, it is embodied by Hassan.

1 How would you define loyalty? Write down your own definition of this (without looking it up).

2 In pairs, **discuss** your definitions and the reasoning behind them.

3 Share your definitions in groups of three of four. How similar or different are they? Can you come up with a common definition?

What is loyalty?

LOYALTY – HASSAN-STYLE

Then I understood: this was Hassan's final sacrifice for me. If he'd said no, Baba would have believed him because we all knew Hassan never lied. And if Baba believed him, then I'd be the accused; I would have to explain and I would be revealed for what I really was. Baba would never, ever forgive me.

(Chapter 9)

In Chapter 9 Hassan again sacrifices himself for Amir, lying that he did indeed steal the watch and money (which Amir had hidden under Hassan's mattress in order to frame him for theft and so force him to leave).

Amir also realizes that Hassan knew that he (Amir) had seen everything that happened in the alleyway between Hassan and Assef, without doing anything about it. Despite this Hassan still sacrifices himself – 'He knew that I had betrayed him and yet he was rescuing me once again'.

Individually, reflect on the following questions:

■ What do you feel is the greatest sacrifice you have made for someone else in your life? What made you do it?

■ What has been the greatest sacrifice anyone has made for you? Why do you think they did it?

As a class, debate the following questions: Is there such a thing as too much loyalty, and taking too much personal responsibility? Was Hassan right to lie and sacrifice himself for Amir in this situation?

ACTIVITY: What was Amir's worst 'sin'?

■ ATL

■ Communication: Read critically and for comprehension
■ Critical-thinking skills: Gather and organize relevant information to formulate an argument

Having read the first section of the novel, consider the following question: What was Amir's worst 'sin' or act in this section of the novel?

Was it:

● **not intervening when he saw Assef and his companions attacking Hassan in the alleyway**
● **not trying to do anything afterwards, such as telling someone what had happened? Rahim Khan tells Amir in Chapter 9 that 'You know, you can tell me anything you want, Amir jan. Anytime.' What else might Amir have done afterwards? What could he have done to support his friend?**
● **his treatment of Hassan afterwards, betraying his friendship and loyalty; for example, in rejecting Hassan's attempts at friendship without giving him any reasons for this, hitting him with pomegranates, and accusing him of stealing his watch**
● **forcing Hassan and Ali to give up their jobs and home, and then leave – causing the break-up of Baba and Ali's relationship**
● **something else?**

1 **In groups of four, write out five cards, as illustrated on page 342, and assign each member one card.**
2 **Each person will argue for two to three minutes that the statement on their card is the worst sin Amir commits.**
3 **To prepare for this, look back at Chapters 7, 8 and 9, and make note of any quotations that are relevant to your argument.**
4 **Decide on three key points that you will make in order to support your argument. Make notes on these points, and find quotations to help illustrate and support each point.**
5 **If you wish, rehearse your speech to ensure you can say everything you want to in the time allowed.**
6 **Each member of the group should now give their speech in turn.** ➤

7 Discuss which argument was the strongest, and why. Do you all as a group agree on what was Amir's worst sin?

Not intervening	Not doing anything after the incident
His treatment of Hassan after the assault	Forcing Hassan and Ali to give up and leave
Something else	

▼ Links to: History

■ Fighters in Afghanistan

In 1979, the Soviet Union invaded Afghanistan. Why? Research the reasons behind the invasion, and the consequences of the Soviet occupation of the country. The following links are a good starting point and will help you better understand the historical context of *The Kite Runner*:

1 A timeline and summary of events in Afghanistan's history is given here: www.bbc.co.uk/news/world-south-asia-12024253.
2 A summary of the Soviet–Afghanistan war is at this link: www.ducksters.com/history/cold_war/soviet_afghanistan_war.php.

ACTIVITY: Reasons to flee

■ ATL

- Critical-thinking skills: Evaluate and manage risk
- Creative-thinking skills: Create original works and ideas; use existing works and ideas in new ways

In Chapter 10, while leaving Kabul secretly in the middle of the night, Amir describes how Kabul had changed for the worse under the occupation of the Soviets.

Imagine you were living in Kabul at this time. Write a diary entry of 500–1,000 words, describing your normal day, but lived within this suspicious and dangerous context:

- **How might your normal activities – such as getting food, going to school, or visiting friends – have changed?**
- How would you react if an adult informant asked you to spy on your friends, teachers and parents? Imagine this happened on the day you are writing about. Describe the incident and your response within your diary entry.
- Your diary entry should contain some reflections on your personal responsibility towards different people or groups – self, family, friends, school, community – during this time. What might those responsibilities be in such a context? How will you carry them out? What may happen as a result of doing so? How have your responsibilities changed since, or during, the Soviet occupation?

What kinds of things might we take responsibility for?

CHANGING CIRCUMSTANCES – CHANGING RESPONSIBILITIES

Chapter 10 describes the journey of Baba and Amir from Kabul following the Soviet Union's invasion of Afghanistan. They travel firstly to Jalalabad in the truck of people smuggler Karim, and eventually on to Peshawar in Pakistan, from where they will travel on to the United States.

When they leave Kabul to travel to the United States, Ali and Baba become refugees. Warfare, political instability and natural disasters are some of the most common reasons why people leave their homes and become refugees.

As in the case of many refugees, Amir and his father had to leave quite suddenly, taking only a few possessions with them.

EXTENSION

To promote the plight of refugees, the International Rescue Committee asked different refugees to share the contents of their bags. Use the search term **What's in my refugee bag?** to find photos and details of the refugees who took part in the project, and the personal belongings they took with them. Choose two of the refugees and write a paragraph for each one, explaining why you think they took the items they did. Do you think their reasons were similar to yours?

ACTIVITY: Fleeing home – what to take?

■ ATL

- Collaboration skills: Advocate for one's own rights and needs
- Critical-thinking skills: Identify obstacles and challenges; evaluate and manage risk

If you had to flee your home very quickly, what would you take?

1 For this, it is important to think about priorities. How might you categorize your possessions? Decide on some categories – these might be 'Need' / 'Want' / 'Might be useful' / 'Don't need or want', for instance, or 'Clothes' / 'Documents' / 'Electronics' and so on. It is up to you to decide on which categories to choose, and how many.

2 List some of your possessions underneath each category heading.

3 Prioritize the categories, and some of the individual items within them – you only need to do this with the most important things each time, as there is a limited number of things you can take in your bag.

4 Decide on the final items that you will take with you when you flee. Share these items, and your reasons for taking them, in groups of three of four. Did you take similar things? Were your reasons similar?

5 A final question: Amir describes in Chapter 10 – though indirectly – what he and Baba took with them when they fled from Kabul. Can you list those things?

◆ Assessment opportunities

In this activity you have practised skills that are assessed using Criterion B: Organizing and Criterion C: Producing text.

ACTIVITY: Refugee voices

Do you think Ali and Baba's personal responsibilities changed once they become refugees?

The photograph above shows refugees carrying their belongings with them as they travel. Imagine you are a television reporter doing a broadcast about the refugees. One of the people in the photograph wishes to speak to you about the responsibilities they have to the members of their family in this situation.

- **You will be the voice of that person. Choose which of the refugees in the above photograph it will be, and write what they wish to say. The speech should be between 1 minute 30 seconds and 2 minutes in length.**
- Rehearse your speech then record yourself as a 'talking head', as if taking part in a television news report.
- In groups of four, share your videos with each other then choose one to be shown to the class as a whole.
- As a class, **discuss** what responsibilities people in this type of situation have towards the family, drawing on the comments you have heard in the various speeches. Think about what the term 'family' could mean in this situation, which family members it may include (immediate or extended?), and where they are.

◆ Assessment opportunities

This activity can be assessed using Criterion C: Producing text and Criterion D: Using language.

ACTIVITY: Perspectives on people smuggling

In *The Kite Runner,* the man who smuggles Amir and Baba from Kabul to Pakistan is called Karim.

1   Skim-read Chapter 10 of the novel again. Make a bullet point facts chart of what we are told about Karim and what he does as a people smuggler.
2   The following sources provide various perspectives on people smugglers.
    ● Newspaper reports: Ghafur Khalil, who used people smugglers to flee from Jalalabad: https://www.mirror.co.uk/news/world-news/calais-migrant-paid-people-smugglers-5942505; Factors which encourage people smuggling: https://goo.gl/Z1fbNV
    ● Feature article: Different groups involved in people smuggling: https://goo.gl/sLLCu6
    ● Video reports: On board a people-smugglers' boat: www.youtube.com/watch?v=xuXBx6NXr5s; Undercover filming of people smugglers: www.youtube.com/watch?v=D-kOU01OmAY
3   Each of the characters listed below must make a 2–3-minute speech summarising: the choices they make in regard to people smuggling; the reasons behind their choices; the possible consequences of those decisions; how they feel about their role. Write the speech for one character. Don't forget to consider their particular context and situation, and how that may impact what they say and do:
    ● a migrant or refugee
    ● a people smuggler
    ● a border or immigration official of a country to which people smugglers take or send refugees
    ● a reporter covering the topic of people smuggling for a newspaper or TV station.

◆ Assessment opportunities

In this activity you have practised skills that are assessed using Criterion B: Organizing and Criterion C: Producing text.

Motifs

In literature, a motif is an image, action or other item with symbolic significance that repeats throughout a work and (unlike a symbol) helps develop a work's theme, and the reader's understanding of that theme.

One of the most important themes in *The Kite Runner* is that of all actions having consequences, which must be faced at some point, and which cannot be escaped. It is often expressed in sayings such as 'What goes around, comes around', or 'We reap what we sow'. Sometimes the idea of 'karma' is quoted, a concept of Hinduism:

> 'Karma is a Sanskrit word whose literal meaning is "action". It refers to the law that every action has an equal reaction either immediately or at some point in the future. Good or virtuous actions, actions in harmony with **dharma**, will have good reactions or responses and bad actions, actions against dharma, will have the opposite effect.'

> Source: www.bbc.co.uk/religion/religions/hinduism/concepts/concepts_1.shtml

People even quote Isaac Newton's Third Law of Motion in this context – 'Every action has an equal and opposite reaction'.

This theme is introduced in the first chapter, when two motifs are used to show how the narrator, Amir, cannot escape or hide from his past actions. Immediately after Rahim Khan telephones Amir, Amir goes for a walk in a park. While there he sees two birds of prey, called kites. Read that paragraph again.

Kites are the first motif: here they are a reminder to Amir of Hassan, the kite runner of the novel's title; and therefore a reminder also of the wrongs he committed against Hassan. When describing the kites the narrator uses a simile when he compares the kites to eyes. This suggests that Amir is not able to hide from what he has done, even years later and on the other side of the world. Eyes are, in fact, continually referred to throughout the novel, making them the second motif here; the author uses eyes to help to convey the idea that one cannot hide or escape one's actions.

The final section of the novel focuses on Amir's return to Kabul, and his efforts finally to face up to his past and what he did to Hassan.

ACTIVITY: Does what goes around, come around?

■ ATL

- Communication skills: Use appropriate forms of writing for different purposes and audiences
- Collaborative skills: Listen actively to other ideas and perspectives

What are your own thoughts on the idea of 'what goes around, comes around'? **Discuss** the following questions in small groups, and makes notes on your ideas.

- **Do you think that your actions influence what will happen to you in the future?**
- **Do you feel that others will be rewarded or pay for *their* actions at some point in the future?**
- **How might it affect the way somebody lives their life if this is something that they do believe?**

The idea of 'what goes around, comes around' has been discussed online in lots of different forums. Some college students responded to this question on a web page at this link, or find another discussion of the subject on a different forum: https://goo.gl/GgYL9d.

Read through these comments and then, using your notes from the previous questions, write a post that you would add to this discussion. Your **comment** should explain your own position on this question, and your reasons for that.

If possible, perhaps someone in your class can set up a class wiki or blog page or something similar, where everyone in the class can add their thoughts on this idea, and can read everyone else's thoughts.

◆ Assessment opportunities

In this activity you have practised skills that are assessed using Criterion A: Analysing and Criterion C: Producing text.

To what extent is it possible to atone for past mistakes?

When making important decisions – usually a decision that cannot be changed once made – people are often afraid they will make the wrong choice and will regret their decision later for some reason. While we cannot look into the future and know with any certainty what will happen, or how an important decision may turn out, we can use 'decision-making processes' to help us make the best decision we can. At their root, these decision-making processes help us to consider the most important factors of the decision and so, by being better informed about our potential choices, we stand a better chance of making the 'right' decision.

EXTENSION

Write out a list of some of the major decisions you think you will need to make in the next few years – this may relate to school, college, family, or be something personal, and so on.

Look at the decision models on page 347: do different decisions require different models do you think? Or does one model work for all decisions?

Choose two major decisions from your list, then **select** two of the models and use each one in turn to work through the decisions you will have to make.

Using the tools in practice should help you to decide on the best one to use for your future important decisions.

ACTIVITY: Choices and consequences

ATL

- Organization skills: Plan strategies and take action to achieve personal and academic goals
- Communication skills: Read critically and for comprehension; make inferences and draw conclusions

Amir's decision not to stand up for Hassan (when he is being attacked and raped by the bullying Assef) is one that significantly affects his life afterwards. Later he questions how it may also have affected the lives of other people:

But I wondered. True, I hadn't made Ali step on the land mine, and I hadn't brought the Taliban to the house to shoot Hassan. But I had driven Hassan and Ali out of the house. Was it too far-fetched to imagine that things might have turned out differently if I hadn't? Maybe Baba would have brought them along to America. Maybe Hassan would have had a home of his own now, a job, a family, a life in a country where no one cared that he was
a Hazara, where most people didn't even know what a Hazara was. Maybe not. But maybe so.

I can't go to Kabul, I had said to Rahim Khan. I have a wife in America, a home, a career, and a family. But how could I pack up and go back home when my actions may have cost Hassan a chance at those very same things?

Individually, think about the following questions and then, in pairs or small groups, **discuss** your responses:

- **What choices have you made which have affected your life?**
- **What choices do you expect to make in the future, which will have a big impact on your life?**
- **How do you feel about making important decisions in life?**

Assessment opportunities

In this activity you have practised skills that are assessed using Criterion C: Producing text and Criterion D: Using language.

ACTIVITY: Decisions, decisions

■ ATL

- ■ Organization skills: Set goals; plan strategies and take action to achieve personal and academic goals; use appropriate strategies for organizing complex information

The majority of decision-making processes outline a pathway that includes these elements:

A number of decision-making process models are included below for you to research and **evaluate**. Copy out the evaluation table below and use it to make notes on the potential effectiveness of each process model, and how well you think each might work for you. Finally, choose the model that you think will work best for you, and give your decisions for this choice.

Decision-making process tool	Your evaluative comments
Decision-making process wheel	
Seven decision-making steps	
Decision flowchart (graphic organizer)	
Decision-making model form (graphic organizer)	
Your choice:	Your reason:

1 The decision-making process wheel

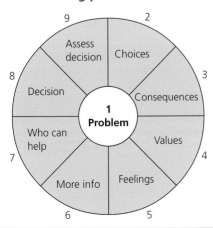

2 Seven decision-making steps

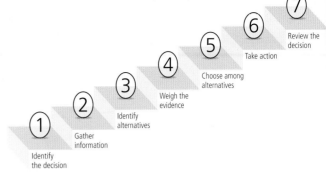

3 Decision flowchart (graphic organizer)

4 Decision-making model form (graphic organizer)

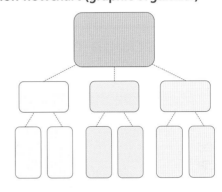

Problem	Goal(s)

Alternatives	Pros ✓ & Cons ✗
	✓
	✗
	✓
	✗
	✓
	✗
	✓
	✗

Decision(s)	Reason(s)

◆ Assessment opportunities

In this activity you have practised skills that are assessed using Criterion A: Analysing and Criterion B: Organizing.

Is there a cultural influence in decision-making?

ACTIVITY: Decision-making poetry

ATL

- Communication skills: Write for different purposes
- Creative-thinking skills: Apply existing knowledge to generate new ideas, products or processes

1 A four-line poem is known as a quatrain. The web page below contains short poems and quatrains on the topic of life choices. Read through some of these – or find your own examples online, and then write your own four-line quatrain about making important choices in life. The format you use for your poem is up to you.

   Short poems on choice:
   http://hellopoetry.com/words/437/choices/poems/.

2 Two poems that examine making choices in life are Robert Frost's 'The Road Not Taken' and Jane Hirshfield's 'The Decision'. Find both of these poems online and then write an essay comparing how each of these poems presents the theme of life-changing decisions.
   You may find it helpful to use the 'Explanation Game' table (page 89) to brainstorm the poems to begin with.

◆ Assessment opportunities

This activity can be assessed using Criterion A: Analysing and Criterion B: Organizing.

ACTIVITY: What might have been?

ATL

- Creative-thinking skills: Use brainstorming and visual diagrams to generate new ideas and inquiries; consider multiple alternatives, including those that might be unlikely or impossible

In the final section of *The Kite Runner* we learn that it is not only Amir who is carrying the burden of an earlier choice, but his father also. Rahim Khan reveals that Hassan was in fact also Baba's son – fathered illegitimately with the wife of his Hazara servant, Ali.

It is explained that Baba decided to keep this a secret because he felt 'It was a shameful situation. People would talk. All that a man had back then, all that he was, was his honor, his name, and if people talked … We couldn't tell anyone, surely you can see that.' (Chapter 17)

Develop a mind map that **hypothesizes** about how the lives of Baba, Amir and Hassan might have been affected if Baba had decided instead to reveal the truth about Hassan.

- **What do you think might have happened to Baba within his community, if it had been known that he had an illegitimate Hazara son?**
- **How might Amir have been affected, at school, in how others treated him, and so on?**
- **How might Hassan's life have been different?**

◆ Assessment opportunities

In this activity you have practised skills that are assessed using Criterion A: Analysing.

ACTIVITY: The cultural impact on what might have been

ATL

- Creative-thinking skills: Revise understanding based on new information and evidence

Baba's main consideration in his decision not to tell anyone the truth about Hassan was a cultural one; in his community and cultural context the consequences of publicly acknowledging a child born by a Hazara woman – one of the lowest social groups – would have been too great. It is worth noting that, when he reveals the secret to Amir, Rahim Khan agrees with Baba's reasoning and decision, though he acknowledges in his letter later that Amir had the right to be angry about it.

In small groups, **discuss** the following questions:

- **What are your views on Baba's treatment of Hassan, as his son?**
- **While Rahim Khan defends Baba, Amir reflects that his father, who saw theft as the worst kind of crime, has stolen 'sacred' things from those closest to him in keeping such a secret – 'from me the right to know I had a brother, from Hassan his identity, and from Ali his honor'. (Chapter 18) Is 'honor' a good enough reason for Baba not to have told anyone about Hassan?**
- **What would happen in your own community, if someone of a higher social status had an illegitimate son with someone of a lower social group?**
- **How much of a difference should the cultural context make to how this question is answered?**

◆ Assessment opportunities

In this activity you have practised skills that are assessed using Criterion A: Analysing.

ACTIVITY: A panel discussion

ATL

- Critical-thinking skills: Gather and organize relevant information to formulate an argument

Your class will be carrying out a panel discussion on the choice that Baba made, the factors that influenced him, and how far cultural pressures should play a part in decisions of such a kind. The discussion should last for 20–30 minutes.

Look online for videos of panel discussions to remind yourself of the format. There are a number of panel discussions online that focus on *The Kite Runner* and its themes, which you might find useful.

The panellists taking part in your discussion will be as follows:

1 **Rahim Khan**
2 **Hassan**
3 **The manager of the gas (petrol) station in the United States, where Baba was working before his death**
4 **One or two members of your class (if more than one, they should have different perspectives on this question).**

Your teacher will assign every member of the class a number from 1 to 4 – these numbers relate to the characters above. You must research and prepare your character's position on the topic of the discussion (or, if you are assigned the number 4, your own), and be prepared to present, explain and defend that position.

The actual panel discussion might take place with student volunteers, or participants can be chosen at random from the classroom. There might even be scope to have panel discussions in groups, or to carry out more than one panel discussion. Or you may as a class have one main panel discussion watched by the rest of the class, which can then **discuss** the issues further more generally afterwards.

◆ Assessment opportunities

In this activity you have practised skills that are assessed using Criterion A: Analysing and Criterion D: Using language.

Panel discussions

A panel discussion is, at its most basic, a group of people gathered to **discuss** a topic in front of an audience. A moderator usually guides the conversation by asking questions and managing the flow of the discussion. When running your own panel, you should think the following:

Before the discussion:

Select, invite and confirm interesting panellists – A diverse selection of experts who are good public speakers and well prepared ahead of the discussion.

Research – You should be able to control the flow of the panel's conversation. Knowing a lot about the topic being discussed, and being aware of the panellists' views/perspectives, will help a lot.

Questions – Prepare your questions ahead of time.

During the discussion:

Introductions – Briefly explain the topic that is about to be discussed, then introduce the panellists to the audience (or ask them to introduce themselves).

Keep the conversation moving – Encourage the panellists to answer each other's questions, or **comment** on each other's statements – 'What do you think of that?' is a good question to help bring another panellist into the conversation.

Q+A? Decide whether you will have audience questions, and when (at the end of the debate? at select points throughout?). Does your audience need microphones for the questions to be heard?

Thank and wish good night – Your discussion should be for a set time – 30 minutes? One hour? At the end, thank the panellists for their participation, and the audience for their attention.

ACTIVITY: Is redemption possible?

■ ATL

- Creative-thinking skills: Make guesses, ask 'what if' questions and generate testable hypotheses

Write down some notes in answer to the following questions and then **discuss** your answers in groups of three or four.

- **If you were to betray a friendship in some way, what could that mean in practice? What kinds of things might you do?**
- **What would be the worst possible way you can think of in which a friend might betray you?**
- **If either of the above happened, would you or your friend be able to put things right afterwards? How? Or why not?**
- **Has anyone ever done anything to you which you could not forgive them for? Why could you not forgive them?**
- **Have you done something to someone else which they could not forgive you for? How do you feel about that now?**

In Chapter 23, Amir receives a letter from Rahim Khan telling him about his father: read the letter again.

Have a class debate on the following two questions:
- **Did Baba redeem himself by the end?**
- **If 'true redemption' is 'when guilt leads to good', does Amir redeem himself by the end?**

◆ Assessment opportunities

In this activity you have practised skills that are assessed using Criterion A: Analysing and D: Using language.

ACTIVITY: Can we put right serious mistakes that we have made in the past?

Early on in this chapter you were asked to complete an activity based on the song *Je ne regrette rien?* (*Do I regret anything?*). This involved considering things that you might regret having done in life, along with whether there is anything you might do at this stage to try to put it right.

You have also just looked at Baba and considered whether he managed to redeem himself by the end of his life, having fathered Hassan, and not told Amir about his half-brother.

Amir is haunted by his failure to try to help Hassan when he was attacked by Assef and his two sidekicks. The choice he made at that point not to do anything has overshadowed everything that has happened since in Amir's life. Its impact is made clear in the very first paragraph of the novel, which we looked at in detail earlier:

"I became what I am today at the age of twelve, on a frigid overcast day in the winter of 1975. I remember the precise moment, crouching behind a crumbling mud wall, peeking into the valley near the frozen creek. That was a long time ago, but it's wrong what they say about the past, I've learned, about how you can bury it. Because the past claws its way out. Looking back now, I realize I have been peeking into that deserted alley for the last twenty-six years."

Earlier you completed a table in response to some of your own regrets. Now imagine Amir has to fill in the table. In the first column he talks of his failure to intervene when Hassan is attacked. What would he say in each of the columns? Write down his responses to the questions in each:

Now read Chapter 22, which narrates the fight between Amir and Assef, before Amir manages to escape with Sohrab.

We are going to consider this particular episode a bit more closely, and look at the question of whether it allows Amir to **atone** for his earlier actions – or inaction …

Write down some notes on the following questions:

1 **Why does Amir accept Assef's challenge at this point?**
2 **Why do you think the author includes a description of Amir's memory of Hassan pointing his slingshot at Assef?**
3 **How does the writer use the following to convey a vivid description of the fight?**
   a **Sensory imagery**
   b **Sentence structure**
   c **Narrative point of view**
4 **Why do you think that Amir, beaten so badly in the fight, feels 'healed' at the end?**
5 **Immediately after this point, Amir is rescued from Assef by Sohrab using his slingshot to shoot one of Assef's eyes out. The two escape as Assef tries desperately to take out the piece of shot.**
   a **Explain the irony in Sohrab's rescue of Amir.**
   b **Do you think Amir atones for his past sins in his treatment of Hassan, by returning to Afghanistan for Sohrab, and standing up to Assef (even if he would probably have been killed without Sohrab's help)? Why?**

◆ Assessment opportunities

In this activity you have practised skills that are assessed using Criterion A: Analysing.

SOME SUMMATIVE TASKS TO TRY

Use these tasks to apply and extend your learning in this chapter. These tasks are designed so that you can evaluate your learning at different levels of achievement in the Language and literature criteria.

THIS TASK CAN BE USED TO EVALUATE YOUR LEARNING IN CRITERION B, CRITERION C AND CRITERION D

Task 1: Creative writing – the telephone call

The Kite Runner begins with the protagonist and narrator, Amir, reflecting on the past, and then on a significant telephone call, which he had received during the previous summer.

Write a short story entitled 'The telephone call'. The story should be about a choice that has been made and the consequences of that choice. Perhaps the call has been made to confirm a decision? Or to reflect on the consequences of a decision previously made?

Your story might begin with the phrase 'Suddenly, the telephone rang.' Or you can use your own opening if you wish. The story should be between 500 and 1,000 words in length.

THIS TASK CAN BE USED TO EVALUATE YOUR LEARNING IN CRITERION B, CRITERION C AND CRITERION D

Task 2: A letter to Amir on how to overcome guilt and regret

This summative assessment involves writing to a grown-up Amir, offering advice on how to overcome guilt and regret.

There is a lot of advice online about how to deal with regret and how to move forward. Spend some time searching for, and reading through, this advice. Make notes for any suggestions, advice or ideas you think might be helpful for Amir.

Imagine that you are a psychologist or life coach and are writing to Amir with advice about how to deal with his guilt. Using the ideas and information from the above websites or others you have found, write a letter of advice to Amir suggesting what he should do.

Remember that you must cite properly and fully any websites or images used as part of the assessment under Criterion B for this task. You must also ensure that you do not use any text directly from any website as if it were your own – quote or paraphrase any text, and cite the source, making it clear whose ideas and/or words these are. You should use the referencing system that your teacher tells you to use, or which is used in general by your school – details and examples for that should be in your school's academic honesty policy.

THIS TASK CAN BE USED TO EVALUATE CRITERION A, CRITERION B AND CRITERION D

Task 3: A literary essay

Show how the theme of parenting is represented in *The Kite Runner*. **Explain** how this might be interpreted or understood in different historical, cultural or social contexts.

Reflection

In this chapter we have explored choices, ways of making decisions, and consequences which may arise from those; including those which help to shape the people we become. Within the context of our own choices and lives, meanwhile, we have explored what 'personal responsibility' might look like, and what it may involve in different situations. We have also considered those choices and decisions which we may later regret and which may cause harm to others, and whether or how far it might be possible to put right mistakes we made earlier. All of this has been explored through various texts, particularly *The Kite Runner*, which provides many examples of choices and consequences, and raises a number of questions about personal responsibility in different contexts. It has allowed us too, meanwhile, to find opportunities to practise a range of writing types including comparative writing, and to look more closely at the nature and purpose of literary techniques such as foreshadowing and symbolism.

Use this table to reflect on your own learning in this chapter.					
Questions we asked	**Answers we found**	**Any further questions now?**			
Factual:					
Conceptual:					
Debatable:					
Approaches to learning you used in this chapter:	**Description – what new skills did you learn?**	**How well did you master the skills?**			
		Novice	Learner	Practitioner	Expert
Communication skills					
Collaboration skills					
Organization skills					
Reflection skills					
Information literacy skills					
Critical-thinking skills					
Creative-thinking skills					
Learner profile attribute(s)	Reflect on the importance of being reflective for your learning in this chapter.				
Reflective					

Glossary

absolve To declare someone free from guilt, blame, or responsibility for something

affectation Pretence; to put on a show

allegory A story that deliberately parallels real-life events in order to convey the nature of those events and to comment on them

alliteration The repetition of the same consonant (not vowel) sound at the beginnings of words

allusion A reference in one work of literature to a particular event or character in another work

ally A person who helps and supports another person

anecdote A short interesting story about something that has happened previously

antagonist The character who opposes the protagonist

anticipation Looking forward to something; feeling excited, curious and so on about something we expect to happen

ardent Enthusiastic

assonance The repetition of vowel sounds

asyndeton A sentence in which a conjunction such as 'and' or 'but' would be expected, but which has been omitted; the effect is to speed up the pace of a sentence, for some kind of effect

autobiography Writing by an author about his or her own life

ballad A long poem that narrates a story in short stanzas

beck A stream

bias Where a preference for a particular point of view is shown

biography Writing by an author about somebody else's life

bismuth A chemical element

blank verse A form of poetry made up of lines that are **iambic pentameters** – each one has ten lines with a particular stress pattern, each beginning with a capital letter and which do not rhyme

caesuras A break in the line of a poem

capacity Ability

catalyst A person or thing that causes something to happen or move forward

chores Dull and boring tasks

climax The point of highest emotion in a story

cobalt A metal chemical element used for making things blue-coloured

colloquial Use of language which sounds like conversation, and is therefore informal in nature

conflict Where two opposing forces come together – conflict can be **external**, which means that it relates to a force (not necessarily human) outside the body, or **internal**, which a person experiences when he or she has competing emotions, thoughts, impulses and so on

conscripted Where a person is forced to join the military services

consensus A general agreement

consonance The repetition of consonant sounds anywhere in words at least twice in quick succession; it differs from **alliteration**, which can be described as a type of consonance, in that alliteration is repeated consonant sounds at the *beginnings* of words

conventions The characteristics that allow works to be categorized in a particular literary genre

countermand To cancel an order made by someone else

criterion (plural **criteria**) A standard that is used to evaluate something; in the MYP, four criteria are used to evaluate/judge student work

curfew A rule that requires everyone to stay at home between particular times, usually at night; it may be used during a war or a period of political trouble

cyclical structural technique Where a writer creates a structure in his or her writing where things end at the same point they began

dark tourism The visiting of sites where something terrible or destructive has happened previously

devil's advocate Someone who pretends to be against an idea or plan in order to get people to consider it further – particularly in an argument or discussion

dharma A cosmic law underlying correct behaviour and social order in the Hindu religion; in Buddhism, it is the nature of reality regarded as a universal truth

direct characterization When we are told something openly/ explicitly/directly about a character

disaffection To stop supporting a cause, or being dissatisfied with what is happening

dramatic monologue A type of writing that shows thoughts passing through the mind of someone who acts as the narrator

dynamic character A character who undergoes a change or development in some way, such as in awareness, personality, attitude

emotive language Carefully chosen words designed to evoke particular emotions in a listener or audience

enjambment Occurs in poetry where the sense of what is being said in a line runs on to the next line without a break: there is thus no punctuation at the end of the line

epic A long narrative poem about the heroic deeds of ancient people and gods

ethos Credibility, one of the three types of appeals (the others being to **logos** – logic, and **pathos** – emotion) that persuasive writing tries to make

euphemism A word or phrase that is used to make something unpleasant, or not very appealing, appear more positive

excreted Removed urine and/or solid waste from the body

exhumation Digging up a dead body from the ground after it has been buried

exonerated Shown not to be guilty of, or cleared of blame for, something

exposition The introduction of important background information about characters, setting, relationships and so on

extended metaphor Where a particular image and others associated with it are referred to and repeated over an extended time in a text

fable A story that often uses animals as characters, and tries to teach a lesson to its readers

falling action All the action that follows a climax, leading ultimately to the resolution

fells Hills

ferro-cyanic A chemical compound that can be used to help make things blue in colour

flashback Where an event from the past is suddenly inserted into a narrative

flat character Characters used in works who have very little depth or complexity to them. Just one or two sides of the character may be shown, and that character does not change over the course of the narrative. A flat character can be used to show a **stereotype**

foot A pair of syllables (see also **meter**)

foreboding A sense that something bad is going to happen

foreshadow To provide a clue about something that will happen later on

foreshadowing A technique where a director or author provides a clue as to something that will happen later on

framing Creating distinct episodes that can be arranged in a particular pattern

free verse A poem with the patterns and rhythms of natural speech, rather than traditional meter or rhyme

genre A particular style or type of literature, such as drama, speech, poetry, etc. A type literature or film that has shared features or conventions

gossip Casual talk about someone else and his or her private life

haiku A traditional Japanese poem, written in 17 syllables divided into three lines of five, seven and five syllables

high angle A type of camera angle used in films, where the camera is placed high up and looks down on whatever it is filming

highbrow Cultured or sophisticated

historic present Writing that is in the present tense, narrating events which have happened in the past. The intention is to try to give an impression to the reader that he or she is present at the events being described

hyperbole Exaggerating something for effect

hypothesis An idea or explanation for something that is based on known facts but has not yet been proved (Source: Cambridge online dictionary – http://dictionary.cambridge.org/dictionary/english/hypothesis)

iambic pentameter Lines with ten syllables and a stress pattern that consists of one short (or unstressed) syllable followed by one long (or stressed) syllable

idiom A word or phrase with a particular meaning, which needs to be known to be understood

imagery The use of images to create particular impressions on readers, or mental pictures in their minds. **Similes**, **metaphors** and **personification** are among the most common types of visual imagery, and **alliteration**, **assonance** and **onomatopoeia** of sound imagery

inciting incident The thing that set in motion the main action of the story

indirect characterization When we identify evidence, then analyse and evaluate it ourselves in order to come up with our own judgement about a character

interpretation Explanation of what a text means. It involves looking at evidence such as literary choices a writer has made in a text to arrive at an argument or opinion as to the meaning of the text and a writer's intentions. Higher-level critical thinking skills such as application, analysis, evaluation and synthesis are generally needed in order to come up with suggestions about the possible meaning or purpose of a text

intervening Intentionally become involved in a difficult situation in order to improve it or prevent it from getting worse

irony Verbal irony is when someone says one thing deliberately when they mean the opposite. Situational irony is where expectations and intentions are different from actual outcomes. Dramatic irony describes a situation in which the audience knows something of what is going on, or what is going to happen, and characters do not

Italian sonnet Also known as a **Petrarchan sonnet**; this sonnet follows a ABBA ABBA CDE CDE rhyme scheme

juxtapose Place next to each other, usually something done by a writer for effect

knacker's yard Abattoir or slaughterhouse, where animals are killed

lee The side of a hill

limerick A humorous poem of five lines, rhyming and with a strong rhythm

loaded language Language that carries positive or negative connotations or associations when used

logos Logic, one of the three types of appeals (the others being **ethos** – credibility, and **pathos** – emotion) that persuasive writing tries to make

long shot A type of camera shot used in films, where the camera is placed at a distance from the focus of whatever is being filmed

meaning Sometimes referred to as 'message', it includes 'layers of meaning', nuance, denotation, connotation, inference and subtext. Meaning is essentially what a text is really trying to say – something that can be apparent on the surface and quite obvious, or which may be more hidden and needing to be uncovered through interpretation and analysis of what has been said and how

metaphor A comparison in which something is stated as *being* something else in a way that cannot literally be the case; the idea being to invite a reader to compare the two things

meter The pattern of stressed and unstressed syllables in a line or lines of poetry. Words are made up of syllables that may be stressed or unstressed. This means that a syllable might be emphasized (stressed) when it is spoken, or not. We can hear where particular syllables in words are being stressed by the way in which the word is spoken. A group of two or three syllables in a particular pattern is known as a **foot**; a sequence of feet, or groups of syllable patterns, make up the meter of a line or lines of poetry

mid shot A type of camera shot used in films, where the camera is placed in the middle distance from the focus of whatever is being filmed

minor character A character who does not appear very much, and is generally created to fulfil specific functions needed by a writer – such as to help motivate actions, indicate an opinion on a main character or their words or actions, provide an audience for a conversation which allows important information to be revealed and so on

mood A particular emotional or psychological state often created by positive or negative descriptive words

mooted Suggested

motif The repeated use of an image, such as that of battles in *The Miracle Worker*, means that the image becomes a motif, an image that reminds us of something important through communicating constant reminders of it

mutual Something which is felt or experienced in the same way by more than one person; something which two or more parties have in common

narrative perspective Who or what is the focus of the narrative

narrative voice Who or what is telling the story

objective Based on facts and not influenced by personal feelings or beliefs

ominous An indication that something bad is going to happen

omission To leave out important information when talking about someone or something, in order to give a misleading impression of that person or thing

onomatopoeia When pronouncing a word makes the sound that the word describes (for example, splash, buzz and so on)

ostracised Excluded from a group of friends, family or society

panning Where a camera is moving across a scene in a film

parallel plotline Where two separate narratives are being told in a text, which switches back and forth between the two

parallel scene Two similar scenes presented for comparison, which have important differences

pathetic fallacy The use of nature to reflect events and feelings, and actions of humans within them

pathos Emotion, one of the three types of appeals (the others being **ethos** – credibility, and **logos** – logic) that persuasive writing tries to make

personification A form of metaphor in which an object or an idea is spoken of as though it has human characteristics

Petrarchan sonnet See **Italian sonnet**

plosive The sound made by saying a letter such as 'd' or 'p', which are known as 'plosives' because of how they are pronounced

point of view The particular perspective brought by a composer, responder or character within a text to the text, or to matters within the text. It also describes the position or vantage point from which the events of a story seem to be observed and presented to us

primary source A source that has a direct or first-hand connection with whatever is being researched

promenading Walking

prose The usual form of language a person uses, which follows grammatical rules and does not generally have a meter or patterns (though these may be included by a writer for effect)

protagonist The main character in a story

protocol Ways of doing things

purpose The reason a writer has for writing a text; the intention a writer might have in terms of how he or she wants an audience to respond to a text

refute State or prove that something is wrong or false

register The use of tone, pace, volume, pitch, inflection, fluency/fluidity, vocabulary, grammar and sentence structure that give the correct degree of formality appropriate for the specific context and audience. The main distinction to make for register is between formal and informal

reportage A non-fiction piece written by an eyewitness who documents and reports what he or she observed

research methodology The methods that a researcher chooses to use in order to carry out some research. There are different possible ways of trying to find out something, and a researcher tries to choose the methods that will lead to answers to whatever the research is aimed at finding out

resolution The end and conclusion of the story, which often sees loose ends tied up and outstanding conflicts resolved

retrospect To think about something in the past, often with a different opinion than was originally formed

rhetorical question A question that does not require an answer but invites thought on the part of an audience

rhyme Rhyme is created by using words that when spoken make sounds which are the same, or very similar. Note that words do not have to be spelled in the same way in order to rhyme

rhymed verse Verse in which the final words of lines rhyme

rhyming couplets When the final words of two successive lines of verse rhyme with one another

rhythm Words are made up of syllables that may be stressed or unstressed. This means that a syllable might be emphasized (stressed) when it is spoken, or not. We can hear where particular syllables in words are being stressed by the way in which the word is spoken. Rhythm is where a writer uses stressed and unstressed syllables to create patterns in lines, which affect the way in which the lines can be spoken, such as how quickly or slowly this can happen, or whether a line might have patterns that reflect the movement of something it is describing – a poet may use patterns of stressed syllables, for instance, when talking about the sea in a way that mimics the movement of the sea

rising action The steps leading up to a climax

round character A character who is more developed, and who is presented with a greater range of 'personality' traits

satire Criticizing something or someone through humorously mocking and making fun of it or them, and highlighting failings

script Contains all of the words spoken by the characters in a play, along with any stage directions

secondary source A source that describes, evaluates, comments or interprets primary sources, but does not itself have a direct or first-hand link to what is being researched

sensory imagery Imagery that appeals to an audience's senses and helps make a scene or description more vivid, giving a greater impression to a reader or viewer that they are actually present in the scene. **Similes**, **metaphors** and **personification** are common examples of sensory imagery that appeals to the sense of sight, while **alliteration**, **consonance**, **assonance** and **onomatopoeia** appeal to the sense of sound. Where a writer is consciously using sensory imagery, references to smelling, touching and/or tasting, in addition to those of sight and sound, may also be found in the text

sententious Moralising or self-righteous

Shakespearean sonnet A sonnet written with a rhyme scheme of ABAB CDCD EFEF GG

shell shock Trauma and psychological disturbance someone can suffer, caused by the stress of taking part in war, and their experiences in that

simile A simile asks a reader to picture one thing as being similar to another and uses the words 'like', 'as' or 'than' to create the comparison in the reader's mind

sobering Makes one feel serious

sociopath Someone who behaves in an extremely antisocial way or has extremely antisocial attitudes

soliloquy The thoughts of a character spoken by the character as if he or she is completely alone, and which are not heard by any other character. A soliloquy provides an insight for an audience into what a character is really thinking and feeling

sonnet A type of poem with 14 lines and a regular (though varied) rhyme scheme

sound effect The creation of sound of some kind for effect; this may be a writer creating particular sounds through use of language techniques, such as **alliteration**, **assonance**, **onomatopoeia** and so on, or a playwright using real sounds for effect – the sound of thunder to create an **ominous** atmosphere, for instance

static character A character who remains throughout a story the same as when they are first presented, and who does not undergo any character development or change

stifle Stop

stream of consciousness Where a character's direct thoughts are written down or spoken in a way that reflects the continuous flow of such thoughts in the reader's mind. This means that the writing may contain incomplete sentences and phrases that do not always follow on from each other, while there may be less punctuation than normally expected in writing; all used to reflect the random nature of thoughts passing through a person's mind

subjective Influenced by or based on personal beliefs or feelings, rather than based on facts

subjugation Being able to use something or someone for particular purposes

suspense A feeling of nervousness or excitement about what might happen

syllable A single unit of sound that must contain either a vowel or the letter 'y'. The sound unit may be within a word, or the vowel may make up a word on its own, as with 'a' and 'I'. All words are made up of individual sound units – syllables

syntax How words are arranged in sentences and phrases in order to convey their meanings

synthesis The highest level of critical thinking in Bloom's Revised Taxonomy of thinking skills. This thinking skill involves bringing together and combining different elements into one. Examples of where it might be used in literature are identifying connections between different texts to make a particular point, and noting in a single text analysis how different references in a text might contribute to the same idea

talisman An object or person considered to bring someone good luck, or to keep them from harm

third-person limited narration The story is told from the (limited) point of view of one character

third-person objective narration A narrator recounts facts about what characters say and do, but does not say anything about their thoughts or feelings

third-person omniscient narration The narrator sees and knows everything

tone The way in which words are spoken. Vocabulary choice, register, sentence structure and sentence type can all provide clues as to a tone that is being used in a text. If the words are spoken, pace, pitch and inflection also help identify tone

ubiquitous Seems to be everywhere

unctuous Flattering

undermining Making something or someone appear weaker

wit The ability to express oneself in a clever and intelligent way, and often a way which might make other people laugh

woo Where someone tries to make a person (usually a woman) like or fall in love with them, because they would like the person to marry them

zest Enthusiasm

zoomorphism Where something or someone is given characteristics or attributes of animals

Acknowledgements

The Publishers would like to thank the following for permission to reproduce copyright material. Every effort has been made to trace all copyright holders, but if any have been inadvertently overlooked the Publishers will be pleased to make the necessary arrangements at the first opportunity.

Photo credits

p.2 *l* © PJF Military Collection/Alamy Stock Photo; *r* © caroline letrange/Fotolia.com; **p.3** *tl* © satori/Fotolia; *bl* © Derek Meijer/Alamy Stock Photo; *tr* © Bundit; Yuwannasiri/Shutterstock.com; *br* © Scott Griessel/stock.adobe.com; **p.4** *tr* © TopFoto.co.uk; *b* © NASA; **p.10** © Sipa Press/REX/Shutterstock; **p.13** © BJ Warnick/Newscom/Alamy Stock Photo; **p.20** © 2004 Credit: TopFoto/Universal Pictorial Press; **p.22** © Everett Collection Inc/Alamy Stock Photo; **p.26** © james mackay/Alamy Stock Photo; **p.29** © United Archives/IFTN Cinema Collection/Alamy Stock Photo; **p.33** © Bettmann/Getty Images; **p.34** © Gary Coronado/Palm Beach Post/zumapress.com/Alamy Stock Photo; **p.37** *t* © JWG/AP/REX/Shutterstock; *b* © Courtesy: CSU Archives/Everett Collection/Alamy Stock Photo; **pp.48, 52** © Nina Leen/The LIFE Picture Collection/Getty Images; **p.49** *t* © Bettmann/Getty Images; *b* © Nina Leen/The LIFE Picture Collection/Getty Images; **pp.54, 55** © Universal/Courtesy Everett Collection/Alamy Stock Photo; **p.56** *t* © AntonioDiaz – stock.adobe.com; *c* © Jozef Polc/123RF; *b* © Pavel Losevsky – stock.adobe.com; **p.58** © AAP Image/Smartartist Management; **p.66** © Universal/Everett Collection, Inc./Alamy Stock Photo; **p.82** *l* © Mauro Fermariello/Science Photo Library; *c* © David Isaacson/Alamy Stock Photo; *r* © Gap Kenya; **p.83** *l* © Mike Kemp/Corbis News/Getty Images; *r* © International Campaign to Abolish Nuclear Weapons; **p.92** © Chris Cooper-Smith/Alamy Stock Photo; **p.101** © Photo 12/Universal Images Group/Getty Images; **p.114** © Everett Collection, Inc./Alamy Stock Photo; **p.117** © John Downing/Hulton Archive/Getty Images; **p.120** © Samo Vidic/Getty Images Sport/Getty Images; **p.123** © schankz/stock.adobe.com; **p.126** © Ed Clark/The LIFE Images Collection/Getty Images; **p.135** © 2017 Data Never Sleeps, Courtesy of Domo, Inc.; **p.136** © From Animal Farm by George Orwell published by Secker and Warburg. Reproduced by permission of The Random House Group Ltd. © 1945/Archive PL/Alamy Stock Photo; **p.144** © Granger Historical Picture Archive/Alamy Stock Photo; **p.147** Rajesh Kargutkar and Sony; **p.163** *bl* © Photodisc/Getty Images/World Landmarks & Travel V60; *tl* Copyright © 2007 Alberto Pomares G./© Alberto Pomares/iStockphoto.com; *br* © Pius Lee/Fotolia.com; *tr* © Moritz von Hacht/iStockphoto.com; **p.164** © Pakhnyushchyy/stock.adobe.com; **p.169** © Interfoto/History/Alamy Stock Photo; **p.174** © REX/Shutterstock; **p.175** © Abbie Rowe. White House Photographs. John F. Kennedy Presidential Library and Museum, Boston; **pp.180, 181, 185** © Gillian Ashworth; **p.188** © George Brewin/Alamy Stock Photo; **p.191** © 3D_creation/Shutterstock.com; **p.194** © The Film Company/AF archive/Alamy Stock Photo; **p.209** © Irina Kogan/123RF; **p.220** *l* © CPC Collection/Alamy Stock Photo; *r* © Hisham Ibrahim/PhotoV/Alamy Stock Photo; **p.222** © Granger, NYC/TopFoto; **pp.225, 228** © Everett Historical/Shutterstock.com; **p.226** *l* © Dorne, Albert, 1904–1965. Less dangerous than careless talk : don't discuss troop movements, ship sailings, war equipment., poster, 1944, [Washington D.C.]. (digital.library.unt.edu/ark:/67531/metadc489/: accessed March 2, 2018), University of North Texas Libraries, Digital Library, digital.library.unt.edu; crediting UNT Libraries Government Documents Department; *c* © National Archives and Records Administration; *r* © Keppler, Victor. Wanted! : for murder : her careless talk costs lives., poster, 1944; [Washington D.C.]. (digital.library. unt.edu/ark:/67531/metadc348/: accessed March 2, 2018), University of North Texas Libraries, Digital Library, digital.library.unt.edu; crediting UNT Libraries Government Documents Department; **p.235** © Historica Graphica Collection/Heritage Image Partnership Ltd/Alamy Stock Photo; **p.242** © Sputnik/TopFoto.co.uk; **pp.253, 311** © Wikipedia; **p.257** © Photofusion/REX/Shutterstock; **p.274** © *I Do Not Come To You By Chance*, Adaobi Tricia Nwaubani, The Orion Publishing Group, London; **p.294** *l* © Michelaubryphoto/Shutterstock.com; *r* © OlegMirabo/stock.adobe.com; **p.295** *l* © panya99/stock.adobe.com; *c* © Stanislaw Mikulski/Shutterstock.com; *r* © George Dolgikh/stock.adobe.com; **p.305** *tl* © Archive Pics/Alamy Stock Photo; *tr* © Hi-Story/Alamy Stock Photo; *b* © Lordprice Collection/Alamy Stock Photo; **p.309** © Historic Images/Alamy Stock Photo; **p.328** © Khaled Hosseini, 06 May 2008, *The Kite Runner*, Bloomsbury Publishing Plc.; **p.337** © DreamWorks/Everett Collection/Alamy stock Photo; **p.340** © Anti-Bullying Alliance; **p.342** © Patrick Robert – Corbis/Sygma/Getty Images; **p.344** © Carsten Koall/Getty Images News/Getty

t = top, *b* = bottom, *l* = left, *r* = right, *c* = centre

Text credits

p.8 Ladder of feedback republished with permission of John Wiley & Sons from Ladder of feedback: David Perkins, 2003. *King Arthur's Road Table: How Collaborative Conversations Create Smart Organizations*; permission conveyed through Copyright Clearance Center, Inc. **pp.11–12** *Seize the Moment* by Helen Sharman and The Orion Publishing Group, London. Reprinted with permission. *Seize the Moment* © Helen Sharman. Reprinted with permission of Diana Boulter, MD at DBA SPEAKERS. **pp.13–15** *I am Malala* by Malala Yousafzai and The Orion Publishing Group, London copyright © 2013 Reprinted with permission. From *I Am Malala: How One Girl Stood Up for Education and Changed the World* by Malala Yousafzai, copyright © 2013. Reprinted by permission of Little, Brown & Company, an imprint of Hachette Book Group, Inc. **p.20** From *Rabble-Rouser For Peace* by John Allen. Copyright © 2006 by John Allen. Reprinted with the permission of The Free Press, an imprint of Simon & Schuster, Inc. All rights reserved. **pp.24–25** *Letter from a Birmingham Jail* by Dr Martin Luther King (1963), p87–88. Reprinted by arrangement with The Heirs to the Estate of Martin Luther King Jr, c/o Writers House as agent for the proprietor New York, NY. © 1963 Dr Martin Luther King Jr © renewed 1991 Coretta Scott King. **p.27** Excerpt(s) from *Freedom From Fear And Other Writings* by Aung San Suu Kyi, edited by Michael Aris, copyright © 1991, 1995 by Aung San Suu Kyi. Used by permission of Viking Books, an imprint of Penguin Publishing Group, a division of Penguin Random House LLC. All rights reserved. Freedom From Fear by Aung San Suu Kyi, edited by Michael Aris (Viking, 1991). Copyright © Aung San Suu Kyi, 1991. Reproduced by permission of Penguin Books Ltd. **pp.29–30** Excerpt(s) from *Diary Of Anne Frank* by Frances Goodrich and Albert Hackett, copyright © 1956 by Albert Hackett, Frances Goodrich Hackett and Otto Frank. Copyright renewed 1984 by Albert Hackett. Used by permission of Random House, an imprint and division of Penguin Random House LLC. All rights reserved. Copyright © 1956, renewed by Albert Hackett, David Huntoon & Frances Neuwirth in 1986. Based upon Anne Frank: The Diary of a Young Girl. Used by permission of Flora Roberts, Inc. **p.44** From *The Miracle Worker* by William Gibson. Copyright © 1956, 1957 by William Gibson/Copyright © 1959, 1960 by Tamarack Productions, Ltd. and George S. Klein and Leo Garel as Trustees under three separate deeds of trust. Copyright renewed © 1984, 1985, 1987, 1988 by William Gibson. Reprinted with the permission of Scribner, a division of Simon & Schuster, Inc. All rights reserved. **pp.58–59** 'Body Imperfect' by Debi Davis, from *The Norton Sampler: Short Essays For Composition 6E*, edited by Thomas Cooley. Copyright © 2003, 1997, 1993, 1985, 1982, 1979 by W.W. Norton & Company, Inc. Used by permission of W. W. Norton & Company, Inc. **p.85** 'Five Ways to Kill a Man' by Edwin Brock. Reprinted with permission. 'The Raven' by Clifford Dyment. **p.86** 'Poverty' by Segun Rasaki. **p.87** 'Man and Beast' by Clifford Dyment. **p.94** 'Harlem' by Langston Hughes © David Higham Associates. Reprinted with permission. 'Green Lions' by Douglas Stewart © The Douglas Stewart Estate, c/o Curtis Brown (Aust) Pty Ltd. Reprinted with permission. 'Mirror' by Sylvia Plath. Reprinted with permission of Faber & Faber Ltd. 'The Ballad of Charlotte Dymond' by Charles Causley © David Higham Associates. Reprinted with permission. 'The Road Not Taken' by Robert Frost from the book *The Poetry Of Robert Frost* edited by Edward Connery Lathem. Copyright 1916, 1969 by Henry Holt and Company. Copyright 1944 by Robert Frost. **p.96** 'Circus' by Karl Marszalowicz. Reprinted with permission of Karl Marszalowicz. 'Thrush' by Roland Robinson. **p.101** 'Suicide in the Trenches' by Siegfried Sassoon. Copyright Siegfried Sassoon by kind permission of the Estate of Siegfried Sassoon. **pp.127–129** *Split Cherry Tree* by Jesse Stuart. Reproduced with permission of Marian Reiner Literary Agency. **pp.138–140, 143, 149, 150, 152, 153, 158, 159** Approximately two thousand two hundred and forty-three (2,243) words from *Animal Farm* by George Orwell (Penguin Books, 2000) Copyright © 1945, Eric Blair. This edition copyright © the Estate of the late Sonia Brownwell Orwell, 1987. From *Animal Farm* by George Orwell. Published by Martin Secker & Warburg Ltd. Reprinted by permission of The Random House Group Limited. © 1945. **p.146** 'International Coastal Clean-up Day'. Reproduced with permission of HT Media. **p.147** 'Doing our bit for the environment' by Mata'afa Keni Lesa , 22 September 2016. **p.167** Excerpt from *This is Botswana* by Daryl and Sharna Balfour. Text by Peter Joyce, Penguin Random House South Africa (Pula Press, Gaborone), 1994, p.16. *Tbilisi* – ed. Maria Bulia and Mzia Janjalia (2006) – p.106; Eka Privalova Centre – Betania – Tbilisi (Bulia M. and Janjalia M. (eds), Kutaisi, Tbilisi, 2006. **pp.173, 174, 175–178** *All the Wrong Places: Adrift in the Politics of Asia*, James Fenton. Reproduced with permission of United Agents. **p.182** *Bou Meng: A Survivor From Khmer Rouge Prison S21* (translated by Huy Vannak) (pp.36–7). **p.188** www.makemytrip.com: Carvela Beach Resort, Goa, hotel details. **p.192** 'Ethical Dilemmas for Classroom Discussion' *The Daily Dilemma Archive* by Charis Denison. **p.194** http://nativeaudiogrrrl.blogspot.co.uk/2011/07/movies-that-made-me-bawl-my-eyes-out.html **p.216** International Baccalaureate eAssessment for MYP English Language and Literature in May 2015 (https://www.ibo.org/news/news-about-ib-schools/release-myp-eassessment-results-from-may-2015-pilot/). Reprinted with permission of International Baccalaureate Organization. http://fra.europa.eu/en/charterpedia/article/11-freedom-expression-and-information © European Union Agency for Fundamental Rights, 2007–2018. **p.223** Scott Howard Phillips: goo.gl/Ps1PRd. **p.229** 'First world war: how state and press kept truth off the front page' by Roy Greenslade, Sun 27 Jul 2014. © Guardian News and Media. **pp.237, 238–240, 248** *All Quiet on the Western Front* by Erich Remarque (two extracts). Reprinted with permission. **p.242** Excerpt(s) from *The Sorrow Of War: A Novel Of North Vietnam* by Bao Ninh, copyright © 1995 by Bao Ninh. Used by permission of Pantheon Books, an imprint of the Knopf Doubleday Publishing Group, a division of Penguin Random House LLC. All rights reserved. *The Sorrow Of War* by Bao Ninh Published by Martin Secker & Warburg. Reprinted by permission of The Random House Group Limited. © 1993. **p.262** Excerpt from *Matilda* by Roald Dahl, text copyright © 1988 by Roald Dahl. Reprinted with permission of David Higham Associates. Excerpt from *Matilda* by Roald Dahl, text copyright © 1988 by Roald Dahl. Used by permission of Viking Children's Books, an imprint of Penguin Young Readers Group, a division of Penguin Random House LLC. All rights reserved. Excerpt from *The Godfather* by Mario Puzo, copyright © 1969, renewed © 1997 by Mario Puzo. Used by permission of G. P. Putnam's Sons, an imprint of Penguin Publishing Group, a division of Penguin Random House LLC. All rights reserved. **p.271** 'Dating customs around the world' by Colleen Crawford. **pp.275–276** From *I Do Not Come to You by Chance* by Adaobi Tricia Nwaubana. Copyright © 2009 by Adaobi Tricia Nwaubana. Reprinted by permission of Hachette Books. *I Do Not Come To You By Chance* by Adaobi Tricia Nwaubani © The Orion Publishing Group. Reprinted with permission. **p.299** 'My Blue Heaven' by Rodney Pybus. **p.310** *The World Set Free* by H. G. Wells. **p.314** Excerpt from *Poems of the Atomic Bomb (Genbaku shishū)*, Written by Tōge Sankichi, Translated by Karen Thornber, Winner of the University of Chicago William F. Sibley Memorial Translation Prize, 2011, https://ceas.uchicago.edu/sites/ceas.uchicago.edu/files/uploads/Sibley/Genbaku%20shishu.pdf. **p.320** 'Technology' by Esther Pang Hui Min. **pp.331, 335, 336, 338, 341, 346, 348, 351** *The Kite Runner* by Khaled Hosseini. Reprinted by permission of Bloomsbury. Excerpts from *The Kite Runner* by Khaled Hosseini, copyright © 2003 by TKR Publications, LLC. Used by permission of Riverhead,